FILM AS FILM:

Critical Responses to Film Art

JOY GOULD BOYUM

New York University

ADRIENNE SCOTT

Fordham University

Allyn and Bacon, Inc. Boston

Library of Congress Catalog Card Number: 77-124941

Printed in the United States of America

Second printing . . . October, 1971

Gloria DeHaven Olivia De Havilland William Demarest Andy Devine Billy De Wolfe Marlene Dietrich Robert Donat Brian Donlevy Philip Dorn Kirk Douglas Melvyn Douglas Betsy Drake Tom Drake Ellen Drew Bobby Driscoll Joanne Dru Margaret Dumont James Dunn Irene Dunne June Duprez Jimmy Durante Deanna Durbin Dan Duryea Ann Dvorak Vera Ellen Faye Emerson Leon Errol Dale Evans Joan Evans William Eythe Douglas Fairbanks, Jr. Glenda Farrell Alice Faye Betty Field Barry Fitzgerald Geraldine Fitzgerald Errol Flynn Nina Foch Henry Fonda Joan Fontaine Glenn Ford Preston Foster Kay Francis Clark Gable Greta Garbo Ava Gardner John Garfield William Gargan Judy Garland Peggy Ann Garner Betty Garrett Greer Garson William Gaxton Leo Genn Billy Gilbert James Gleason Paulette Goddard Thomas Gomez Betty Grable Gloria Graham Farley Granger Cary Grant Bonita Granville Katherine Grayson Richard Greene Sydney Greenstreet Charlotte Greenwood Jane Greer Edmund Gwenn Alan Hale Jonathan Hale Jon Hall Margaret Hamilton Rex Harrison Hurd Hatfield June Haver June Havoc Sarah Hayden Sterling Hayden Gabby Hayes Dick Haymes Louis Hayward Susan Hayward Rita Hayworth Van Heflin Sonja Henie Wanda Hendrix Katherine Hepburn Paul Henreid Jean Hersholt Daryl Hickman John Hodiak Fay Holden William Holden Celeste Holm Tim Holt Skippy Homeier Bob Hope Miriam Hopkins Lena Horne Edward Everett Horton Leslie Howard Trevor Howard Rochelle Hudson Mary Beth Hughes Marsha Hunt Ruth Hussey Walter Huston Betty Hutton Robert Hutton Frieda Inescort José Iturbi Claude Jarman, Jr. Gloria Jean Van Johnson Allan Jones Jennifer Jones Victor Jory Louis Jourdan Arline Judge Boris Karloff Roscoe Karns Danny Kaye Cecil Kellaway Gene Kelly Nancy Kelly Patsy Kelly Paul Kelly Evelyn Keyes Guy Kibbie Patric Knowles Kurt Kreuger Otto Kruger Alan Ladd Arthur Lake Veronica Lake Hedy Lamarr Dorothy Lamour Elsa Lancaster Carole Landis Jessie Royce Landis Lola Lane Priscilla Lane Rosemary Lane Angela Lansbury Charles Laughton Peter Lawford Vivien Leigh Sheldon Leonard Joan Leslie Gene Lockhart June Lockhart John Loder Carole Lombard Peter Lorre Anita Louise Robert Lowery Myrna Loy Bela Lugosi Paul Lukas Keye Luke John Lund William Lundigan Ida Lupino Jimmy Lyon Diana Lynn Fred MacMurray George Macready Guy Madison Marjorie Main Frederic March Margo Hugh Marlowe Tony Martin Herbert Marshall Arthur Marx Julius Marx Leonard Marx James Mason Ilona Massey Raymond Massey Victor Mature Marilyn Maxwell Virginia Mayo Mike Mazurki

Lon McCallister Charlie McCarthy Joel McCrea Hattie McDaniels Roddie McDowall Dorothy McGuire Victor McLaglen Horace McNally Adolphe Menjou Una Merkel Burgess Meredith Ray Milland Ann Miller Carmen Miranda Robert Mitchum Ricardo Montalban Maria Montez George Montgomery Robert Montgomery Victor Moore Agnes Moorehead Dolores Moran Dennis Morgan Frank Morgan Robert Morley Wayne Morris Alan Mowbray Paul Muni George Murphy J. Carroll Naish Mildred Natwick Richard Ney David Niven Lloyd Nolan Jack Oakie Merle Oberon Margaret O'Brien Pat O'Brien Virginia O'Brien Donald O'Connor Una O'Connor Maureen O'Hara Dennis O'Keefe Laurence Olivier Michael O'Shea Maureen O'Sullivan Maria Ouspenskaya Gale Page Eugene Pallette Lilli Palmer Franklin Pangborn Cecilia Parker Eleanor Parker Larry Parks Gail Patrick John Payne Gregory Peck Susan Peters Walter Pidgeon Dick Powell Eleanor Powell Jane Powell William Powell Tyrone Power George Raft Luise Rainer Claude Rains Ella Raines Vera Hruba Ralston Basil Rathbone Gene Raymond Ronald Reagan George Reeves Anne Revere Marjorie Reynolds Edward G. Robinson Ginger Rogers Roy Rogers Gilbert Roland Ruth Roman Cesar Romero Mickey Rooney Charles Ruggles Gail Russell Ann Rutherford Peggy Ryan Robert Ryan Sabu S. Z. (Cuddles) Sakall George Sanders Lizabeth Scott Randolph Scott Johnny Sheffield Ann Sheridan Dinah Shore Sylvia Sidney Simone Simon Jean Simmons Frank Sinatra Penny Singleton Walter Slezak Everett Sloan Alexis Smith C. Aubrey Smith Kent Smith Gail Sondergaard Ann Sothern Barbara Stanwyck Robert Sterling Craig Stevens Mark Stevens James Stewart Dean Stockwell Lewis Stone Gale Storm Margaret Sullavan Akim Tamiroff Elizabeth Taylor Robert Taylor Shirley Temple Phyllis Thaxter Gene Tierney Laurence Tierney Ann Todd Sidney Toler Franchot Tone Audrey Totter Spencer Tracy Arthur Treacher Claire Trevor Sonny Tufts Lana Turner Vali Conrad Veidt Lupe Valez Eric von Stroheim Nancy Walker Robert Walker Ruth Warwick John Wayne Clifton Webb Virginia Weidler Johnny Weissmuller Orson Welles Dame May Whitty Richard Widmark Cornell Wilde Esther Williams Charles Winninger Jane Withers Monty Woolley Teresa Wright Jane Wyatt Jane Wyman Keenan Wynn Loretta Young Robert Young Vera Zorina and all the other idols of our Saturday afternoons

who let us play

CONTENTS

PART I/THEORY

PART II/PRACTICE

PREFACE

This is not a book about what makes for good film. Instead, it is a book about what makes for good film criticism: for sound experience and the valid explication of that experience. Still, it would be absurd to claim that a book which talks about film criticism does not imply a theory of film, and although this theory is merely implicit throughout the text, it is perhaps wisest and most honest to make it explicit here.

For us, a film has no mode of existence in itself. It comes into being only as a partner in a cooperative venture with an audience, contributing the raw material from which each viewer creates his work of art. The perfect film is the one which makes everyone's work of art the same work of art in that it is so finely fashioned, so in charge of its own possibilities, that it precisely structures the shape of the film which the partnership will produce. From this point of view, the worst film is that which allows the viewer the greatest possible freedom in the realization of his work of art. Taken to its extreme, such a "movie" would simply be raw stock run through a projector.

For us, criticism most conveniently begins with the assumption that the film we are about to experience is perfect: each detail, every nuance in the film will be accepted as contributing to the whole, as essential to our creation of a coherent work of art. What this means is that when we encounter a detail, a sequence even, that cannot be worked into the totality of the experience, we blame first our understanding, and only afterwards, the film. We know this is difficult and that there are formidable temptations to dismiss as failed art films with puzzling aspects. It is easier to reject a film than to take the trouble to reconstruct—perhaps totally—our original experience. But there are no shortcuts, no five easy lessons to good criticism.

It is true, alas, that the perfect film does not exist, but nevertheless a large number of the most serious errors in critical judgment would have been avoided had the viewer assumed he was experiencing a perfect film and was therefore obligated to wrestle with the problems he encountered. And this is especially relevant to a quickly developing medium in which the critic must often relinquish whatever criteria he has developed from the past (no matter how recent) in favor of newer, more immediate ones demanded by the present experience.

In terms of evaluation, then, we would hold that each film establishes its own criteria of excellence. But we are not so much interested in evaluation as we are in understanding, in explication. And when we talk about a perfect film, we are not setting up an ideal construct against which other films can or should be measured, but are establishing a first principle of criticism—an attitude which operationally should result in more valid film experience.

. . . . .

This book consists of two parts. In the first chapters, we discuss problems inherent in establishing film as an art form and isolate inhibiting aspects of the film experience and thus of the criticism of film. The second part comprises a collection of critical writings concerning twenty-five films. The selection of films was largely arbitrary; some of the films we think are highly successful works of art; some are special favorites; others are interesting above all for the problems they have raised in their receptions; but for the most part, we have selected pragmatically those films which appear with great frequency in film courses. In general, our selection is heavily weighted in favor of the sixties; this is primarily so because much of the interesting criticism, as distinguished from theoretical writings on film, dates from this period. Each piece of criticism was selected because it pointed to problems inherent in the experience with a particular film, because it raised a general problem in film aesthetics, or sometimes merely because it seemed to dovetail so neatly with other criticism of the same film. The criticism should not be seen as representative of a particular critic's usual standards; in some cases, we have chosen writings which may even belie his general attitude toward film. It should be noted too that some of the criticism was written hurriedly, under the pressure of daily deadlines, while other pieces were published in quarterlies, allowing the critic considerable time and space in which to develop his arguments. Nor should the questions we raise (below the criticism) be understood as anything other than what they are: aids to the reader in sharpening his own critical perceptions. These questions vary greatly in the degree of their sophistication, having been occasioned by a wide range of issues arising from both the film encounter and the nature of the criticism itself.

Finally, we should make clear that our selection of criticism does not pretend to be comprehensive; one glaring omission in our sources is *Cahiers du Cinema,* since there were no available English translations of relevant materials. An obvious bias, moreover, is a geographical one. We are in New York and thus most familiar with criticism produced here.

. . . . .

We should like to acknowledge our debt to our teacher, Louise M. Rosenblatt, who did for us what we hope this book will do for others. By making us conscious of our critical presuppositions and by forcing us to articulate these biases and to examine them, she enabled us to arrive at what we believe to be a sound basis for criticism. We would also like to thank Asmund Boyum for his continuing encouragement and his patience and especially for his good will.

J.G.B.
A.S.

PART I

Theory

FILM: ITS STATUS AS ART

The editors of the fifteenth edition of the *Encyclopedia Britannica,* published in 1947, recognized that motion pictures were important—important enough to warrant a sixteen page discussion and twenty-one pages of plates. Yet, their use of these thirty-seven pages strikes us today as somewhat curious. Three pages of text and four pages of plates, for example, are devoted to a discussion of make-up, by Percy Westmore, which contains such aesthetic material as the following: "The need for thoroughness in the art of make-up cannot be overemphasized. . . . You first determine the shape of your face which may be one of the seven basic types . . ."; and we find under the caption "Order of Make-up Application": "First cleanse the face thoroughly with cold cream, then wash with warm water and mild soap. . . ." Most of the remainder of the text is concerned with the production of film: descriptions of motion picture sets, a paragraph defining the duties of a director and his ultimate responsibility to the producer, a list of studio departments, discussions of the distribution of scripts, of the projection room, and of the type of lens used on movie cameras. Although the word "art" and its derivations appear from time to time (e.g., Cecil B. De Mille, author of much of the article, refers to the director as "executive artist"), there is literally no talk of the aesthetic qualities of the product itself. It is as if the article on the novel were to be devoted to the history of the printing press, the development of publishing houses, techniques of book production (such as jacket design, typography), and means of distribution.

The interesting question here is why the *Britannica* should take this approach to motion pictures at a time when, although admittedly few in number and limited in distribution, there were already published some very serious works on film—Spottiswoode's *A Grammar of the Film,* Arnheim's *Film as Art,* Eisenstein's *The Film Sense,* to name just three—and why it would select a figure such as Cecil B. De Mille as authority in the field. True, De Mille has been involved broadly in motion pictures and is well known as both producer and director. Not surprisingly, the *Britannica* describes him not as a director but as a producer, thus suggesting that he makes movies in the sense that the firm of Knopf makes books. Knopf, however, has the status of being the publisher of Mann and Camus; De Mille, on the other hand, is associated with *kitsch* (or commercial art) and with financial success. What the *Britannica* is doing then is to make official an attitude toward film which is common to most filmgoers. The student in a film course need only recall the response of many of his friends to the announcement that he was to take a film course. It is clear that, for the vast majority of people, the film is neither academically respectable nor an art form.

Art and Profit

In discussions of most art forms, there exists the general agreement that the form is an art, and everyone recognizes it as such when they see it. Making movies is a business; writing novels is not, and business is not art. The motion picture industry (think of a phrase like novel writing industry) itself, of course, established the view of film as commodity with its quick-buck aura, its trade magazines with daily publications of a film's gross, its emphasis on the star system and its stars' fantastic earnings, its publicity techniques, and its gossip columns. And while the image has been reinforced for us by the artist fleeing Hollywood à la F. Scott Fitzgerald and by such novels as *What Makes Sammy Run?* and *The Deer Park,* it is difficult in any case to reconcile the image of the sound stage with that of the ivory tower.

Still, we do not deny that Dostoevsky is an artist because he wrote for quick cash; and the most severe critics discount Dickens' economic motives when they declare him to be a great novelist. Art frequently makes a profit. Further, to become overly entangled in the question of whether film is art or commerce is to become embroiled in an "intentional fallacy." It is surely not the film maker's *intention* which should occupy the interest of the film critic, but rather the film maker's *product,* the film. Since it is exceedingly difficult to assess the film maker's intention—are we to ask Cecil B. De Mille if he made *Samson and Delilah* for art or money?—we must of necessity disregard it.

The Search for the Artist

The commercial aspect of motion pictures is only one of the obstacles to our acceptance of film as art. A major problem is that a film is a group production. Indeed, in order to see film as art, it seems necessary psychologically to see it as the work of a single creator. The director, the man whom Cecil B. De Mille sees as "executive artist," is *the* artist, according to recent theories of film, particularly those proposed by *Cahiers du Cinéma.* The concept is a comfortable one when faced with the films of Antonioni, Fellini, Bergman, even Hitchcock and Orson Welles; but will it hold when applied to films where the director has exercised less control, has had little to do with either the screenplay or editing or both? Of course, the less sophisticated end to this same search for an artist was the movie star. And in America, this still holds to a great extent. The *pièce de résistance* of the gala evening in April at the Santa Monica Civic Auditorium is the award for best actor, and few of us even take interest in the best director except as clue to this final, most important award. While we might argue that we go to see a Fellini rather than a Marcello Mastroanni film, we cannot in truth claim that we are off to see a movie directed by Billy Wilder; for most, the interest lies in Jack Lemmon or in Marilyn Monroe.

A chief difficulty, then, is the group as artist. Add to it the further hindrance of the credibility of the machine as artist (Can a computer write poems?), and we are faced with accepting a business undertaking manufactured by a group as a work of art.

The Mass Audience

A third and complex problem is the mass audience—traditionally essential to the distinction between fine art and *kitsch.* In recent years, we have become preoccupied with making further distinctions: between high cult and mass cult, between mass cult and mid cult, between lowbrow and highbrow. If it's a best-seller, if it's entertaining, it's simply not art. Fifty million Frenchmen can't love art. Historically, then, film only began to assume status as a potential art form (in this country, at any rate) with the creation of the "art house." And in New York City, where a film will often play simultaneously at a small, eastside art theatre and at a more "commercial" Broadway theatre, long lines will form at the art house while the larger westside theatre will play to nearly empty houses. It was only when "movies" became "films," and even better, "the cinema," that audiences began, in any large number, to go to films for more than mere entertainment. This is significant in a country with a Puritan ethic where art and entertainment are mutually exclusive terms. The art house demanded a sacrifice: cigarettes were taboo and there was no popcorn. The price of tickets was outrageously high and the audience had to arrive at the beginning of the show. Now that movie going became uncomfortable and stuffy, motion pictures could be art.

Good Films and Bad Movies

Yet, not all films were worthy of the epithet, "art." Americans have tended to simplify the selection process by reserving the status of art for films they like, while regarding movies they do not like as "trash." Unlike literature, painting, and music, films have the distinction of being without "bad art." A film is either art or it is not film. It is non-art; it is trash; and it is probably a "movie." Furthermore, it is most likely a Hollywood movie, since for the most part in America, the distinction between art and non-art has been further simplified by classifying Hollywood products as "commodity," and foreign films as "art." It was necessary for the French critics to draw the attention of American film critics to the virtues of Hitchcock. The French, interestingly, regard all films as art and, consequently, astound the English-speaking world with their reverence for such an apparently commercial film figure as Jerry Lewis. It will be amusing to see if Jerry Lewis, *l'artiste-directeur,* follows in Hitchcock's footsteps and ultimately receives serious critical attention in this country.

It would seem unlikely, if for no other reason than Jerry Lewis' comparatively recent arrival on the film scene. The nostalgic element is not to be discounted. We will stay up half the night to see Humphrey Bogart in *The Maltese Falcon.* Again, it was the French who started the great Bogart craze, but would it have been so readily accepted in America if there had not been a whole generation of moviegoers-become-intellectuals who were consciously comparing their adult responses to Bogie with their Saturday-afternoon-when-we-were-eight response? The French have aided us in transforming *kitsch* into art, and our sentiments have encouraged the process. Further, to resee at a later point in our lives that which we retain in memory is to complicate our responses and evaluations enormously. We are continually holding before ourselves a twofold image: one of the film and another of our first experience with it. And frequently, it is in fact our embarassment over our primary psychological response that may well lead to our readiness to accept film as art.

The Lack of Tradition

The institution of the film course, literary critics converting from novels to film, philosophers leaving Camus for Mae West, all signal the intellectual coming of age of film—ironically, when film itself is being recorded on video tape. And perhaps television was a prerequisite for the new status of motion pictures in the same way that it functioned to put comics between hard covers and to give them the Penguin Books' stamp of respectability. Television did, after all, diminish the massness of the film's mass audiences, while at the same time it helped to encourage with the Late and Late Late Shows that delightful aura of nostalgia. There is a real possibility, of course, that some of the aesthetic interest films now command is, as we have implied, only a disguised defense of the Saturday mornings and afternoons of the pre-television children; but it is noteworthy how they have convinced the generation that followed them—those now enrolled in film courses, those now making their own films, most likely the reader of this book—that films are worthy of this kind of attention.

The problem is that much of this attention, seemingly intense though it may be, is at base not only hit or miss but also unstructured and uncodified. For while there may exist a tradition of the film, surely there is no tradition for its criticism. The landmarks of literature on the film—Pudovkin's *Film Technique and Film Acting,* the works of Eisenstein and Arnheim mentioned earlier—are all books concerned with technique and as such provide a telling contrast between the interests of professionals in the field and those of movie audiences. Except for the small audience created in most part by this criticism itself, people who go to motion pictures are totally uninvolved with film technique. What interests them and concerns them and, in fact, invites their attendance is the story—the human element—the relation to or distance from reality of the characters and their experiences. And this dichotomy between the concerns of the professional and those of the mass audience are nowhere as pronounced as they are in film. The critic of novels, for example, will only very rarely make a point about technical aspects of a literary work, such as the pattern of metaphors, which do not immediately relate to the *effect* the total work has on the reader. Too often, the film critic will become so engrossed in technique that he seems to forget not only the human qualities of films and their audiences but the audience, itself. Indeed, focusing on technique is a way of ridding the film critic of the burden of the film's mass audience as an obstacle to the acceptance of the film as art. What the mass audience, after all, does not understand is what seems to make motion pictures art. *Ulysses* may have been a best-seller, but no one understood it. Faulkner's novels, at the time he won the Nobel Prize, were, because of their intricacy, mostly out of print. Talking about technique, moreover, is to indicate that film is serious and self-conscious business. Then, too, the critic may concentrate on technique: first, as a reaction to, as well as a way of distinguishing his work from, the kind of daily reviewing that has formed the bulk of film criticism up to now and that sees nothing but the story line and its moral acceptability; and second, and more significantly, as a way of establishing criteria to which all film critics may agree. Clearly, a pan to the left is a pan to the left. Human elements are not so readily standardized; one man's fear is another man's joy. Criteria, after all, emerge from a sense of tradition and a definition of the nature of the art form itself. And what makes film different from poetry and the novel and the drama *is* its technique; human quality it shares with all.

As indicated earlier, this lack of a secure tradition is a basic problem in discussing motion pictures. In search of a past, there are those, for example, who see film as an extension of drama and who consequently evaluate it in terms of the criteria traditionally reserved for this art. Thus, they will focus on dialogue, conflict, characterization. Others see the film as an extension of still photography, itself a very new art form, which has borrowed the vocabulary and criteria of painting, and thus tend to talk about film in visual terms. Still others see it as a narrative form stemming from epic and novel and evaluate it as a literary work. It is these especially, viewers who essentially refuse to accept film on its own terms and as a new art form, who are perhaps best countered by an emphasis on what is unique in film: its technique.

Film As Art

Up to this point, we have tried to explore the status of film. We have been, in effect, trying to find an authority for deciding that films are or are not art. Traditionally, art is distinguished from non-art in many ways: by intention, by the audience's response, by the manner in which it is spoken about, by the qualities inherent in the thing itself. We have discussed the futility of searching for the film maker's intentions as a guide; first, the film maker is not a reliable source of information and second, even if he were, it is fallacious to assume that products correspond exactly, if at all, with intention. The reader himself knows the gap that exists between what he intends to do and what is accomplished. The film maker becomes just another viewer once he has made the film. What we say about a film must come from the film itself and not from statements about it.

We have also seen that the audience's response is unreliable as a touchstone for art, in that it is not consistent. Most American audiences do not respond to Jerry Lewis' films as art; is *Cahiers du Cinema* wrong? For that matter, is Antonioni's *Blow-Up* a work of art? There is no unanimity in the audience or even among critics. Further, this way of defining art is clearly useless and unsatisfactory, since there is no inclusive definition of the sort of response that should be elicited by a work of art.

The third mode of definition that is based upon the viewer's approach to film is somewhat more satisfying. We have seen the concern of critics to establish film as an art by concentrating on technical matters. It is possible to apply equal energy to the technical aspects of comic books; does this make them art? Probably not, but the fact remains that this energy is not expended on comic books and is expended on film. If we recognize that art is not something that can be defined in any absolute sense, that we cannot say with complete authority "this is art" or "this is not art," then one of the most fruitful ways we have for identifying an "art form" is by exploring the ways in which it is treated. If a community of experts talks and acts as if something were art, then it is. If the enlarged comic figures of Roy Lichtenstein hang in the Guggenheim Museum, they are art, even if my mother and your Uncle Sam don't believe it. To paraphrase Lionel Trilling, art is not a democracy. And if movies are shown in art houses and at The Museum of Modern Art, they too are art.

We now come to the film itself and its qualities. Again, we can only adopt a pragmatic position since there are no absolute criteria existing which tell us precisely what art is. If we will agree that photography is art, that drama is art, that painting is art, that literature is art, then we are forced to admit on the principle of guilt by association that film is art. There is something about film that is reminiscent of these other art forms. Finally, we come to the most substantial argument of all: films have had an enormous impact on our culture and on our citizens—on us. We want to have, need to have, some way of understanding film and its impact and to view it merely as a mass medium is to focus, à la McLuhan, on the medium itself rather than on its content. And while, of course, the medium is part of the message, it is perhaps the least interesting and certainly the most easily comprehended aspect of it. We must recognize the way technological aspects of film affect its form and our responses to it, but to focus on technology alone is to fail to distinguish one film from another—*The Dolly Sisters* from *La Dolce Vita.* And let us not confuse technology, that which concerns the *Britannica,* with technique. In aiding us to make these distinctions and to make them most wisely, it is perhaps the principles of criticism usually associated with art forms that are most suitable. And to apply these principles, it is clear that we must consider film as art.

THE CRITICAL ACT or I JUST SAW BARBARELLA: IT WAS GREAT

I Just Saw Barbarella

If taken literally, as it almost always is, "I just saw Barbarella" is a nonsense statement. We forget that this is a metaphor, that no one has even *seen* a film, since to *see* a film is to suggest that a spectacle of images and a parade of sound has a life of its own, distinct from the life which the viewer brings to it. It is to suggest that the viewer is a passive recorder of these images, when in fact he must, in order to *see* anything, organize and invest with significance the patterns of lights and darks and sounds projected before and around him. We think of this process, if we think of it at all, as automatic, but there is good evidence that considerable cultural training has gone into our ability to effect this organization. Marshall McLuhan tells us, for example, of primitive tribes who, totally unfamiliar with electric circuitry, are unable to *see* a film. (See *Understanding Media: The Extensions of Man,* Chapter 29: "Movies: The Reel World.") They cannot synthesize the shadows and forms on the screen. They cannot connect the conventions of these mobile two dimensional images to the world out there. We can do this, and probably more easily than our parents could, since most of us from the time we were infants, have been exposed to the television image, which approximates that of the film. The fact that we can organize sounds, that we can so very easily make these connections between conventional patterns and our intellectual and emotional pasts obscures the tremendous amount of work we are in actuality doing. This might be best understood if we consider ourselves in the act of walking. It would seem to us an effortless physical act; nevertheless, if a physiologist were to describe the complex workings of our muscular and neurological systems, we would discover the considerable amount of exertion involved in this seemingly easy process.

The point is that film is not merely out there to be seen; it is rather something which we must create. But while it is not simply those lights and shadows on the screen, neither is it only our response to it. It is instead a third entity, a combination of, a function of our perceptions *and* those lights and shadows. What we register is thus our own creation, an imaginative construction stimulated and controlled by what we see and hear. Twenty people "see" *Barbarella.* The result: twenty distinct organizations of sound and sight which exist somewhere between the reflection on the screen and the viewer before it, and it is this that we call the film.

It Was Great

If we examine the comments that we make after having imaginatively constructed a film, we will note that they tend to be evaluative ones: "It was great"; "It was terrible"; "It was boring." Ostensibly comments about an objective structure—the celluloid strip and its sound track—they are, in fact, comments about ourselves, and, as such, are the clue to our own central roles in the creation of film. When we say "It was great," we are actually saying "I liked it." And "I liked it" (or its antithesis, "I disliked it") may, depending on its context, become the first step in the critical act. In any case, it remains a very small one, since unless the question "Why did I like it?" follows, an act of criticism has not been initiated. "I like it," when it stands alone, is only a grunt of approval and while one has every right to grunt, let us not mistake it for other than it is. "Why did I like it?" demands development and will invariably lead to further questions about one's self as well as to those about the celluloid strip. Since these are the two ingredients of film, film criticism has begun.

Let us return to those twenty people who created twenty films, all called *Barbarella.* Which *Barbarella* is the best *Barbarella?* More basic, *is* there a best *Barbarella?* Is there a single best experience to be put together by the viewer in his encounter? Or, are all twenty creations, all twenty *Barbarellas*, equally good? For openers, let us replace the word "good" with the word "valid." And let us also suppose that one of our viewers is a member of Mr. McLuhan's tribe and another is a college student. Whose experience will be more valid, that of the student who has seen a movie about a woman who travels in space or that of the tribesman whose response has produced no story at all? And what of the viewer who offers us as his film a visit to the North Pole? Which of these compositions is most valid? Clearly, that of the student. We know the answer intuitively, and if we can translate this intuition into working critical principles, we will have made a giant step in the direction of meaningful criticism. Why do we prefer the film of the student? Because it does not, as does the tribesman's film, completely ignore the images on the screen nor does it, as that of the viewer who creates a film about the North Pole, seem to be a free association upon a single scene. As limited a statement as it is, that of the college freshman seems to account for more aspects of the projected images than those of the others. What this suggests, then, is that the best critic is one who creates a film which most consistently utilizes the visual and aural stimuli that are given, neither adding to them, nor ignoring any of them. What this says, too, is that these patterns serve as an objective reference against which statements about the experience they contribute to may be tested. Here then is our first and perhaps most overwhelming, critical principle. A sound imaginative creation of a film is one which can be supported with evidence from the celluloid strip. And as simplistic as this principle may sound, evidence is frequently elusive. There are many problems in getting at it—problems inherent in the medium itself and problems in our own individualities.

Problems Inherent in our Own Selves

1. The first and most obvious difficulty may be called the *necessity of understanding*. We mentioned earlier the tribesman who could not *see* the motion picture. Each reader of this book is sufficiently educated so that such a problem is not relevant to him. Beyond this however, the viewer must have enough intelligence to make sense of

the language he hears and the sequence of events before him. He must be able to recognize the same personality despite greying hair and change of costume. He must be able to identify a place he has visited before, although now viewed from another angle. He must recall the sled seen at the outset of *Citizen Kane* if the conclusion is to be comprehensible to him. In other words, he must be awake to his experience both figuratively and literally.

2. A second difficulty lies in the *private associations* the film may induce from a particular viewer. Let's say my grandparents lived on a farm in Iowa and I spent my happiest summers there as a child. When in *North by Northwest,* Cary Grant is attacked while alone in a cornfield, I feel, instead of the terror the harrowing scene invites, the kind of gentle warmth I associate with ripening corn. Or let's suppose I am dreadfully afraid of dogs. Whatever their actions, neither Lassie nor Rin Tin Tin seem heroic or beloved to me. In both these instances, the personal associations of the viewer have so obliterated the film that it can no longer serve as material from which he can construct a legitimate experience. The film is nonexistent and the viewer may as well be walking down a street as sitting in a movie theatre.

3. A third and related difficulty lies in *culturally induced associations.* When John Barrymore playing the good thief in *Grand Hotel* is killed by the selfish tycoon, Wallace Beery, I may read his death as an embodiment of the moral lesson, crime does not pay, rather than seeing in this event the appropriate end of failure. When Ingrid Bergman follows her husband in *Casablanca* and leaves her lover, Humphrey Bogart, I may perceive this as a happy ending since the culture has taught me that marriage is sacred. Now of course film makers, whether American, European or even of more distant cultures, aware of the likelihood, in fact of the inevitability, of such associations—and indeed sharing many of them—may consciously use them both as economical means of advancing a story and as commercial ways of insuring certain responses. When such beautiful people as Warren Beatty and Faye Dunaway are cast as two hardened criminals, Arthur Penn, the director, can be sure that we will not rejoice at their death and condemn them heartily for their actions. By relying on our cultural response to physical attractiveness, he can be sure that most of us will replace crime does not pay with beauty does. Thus, what might have been merely inevitable comes as a shock. When, to take another example, Scarlett O'Hara asks what will become of her and begs Rhett Butler to take her back, we

expect he will, and director Victor Fleming is aware of our expectations (as was Margaret Mitchell). Rhett's "Frankly darling, I don't give a damn" jolts us then and the surprise rejection it contains and not its use of a four-letter word explains the extraordinary memorability of the line.

Of course, the problem with *culturally induced associations* does not lie in their manipulation but in the way they may work towards the distortion of meaning. When we insist that the children in *Lord of the Flies* are sweet and innocent things (as our culture suggests all children are), we are emphatically denying the sense projected before us.

4. Closely akin to the culturally induced association, but distinct in the possibility of its being private as well, is the *reverberating heart string*. When the young hero of *The 400 Blows* stands defeated at land's end and we insist that tomorrow everything will be all right, we are indeed substituting a flowery and unfounded optimism for the harsh pessimism implicit in the scene. When we insist that there is something wrong with the children who play *Forbidden Games,* we are refusing to relinquish our sentimental view of children, and, more significantly, refusing the material offered. Our film will be made of other stuff.

Essentially unrelated, but mentioned at this point because so often seen as connected to and sometimes, in fact, confused with the *reverberating heart string* is the inability or unwillingness to talk about a film. Usually, such ineffable experiences arise from the sensation of exquisite beauty or from intense identification or from the recognition of a particularly painful insight. The problem here, however, lies not so much in experiencing the film as it does in the examination and expression of the experience. Certainly, we cannot reasonably demand of every filmgoer that he explore and verbalize his experience; but we can and indeed must demand that students and critics of film do so.

5. From the very opposite kind of response rises a fifth difficulty, that of the *refusal to feel*. A viewer whose psychology is of this kind would deny the beauty of a film such as *Umbrellas of Cherbourg* because of its lush colors and puristic love affair. He would insist that life just isn't like the life in *A Man and a Woman* or that people don't die for love's sake as they do in *Elvira Madigan*.

6. *Intellectual commitments* constitute another difficulty. An overly firm commitment to a particular system of beliefs can frequently

distort meanings or, in instances where meanings are recognized, force their rejection on the grounds of disagreement. For example, a persistent preoccupation with psychoanalytic insights would turn the adult male of *Sundays and Cybele* into a psychopath because of his affection for a young girl. If your moral system holds that adultery is a sin, you must condemn the relationship dramatized in *Brief Encounter.* If you are deeply concerned with civil rights and the abuse of minority groups, you may go so far as to see *King Kong* as an allegory of slavery.

7. *Aesthetic presuppositions*—general assumptions about what makes for art—are essentially a special kind of *intellectual commitment,* but because they are so explicitly central to criticism, they demand separate treatment. There are some aesthetic commitments that are so clearly skewed, they can be dismissed as lunatic fringe. "The film prostitutes itself if it is in color" is harmless because it is not widespread. It will not often interfere with the experiencing of color films. The same holds true for a bias such as Rudolph Arnheim's against the "talking film" when sustained in the present. For although an occasional silent may appear—like *The Spy*—sound has by now become such an integral and integrated part of the total film experience that to reject it almost constitutes a dismissal of the medium itself.

Many *aesthetic presuppositions,* however, do not derive so clearly as do these from theoretical considerations of what film should be, but instead from concepts of art in general (and especially, art with conceptual content). Such *aesthetic presuppositions* are not in themselves barriers to the realization of film; indeed, it would be virtually impossible to organize the experience of film without them. But any filmgoer who has *aesthetic presuppositions* (which may also serve as aesthetic criteria) that cannot be adapted to the demands of a particular film is in big trouble. And the fact remains that there are some *aesthetic presuppositions* which seem repeatedly to lend themselves to abuse.

If, for example, a filmgoer has a didactic bias—films have messages—and goes to see *Goldfinger,* he will be hard pressed to find the message. He finally decides, though, that the film does have a message: "Hoarding is dangerous." He can stop right there, which is bad enough, for surely he has not allowed the celluloid strip to play much of a part in his experience with *Goldfinger.* But chances are he will not stop there, but will go on to say, "What a stupid message. What a lousy film."

The belief that great films have great themes is a more subtle *aesthetic presupposition.* "Great" here obviously shifts in meaning. When it qualifies "film," it points to that which is exceptional; when it describes "theme" (in itself a highly equivocal term, sometimes confused with message, sometimes with subject, but in this context nearly synonymous with meaning), "great" equals universal. Exceptional films then are those that have universal meanings. *The Maltese Falcon* most probably does not express a "great theme." Must it then be seen as unexceptional, or as exceptional in only a very limited sense? As an exceptional genre film, let's say, a fine film of its kind? A sufficiently firm commitment to the great theme will force the conclusion that it is not fine anything, since entire genres can be dismissed on this principle. More significantly though, a commitment to the great theme may compel the critic who has, despite his bias, perceived *The Maltese Falcon* as exceptional to discover in it a universally significant comment on greed, let's say, and thus involve him in an essential distortion. On the other hand, the identical commitment may lead to inflated assessments of films such as *The Pawnbroker* or even *Exodus* which, whatever their aesthetic quality in general, at least attempt to express great themes.

It may well be true that one film, all other things being equal, is by virtue of its theme a greater work of art than another film. After all, doesn't this presupposition arise from the great humanistic tradition? But the point is that wholesale application of this *aesthetic presupposition* (as of any other) is in a sense like having to sit behind an enormous pillar when viewing a film.

8. A very special kind of difficulty lies in the matter of how much experience and how much information a viewer brings with him. The issue here is not really one of understanding. It is rather one of *not being with it.* For example, if you have never seen a Busby Berkeley musical, the shot of the chorus line forming a swastika in *The Producers* loses much of its force for you. If you've never seen a Bogart film (highly unlikely, of course) the presence of the Bogart poster in *Breathless* cannot arouse the associations and meanings its depiction clearly invites. If you have never seen the Marx brothers and, even more, if you are unprepared for inter-film references, you cannot appreciate the use of the name Chico in *Shoot the Piano Player.*

9. Finally, we come to what is probably the most widespread kind of difficulty, that of *failure in aesthetic perception.* In great part,

this is a matter of education. We may be trained to perceive principles of composition, organization, unity, color, and texture. But we may also have acquired these sensitivities in a less structured fashion. We speak of a *sense* of rhythm, a *sense* of balance, of movement, and of design, suggesting that these are inborn faculties. Whatever the explanation, the quality and intensity of our sense perceptions vary greatly. A viewer may simply fail to see the extraordinary pattern of John Ford's famous and much imitated shot of the Indians overlooking the plains in *Stagecoach.* A viewer may overlook the carefully sustained pacing of a typical Hitchcock film, as *The Birds,* where the first section of the film is purposefully calm and slow. He may be unable to feel the claustrophobia established by Roman Polanski's use of shots which are restricted and close and clipped at the outset of *Rosemary's Baby.* While *failure in aesthetic perception* is unlikely to be limited to the film but will also characterize a particular viewer's response to paintings and literature as well, there are aesthetic qualities special to film itself which lead to unique difficulties in apprehension. Only a viewer with highly developed sensory responses will consciously observe the shadowlessness of the trees in *Last Year at Marienbad* or the continuous tracking shot of the traffic jam in *Weekend.* Less sensitivity is required to note the flanking of the very short Cabiria by two towering prostitutes on the Via Veneto or to hear the motifs associated with each character in the *Umbrellas of Cherbourg.* And while it is possible to overlook the first person camera in Robert Montgomery's *Lady of the Lake,* on the other hand, it is almost impossible without extreme sensitivity to visual imagery and extraordinary quickness of perception to notice the sign on the truck advertising *Cahiers du Cinema* in Truffaut's *Shoot the Piano Player.* And since these difficulties are, as we have suggested, special to the film medium, we have arrived at a variety of problems wholely different from those encountered in other art forms.

Problems Inherent in the Film

1. The first difficulty in this category lies in the *use of conventions.* Film, as all other art forms, relies on certain conventions of form and content. When the Indians appear on the crest of the mountain, the film is announcing that they will attack. Rain and storm signal danger, and Transylvania, in turn, signals rain and storm. A black hat

in a cowboy film informs us that we have met the badman. A German accent until at least 1950 was a clue to the villain. These seem very obvious, but they do depend in great part on our past experience with films. For example, it is only because we have been conditioned to the flashback device that we know the little blonde girl in *Rachel, Rachel* is Joanne Woodward as a child. We know, too, because we have seen the technique before, that a darkened screen, following a kiss and followed by a sunny morn means a couple have had sexual intercourse. Interestingly, our familiarity with conventions and our conditioned responses to them can serve to force unwarranted interpretations. An excellent example is in *Blow-Up* when the cut indicating time passage in the scene between David Hemmings and the half-dressed Vanessa Redgrave is automatically assumed to mean intercourse has taken place, simply because such cuts have signalled this in the past. There is nothing, however, in the scene itself to suggest this; in fact, there is considerable evidence against it, such as the consistency of Miss Redgrave's distinctive costume before and after the cut.

2. Closely related to the use of conventions is a high degree of *technical consistency* in films which has tended to invite strong formal expectations on the part of the audience. We expect a film to be of a certain length, to see it all at once and not on separate days as we had to see *War and Peace.* We were, until Truffaut began making movies, largely unprepared for stills in the midst of a motion picture, and despite this exposure remain even less ready for the inertia of Andy Warhol's camera. Because we anticipate consistency in the quality of the film, we are jarred by such shifts as those in color (as ancient an innovation as it is), and in photographic texture, as in *The Naked Night.* We have been trained to accept illusion as reality and are shocked when the illusion is destroyed, or at least modified, by the direct address of a film character and the visual statement that film is film in Godard's *La Chinoise.* We expect clarification, answers to questions, and are consequently troubled by the unresolved disappearance of the girl in *L'Avventura* and by the unexplained marble slab in *2001.* The point is that film has established these expectations and in recent years has been violating them more and more as it has increased in self-consciousness and seriousness. In much the same way as we have come to revise our notions of what shape a poem must assume, or even what constitutes art, we must rethink our attitudes toward film.

3. Richard Burton has been applauded for his bravery in playing a homosexual. Barbara Stanwyck, less courageous and apparently more committed to her screen image, refused a similar role in *The Killing of Sister George.* Although the daring of Burton would seem to lie in the acceptance of a certain kind of role, one that might be morally reprehensible to his following, it really lies in his assumption that he can act so well and so dynamically that the audience will be able to overcome its highly structured view of the super-heterosexual. We can blame the star system but whatever its source, we come to a film with deep preconceptions as to the nature of its star—in other words, we confront the difficulty of the *actor as barrier* to our understanding. Humphrey Bogart cannot be purely evil. Bette Davis is never innocent. It's a cliché by now that part of the convincingness of European films can be explained by the introduction of new faces, of people we do not know and can associate only with their immediate roles. (Ingmar Bergman's films of course must be excepted here.) But there is still another effect. The European film with its cast of unknowns becomes more puzzling. When Gregory Peck appears in a crowd of extras we know it is he to whom we must be attentive. We do not have the same response to Henri Serre (Jim in *Jules and Jim*).

4. Currently, the same response—the preconceived idea of what we will be given—has been carried over from stars to directors. *Belle du Jour* was made by Buñuel. It must be good. *Secrets of Women* was directed by Ingmar Bergman. It must be serious, heavy, obscure. *Mr. and Mrs. Smith* was directed by Alfred Hitchcock. We wait throughout and unsatisfied for the mystery to develop.

This tendency to set up the *director as barrier* operates somewhat more subtly, and surely more pervasively, among adherents to the *auteur* theory of film. The point is that viewing the director as the single artist of a film will often lead to pushing and pulling film experiences so that the *oeuvre* of this artist can be discussed. What we do here, generally, is to take our past experiences of a director's films, draw from them qualities which we transform into *aesthetic presuppositions,* and apply them (all too frequently with extraordinary rigidity) to the film of his we next may view. And this is not simply a matter of evaluation ("The film is bad Fellini"; "This is inferior Truffaut"); it is much more one of distorting our experiences in order to leave our presuppositions in tact.

5. Films share with novels the quality of being judged and recommended. We rarely go to a film or read a book without someone's

opinion, whether negative or positive, preceding our experience and frequently coloring it. But film sharply departs from literature in the nature of the atmosphere in which it is experienced. A book is read by a reader who is alone, or at least alone in the experiencing of the book. A *film is a social event.* It is seen by groups, and the group with which it is seen alters the experiencing of that film, since the audience provides a simultaneous feedback to the viewer. Thus, *Dr. Strangelove* was a very different motion picture in the two theatres in which it was shown for its premiere engagement in New York City. In an eastside art house, seats were hard to come by, the theatre was always crowded, and there was much laughter. In a larger Broadway house, the theatre tended to be only half full and the audience, much less with it, laughed very little. *Dr. Strangelove* was a much more comic film on the eastside than on the west, and the difference was clearly reflected in discussions of the film among those who had seen it in these varying situations. The point is laughter is contagious. And the canned giggles and guffaws of radio and television make the point. Very frequently, we have to be told what's funny.

6. The special ability of film to provide *the illusion of reality* makes it a strikingly compelling medium. It also, however, brings to the experience of film one of its greatest difficulties: the belief that a movie must be "true-to-life." And although this notion pervades attitudes towards other art forms, it does not lead to the same confusion it does with film. A novel is, after all, words in a very small package, while the film is so easily confused with real life. So that while we tend to say, for example, that a novel is not true-to-life because we do not believe the humanity of its characters, or the situations in which they find themselves, or because the experiences the novel provides are ones unlikely to be met in the world-out-there, when we say a film is not true-to-life, we mean this but something else as well.

For instance, when we remark that *The Umbrellas of Cherbourg* is not true-to-life (and if we offer this as negative criticism we are, of course, misunderstanding the whole spirit of the film), we are essentially saying two things: we are saying that the events, and probably the emotions, it relates seem false to what occurs in real life as we know it; but we are also saying that the movie doesn't *look* real—that the wallpaper in our homes doesn't match our clothing, that the colors of brick walls we happen to pass do not harmonize so consistently with our moods and situations, and that people do not sing to each other; they talk. Similarly, when we perceive Italian films as more realistic than American ones, it is very often because the world of these foreign films—the total environment projected on the screen before us—is unidealized and thus totally recognizable to us as an image of the world-out-there. The Rome, then, of *The Nights of Cabiria* is consistent with our own vision of reality, while the Rome, let's say, of *Three Coins in a Fountain* is idealized, romanticized, and finally false.

"People look like real people in foreign films." And on that ground, the movie is more true-to-life. This may very well be a valid observation. But one must restrict this comment very carefully to matters of appearance. For while the set may be actual—the film shot on location—while the actors may wear little make-up, one may easily be deceived into mistaking a superficial, pictorial reality for other than it is, as a faithful portrayal of life. Because *Marjorie Morningstar* was filmed in New York City, because its characters live on Central Park West where their real life counterparts in fact do, and because it gives us the illusion of authenticity in other ways as well (the Bar Mitzvah and the Catskill hotel), we may be conned into seeing the movie as true-to-life in a more basic and philosophic sense. Because the kitchen in *Who's Afraid of Virginia Woolf* looks very much lived in, we may on this basis alone fall into the trap of believing the film is true-to-life.

The point is that visual authenticity gives only *the illusion of reality.* It must not be confused with the faithful representation of human experience, any more than it must be confused with reality itself. The film may seem to be reality, but if it were reality it would cease to be film and become life and then where would we be?

• • • • • •

The problems we have listed—as generalized, as oversimplified, and perhaps as arbitrary in their arrangement as they may be—suggest that difficulties in the reconstruction of images and sound into meaningful film experience fall into two general categories: those which arise primarily from our own individual psychologies—our individual preconceptions—our individual tastes, if you will; and those which arise from the nature of film itself. Despite their source, however, these are the problems inherent in the encounter of film and viewer, and they are reflected in the way we talk about film and in the way professional writers talk about it. When Dwight MacDonald suggests that *L'Avventura* is less effective than it might have been because the wrong girl got lost, what we see at work seems a peculiarly personal response to Monica Vitti rather than an aesthetic response to the film. When Stanley Kauffmann remarks without development that in Franco Zefferelli's version of *Romeo and Juliet,* important scenes are omitted, he may well be saying no more than that scenes he personally likes have been cut. What is important is that we be on guard, both when speaking ourselves and when listening to others, against failed judgment and attempt to discover what criteria are actually at work in these judgments. Earlier, we suggested that in films the problems of criticism are dramatized more than in other arts because of the medium's newness, because of its tentative status, and its consequently unstructured criteria.

Still another difficulty remains to be noted. Despite the plethora of books on film and despite the growth of serious film magazines, most writing on films takes the form of the daily or weekly review. And while in the field of literary criticism, the articles of Charles Poore and Thomas Lask are not confused with the work of F. R. Leavis, no such distinction holds true in film criticism. In part, this is due to the limited body of serious film criticism. But more important is the marked tendency of the film critic to restrict himself to current releases, whereas the serious literary critic almost never works within such limits. The reasons for this are obvious; if Lionel Trilling chooses to discuss Dickens, the reader of his criticism may pick the volume off his shelf and check the critic's statements against the novel. No such luxury is afforded the student of film. If Andrew Sarris were to discuss, for example René Clair's *Sous les Toits de Paris,* the student in considering Sarris' remarks must—if the film is not presently being shown—rely on a distant experience. Even more significantly, if the student has never seen the film, he has no immediate way of doing so. He cannot go to the public library. And what of the critic himself? He too must rely on what is currently being screened. How can he responsibly discuss a work he has not viewed for ten years, if at all? Still another problem is one that is analogous to that of reliable texts in literature. Any literary scholar knows that he cannot depend on a popularized edition of Shakespeare when attempting serious analysis. But how reliable are the prints of many classic films?

Film talk then is deeply committed to the moment. In the context of a film course, however, one has a special advantage: films, selected from the productions of many years, are shown, and we have the opportunity to examine present responses and past ones—to contrast, to consider, to compare—above all, to *see*. Here, then, are groups of reviews: critical pieces hopefully concerning films you are now studying.

PART II

Practice

ACCIDENT

Hollis Alpert, *SATURDAY REVIEW*
April 24, 1967

Where It's Happening

As Bob Hope made amply clear during the recent Academy Awards telecast, the scene of film-making excellence is the London area, where several active studios fringe the city. It can hardly be accidental that a preponderance of the best directors, actors, and writers is concentrated here, and it seems to be more a matter of atmosphere than geography that helps to account for a level of quality beyond the present capabilities of Hollywood. Indeed, two American companies —Columbia and Universal—are firmly embarked on production programs aimed at taking advantage of the London-based talent pool, and all of our majors appear to look with favor on projects that originate in England. The results are not only apparent at Academy Award time; the box office, too, is responding briskly to such films as *Blow-Up, Alfie,* and *Georgy Girl,* as well as to the award-showered *A Man for All Seasons.*

Not only is the direction of the above films of an accomplished nature, but the acting, too, is exemplary. The genuine stars, it is becoming all too clear, are the members of the Redgrave clan and such disparate types as Paul Scofield, Michael Caine, David Hemmings, and Albert Finney. While Hollywood hopefully continues its search for "talent," often with its eyes focused on legs and bosoms, each new British film of distinction manages to display someone new and more genuinely exciting. And veterans such as James Mason also shine anew from time to time. (1)

Now *Accident* has come along, a remarkably atmospheric (2) film that examines some of the erotic tensions in a middle-aged academic community and exhibits the rare finesse of its director, Joseph Losey. Mr. Losey has been an in-and-outer. From the hothouse decadence of *The Servant* of a few years ago, he found himself out of his element with a James Bond parody called *Modesty Blaise*. But he is back on the track again with *Accident,* in many ways his best film. Again he has had the script help of Harold Pinter, as he did for *The Servant,* and his star is again Dirk Bogarde, who is somehow an enormously sensitive actor when directed by Losey.

Based on a novel by Nicholas Mosley, Pinter's script is of the evocative kind that concentrates on images rather than dialogue. Wordiness is definitely not one of the handicaps of *Accident,* and, in fact, it might be complained that the characters express themselves in all too clipped a British manner. Losey, an American long based in England, is, however, undoubtedly putting on a bit his hosts and getting some humorous bite out of their habits. (3) Only one stark event provides the action phase of the film—an Oxford philosophy student (Michael York) is killed in an automobile accident—and the rest is all a studied portrayal of the possible causes of the accident and its disturbing effects on the lives of several people.

There is a girl, of course, an Austrian student of some sort of aristocratic lineage, as is the philosophy student who wants to marry her. And she, passive, beautiful, and sexually amoral, causes a vast yearning in the breast of a middle-aged Oxford don (married, two

---

1. How relevant are these first two paragraphs to an understanding of *Accident?*

2. How useful is the word "atmospheric" in this context?

3. Is Alpert complaining? Is he saying that more dialogue would help to clarify his experience of the film? And, how does Alpert know that Losey is "putting on" the English?

children, another on the way), and succumbs to the seduction of another Oxford professor who plans to leave his wife for love of her. A perfectly ordinary academic situation, in other words, explored often enough by novelists. But it is what Losey does with it that counts. Quietly building his tensions incident by incident, getting a quality of recognition of an almost painful kind in each scene, he exposes the discontents, torments, and fears of his people. Eventually the quiet don (Dirk Bogarde) commits himself to a shameful, shocking ravaging of the girl, and his pitiableness is evident even to himself.

Actually, there are contrivances in the story. The accident is too neatly arranged—the student dies, and the girl, who is driving, lives—but since the accident serves as a framework only, this doesn't matter too much. What fascinates is the intimate contact we are given with presumably prosaic lives. And here the acting helps enormously. Bogarde is fully believable; Stanley Baker as his friend, a flashy academic sort, equally at home at Oxford or on television as a witty pundit, reveals himself to be a first-rate actor; and Michael York, who is new, is another in the increasing list of British male discoveries. There is another estimable performance by Vivien Merchant as the don's wife, and the only weak member of the cast is Jacqueline Sassard, as the girl who unwittingly causes all the emotional havoc in the scholarly backwaters. She is stiff and ill-at-ease. But, aside from a couple of directorial indulgences—and that choice of Miss Sassard—Losey's film is subtle, revelatory, and, on the whole, distinguished. (4)

---

4. Has Alpert demonstrated that *Accident* is "subtle, revelatory . . . distinguished"?

Judith Crist, *NEW YORK WORLD JOURNAL TRIBUNE* April 18, 1967

The Agony beneath the Skin Revealed with Surgical Skill

"Accident," the second Joseph Losey-Harold Pinter screen collaboration, is, like "The Servant," a film to watch with fascination and brood about afterward. And if ultimately we are left to question whether it is worth the brooding, at very least we are left also with the satisfaction of having watched two master craftsmen at work.

In his adaptation of Nicholas Mosley's novel, Mr. Pinter proves his genius for capturing the essence of our society in the small-talk veneer of our lives, in probing to the heart of the matter with needle-pricks that barely blemish the skin, in turning the commonplace into a portentous suggestion of all the human agony that feeds on its own secrecy. And the vivid camera eye of Joseph Losey's direction observes, implies and challenges us to see beyond its own visualizations.

Out of the Wreckage

The film literally starts off with a bang—the auto accident near the home of an Oxford don. Two of his students were in the car; William, a golden boy, is dead. The don, Stephen, pulls the dazed survivor, Anna, from the wreckage, takes her into his house, lets the police conclude that only the boy was in the car and then, watching the girl's troubled sleep, recalls the beginning of their relationship.

Conventionally, then, with flashback, we are introduced to those involved with the boy and girl—Stephen, drawn to both by their youth and the malaise of his oncoming middle age, fighting his desire for the enigmatic and exotic girl; Charley, his successful extroverted colleague and friend, whom he envies for his physical, intellectual and sexual athleticism; Rosalind, his sensitive and pragmatic wife, aware of Stephen's vulnerability during her pregnancy with their third child, aware of the pathetic frailties and stupidities of married men of a certain age.

A Summer Sunday

Thrust among the three "mature" adults are the boy, only vaguely aware of the challenge his youthful prowess and aristocratic background put upon the men, and the girl, sloe-eyed and impassive, aware of her status as focus of desire but seemingly devoid of initiative in stimulating it. And in a triumphant sequence of the film, the five spend a desultory and languid summer Sunday at Stephen's home, with sports and drink and small-talk to hide the building pyramid of emotion, the smoldering suspicions and resentments and jealousies, the minor wounds inflicted in passing and quick to fester. These are relatively decent people accidentally—by pure chance—involved with each other, tearing at each other's hearts and guts with a "tennis, anyone?" superficiality.

The center of interest is the involvement of the two men with the girl, an ultimately overt and abandoned involvement on Charley's part. But it is Stephen, an intelligent and considerate and responsible man, a devoted and honest husband, who—by pure chance, literally the auto accident—can turn to total amorality, commit an indecent act and leave the surface of his life unrippled.

The outer lushness and surface calm of their lives in Oxford and its environs is counterpointed with the frustrations of Stephen's attempts to compete with Charley as a television pundit or to rekindle an affair with a past mistress, with explosions of physical violence in sports (with a "traditional" game of indoor rugby permitting don and pupil to do physical battle for the girl), with emotional outbursts in the still of night or in the dreariness of a sodden country garden.

The Way It Is

This is the way it is with us (1)—and the stolidity and intelligence of Dirk Bogarde's Stephen, Stanley Baker's Charley, Vivien Mer-

---

1. What are we being told when Miss Crist says, "This is the way it is with us"? Are you convinced?

chant's Rosalind and Michael York's William add conviction. We destroy each other—by accident. We are victims of our instincts that are unleashed—by accident. True. Too true, perhaps. So true, in fact, that we wind up with a suspicion that Messrs. Losey and Pinter could not be stating the obvious so obviously.

They state it in fascinating cinematic terms, (2) filling the eye, alerting the ear to every nuance, titillating the intellect. But they leave the emotions unscathed. "Accident" is for watching, and even the brooders among us will settle for that on the Losey-Pinter level. (3)

---

2. Have we any clue to what the "fascinating cinematic terms" might be? Note that Miss Crist, like Mr. Alpert, fails to mention that the film is in color.

3. In this review, Miss Crist focuses heavily on the plot of the film. To what extent *is* the plot the film? And perhaps more significant, to what extent does a movie like *Accident* with its particular ambiguities invite us to focus on plot? Does Miss Crist's comment from her Sunday review of the same film, "The era of read-it-yourself moviemaking seems to be upon us with a vengeance . . ." provide us with too facile an answer to this question?

Andrew Sarris, *THE VILLAGE VOICE*
May 18, 1967

"ACCIDENT" (at Cinema II) leaves too little to accident. Joseph Losey and Harold Pinter achieve precision at the expense of preciseness. The cutting is razor sharp. The camera moves with cool, cruel logic. The dialogue is almost turgid in its terseness. "Accident" is the most fascinating slice of stilled life since "Blow-Up." Losey and Antonioni find difficulty in breathing life into landscapes. Their characters inhabit the world without living in it. Losey and Antonioni

---

are brilliant but incomplete artists(1). Renoir, Ophuls, Mizoguchi dig and dig into their material until they find all the tunnels of communication linking their characters. Losey and Antonioni take an aerial view of the terrain and curse the camouflage for obscuring their view of humanity.

"The Servant" was more Losey than Pinter. "Accident" is more Pinter than Losey.(2) Losey's talent was better served in "Modesty Blaise," Pinter's in "The Quiller Memorandum." The structure of "Accident" is too complex for melodrama, but its statement is too elliptical for tragedy. The cast is dominated by Stanley Baker and Dirk Bogarde as two Oxford dons middle-aged to the point of medievalism. The women are incidental. Vivien Merchant's pregnant wife is enigmatically earthy. Delphine Seyrig's desperate bachelor girl is enigmatically abstracted. Jacqueline Sassard's poltergeist princess is enigmatically mediocre. Michael York's young aristocrat dies as meaningless as he has lived and loved, and a new-born baby has difficulty breathing.

"Accident" is at its best when its characters are too tired to talk. Or too disgusted. The clipped dialogue does not suggest the profundity of something unspoken, only the aimlessness and incompleteness of the speaker's feelings. The characters are all power-oriented and yet disconnected. Bogarde envies Baker's prowess on brains-trust television even though the medium is a mess. Bogarde feels cuckolded when he discovers Baker's prowess with the poltergeist princess. Cuckoldry descends to complicity. Bogarde comes to pity the compulsiveness of Baker's prowess. Bogarde and Baker collaborate on a seduction. Baker provides the consummate style of consummation. Bogarde assumes all the anguished guilt.

"Accident" is the story of a sexual fantasy shared by two middle-aged intellectuals. The fact that Jacqueline Sassard's poltergeist princess is a mediocre fille fatale is undoubtedly intentional but still miscalculated.(3) The audience is not implicated in passionate long-

---

1. The phrase "incomplete artist" has an objective ring. Does Sarris at any point tell us what makes for incompletion? If so, what?

2. Is Sarris saying here that the film is more the creation of the screen writer than of the director, or are Pinter and Losey labels for style or tone? In either case, is there a value judgment implied?

3. How does Sarris know the mediocrity is "undoubtedly intentional"?

ing. It remains detached from the protagonists. It is chilled by the absence of genuine temptation. It is bored by the suppression of psychological investigation. The world is not yet so weary that no prospect pleases. Or is it? What are we all really after? Where is all the fullness of our own lives that Losey and Pinter (and Antonioni) allegedly neglect? Losey and Pinter strike too close to home and hearth in "Accident." Theirs is a world that would rather die than grow old. It is our world. It is us.

Joseph Losey may not exactly thrive on controversy, but he seems to arouse it on every level from the most vulgar to the most esoteric. Originally an exile from the Hollywood blacklist, he seemed by all indications to belong to the committed Left. In quick succession, he was embraced by a rightist faction in Cahiers du Cinema, enthroned by Movie, and repudiated by Sight and Sound. Realist critics have always resisted the intensity and sweep of his style, the steady hysteria of his actors, the violence of his plots. By any standards, Losey's is a technique that calls attention to itself or, more properly, to the personal feelings of Joseph Losey.

Losey has spent most of his career on commissioned projects that mixed melodrama with social significance. The movies of his Hollywood period—"The Boy with Green Hair," "The Lawless," "The Prowler," "M," and "The Big Night"—have gained in interest over the years as the exaggerations of a style have become more expressive of an era. The stage director of Charles Laughton in Bertolt Brecht's "Galileo" and the screen director of Harold Pinter's scripts for "The Servant" and "Accident," Losey seems always to have aspired beyond the presumed limitations of genre movies. The High Art Game is an understandable temptation to the movie director, particularly in the culturally beleaguered Anglo-American cinema. Indeed, "The Servant" and "Accident" have done more for Losey's general reputation than all his other pictures put together. (4)

Ironically, Losey's personality comes through more clearly and forcefully in such relatively neglected works as "Time Without Pity," "Chance Meeting," "The Concrete Jungle," "King and Country," and "Modesty Blaise." Like many directors, Losey seems more effective when he transcends conventions than when he avoids them altogether.

---

4. What view of film art is implied by Sarris' devotion of three paragraphs to Losey's career? Do they help us to understand *Accident?*

Genre movies give him the distancing he needs to writhe expressively on the screen. By contrast, movies about Life and Time and The World seem to make him relatively subdued, functional, and impersonal. Losey's dilemma is not unique. With "Accident," Losey has escaped the clutches of the cultists only to fall into the hands of the snobs.

Andrew Sarris, *THE VILLAGE VOICE* June 8, 1967

Second thoughts on "Accident" have crept into a corner of my critical conscience, and refuse to be dislodged. How does one do justice to troublesome artists like Losey and Pinter? The slightest hint of critical doubt becomes a damaging pan. As it is, Donen and Raphael ("Two for the Road") were treated more generously here than were Losey and Pinter. Though Donen and Raphael gave me more than I expected, and Losey and Pinter gave me less than I expected, the difference between "Accident" and "Two for the Road" is the difference between personal art and manipulative entertainment. I had the same trouble last year with Losey's "Modesty Blaise" and Wyler's "How to Steal a Million." When you add everything up in the ultimate scale of values, Losey is more interesting than Wyler and Donen put together. The immediate experience, however, still raises perplexing questions.

"Accident" is full of meanings to which I did not respond emotionally. Losey himself has spoken of the death-defying arrogance of the British aristocracy, but I didn't feel it in Michael York's characterization even when it was superimposed on his death-mask. I didn't understand the point of the violent indoor game in "Accident." I didn't respond to the moral problems posed for the two Oxford dons. I didn't even understand what the moral problems were supposed to be. Adultery? Come now. It may not be good form to seduce your students, or even to let your students seduce you, but once this

---

breach of moral custom is observed, the investigation of individuals must continue. In "Accident," sentence is passed before any witnesses have testified. The flashback structure sees to that. Death haunts all the characters from their first entrance to their last exit. Death and indifference. Alexander Knox's Provost never finishes a story and can barely remember that he has a daughter languishing in London.

The trouble is that Stanley Baker and Dirk Bogarde dominate the proceedings so completely with their performances that I see everything from their point of view. One of the most beautiful shots in the film shows Stanley Baker's "turning off" from everyone around him at the kitchen table. As his mind wanders, mine wanders with it. Certainly Jacqueline Sassard's personality is too pallid to make me speculate about her attitude. She remains a boring enigma throughout the film. The Marienbad interlude with Delphine Seyrig has its moments, particularly when the lonely bachelor girl wriggles coyly into her coat with a movement of desperate flirtatiousness, but the episode fails as a whole because it seems so carefully contrived to prove something.

Losey and Pinter ridicule the meaning game as applied to their work, and I see no reason not to take them at their word. My objection to "Accident" is that it never takes off beyond the conscious intention of its creators. Losey and Pinter have calculated closely and shrewdly, but their characters have become suffocated from an excess of artistic sensibility. Even the tennis game is made to count for something by being deviously meaningful as opposed to Antonioni's obviously meaningful tennis masquerade in "Blow-Up." Both Losey and Antonioni play with the possibilities of suspense, but they don't really believe in it. Still, "Accident" and "Blow-Up" remain the most striking testaments modern cinema has given us the past season, and if there are any better performances than Baker's and Bogarde's in "Accident" this year I will be very deliriously surprised (1).

---

1. Is Sarris apologizing for his previous review?

Brendan Gill, *THE NEW YORKER*
April 15, 1967

Inside the Redoubt

Joseph Losey's admirable new movie, curtly entitled "Accident," begins and ends with long shots of a snug, rosy brick, many-windowed Georgian house set in the green countryside a few miles from elmy Oxford. The master of the house is a good-looking don, skittishly approaching the middle years; his tacky, sensible wife, less good-looking than he is and bitchy enough when the occasion warrants, is about to bear their third child. One of the undergraduates whom the don tutors is an athletic aristocrat, who has fallen in love with a severely beautiful Austrian princess, also an undergraduate. The princess being exceptional in her sexual ambitions as well as in her looks, the aristocrat proves insufficient booty; she makes a prize of one of the don's colleagues—not a very savory chap and so not much of a prize—and does her best to place the don himself under her rule, which is all the more imperious for seeming so permissive. The rosy house stands for that private redoubt of domesticity in which the conventional kindnesses offered to outsiders—food, drink, talk, a night's lodging—can be taken unfair advantage of only at high cost. For domesticity, though it gives a smiling welcome, is hostile to strangers, and the embrace it offers is a form of courteous exclusion, warning "Thus far and no farther." The princess is a threat to the house, and sooner or later the evil she brings into it must be purged—in this case, by the sacrificial death of an innocent, in the accident that gives the picture its name. The unuttered, invisible motto of the don's house, and indeed of every house, is that marriage and the family are imperfect and sometimes horrifying inventions but that they are all we have; we tamper with them at our peril.

The screenplay of "Accident" is by Harold Pinter, who has based it on a novel by Nicholas Mosley. Mr. Pinter is fantastically clever at presenting family scenes that, under a smooth surface, are so charged with the ability to ravage and destroy that even Count Dracula might hesitate to pull up a chair and join the group. In a characteristic scene in "Accident," Mr. Pinter sketches for us a pleasant, lazy Sunday in the country: drinks, lunch, tennis, an hour or so of dozing and idle chatter on the lawn, more drinks, perhaps a walk, a pickup supper, drinks again . . . It is so harmless and so commonplace, but somewhere along the way the gates of Hell have secretly, silently swung ajar, and devils swoop and chitter like swallows in the evening air. Mr. Pinter appears to believe that evil is an entity and that man is capable of being invaded and possessed by it—we are fallen creatures who slowly bleed ourselves to death by the infliction upon each other of innumerable small spiritual injuries. Mr. Pinter conveys this progressive, irreversible disaster with words, and Mr. Losey conveys it with precise pictorial correlatives. The two men make an exceptionally gifted and intelligent team, and I hope they will go on working together for a long time to come. (An earlier Losey-Pinter collaboration was that brilliant study of corruption "The Servant," in which, as in "Accident," a house played a role so important that it became, in effect, one of the leading characters.)

In the cast of "Accident" are Dirk Bogarde, as the don; Vivien Merchant, as his wife; Jacqueline Sassard, as the princess; Stanley Baker, as the don's shady, aggressive colleague; Michael York, as the aristocrat; and Delphine Seyrig, as a lonely ex-girl friend of the don. Mr. Bogarde and Mr. Baker give superb performances; I wish I could say as much for Miss Sassard, a newcomer to whom the adjective "promising" does not instantly affix itself. We also catch a glimpse of Mr. Pinter, playing the role of a high-powered television executive in London; he is extremely funny. The excellent camerawork in "Accident" is by Gerry Fisher. (1)

---

1. A tenet that is repeated in this text is that the best criticism is that which accounts for the most elements in a film and omits the least. In this review, the focus would seem to be on a single element, the house. Does this apparently exclusive attention to a single element constitute bad criticism? Or does the reviewer manage to use the house to provide both an organizing principle and a key to the essential meanings of the film?

Tom Milne, *SIGHT AND SOUND*
Spring, 1967

Third time lucky, as they say. For if *Muriel* and *La Guerre est Finie* were rather less than fairly treated by the critics, *Accident* has been justly acclaimed as masterly in its exploration, through a dislocated time structure, of the turbulent emotions lying unspoken and unperceived beneath a calm surface. Not that Losey is content simply to follow Resnais: making graceful acknowledgment of his debt, he pushes even further along these new paths. In *Accident* there is no mysterious lover from the past, no haunting loyalty for a lost cause, to lend dramatic echoes to the situation: simply a banal incident, involving more or less banal people, whose clipped, glancing conversation is never of the slightest apparent consequence. And Losey's style is all his own: a return to the simplicity of his early films, with the later baroque splendours still lending their riches, but reduced to order by firmness of line. Starting with an accident and ending with its echo, constructed out of a chain of interlocking emotions which lead right back where they started from, gradually generating a beam of light to illuminate the central situation before it dies away again, *Accident* is as simple, as baffingly perfect—and as difficult to take apart—as a circle. (1)

"All you need is a starting point. Here, for instance, on this lawn," says Charley (Stanley Baker) in one of the key scenes, the long, lazy summer afternoon when the characters are almost provoked into burning their social boats in speech. So all right, let's start on the lawn. Five adults (and two children) pottering happily about on a hot, endless summer Sunday, probably not thinking about anything in particular: the youthfully middle-aged Oxford don, Stephen (Dirk Bogarde), who would like to be having an affair with one of his

---

1. Consider the criterion of perfection Milne establishes here. Is the implication that, suggested by the experience of *Accident,* it applies only to this film, or does it seem to have a more general application?

pupils, the beautiful Austrian student Anna; his wife Rosalind (Vivien Merchant), contentedly pregnant, but still lazily watchful; his friend Charley who, unknown to him, is in fact having an affair with Anna; another pupil, William (Michael York), who is going to marry Anna; and Anna herself (Jacqueline Sassard), something of an enigma, not exactly throwing herself at Stephen's head, but obviously interested.

Suddenly, while casually describing these people basking on the lawn as part of his explanation of the process of observation which goes into writing a novel, Charley shatters the air of drowsy serenity—"... and Stephen is having an affair with a girl at Oxford." Maybe a joke, maybe not, but no one cares to pick it up, and after an embarrassed pause, serenity returns and the afternoon continues as before. But not quite as before. Charley's remark has radiated secretly, and the casual round of tea, tennis and strolling conversation now conceals an alert, growing sexual competition as, wordlessly and almost unaware of what they are doing to each other, the three men begin to fight for Anna.

These people are all friends, civilized, comfortable and urbane, capable of assessing their own behaviour and of attributing reasonably accurate motives to the others; but between them lie dark areas which they do not recognise, abrasions on a cool surface. When Charley, for instance, becomes aware of the electricity sparked off by his remark, and adds to it by calling to Stephen to ask if he has heard, is he conscious of the real extent of his malice? Equally, when Stephen mutters 'yes' as he bends busily over the flower-bed he is weeding, and his wife's voice echoes 'YES!' with quizzical clarity from another part of the lawn, is she aware that she is striking a match under Stephen's smouldering guilt? The remarkable thing about the film is that one can interpret the characters and their motives almost any way one likes. (2) Charley, for example, may know that Stephen is attracted by Anna; or his remark may merely have been a shot in the dark;

---

2. Seen as a defect by several other critics, the extreme ambiguity of *Accident* is for Milne one of its great virtues. Does this seem an issue of personal taste replacing critical judgment—that is, one critic enjoys ambiguity and another doesn't? Or does Milne convince you that he has looked to the film to discover the criteria by which it can be judged and found that *in this particular instance,* ambiguity is central to the experience of film.

or it may even have been a wry joke at his own expense. One never really knows which. But the point is, here as throughout the film, that what matters is not the remark (situation, emotion, gesture) itself, but the way it brings new, unexpected facets to light.

The signs are discreetly posted for us in the opening shot, as the camera stares motionlessly at the façade of Stephen's house. The night is dark, a plane passes overhead, a bird cries, a typewriter chatters faintly inside, and the camera begins to track slowly towards the house, away from the roar of an approaching car which gradually splinters to a screeching crash. Unexpectedly, the camera continues tracking forward steadily, almost wilfully oblivious, until the front door opens and Stephen emerges to investigate. The accident in which William is killed, in other words, is one thing; what Stephen makes of it is another. And this distinction is underlined by the sense of abrasion between sound and image. First, the peaceful contemplation of the house shattered by the sounds of the crash; then the dream-like quiet of the two bodies lying in the car, shattered by the sound of Stephen's shoes scraping harshly on the metal sides, his voice grating on the still air. (3)

Brilliantly shot to accentuate the atmosphere of bewilderment and mystery (rapid track along a grassy verge, (4) passing footsteps, inset shots of startled horse and pale moon glaring down), the accident is made to seem a key. And Stephen, after his initial guilt about William's death ("Don't! You're standing on his face!"), takes it as such, building round it a drama which will bring Anna to him. He assumes she was driving, shelters her from the police, and then makes love to her, tacitly expecting her to respond. In fact there is no mystery about the accident, it is a key to nothing. Anna leaves for home because William is dead and there is nothing left for her in Oxford; if there are darker, more secret reasons for her departure—her disillusionment with both Charley and Stephen—these were settled long before the accident.

Losey makes this clear in two ways. First, by his demystification of the accident. The last shot of the film, which in a way brings it full circle, is again of the façade of the house, by daylight this time, as the

---

3. Note the detailed observation here of sensory experience.

4. Milne makes several references here to tracking. What is a tracking shot?

front door closes, a dog runs down the drive to the road, and a car crashes. Seen in broad daylight (no moon, no horse, no shadows), the accident is simply an accident; and by implication the only fact of the first accident is that William dies. Secondly, there is the aftermath of the scene on the lawn. By snubbing William and accepting Stephen's invitation to go for a walk, Anna has made her intentions as plain as she can. But Stephen is still held back by his inhibitions, and nothing happens. Their hands rest on a gate, close but not touching; after a time, as though giving up, Anna says "Shall we go back?" And as they turn back to the house, the camera stays where it is, gazing at the empty landscape as though lamenting the end of the affair. It is, in fact, the end. The next time Stephen meets Anna is when he returns unexpectedly from London to find her sleeping with Charley; and the time after that she announces her engagement to William. The accident is merely a postscript to a chapter already closed. (5)

The strange, hypnotic quality in this shot of an empty landscape suffuses the whole film, so that as one watches scene after scene unfolding in the serene stillness of an Oxford summer, one is constantly made to sense the extraordinary beneath the ordinary. A shot of a man standing in the distance with a raised umbrella on a bright sunny day contains an indescribable charge of latent menace. It is only later that one realises why, when we discover that the man is Stephen, that the umbrella is a protection against garden sprinklers, and that he is nerving himself to face Charley's distraught wife, Laura, who is being driven mad with grief and jealousy. But the charge works both ways: Laura, in her unsuitable black oilskins, becomes identified with the black figure poised against the house with raised umbrella, awkward and out of place, deprived of any sense of belonging.

The film is studded with these strange, apparently meaningless shots, which hover indelibly in the mind until they are completed (it is only later, for instance, that one realises that the long-held shot over the gate marks the last moment at which Stephen might have achieved happiness with Anna). Here one comes up interestingly against the question of time in the film. Although the main body of the action is a flashback—or rather, a series of flashbacks—occa-

---

5. Does the evidence Milne presents here convince you of the validity of his interpretation?

sioned by the accident and describing Stephen's recollection of the events which led up to it, the time sequence appears to be fairly simple. With one exception, the various scenes are recalled in logical (and almost certainly chronological) sequence, as in a conventional narrative. And the exception—the intercutting of Stephen's visit to Laura with his visit to his own wife after she has gone to stay with her mother—is again perfectly logical: the scenes with Laura are conjured in his mind as he talks to his wife. Time is allowed to be sequential, but on other levels is completely annihilated.

Twice during the course of the film, a clock chimes out, and at each stroke the camera marks time derisively by jumping along a row of grinning gargoyles on the college wall. Elsewhere, climactic points —Stephen's return home from London to find Charley and Anna sleeping together, his departure from the college after Anna has left to catch her plane—are marked by insistently chiming clocks which seek to place their seal on things. But in this story, nothing can be defined or limited in this way. An emotion exists independently of time, perhaps remaining constant, perhaps growing weaker or stronger as more illumination is thrown on it. William's jealousy of Stephen, for instance, is most clearly illuminated during the Eton-type wall game at his aristocratic home, when his light emphasis of "I think *you* should go in goal" indicates that he is assigning the most dangerous position to his rival; but the same jealousy, dark, unconscious, and as yet without illumination, exists much earlier, before he has even met Anna, when he refuses to let Stephen effect an introduction.

A more complex instance comes in the sequence with Francesca, the old flame whom Stephen looks up during his visit to London for a television interview. Here the illumination is not exterior (fed by external events or actions) but purely interior. From the way her name is introduced by the man at the TV studio in a sort of cross-talk act ("Do you ever see Francesca? The Provost's daughter? The daughter of the Provost?"), one is led to expect something hard and sharp, a sort of part-time college whore, perhaps; later, this impression is strengthened by Rosalind's indifference and the Provost's knowing leer. But in fact the scenes of their evening together have a tender, candle-lit quality, a dream of pure romance, as Francesca (Delphine Seyrig) flits gracefully to and fro in her room, or is seen shimmering through a delicately rain-spotted restaurant window. The accompanying dialogue, much more down-to-earth ("I'm in consumer research, did you know?") and much more strained in its quest for romance

("You don't look a day older"—"Oh really? I'm ten years older"), is significantly dissociated from the images, as though it had nothing whatsoever to do with them. In recollecting this scene, Stephen is obviously creating the perfect romance, an amalgam perhaps of his first love for Francesca, his love for his wife, the love he hopes for with Anna.

The feeling that this sequence is fabricated in recollection by Stephen for his own pleasure is increased by the fact that, whereas the rest of the film is shot with a diamond-sharp clarity, the Francesca scenes have much softer, gauzier tones. By extension, therefore, the scene in the TV studio—at first glance the only unsatisfactory one in the film because it feels like a Losey-Pinter self-parody—is also fabricated: its thin, two-dimensional texture, its note of hysteria, is the way Stephen remembers it, as something grotesque, best left unexplored. In it one finds none of the tiny, indefinable details which lend their weight to the texture of the rest of the film: the automatic gesture with which Stephen pushes the rockinghorse as he passes on the way to the room where Anna has been sleeping with Charley; the sudden flood of light as a cloud passes over at the start of his walk with Anna; the abrupt stutter by the train which has been puffing away steadily in the distance during the accident. (6)

In a way, of course, being Stephen's recollection, the whole film (with the exception, naturally, of the accident and last scenes) is his fabrication, with Charley being beastly, Anna provocative, Rosalind patient, and William callow. (It is interesting, in fact, to note the disparity between the dignified, hesitant Stephen of the flashbacks, and the man who virtually rapes Anna after the accident.) But the characters refuse to be limited by what we are shown of them. The whole film is put together virtually without transitions, using only direct cuts, (7) and as with Resnais, it is in the gaps that the real story is told.

Stephen's whole situation, for instance, his fear of sinking into staid middle-age, is conveyed in the cuts linking three brief scenes:

---

6. At this point, and indeed throughout the discussion, Milne indicates his sensitivity to the visual modulations in the film as well as to its particular use of sound. Does his perceptiveness in itself constitute support for his analysis?

7. What is a direct cut? And what other kinds of transitions might have been used?

from Rosalind at home (jokingly saying "I'm not too old for you") to a languorous Anna in his study ("Write me an essay on what the problem seems to you"), to the dons' common-room (with the Provost preparing to launch yet again into his pet story). Similarly but more obliquely, the intercutting of Stephen's visits to Rosalind and Laura effects a curious kind of osmosis between the two women: Laura, distraught but struggling to conceal it, evokes the tension which must lie beneath Rosalind's air of calm competence. Further: this osmosis (if that is the word) is only complete when one adds to it the identification made earlier between Rosalind and Anna and which has since been hanging fire (the scene in which Stephen is deceived by the hem of a dressing-gown whisking out of sight into thinking that Rosalind is Anna: and its complement when he discovers Anna on his staircase, dressed exactly like Rosalind). If the Francesca sequence is a male dream of love fulfilled, the film also adumbrates a female dream of love betrayed.

More, perhaps, than any other Losey film, with its bland surface being invisibly gnawed away from within, *Accident* forces one to look and look again, to make connections where none are apparent. Perfectly served by his entire cast (invidious to single out names, but Stanley Baker and Vivien Merchant are miraculously good), by his designer (Carmen Dillon), cameraman (Gerry Fisher) and script writer (Pinter), Losey has made a film in which nothing is signalled, nothing given away. As with *Muriel,* you have to do your share of the work, watching patiently and absorbedly as the characters live their lives, cook their omelettes, exchange their trivial chat, and be rewarded almost constantly by the moments of glittering illumination. (8)

---

8. Whether or not one is convinced by the critic, this piece of criticism stands as an excellent model of explication. Generalizations are supported throughout by specific details drawn from the experience of the film.

THE BIRDS

Brendan Gill, *THE NEW YORKER*
April 6, 1963

(1) Alfred Hitchcock's "The Birds" is a sorry failure. Hard as it may be to believe of a Hitchock, it doesn't arouse suspense, which is, of course, what justifies and transforms the sadism that lies at the heart of every thriller. Here the sadism is all too nakedly, repellently present; we watch with horror as a small town on the California coast is besieged by vast flocks of birds, which appear bent on expunging the human population by pecking it to death. Whether they succeed we never find out—we're merely shown their fearful ability to draw blood, and left to make what we can of the mystery of their sudden murderous intent. If this picture is a hit, the Audubon Society has an ugly public-relations problem on its heads. At the moment, I wouldn't willingly find myself alone with an indigo bunting, much less a great big scowling robin. In the cast of "The Birds" are Jessica Tandy, Rod Taylor, Suzanne Pleshette, and a blond ex-model named

---

1. The reader can, almost without reading the review, know what attitude Gill has toward this film. What does the length of this discussion suggest?

Tippi Hedren. Miss Hedren is so new a newcomer that Universal has boasted in print of her having no previous acting experience whatever. Not everything about this picture is hard to believe. (2)

---

2. On what grounds does Gill reject the film?

Paul Mayersberg, *THE LISTENER AND BBC TELEVISION REVIEW* September 12, 1963

The Beak and the Eye

The position of the spectator in relation to the action of a movie is, perhaps, the cornerstone of the aesthetic of film. Wherever the camera goes, the spectator must go with it. If the camera looks down on a particular action, the spectator looks down. If the camera looks up at a face, the spectator inevitably finds himself looking up. The director of a film literally directs the spectator's eye. This means that the spectator's emotional and intellectual response to the action on the screen is dictated by the director's choice of camera position. There are, naturally, other elements involved in the spectator's response, such as the story, the acting, the very words that are spoken. But these are all part of the action itself: the camera is outside the action. It may worm its way in, and become an inseparable part of what is happening, but its role is none the less that of a commentator recording and describing the action. In my opinion, if the director's viewpoint is not expressed in the position of the camera, then it has not been expressed in terms of film.

The degree to which the spectator is directed how to respond to what he is watching varies in relation to the personality of the individual film-maker. Directors like Otto Preminger, Roberto Rossellini, and Jean Renoir allow the spectator considerable freedom in

---

his response to the action. They have at least one characteristic in common: the desire to be as impartial as possible. This does not mean that they do not have a viewpoint at all, but simply that it is an impartial one. Such a viewpoint requires a camera style that makes the action as lucid as possible so that the spectator is allowed a degree of freedom to interpret the significance of the action and the motives behind it. It is not surprising that Preminger's *Advise and Consent,* Rossellini's *Vanina Vanini,* and Renoir's *Le Caporal Epinglé,* which are their latest films to reach Britain, are concerned thematically with questions of freedom.

In these films the camera tends to be detached from the action, for the sake of impartiality and also to let the spectator see as much of what is happening as is possible. There are very few inserted close-ups or reaction shots: the camera, like the film-maker, maintains a certain distance from the action. If one said that the spectator walks freely round Preminger's movies, nudging and prodding them, examining his responses as he goes, one might say that the spectator is enticed inside Hitchcock's films, whereupon the door is slammed shut and the movie begins to rotate round him. Two hours later he is allowed out, bruised black and blue and sick with dizziness. Alfred Hitchcock is at the other end of the scale to Preminger. Where Preminger is content to place the spectator on the perimeter of the movie, Hitchcock needs to force him into the action itself.

The Birds is Hitchcock's latest and most fantastic experiment with the spectator. The film begins outside a pet shop in San Francisco. Melanie Daniels, a smart play-girl with a rich father arrives to collect a myna bird to give to her aunt as a present. She pauses outside the shop to look at the sky where a flock of wild birds are circling high above her, remote and harmless. As she enters the shop we see hundreds of caged birds on display. This, Hitchcock is saying, is the conventional domestic relationship between birds and man. The action soon moves from the city of San Francisco to the open coast landscape of the small town of Bodega Bay. The change in the landscape from concrete buildings for people and metal cages for birds to wooden buildings and the open air reveals the intention of the movie (1). As the film progresses Hitchcock removes the shrouds of convention and domesticity that hide the true relationship between

---

1. Note Mayersberg's use of "intention" here. The film reveals the intention rather than the intention revealing the film.

man and nature. When the birds do begin to attack, the inhabitants of Bodega Bay find it impossible to defend themselves and are forced to retreat inland. For centuries man has been shooting and caging birds. Now it is the birds' turn.

This is a rational explanation of the movie, but clearly, as a rational explanation it will not do. Hitchcock is fully aware of this and at no point in the film does he 'explain' the bird attacks. In one scene at a bar a drunk mutters 'It's the end of the world'. This is perhaps the nearest Hitchcock comes to an explanation within the film itself, but he has admitted to an interviewer that he sees *The Birds* as a vision of Judgment Day. (2) Though the spectator takes the action literally while he is watching it, and it is frightening at times, I think it is inevitable that he should ask himself what it all means when he leaves the cinema.

The first step is to decide on the nature of the birds themselves. And it is here that the spectator questions his own position in relation to the action. When one sees hundreds of birds attacking a few human beings, one's natural instinct is to side with one's own species. The birds appear to attack people wantonly and ferociously, but Hitchcock has assiduously avoided shots of ferocious-looking birds. Since many birds look quite nasty in close-up it is surprising that Hitchcock has completely eschewed this image. Moreover, the birds do not attack at every conceivable opportunity, as one might imagine. For long periods, as they are gathering, they just sit and stare. Then suddenly they attack, and for no apparent reason they stop and fly away. Then they mass and attack again. Undoubtedly, there is a fundamental mystery in their behaviour, because when we do see the birds sitting and watching the humans they look frankly passive. The collective feeling that Hitchcock has captured for the birds is: if you leave us alone, we'll leave you alone.

So the natural deduction is that the birds are not launching their attacks without some reason. And if they have a reason it could follow that they are in the right, and that the human beings one

---

2. Is Hitchcock's interpretation of *The Birds* necessarily any more valid than, say, Brendan Gill's or that of any other filmgoer? And if his interpretation is more valid, is this because he is the director of the film? Or is he just like any other critic who must justify his interpretations under the rules of evidence common to us all?

instinctively sides with are in the wrong. This, again, is perhaps too blunt an interpretation because the birds destroy life, and that cannot be right. One point which is certain is that the birds are not what they seem to be at first; and therefore the spectator's attitude to the attacks is an ambiguous one. (3)

I can explain the true nature of the birds more clearly through an analogy with the Anthony Perkins character, Norman Bates, in Hitchcock's last film, *Psycho.* Norman constantly appears as birdlike. Hitchcock concentrates on his eyes, on his profile, on his long arching neck. The knife with which he stabs his victims is an enormous flashing beak. In the murder scenes he always stabs downwards, in a pecking movement, despite the fact that this is not the most effective method of stabbing someone to death. Norman Bates is a schizophrenic: part of the time he is Norman, but when he commits murder he is effectively his mother. He is not a wanton killer: he kills because he cannot help himself, because he is psychologically disturbed. Similarly, the birds are disturbed. This time, however, we do not know the reason; but like Norman they are compelled by some impulse they cannot control. Like Norman, they are schizophrenic. At the end of *Psycho* we have considerable sympathy for the man, and in theory at least we should have the same sympathy for the birds. The birds act as if they were a single character and Hitchcock treats them as such. (4)

The divided allegiance of the spectator in *The Birds* is an expression of this schizophrenia. Norman Bates, referring to his collection of stuffed birds, said: 'I think only birds look well stuffed because they are passive to begin with'. Like the birds the audience is passive—to begin with. Throughout the film Hitchcock alternates the position of the spectator from passive observer to active participant. The relationship between the birds and the people in the movie has a parallel in the formal relationship of the spectator to the action on the screen.

Perhaps the most characteristic camera position in *The Birds* is the high-angle, overhead shot. When the birds attack Bodega Bay in

---

3. Note Mayersberg's closely reasoned argument. He does not merely state that the "spectator's attitude to the attacks is an ambiguous one." He compiles evidence from the film to try to prove his statement. Does he convince you?

4. How relevant is this analogy with Norman Bates?

broad daylight an assistant at a petrol station is knocked over while filling up a car. The escaping petrol flows down the street. A man getting out of his car pauses to light a cigar and drops the match on to the petrol. Suddenly, Hitchcock inserts a very high-angled shot looking down on the town. The main street is marked out on this map-like image as a river of flame. The shot is held as a bird flies in, then another bird and another. This overhead bird's-eye view is repeated during the bird attacks when the camera looks straight down on Melanie Daniels as she is trapped inside a telephone booth. Now the camera is much closer and more oppressive, suggesting the hysteria that comes with the attack from the sky.

The bird looking down has a natural corollary in the people looking up. At the end of the last bird attack on the house where Melanie is staying the camera points up at the oak-beamed ceiling as the characters' faces slowly move into the frame. As the camera tracks back still pointing up, the ceiling is given an appearance of terrible weight as if it is closing down on the room. The characters' fear of the birds in the sky has been transferred to the ceiling of the room.

Transference Theme

The theme of transference is central to Hitchcock's work. It takes many forms: the transference of feeling from people to inanimate objects via the camera, as in this shot of the ceiling; the transference of guilt from mother to son in the schizoid personality of Norman Bates; the transference of the experience of the action from the characters to the spectator. When Melanie is trapped in the telephone booth she finds herself in the predicament of the birds in the pet shop—inside a cake. When she comes to Bodega Bay she brings a pair of caged love-birds as a present for the small sister of a man she met in San Francisco. The shots which show her delivering the birds to his house on Bodega Bay comprise a sequence of overlapping forward and reverse tracking shots. This form is usually reserved for moments of high tension in Hitchcock's movies, as for example Vera Miles approaching the house in *Psycho*. There is some tension in Melanie's attempt to put the birds in the house and get away without the man seeing her, but this is rather domestic and hardly worthy, one would have thought, of such dramatic treatment. No: the point is that here the camera is revealing something more sinister. The patterns of overlapping tracking shots are later associated with fear of the birds. They recur in the scene where Melanie and Mitch Brenner, the man she came to see, have to walk past a line of birds sitting on a fence.

Why should the spectator fear the love-birds in a cage? Why should Hitchcock make such a dramatic point out of Melanie's arrival? The reason is that Melanie is responsible in some mysterious way for the bird attacks. At one point a townswoman addresses her: 'Why are they doing this? They said when you got here the whole thing started. Who are you? Where did you come from? I think you're the cause of all this. I think you're evil'. Hitchcock provides us with a number of clues about Melanie. First, as she races along the coast road in her Aston Martin towards Bodega Bay we hear the screech of brakes and tyres with almost every shot of her driving, and the sound of that screech is identical to the seagull's cry that we hear later on when they attack. Second, the image of Melanie peering round a cage in the bird shop and later over the prow of her outboard motor boat emphasizes her eyes. When she crosses the bay in the boat she cocks her head to one side in the manner of a bird. At that moment a seagull swoops and cuts her head.

The character of the apparently innocent person who enters into a nightmare world by chance is not new in Hitchcock's work. For example, James Stewart in *Rear Window* seems at first to be the conventional hero accidently overlooking a crime and bringing the murderer to justice. But, like Melanie Daniels, he is in reality the progenitor of the crime. Sitting alone, confined by a broken leg, bored, he has dreamt up a crime for someone else to commit. He wants action and he gets it. As it turns out, the murderer is not the savage killer he would like to imagine, but a weak husband who cannot stand his wife's nagging.

When asked to describe the theme of *The Birds* Hitchcock replied in a single word: 'complacency'. The birds assault the complacency of man symbolized in his belief that birds are harmless. Melanie is complacency itself, so it is not surprising that she should be the centre of the attack. Like James Stewart in *Rear Window* she has brought the nightmare and she has to experience it personally. Melanie is finally attacked by scores of birds and pecked unconscious, just as Stewart has to face the murderer himself and is finally pushed out of his apartment window. Stewart's weapon is a flash-gun, Melanie has a torch. The flashes and beams of light are the sole weapons for fighting the darkness and evil. And, of course, they are not powerful enough, because evil in Hitchcock's world is stronger than good.

In one scene in *The Birds* Lydia, Mitch's mother, remembering her dead husband says: 'I wish I were a stronger person . . . it's terrible how you depend on someone else for strength . . . and then suddenly all the strength is gone and you're alone'.

When Melanie brings the love-birds she brings the wild birds. The caged birds symbolize man's sentimental view of birds. When Melanie, Mitch, Lydia, and the small sister leave their house they take the love-birds with them. Despite the bird attacks these people have learned almost nothing about themselves. To the end they cling to their sentimental belief that the caged birds are the real birds and the wild birds part of some fantastic nightmare. (5)

The love-birds are symbolic, not only of man's dream-picture of birds but of his dream-picture of love. The relationship between Mitch and Melanie is based on parallels with their respective parents. Mitch's mother, Lydia, is in the great tradition of Hitchcock's mother figures, of which Mrs. Bates in *Psycho* was the most fearful example. Lydia has upset Mitch's life to the extent that he cannot feel free to love another woman. His relationship with Melanie is a kind of token love affair completely devoid of the sexual fireworks that Hitchcock goes in for in *North by Northwest* or *To Catch a Thief*. Melanie's relationship with her father is of the spoilt child self-indulgent parent kind. Her mother ran off with another man when she was very young.

A Tragedy of Uselessness

The Birds is a tragedy of uselessness. It is useless to try to defend oneself against the birds. It is useless to initiate a relationship you cannot support emotionally. The birds themselves are useless: 'Look at the birds of the air, they do not sow or reap.' And like the birds Melanie is useless, a rich, aimless playgirl. Bodega Bay is a dull, useless little town. One is tempted to question the usefulness of the film. Is it not an elaborate and highly personal game of Hitchcock's that is the ultimate in art for art's sake? The answer, I am certain, is 'no'; and the reason lies in the part played by the spectator in the action.

---

5. Note throughout this entire section the evidence of Mayersberg's very highly developed aesthetic perceptions and his underlying assumption that camera and sound do more than merely further plot.

If it were necessary to justify the cinema as an autonomous medium of expression *The Birds* is the film to cite.

Unlike many other films *The Birds* does not depict characters who in the course of the action come to terms with their destiny. Hitchcock strips their illusions from them for our benefit rather than theirs. It is the spectator who comes to terms with the destiny of the characters. The action throughout is aimed at the spectator: we are waiting, if for nothing else, for the ruffling of Melanie Daniels's immaculate appearance and for the shock that will destroy her complacency.

And because we are waiting for it to happen to her we are also waiting, perhaps unconsciously, for it to happen to us. When she is finally attacked we see the birds attacking her, but we also experience the attack directly. The camera is placed subjectively from time to time and the birds are attacking us. As in the combination of forward and reverse tracking shots that are associated with the fear of the birds, we, in the place of the camera, watch and participate. Like Norman Bates we are voyeurs. But we are not content to watch, eventually we must participate. It is not for nothing that the birds resemble thousands of spectators: we all want to be in at the kill. We want not only to see with our eyes but to destroy with our beaks.

Andrew Sarris, *THE VILLAGE VOICE* April 4, 1963

"The Birds" is here (at the Palace and Sutton), and what a joy to behold a self-contained movie which does not feed parasitically on outside cultural references—Chekhov, Synge, O'Neill, Genet, Behan, Melville, or what have you. Drawing from the relatively invisible literary talents of Daphne DuMaurier and Evan Hunter, Alfred Hitchcock has fashioned a major work of cinematic art, and "cinematic" is the operative term here, not "literary" or "sociological." There is one sequence, for example, where the heroine is in an outboard motor boat churning across the bay while the hero's car is racing around the shore road to intercept her on the other side. This race, in itself pure cinema, is seen entirely from the girl's point of view. (1) We see only what she can see from the rowboat. Suddenly, near shore, the camera picks up a sea gull swooping down on our heroine. For just a second, the point of view is shifted, and we are permitted to see the bird before its victim does. The director has apparently broken an aesthetic rule for the sake of a shock effect—gull pecks girl. Yet this momentary incursion of the objective on the subjective is remarkably consistent with the meaning of the film.

More Victims

The theme, after all, is complacency, as the director has stated on innumerable occasions. When we first meet each of the major characters, their infinite capacity for self-absorption is emphasized. Tippi Hedren's bored socialite is addicted to elaborately time-consuming practical jokes. Rod Taylor's self-righteous lawyer flaunts his arrogant sensuality. Suzanne Pleshette, his ex-fiancee, wallows in self-pity, and Jessica Tandy, his possessive mother, cringes from her fear of loneliness. With such complex, unsympathetic characters to contend with, the audience quite naturally begins to identify with the point of view of the birds, actually the inhuman point of view. As in "Psycho," Hitchcock succeeds in implicating his audience to such an extent that the much-criticized, apparently anti-climactic ending of the film finds the audience more blood-thirsty than the birds. (2) Although three people are killed and many others assaulted by man's fine feathered friends, critics and spectators have demanded more gore and more victims.

---

1. What constitutes "pure cinema" for Sarris? Films are often accused of being uncinematic, of being "literary." What would make a film literary? Does the stillness of the camera in early films, the considerable amount of dialogue in, let's say, a movie directed by Preston Sturges, make for literary film?

2. Is Sarris talking here about Hitchcock's manipulation of conventions or is he offering an observation on the cruelty of man to man?

Into the Fantasy

In "Psycho," if you recall, there is a moment after Tony Perkins has run Janet Leigh's car into a swamp when the car stops sinking. One could almost hear the audience holding its breath until the car resumed its descent below the surface. At that first intake of breath, the audience became implicated in the fantasy of the perfect crime. In "The Birds," the audience is similarly implicated, but this time in the fantasy of annihilation. The point Hitchcock seems to be making is that morality is not a function of sympathy, but a rigorous test of principles. If we can become even momentarily indifferent to the fate of a promiscuous blonde (Janet Leigh in "Psycho") or a spoiled playgirl (Tippi Hedren in "The Birds"), we have clearly failed the test.

As symbols of evil and disorder, Hitchcock's winged bipeds lend themselves to many possible interpretations—Freudian, Thomistic, Existential, among others—but the imaginative spectator can draw his own analogies. What is beyond speculation is the strikingly visual potential of the subject.(3) One penultimate shot of a row of blackbirds perched magisterially above the fearfully departing humans is worth a thousand words on man's unworthiness. Hitchcock's dark humor is as impressive as ever on both human and ornithological planes. There is something indescribably funny in the familiar gesture of a man winding up to throw a rock at some crows before being deterred by his prudent girl friend. Her "let sleeping birds perch" philosophy explodes its grotesque context into half-fragmented memories of human presumption.

Love Birds

Yet, in the midst of all the human guilt, the idea of innocence survives. When the survivors of the bird attacks venture past thousands

---

3. Sarris seems to be saying here that the meaning of a symbol doesn't really matter as long at it is a symbol which the audience can immediately perceive as such. Is he then arguing for ambiguity for its own sake, or is he simply dismissing meaning as relevant to cinema?

of their erstwhile enemies, now ominously passive, the hero's eleven-year-old sister asks him to return to the house for her caged love birds. "They did no harm," she insists. The audience fears and anticipates the worst, but nothing happens. The caged love birds do not arouse the free hordes of the species. Instead, these two guiltless creatures seem to clear the path to the car as if the rediscovery of innocence were yet the only hope of the world.

"The Birds" finds Hitchcock at the summit of his artistic powers. His is the only contemporary style which unites the divergent classical traditions of Murnau (camera movement) and Eisenstein (montage). (Welles, for example, owes more to Murnau, while Resnais is closer to Eisenstein.) If formal excellence is still a valid criterion for film criticism, and there are those who will argue that it is not, then "The Birds" is probably the picture of the year.(4)

---

4. Has Sarris convinced us of the film's "formal excellence"? Even more significant, is he implying that formal excellence is the only criterion?

Dwight MacDonald, *ESQUIRE*
October, 1963

Mostly on Bird Watching

The only point of interest about *The Birds* is that it's by Alfred Hitchcock, who once had a deserved reputation as a master technician. If the director's name had been, say, Albert Hotchkiss, I should have noted "tedious and amateurish . . . perhaps the most spectacularly untalented newcomer since Allen Baron," and let it go at that. But since it's Hitchcock and not Hotchkiss, something more elaborate seems in order. As Brutus said to Cassius about another large figure,

"Let us be sacrificers but not butchers. . . . Let's kill him boldly but not wrathfully,/Let's carve him as a dish fit for the gods."(1)

Hitchcock's best films were distinguished by [1] technical brilliance, [2] persons and scenes that were superficially lifelike, [3] economy of means, [4] tight, logical plots. *The Birds* is a negative print of these qualities.(2)

[1] I counted just two cinematic coups. One was the first bird attack: the heroine is rowing across a bay; suddenly a sea gull screeches down and rips her forehead open—the shock, the quick cutting, the changes in point of view, here we had the old master for a moment. The other was the gradual massing of the crows outside the school: the heroine is sitting on a bench, her back to a jungle gym on which one crow is perched; another flies up, settling down silently, then another, then a series of cuts between the unaware girl and the bars of the jungle gym which become blacker and blacker with dozens, scores, hundreds of ominously quiet crows. For the rest, Hitchcock's technical ingenuity is limited to multiple-exposure trick shots—371 is the figure he gives—that don't work very well.

[2] Everything looks fake, partly because of poor color (and is color ever right for a thriller? it was merely distracting in *Vertigo*) which makes the outdoor shots look like postcards and the interiors like color spreads in *Life*.(3) The leads all act atrociously. This may be partly due to a script that gives them lines as unconvincing as their stock characters. But why must each play badly in a different style? 'Tippi' Hedren, a glacial model in whom Hitchcock discovered talents that don't show up on the screen, plays in the stiffest tradition of junior-high dramatics. Rod Taylor is run-of-the-mill Hollywood—might do as the hero's loyal sidekick in a B Western. Jessica Tandy overplays her role in *haut*-Broadway style. They can't make contact. Even the bit parts, once a Hitchcock specialty, have become labored, over-shrill, as in the lunchroom scenes.

[3] The old, or classic, Hitchcock followed Poe's recipe for the short tale: every sentence must contribute to the specific effect the

---

1. What is your reaction to this first paragraph?

2. Note here that MacDonald sets up his criteria very clearly.

3. Would you classify MacDonald's comments about the inappropriateness of color for a thriller as a legitimate *aesthetic presupposition?*

writer wants to produce. This effect in Hitchcock's case as in Poe's—both are Pavlovian experimenters on the nerves of their audiences—is always the thrill, the Baudelairean *frisson.* In his better films the human aspect is sketched in only enough to engage the viewers' empathy and to lend plausibility to the unpleasant little surprises he has in store for them. But in *The Birds,* background has become foreground: we must sit through a half hour of pachydermous flirtation between Rod and Tippi before that sea gull attacks, and another fifteen minutes of tedium, mostly centering around Rod's old girl friend, who plays badly in still a fourth style—sentimental method—before the birds get into action again. If one adds later interrelations between lovers, mother, girl friend and a particularly repulsive child actress,(4) about two thirds of the film is devoted to extraneous matters. Poe would have been shocked. Human situations, in short, are developed far beyond the modest needs of a thriller, so far indeed as to produce a kickback. Since, as Charles Higham observes in the Winter *Film Quarterly,* Hitchcock has never been any good with this sort of material, his elaborate attempt to make us believe his puppets are people merely convinces us they are phonier than his trained birds.

[4] As for that logic of plot and motivation which, as Poe and (the old) Hitchcock understood, is essential to enforcing belief in a fantastic story, consider:

¶ Tippi warns a teacher that crows are massing outside the schoolhouse; their jointly worked-out response to the threat is not to put the kids into the cellar but to march them outside to walk home. To no one's surprise but Hitchcock's, the birds come shrieking like Stukas on the helpless little column.(5)

¶ As the final mass attack on the house begins, it turns out that Rod has forgotten to block up the chimney (although a destructive flood of sparrows had poured out of it only the day before) and also to put

---

4. Is MacDonald's "particularly repulsive child" a case of *private associations* or the *actor as barrier?* Is it possible to establish objective criteria for repulsion and attractiveness?

5. Clearly, taking the children out of the schoolhouse is irrational behavior, and thus in MacDonald's terms, a "violation of the logic of the plot." But Mayersberg would probably say that this irrationality is necessary, if the "spectator's attitude to the attacks" is to be an "ambiguous one."

up the shutters. He repairs these negligences, though at the cost of some wounds recorded in interesting closeups.

¶ Later there is a lull, after a specially determined onslaught (could gulls actually drive their beaks through a thick oak door?) and Tippi wanders upstairs for no special reason. Hearing noises in the attic, she naturally opens the door and sees a great hole in the roof, with hundreds of birds sitting around. Her natural reaction is to enter the room, carefully closing the door behind her. She is at once pecked into insensibility (splendid color shots of her blood-streaming face and hands). Rod rescues her in the nick of time (more blood and grue) and she ends up on a sofa no worse for her experience than a stagy bandage on her stagy brow.

¶ Throughout the film everybody behaves with similar idiocy; we are supposed to believe, for instance, that a community of farmers and fishermen—tough, practical folk, one might assume—can devise no better defense, like maybe guns, than running around hysterically every time the birds make a pass. Tippi is an effete city type but still she might be supposed incapable of asking, after a flock of gulls have dive-bombed a picnic: "Mitch, this isn't usual, is it?" This helplessness is necessary, of course, so that Hitchcock can get plenty of those shock closeups he seems to dote on in his old age, but it destroys that elementary logic a thriller must have to be thrilling. The only characters in the film who aren't birdbrains are the birds. How did those crows, for instance, come to pick just the right hour to congregate on the jungle gym? They must have known when school's out. We've lost one more insult.

BLOW-UP

In the September 7th, 1967 issue of *The Villager,* Walter J. Carroll wrote: "Is there no one who, having seen *Blow-Up,* has the courage to admit they couldn't get anything out of it at all?" Cowardice or not, apparently many filmgoers got quite a lot out of *Blow-Up,* and given the opportunity, wrote about it, too. What follows then, together with the reviews by Pauline Kael and Richard Goldstein that stimulated them, are the responses of filmgoing readers who, happily, direct themselves to inquiry very much in the spirit of this text. The usual questions would be merely redundant here.

Pauline Kael, *THE NEW REPUBLIC*
February 11, 1967

Tourist in the City of Youth

Some years ago I attended an evening of mime by Marcel Marceau, an elaborate exercise in aesthetic purification during which the audience kept applauding its own appreciation of culture and beauty, *i.e.,*

From *Kiss Kiss Bang Bang* by Pauline Kael, by permission of Atlantic-Little Brown and Co. Published in Great Britain by Calder & Boyars, London, 1970.

every time they thought they recognized what was supposed to be going on. It had been bad enough when Chaplin or Harpo Marx pulled this beauty-of-pathos stuff, and a whole evening of it was truly intolerable. But afterward, when friends were acclaiming Marceau's artistry, it just wouldn't do to say something like, "I prefer the Ritz Brothers" (though I do, I passionately do). They would think I was being deliberately lowbrow, and if I tried to talk in terms of Marceau's artistry versus Harry Ritz's artistry, it would be stupid, because "artist" is already too pretentious a term for Harry Ritz and so I would be falsifying what I love him for. I don't want to push this quite so far as to say that Marceau is to comedians I like what Antonioni's new *Blow-Up* is to movies I like, but the comparison may be suggestive. And it may also be relevant that Antonioni pulls a Marceau-like expressionist finale in this picture, one of those fancy finishes that seems to say so much (but what?) and reminds one of so many naïvely bad experimental films.

Will *Blow-Up* be taken seriously in 1968 only by the same sort of cultural diehards who are still sending out five-page single-spaced letters on their interpretation of *Marienbad?* (No two are alike, no one interesting.) It has some of the *Marienbad* appeal: a friend phones for your opinion and when you tell him you didn't much care for it, he says, "You'd better see it again. I was at a swinging party the other night and it's all anybody talked about!" (Was there ever a good movie that everybody was talking about?) It probably won't blow over because it also has the *Morgan!-Georgy Girl* appeal; people identify with it so strongly, they get *upset* if you don't like it—as if you were rejecting not just the movie but *them.* And in a way they're right, because if you don't accept the peculiarly slugged consciousness of *Blow-Up,* you *are* rejecting something in them. Antonioni's new mixture of suspense with vagueness and confusion seems to have a kind of numbing fascination for them that they associate with art and intellectuality, and they are responding to it as *their* film—and hence as a masterpiece.

Antonioni's off-screen conversation, as reported to us, is full of impeccable literary references, but the white-faced clowns who open and close *Blow-Up* suggest that inside his beautifully fitted dinner jacket he carries—next to his heart—a gold-edged gift edition of Kahlil Gibran. And from the way people talk about the profundity of *Blow-Up,* that's probably what they're responding to. What would you think of a man who stopped at a newsstand to cluck at the cover girls of *Vogue* and *Harper's Bazaar* as tragic symbols of emptiness and sterility, as evidence that modern life isn't "real," and then went ahead and bought the magazines? Or, to be more exact, what would we think of a man who conducted a leisurely tour of "swinging" London, lingering along the flashiest routes and dawdling over a pot-party and a mini-orgy, while ponderously explaining that although the Mod scene appears to be hip and sexy, it represents a condition of spiritual malaise in which people live only for the sensations of the moment? Is he a foolish old hypocrite or is he, despite his tiresome moralizing, a man who knows he's hooked?

It's obvious that there's a new kind of non-involvement among youth, but we can't get at what that's all about by Antonioni's terms. He is apparently unable to respond to or to convey the new sense of community among youth, or the humor and fervor and astonishing speed in their rejections of older values; he sees only the emptiness of Pop culture. All we can tell is that he doesn't understand what's going on—which is comprehensible, God knows, because who does? But then shouldn't he spare us the attitudes worthy of a *Time* essay or a Reagan speech?

Those who enjoy seeing this turned-on city of youth, those who say of *Blow-Up* that it's the trip, it's where we are now in consciousness and that Antonioni is in it, part of it, ahead of it like Warhol, may have a better sense of what Antonioni is about than the laudatory critics. Despite Antonioni's negativism, the world he presents looks harmless, and for many in the audience—and not just the youthful ones—sex without "connecting" doesn't really seem so bad—naughty, maybe, but nice. Even the smoke at the pot-party is enough to turn on some of the audience. And there's all that pretty color which delights the critics, though it undercuts their reasons for praising the movie because it's that bright cleaned-up big-city color of I-have-seen-the-future-and-it's-fun. Antonioni, like his fashion-photographer hero, is more interested in getting pretty pictures than in what they mean. But for reasons I can't quite fathom, what is taken to be shallow in his hero is taken to be profound in him. Maybe it's because of the symbols: do pretty pictures plus symbols equal art?

There are the revelers who won't make room on the sidewalk for nuns (spirit? soul? God? love?) and jostle them aside; an old airplane propeller is found in an antique shop; the hero considers buying the antique shop; two homosexuals walk their poodle, etc. Antonioni could point out that the poodle is castrated, and he'd probably be acclaimed for that, too—one more bitter detail of modern existential agony. There is a mock copulation with camera and subject that made me laugh (as the planes fornicating at the beginning of *Strangelove* did). But from the reviews of *Blow-Up* I learn that this was "tragic" and "a superbly realized comment on the values of our time" and all that. People seem awfully eager to abandon sense and perspective and humor and put on the newest fashion in hair shirts; New York critics who are just settling into their upper-East Side apartments write as if they're leaving for a monastery in the morning.

Hecht and MacArthur used to write light satirical comedies about shallow people living venal lives that said most of what Antonioni does and more, and were entertaining besides; they even managed to convey that they were in love with the corrupt milieu and were part of it without getting bogged down. And Odets, even in late work like his dialogue for *Sweet Smell of Success,* also managed to convey both hate and infatuation. Love-hate is what makes drama not only exciting but possible, and it certainly isn't necessary for Antonioni to resolve his conflicting feelings. But in *Blow-Up* he smothers this conflict in the kind of pompous platitudes the press loves to designate as proper to "mature," "adult," "sober" art. Who the hell goes to movies for mature, adult, sober art, anyway? Yes, we want more from movies than we get from the usual commercial entertainments, but would anybody use terms like mature, adult, and sober art for *The Rules of the Game* or *Breathless* or *Citizen Kane* or *Jules and Jim?*

The best part of *Blow-Up* is a well-conceived and ingeniously edited sequence in which the hero blows up a series of photographs and discovers that he has inadvertently photographed a murder. It's a good murder mystery sequence. But does it symbolize (as one reviewer says) "the futility of seeking the hidden meanings of life through purely technological means"? I thought the hero did rather well in uncovering the murder. But this kind of symbolic interpretation is not irrelevant to the appeal of the picture: Antonioni loads his atmosphere with so much confused symbolism and such a heavy sense of importance that the viewers use the movie as a Disposal for intellectual refuse. We get the stock phrases about "the cold death of the heart," "the eroticism is chilling in its bleakness," a "world so cluttered with synthetic stimulations that natural feelings are overwhelmed," etc., because Antonioni *inspires* this pompous jargon.

When the photographer loses the photographic record of the murder, he loses interest in it. According to *Time,* "Antonioni's antihero"—who is said to be a "little snake" and "a grincingly accurate portrait of the sort of squiggly little fungus that is apt to grow in a decaying society"—"holds in his possession, if only for an instant, the alexin of his cure: the saving grace of the spirit." (My Webster doesn't yield a clue to "grincingly"; an "alexin" is "a defensive substance, found normally in the body, capable of destroying bacteria.") In other words, if he did something about the murder, like going to the police, he would be accepting an involvement with the life or death of others, and he would find his humanity and become an OK guy to *Time*. (Would he then not be a representative of a decaying society, or would the society not then decay? Only *Time* can tell.)

This review, and many others, turn the murder into something like what the press and TV did with the Kitty Genovese case: use it as an excuse for another of those what-are-we-coming-to editorials about alienation and indifference to human suffering. What was upsetting about the Genovese case was not those among the "witnesses" who didn't want to get involved even to the degree of calling the police (cowardice is not a new phenomenon) but our recognition that in a big city we don't know when our help is needed, and others may not know when we need help. This isn't a new phenomenon, either; what is new is that it goes against the grain of modern social consciousness, *i.e.,* we feel responsible even though we don't know how to act responsibly. The press turned it into one more chance to cluck, and people went around feeling very superior to those thirty-eight witnesses because they were sure *they* would have called the police.

The moral satisfaction of feeling indignant that people take away from these cases (though I'm not sure that *Time's* moral is what Antonioni intended; probably not) is simple and offensive. Do all the times that the police are called when they are or aren't needed prove how humanly involved with each other we are? The editorial writers don't tell us. And they couldn't do much with the West Coast case of the young academic beaten, tied to his bed, moaning and crying for help for days before he died. His friends and neighbors heard him all right, but as that's how he customarily took his pleasure, they smiled sympathetically and went about their own affairs, not knowing that this time the rough trade he had picked up to beat him had been insanely earnest.

The quick rise to celebrity-status of young fashion-photographers, like the quick success of pop singers, makes them ideal "cool" heroes, because they don't come up the slow, backbreaking Horatio Alger route. And the glamour of the rich and famous and beautiful rubs off on the photographer who shoots them, making him one of them. Antonioni uses David Hemmings in the role very prettily—with his Billy Budd hair-do, he's like a pre-Raphaelite Paul McCartney. But if we're supposed to get upset because this young man got rich quick—the way some people get morally outraged at the salaries movie stars make—that's the moral outrage television personalities specialize in and it's hardly worth the consideration of art-house audiences. Yet a surprising lot of people seem willing to accept assumptions such as: the fashion photographer is symbolic of life in our society and time; he turns to easy sex because his life and ours is empty, etc. Mightn't people like easy sex even if their lives were reasonably full? And is sex necessarily empty just because the people are strangers to each other, or is it just different? And what's so terrible about fast, easy success? Don't most of the people who cluck their condemnation wish they'd had it?

Vanessa Redgrave, despite an odd Mod outfit, has a tense and lovely presence, and because she has been allowed to act in this film (in which almost no one else is allowed to project) she stands out. However, someone has arranged her in a wholly gratuitous mood—laughing with her head back and teeth showing in a blatant imitation of Garbo. It's almost a subliminal trailer for *Camelot* in which, according to advance publicity, she will be "the Garbo of the Sixties." This little deformation does not stick out as it might in another movie because this movie is so ill-formed, anyway. The exigencies of the plot force Antonioni to alter his typical "open" construction (famous partly because it was the most painstakingly planned openness in movie history). In *Blow-Up* he prepares for events and plants characters for reappearances when they will be needed, but limply, clumsily; and he finds poor excuses for getting into places like the discotheque and the pot-party, which "use" London to tell us about dehumanization. In some terrible way that I suppose could be called Antonioni's genius, he complains of dehumanization in a dehumanized way, and it becomes part of non-involvement to accept a movie like this as "a chronicle of our time."

Just as *Marienbad* was said to be about "time" and/or "memory," *Blow-Up* is said (by Antonioni and the critics following his lead) to be about "illusion and reality." They seem to think they are really saying something, and something impressive at that, though the same thing can be said about almost any movie. In what sense is a movie "about" an abstract concept? In *Marienbad* and in *Blow-Up,* by reducing it to silliness. It's likely that what Antonioni and the approving critics mean is that high fashion, Mod celebrity, rock and roll, and drugs are part of a sterile or frenetic existence, and they take this to mean that the life represented in the film is not "real" but illusory. What seems to be implicit in the prattle about illusion and reality is the notion that the photographer's life is based on "illusion" and that when he discovers the murder, he is somehow face to face with reality." Of course this notion that murder is more real than, say, driving in a Rolls Royce convertible, is nonsensical (it's more shocking, though, and when combined with a Rolls Royce it gives a movie a bit of box-office—it's practical). They're not talking about a concept of reality but what used to be called "the real things in life," *i.e.,* the solid values they approve of versus the "false values" of "the young people today."

Antonioni is the kind of thinker who can say that there are "no social or moral judgments in the picture:" he is merely showing us the people who have discarded "all discipline," for whom freedom means "marijuana, sexual perversion, anything," and who live in "decadence without any visible future." I'd hate to be around when he's making judgments. And yet in some sense Antonioni is right: because he doesn't *connect* what he's showing to judgment. And that dislocation of sensibility is probably why kids don't notice the moralizing, why they say *Blow-Up* is hip.

The cultural ambience of a film like this becomes mixed with the experience of the film: one critic says Antonioni's "vision" is that "the further we draw away from reality, the closer we get to the truth," another that Antonioni means "we must learn to live with the invisible." All this can sound great to those who don't mind not knowing what it's about, for whom the ineffable seems most important. "It's about the limits of visual experience. The photographer can't go beyond make-believe," a lady lawyer who loved the movie explained to me. "But," I protested, "visual experience is hardly make-believe any more than your practice is—perhaps less." Without pausing for breath she shifted to, "Why does it have to mean anything?" That's the game that's being played at parties this year at Marienbad. They feel they understand *Blow-Up* but when they can't explain it, or why they feel as they do, they use that as the grounds for saying the movie is a work of art. *Blow-Up* is the perfect movie for the kind of people who say, "now that films have become an art form . . ." and don't expect to understand art.

Because the hero is a *photographer* and the blow-up sequence tells a story in pictures, the movie is also said to be about Antonioni's view of himself as an artist (though even his worst enemies could hardly accuse him of "telling stories" in pictures). Possibly it is, but those who see *Blow-Up* as Antonioni's version of 8½—as making a movie about making a movie—seem to value that much more than just making a movie, probably because it puts the film in a class with the self-conscious autobiographical material so many young novelists struggle with (the story that ends with their becoming writers . . .) and is thus easy to mistake for the highest point of the artistic process.

There is the usual post-*Marienbad* arguing about whether the murder is "real" or "hallucinatory." There seems to be an assumption that if a movie can be interpreted as wholly or partially a dream or fantasy, it is more artistic, and I have been hearing that there is no murder, it's all in the photographer's head. But then the movie makes even less sense because there are no indications of anything in his character that relate to such fantasies. Crowther has come up with the marvelously involuted suggestion that as the little teeny-bopper orgy wasn't "real" but just the hero's "juvenile fantasy" the Production Code people shouldn't have thought they were seeing real titbits on the screen.

What is it about the symbolic use of characters and details that impresses so many educated people? It's not very hard to do: almost any detail or person or event in our lives can be pressed into symbolic service, but to what end? I take my dogs for a walk in New York City in January and see examples of "alienation." An old Negress is crooning, "The world out here is lonely and cold." A shuffling old man mutters, "Never did and never will, never again and never will." And there's a crazy lady who glowers at my dogs and shouts, "They're not fit to shine my canary's shoes!" Do they tell us anything about a "decaying society"? No, but if you had some banal polemical, social, or moral point to make, you could turn them into cardboard figures marked with arrows. In so doing I think you would diminish their individuality and their range of meaning, but you would probably increase your chances of being acclaimed as a deep thinker.

When journalistic details are used symbolically—and that is how Antonioni uses "swinging" London—the artist does not create a frame of reference that gives meaning to the details; he simply exploits the ready-made symbolic meanings people attach to certain details and leaves us in a profound mess. (The middlebrow moralists think it's profound and the hippies enjoy the mess.) And when he tosses in a theatrical convention like a mimed tennis game without a ball—which connects with the journalistic data only in that it, too, is symbolic—he throws the movie-game away. It becomes ah-sweet-mystery-of-life we-are-all-fools, which, pitched too high for human ears, might seem like great music beyond our grasp.

THE NEW REPUBLIC
February 25, 1967

Correspondence

Sirs:
When a film critic consumes close to 4,000 words in putting down one of the world's great directors, something bordering on an obsession must be involved. I am referring to Pauline Kael's longwinded review of Antonioni's *Blow-Up* (February 11).

Her critique has all the earmarks of a carefully planned hatchet job, with its petty picking at minute details and scenes, its belaboring of irrelevancies outside the film, and its shrewdly placed allusions to film classics which have nothing in common with *Blow-Up.* In addition to all the lint-picking, Miss Kael apparently, before writing the review, read everything that had been said in print about the film, then strung together what appeared to be overly arty interpretations from Bosley Crowther to *Time.* Of course this is a familiar method of the "put-down"— if you're an inverted snob, simply lift out of context all the comments of the film critics which run counter to your anti-art premises (pooh-poohing of symbolism, levels of meanings, etc.), then comment on the comments. In this way you can

---

easily demonstrate that every critic except Pauline Kael is precious, overintellectual, and just too too artsy.

What irritates me most about Miss Kael's review is its preoccupation with what's In and what's Out, what's culturally and artistically fashionable and unfashionable, and what's Hip and what's Square. I just wonder if all these fringe trappings are really important and pertinent. James Agee thought not. In fact, may I suggest that Miss Kael re-read *Agee On Film* before reviewing the next movie by Fellini, who I assume is the next genius to be put on the block.

Burling Lowrey
Washington, D.C.

Ronald Reagan's comment on California redwoods might apply, with a little paraphrasing, to Pauline Kael: read one review and you've read them all. I was ready when she got around to Antonioni's *Blow-Up*. First, she reached into her rich store of personal (apocryphal?) experiences to find stupid statements by her (stupid?) acquaintances illustrating all the worse reasons why people go to movies, silly interpretations and, by contrast, Miss Kael's sturdy common sense, intellectual astuteness, and aesthetic sensitivity. Then she told us that *Blow-Up* did not sufficiently "entertain"; perish the thought, apparently, if a film provokes reflection and discussion. As usual we benefited from her numerous "titbits," as she put it, about life, love, art, modern man, *etc., etc.,* which are supposed to have something to do with the little she says about the movie. By this time we are again aware of her characteristic tone: so, so *chic* but never, never "in" or "out." Superior and patronizing? Yes. Communicative? Hardly. I am beginning to think that she, like Mary McCarthy, has begun to write satire without realizing it.

She tells us that *Blow-Up* has bad photography and poor color. *That,* I admit, is new. We learn that it is confused, disjointed, and cliché ridden. The "reviewers," "New York critics," "hippies," "kids," and "middle-brow moralists" (who seem to be the only ones frequenting theatres these days) cannot see, as of course she can, that Antonioni is a shallow thinker, a sentimentalist, a moralist, and all those other things we were not aware Antonioni was. She almost, but not quite, succeeds in pulling the wool over our eyes by using the device of ridiculing the critics who have praised *Blow-Up* as a way of criticizing Antonioni.

Miss Kael prefers two kinds of movies: those by Godard and non-think Hollywoods that "entertain." Gone are the good old days for us movie fans; gone too are the good old days for Miss Kael. Nobody makes a decent film anymore. Oh yes, there was *The Bible.*

Robert C. Twombly
University of Wisconsin

It is perhaps fit, when a film appears to be rather more concerned with photographs of an event than with the event itself, that the review of this film should be rather more concerned with other reviews of it, than with the film itself. Should this have been Miss Kael's oblique intent, her discussion of *Blow-Up* would have been fine irony. But I do not credit her with so subtle an achievement. Rather, I feel that she failed utterly to distinguish between what people have said about the film, and what the film itself says, and so has misread the shallowness of the comment as the shallowness of the film. And incorrectly assuming that the cocktail-party commentary correctly describes a film, she has undertaken a severe rebuttal of the film which ought instead to have been reserved for the fashionable, misperceptive, cozy chatter about alienation and contemporary despair. So, in place of the perceptive analysis of a deep film, which we have a right to expect in your journal, we find a waspish, irrelevant, acutely self-congratulatory and unspeakably vulgar snapping away at views which are less those of Antonioni than of his self-styled admirers. The catchwords of the day, when they blind us to the works they are intended to clarify, exercise a destructive power disproportionate to their intrinsic frivolity. It would be a disaster if so great a work as Antonioni's should become so identified with what people of the moment say about it, that it should fail to survive the shifts in pseudo-intellectual fashion which are the destiny of catchwords. Miss Kael tightens this identification, and so contributes to the suffocation of a masterpiece. . . . If Miss Kael's review is an index of the intellectual level at which she operates, however, she had better suspend assignments until the next Ritz Brothers confection. Who possibly could care whether she (really) likes Harry Ritz?

Arthur C. Danto
Columbia University

I fail to understand how Miss Kael can write for three whole pages before even mentioning the theme of illusion and reality, which, as far as I'm concerned, is primarily what *Blow-Up* is about—though not in the way Miss Kael sees it. Why even discuss the point of which is more "real"—murder or driving in a Rolls Royce convertible? A thief, yes? We see a dirty man in torn-up clothes carrying a lunch pail, exchanging words with equally impoverished-looking men, and finally running suspiciously towards a very expensive-looking car. Obviously he's a thief! But is he? As it turns out, he's not a thief at all! he's a wealthy photographer. You say we were caught up in an illusion?

Later we see the same man at his studio wildly snapping pictures of a seductive model, but doing so in a position of copulating. Of course we laugh. How can we help it when faced with the strange juxtaposition of the (supposedly) most objective of activities (photography) and the most subjective of human endeavors (making love). . . . I don't think Antonioni is asking us to intellectualize about the "abstract concept" illusion and reality. Rather, he involves us in an experience which forces us to contemplate the *un*certainty of what we feel most certain of.

It is disappointing (if not incredible) that Miss Kael cannot perceive what the last scene is saying. As the photographer watches the clown's tennis game, certainly he *knows* there is no tennis ball . . . but then . . . maybe there is. What could be more fitting at the end than that we should hear, amidst the rustling leaves, the sound of a tennis ball . . . not really so different from the sound of a clicking camera.

Nannette Cochran
Berkeley, Calif.

If the readers can accept the surreal dream-logic of Pauline Kael's comments on *Blow-Up* then her blast of "Anti-Onionism" makes amusing reading. This logic is based on a series of unrelated and often conflicting a priori assumptions:

1. Movies are made for children and cannot be taken seriously as art. ("Who the hell goes to movies for 'mature,' 'adult,' 'sober' art, anyway?")

2. Movies have no themes nor serious content. ("In what sense is a movie 'about' an abstract concept?")

3. *Blow-Up* is about nothing. (This is an inferred assumption derived from the unassailable fact that she cannot figure out what the picture *is* about.)

Based on this syllogism one would conclude that logically Miss Kael would have admired *Blow-Up.* However, the only utility she seems to find for the film is to employ it as a club against all the critics who disagree with her. She scarcely stoops to criticize the film at all. In an age of non-books and anti-novels she stands high on the list of non-critics.

Far too often, Miss Kael tends to damn a picture for some preconceived notion she holds somewhere (generally unstated) of what it should have done. She makes little effort to discover what the film attempts to do. The idea of viewing a film twice is evidently inimical to her (particularly since you only get credit for dropping the same name once) as her comments on *Blow-Up* indicate. Since one of the qualities of art is that it gives sustained pleasure, her view of films is perfectly consistent.

The history of all the arts is filled with strident, shrill, smug hissings. Every new experiment has been greeted with similar "Crokeries." And if we remember that John Wilson Croker is now primarily remembered for his attacks on Keats, we can only hope that Miss Kael, in a similar manner, has also earned her place in posterity.

Regina K. Fadiman
Los Angeles, Calif.

Rarely have I been so impressed with magazine writing as I have been with Pauline Kael's articles on *Sand Pebbles* and *Blow-Up.* Her ability lies not only in expostulating an intelligent review of the movies themselves, but relating them to our culture in general and to the movie culture in particular. . . .

I don't even agree with her, at least not always. It is her perspective, her refusal to be conned, that I most enjoy.

Sidney Tatz
Flushing, New York

Richard Goldstein, *THE VILLAGE VOICE* December 29, 1966

The Screw-Up

The total flaw in Michelangelo Antonioni's "Blow-Up" is non-participation.

The master of cinematic ennui has never been content to let a story tell itself. It has always been Antonioni's movie, as though the writer-director had steamed the very camera-lens with his own icy breath.

Cinematic style is no accident and Antonioni's presence in every frame of every weighted scene has become a personal hallmark. His face shines against the glass walls of the ultra-distant skyscrapers he loves to surround his actors with. It is his hand guiding those stealthy Vitti-Moreau-Redgrave hips as they sway to the beat of boredom. His mouth behind every pout. His chicken in everybody's pot.

Antonioni appears more deliberately in his films than even Alfred Hitchcock, whose cameo roles have become an insider's guessing game. Nobody has to guess where Michelangelo appears in "L'Avventura"—or in "Blow-Up." He is the Big Brother of Blue Funk. He is every moviegoer's Wizard of Oz.

Now, in this latest film, the old maxim is truer than ever. On the set, the actors come and go . . . talking Michelangelo. Because "Blow-Up" is another Antonioni treatise. If you groove on them, as I usually do, you'll find those plexiglass pauses in conversation even more intriguing this time around. But don't settle back expecting the real story behind swinging London.

Antonioni has always been a controversial commodity in cinematic circles. He's always thrown the "pros" in shiny suits and sunglasses into a rage. He's always charmed the theorists because, as an architectural director, he sees so much as an extension of life-style.

But before the pros and cons of his latest Statement of Policy are tabulated, let's get one thing straight; "Blow-Up" is pure Antonioni, and only Antonioni. Its intention, its execution, its conclusions, make "Blow-Up" vintage malattorio Italiano. But the only way to excuse the gross inaccuracies with which the film treats its subject is to condone its excesses as poetic license. Don't anybody think "Blow-Up" is good journalism.

Antonioni makes a praiseworthy first attempt to evaluate the world of pop culture. As his locale, he chooses London: Where else but a city where Billy Graham got booted out of Soho by a stripper, where Kenneth Tynan said "fuck" on the air. If London looks like an Antonioni city, if the photographers and their models look like Antonioni people, it is not because things are as they seem. There are two ways to make a film: you can either make a movie about the subject or make a subject about the movie. The master of melancholia has choosen the latter approach, and in making this choice of doctrine over fact has given us, not a swinging city, but a ghost town in which characters and events are mirages, and the only reality is moral, not situational. This London is strangely reminiscent of Antonioni's Rome, even though the director was careful to capture visual essences of the scene—Bobbies, Bentleys, and brollies, all in the proper proportion. The parties are like the exercises in ennui we sat through in "La Notte," the long futile walks like the ambivalent search in "L'Avventura," the "new London" landscape like the electric lamp posts in "Eclipse," the grassy knolls like the neglected sprigs of nature in "The Red Desert."

What we never saw in Antonioni's Rome were the street stalls, the pasta places, the vulgar hot breath of the old quarters.

All this working culture has been screened out, so we could perceive the lectures on anomie in a rarified atmosphere, where culture cracks like a bloated vein, leaving everyone to swim in a pool of superficial blood.

They suffer; they flounder; they drown. And we watch fascinated because it is an arresting concept. Antonioni the artist peoples his own cities with his own morality of despair; existentialist angst fairly oozes from the underground.

But it isn't London. The similarities between the "swinging" city we see here, and the "eternal" city in films past, should hip audiences to the real locale of "Blow-Up." It is a London of the mind. Its convolutions are the turns of a master moralist. Its languid stench of corruption is an imagined flow. Its crystal teardrops, drip drying against a snow-powdered cheek, have nothing to do with real fashion; they are mod from Michelangelo's own boutique.

Problems of geography and age leave gaping holes in the credibility of "Blow-Up." The whole film smacks of frenzy Italian-style. And the fog you see settling over those switched-on streets is not London pea soup, but the heavy-rasping breath of an old man telling us how groovy it is to be young.

The Antonioni technique, like the worst Italian cooking, means deep frying a piece of meat in an oily overwriting, then dousing it in a stinging sauce of symbolism. And the whole thing drips with cheese.

This inability to cook a piece of meat unadorned is most apparent in the handling of the murder, central to the plot of "Blow-Up." Our photographer-protagonist discovers the crime in a series of photos he has taken on one of those clinging London greens. Slowly, painfully, he enlarges a suspicious section of film and—shades of Zapruder—we see, hidden in the underbrush, the hideously barren outline of a man's face, and to one side a gun.

The sudden jolt is stunning. Antonioni has never dealt with murder before, but he approaches the crime with a master's eye. The subsequent confrontation on the green, between victim-corpse and photographer-corpse, is chillingly reminiscent of Bergman's open-grave scenes. There is the same deja-vu, the same I-am-a-voyeur-at-my-own-funeral-compulsion. The audience feels the rush of symbolism and reacts—not to the line, but to the situation—by getting the point.

But what follows is a travelogue through the bi-lanes of Chelsea, an early morning mock-tennis game, and lots of pregnant walking. Through it all, the only sound we hear is the director, hammering away at our perception with his SUPER-MESSAGE: Get it? He realizes life is a travesty? Get it? Post-industrial-pre-subliminal-quasi-crotical-funk? Get the message? Yes, we see. All those costumed people playing tennis—it's all a game.

But Antonioni's divesting of situation with symbolic meaning often contradicts the realities involved. A carload of students tearing down those narrow London lanes disguised as harlequins is a ready made allegory, and so we see these personifications of sad-sin, tearing through the early morning gloom at the start and finish of "Blow-Up." At the end of the film, they give our photographer-everyman his inevitable epiphany. They are the soul of Mod London—the pastel colored inevitable, the massless masses, the all-night parchesi players, the new chic, the new cool, the new religion—aloneness.

But—hold on a sec with all that literary overkill. Those kids are participants in an old tradition. They're students on a rag, which means they dress up and collect money for their pranks. The profits go to charity. It's all very much like a UNICEF for Halloween and quite the opposite of symbolizing anomie, it actually signifies cultural integration.

Compare the meaning of rag-week, with the overcoat Antonioni adds, and decide for yourself whether the moral is necessarily the real. The example is only one illustration of a director's unwillingness to allow the perception of reality to interfere with the construction of art. There is a rock 'n' roll scene in "Blow-Up" which makes vicarious use of the Yardbirds. Our hero wanders into a youth club—what's a latter-day inferno without a discotheque called Satan's Jaw, right—and lingers among the catatonic dancers. It is a scene out of "Marat/Sade," and it bears no resemblance to any London youth club I have ever seen. The music is there; the kids are there; but between the sound and the action falls that heavy clapboard called Art. And so, everyone limps, droops, and sighs profoundly. The sick soul of Europe party, in youth drag. And when one of the Yardbirds stomps on his guitar (I'm told he got splinters in his fingers from this cameo performance, which is understandable because pop musicians don't customarily vent their spleen on as personal a treasure as their instruments) and throws the stump into the audience, the catatonia becomes manic; the kids scream a lot and fight over the guitar. The photographer seizes it, races out into the street, then drops it spitefully into the gutter. Some kids pick it up, puzzled at its lack of significance (they don't know whose guitar it is) and drop it again. So, Mick makes a good point about totem and taboo in teen culture, but he does it with a lack of understanding that can only be called Parental.

Then there's a pot party. The denizens, the opiated orgasm, all that Anglo-Saxon limp-wrist submission. But what have we here? —a real crew of kiddies gathered around a supply of giggling, dragging, generally oh-wowing. The whole room tilts and clouds. Everyone is laid out in one reverie or another. The photographer approaches a model and says: "I thought you were in Paris." Her eyes narrow to freaked-out slits. Darling, she drawls, through hookah-teeth: "I am in Paris."

Now, a trip across the channel is an awful lot to ask of even the best pot, and so is a crowd of slumped and fagged-out people. Nonetheless, Mick's pot-party makes the opium dens of China look like milk bars. And, intimates will tell you that the director—always out for authenticity—threw a real pot party, all night in a Chelsea flat. Of course, you put a bunch of stoned people in front of a movie camera and you get acting. Even Andrelo knows that.

It's stretching a point to compare "Chelsea Girls" to "Blow-Up" because Warhol's church is the boutique and Antonioni's boutique is the church. But as a serious cinematic attempt to grapple with the phenomenon of pop—with the men and women who really make it move around us—Warhol's film avoids all the traps "Blow-Up" falls into. If Warhol is a permissive parent Antonioni is a veritable Jewish mother hovering over every frame until it is all constructed, shipped and packaged into a do-it-yourself gospel. This is fine for a closet drama where you're willing to sit and be screamed at, but it washes off a scene like fingerpaint.

It leaves the real London crying for real analysis. Because, there is a life style on that sceptered isle that is puzzling all of us, and yet, moving us to copy. It is a mode far beyond the rudiments of fashion; to get hung up with all that asexual longhaired mod, the way Mick did, is to miss the point. Londoners have refined the creation of image to an art; everybody does it every day. But underneath all that fab gear from the King's Row lies the real soul of the swinging city—and it is just as mysterious and elusive as that murderer who lurks in Antonioni's shadow.

THE VILLAGE VOICE
January 5, 1967

Correspondence

Spooky Film

The fatal flaw in Richard Goldstein's review of "The Blow-Up" (Voice, December 29) is his incredible involvement in his own language—coupled with a certain naivete which would almost be charming—if naivete were not by nature a journalistic sin. "The Blow-Up" is indeed a London of the mind—and a New York of the mind, and a Paris of the mind—a reality of enough minds to make one shiver. It's a pretty spooky film.

Cabell D. Smith
East 55th Street

Sub-Hippie Newspeak

. . . It was something of a shock to come up against the sub-hippie newspeak of Richard Goldstein on the same film. A double shock to me, as I had found his dissertations on pop culture in the past to be most illuminating.

After explaining, via verbal convolutions that would put Tom Wolfe to shame, what a personal craftsman Antonioni is, he complains that "Mick" (almost as obscene an abbreviation as New York Times sharpie Rex Reed's reference to Otto Preminger as "The Big O") didn't capture the swinging city as a result of this highly personalized form of self-expression. Does Mr. Goldstein think for one moment that an impersonal documentarist of the assembly style like David L. Wolper, for example, could bring back anything valid concerning the contemporary London scene?

Of course Antonioni could have taken the easy way out and rushed into London like Jean Rouch or the Maysles brothers—into real rock and roll spots, real pot parties, etc. But then where would that have gotten him, or his characters, or his story? Antonioni takes our knowledge of such phenomena for granted, and is thus free to recreate such environments on his own terms. There is a direct line between the high class prostitute with the ripped dress sequence in "L'Avventura," the stock market crash in "Eclipse," and the instrument smashing session in "Blow-Up." The latter was no more "about" rock and roll than its predecessors were "about" financial investment and prostitution.

Mr. Goldstein's interpretation of the tennis court revellers is just as superficial. These figures are hardly "lost souls," they are quite happy during both their appearances, and Antonioni makes it quite clear that their party is never over. Antonioni has not conjured up a dime-a-dozen message movie of the Stanley Kramer garden variety, but a painful confrontation of self coming to terms with both the extents and limits of his art. The evocations of London are icing on the cake, means to an end.

"Life is a travesty, post-industrial—pre-subliminal-quasi-erotical-funk" etc., etc., ad nauseum are "interpretations" to be filed away for another day, another review (of Donovan perhaps). As for Mr. Goldstein: Stay off the movies, son. It's a medium with a message, but there are artists too.

David Ehrenstein
Flushing

Misguided Enthusiasm

I read through Goldstein on "Blow-Up" (Voice, December 29) twice hoping that the second time around it would appear as something other than it apparently is: a classic sophomoric criticism of a work of art based on the you-didn't-make-the-kind-of-picture-I-would-have-made-if-I-were-making-that-picture-approach. It came off as badly on second reading.

Mightn't we have been spared this jejune outburst of misguided enthusiasm?

Fred Vassi
Thompson Street

Joseph Morgenstern, *NEWSWEEK*
January 2, 1967

The Colors of the Soul

Never before BLOW-UP has Michelangelo Antonioni, the cinema's bravest spelunker of the soul, come up from the depths with such a marvelous story and such gorgeous pictures of the cavernous emptiness inside modern man.

His first English-language film is entertaining, as well as enlightening, and not because he decided to put on a happy face for American financiers. Antonioni's people are no less tormented or perplexed, no better oriented in the allegedly real world than they were in "La Notte, "L'Avventura, "The Eclipse" or "Red Desert." The change has taken place in the director's artistry. More certain of his own techniques, perhaps more nearly at peace with himself, he seems to have opened himself to the vitality, variety, humor and complexity of life, however barren it may seem to those who live it.

Much of his success derives from his choice of a hero, a young British photographer who nips about London in a Rolls-Royce convertible trying to catch reality with his little Nikon. Not for him the old Kodak slogan, "You push the button, we do the rest." This fellow pushes buttons and does everything else, crawling all over his high-fashion models in close-up communion with their extinct spirits, pulling them like taffy, brutalizing them—"C'mon, now, work! Work! Work! Work!"—and finally driving one of them and himself to the synchronized flash of an orgasm.

Essence of Being

Here in the fashion photographer's studio, among the monochrome gauzes, the sky-blue sheets and gaudy feather boas, Antonioni has found his most telling expression of dehumanization and thingness in the switched-on society. Here is where all the intellectual generalizations become specifically true, where pose is the essence of being, where people are props and props the reality, and he has filmed its disconnections, silences and unearthly minuets with flabbergasting virtuosity. (1)

Outside the studio, however, complications arise for the hero and for Antonioni as well. There are real people to make pictures of; people can lead to feelings, and what is the correct exposure for a feeling? There are lovers in a park, running through alleys of rustling trees. Snap goes the shutter, slap goes the reflex mirror. But back in the darkroom, whence final enlightenment comes, a blow-up reveals that things were not what they seemed, that the frolic on the greensward was a set-up for murder.

It should quickly be added that "Blow-Up" is no more a picture about murder than "L'Avventura" was a detective story about a missing girl. Antonioni traffics in feelings, not plots. While other directors are busy teaching new dogs old tricks, he is working with the slippery eels of emotion, and the work is not easy. He has not yet achieved a synthesis of feelings, story and structure. A few scenes, though delightful in themselves, dangle loosely from the body of the film: the photographer rummaging through a junk shop, the photographer rampant on a field of kraft paper with a couple of naked postulants to mannequinhood, the subplot involving Sarah Miles as the mistress of an abstract painter. (2) Some of the dialogue unfortunately becomes self-conscious. A final mime sequence, in which an invisible tennis ball becomes more real than any photo of

---

1. Morgenstern convinces the reader that he is correct in viewing the studio as a symbol of dehumanization. How does he do this?

2. After seeing *Blow-Up,* do you agree the scenes cited here "dangle loosely," or is it rather that Morgenstern cannot fit them into his view of the movie? Note here that Morgenstern assumes he must come up with some interpretation which will unify the whole film. And this is extremely difficult to do at times, most especially with a highly suggestive work such as *Blow-Up.* While one admires the critic's commitment to this principle, it might have been wiser for Morgenstern to have admitted that he was having difficulty, instead of stating with insufficient support that the scenes failed to contribute to the whole.

it could ever be, is matchlessly magical as a separate short subject, yet strangely clumsy as a symbolic carnival coda in the style of Fellini.

What matters most, however, is what Antonioni has achieved. His direction of actors is remarkable. David Hemmings, as the photographer, puts every other male performance of the year in deep shade. Vanessa Redgrave, as the girl in the park, is a model of intelligence and tightly controlled energy. "Blow-Up" confirms what "Red Desert" suggested, that Antonioni is the master of the age in his use of color, and his uncompromising quality control of every print that leaves the laboratory suggests that other directors who get mediocre results from the same film and cameras are simply mediocre workmen.

Mindlessness

Most exciting of all, "Blow-Up" shows a great enlargement of Antonioni's already enormous talents. He is alive to new possibilities, taking new chances. Even when he loses, on parts that refuse to join the whole, his stuff is often so rich that he really wins. One such scene is spent on a rock 'n roll guitarist in mortal combat with his loudspeaker. The thing has developed so much static that it threatens to drown out the music. Man turns on machine and beats it into submission with his guitar, and this struggle against the mindlessness of matter is a valiant and memorable one, even if the man has nothing to show for it in the end but a sullen silence and the broken neck of his highstrung love.

Brendan Gill, *THE NEW YORKER*
December 31, 1966

After a brilliant beginning, Michelangelo Antonioni's "Blow-Up" dwindles down and away into failure, and for a reason that would no doubt strike its maker as ironic. In the past, critics of his pictures have complained that they lacked a strong story line—that their evasive meanderings in time and place were a bore, and that boringness was no less irritating for being perhaps intentional. In the present movie, which is Mr. Antonioni's first English-speaking production, a strong and realistic story line lies embedded in the very heart of an otherwise lyrical, non-realistic study of contemporary English life, and this, though not boring, is a crucial mistake. (1) What it amounts to is an unlucky mingling of true Antonioni with imitation Hitchcock, and the two parts cannot be made to seem one. The hero of "Blow-Up" is a young fashion photographer—one of those lank London braves, sprung from the lower depths, whose caste signs are birdnest hair, blue jeans, expensive cars, and an almost total lack of feeling. For this zombie-like creature, well played by David Hemmings, the cameras he carries are not merely his livelihood but who he is and all he is; with their help, his days and nights are passed in a trance of profitable professional voyeurism. This trance, which Antonioni delineates with his usual suave beauty of imagery, is broken by the accidental arrival in his life of a pretty girl who may be a murderess. The girl, enacted with understandable uncertainty by Vanessa Redgrave, never gets an opportunity to reveal her true nature to us, much less to the photographer, (2) for, having launched a conventionally piquant little mystery story, Antonioni characteristically abandons it, and the picture slips into fantasy and closes with a pretentiously symbolic tennis match, played without rackets or ball. "Blow-Up" was shot in color and Antonioni's London is, as you would expect, exquisite. The director of photography was Carlo Di Palma.

---

1. How can we reconcile the reviewer's perception of "a strong and realistic story line" with the ambiguities so stunningly underscored by other commentators? Is it possible that the critic is using "story line" in a very special and eccentric way? Incidentally, is the critic necessarily wrong simply because he is a minority? Is criticism a democracy where majority rules?

2. Is the critic suggesting that the girl *should* reveal her true nature?

Selections from Stanley Kauffmann's National Educational Television review

... [*Blow-Up*] is about photography: it treats photography both as subject and as medium. And since film itself is a photographic medium, we are confronted with a comment on a comment on a comment. Part of the relation between the story, which is certainly cryptic, and photography as such is the paradox of the camera, which sees all, sees more than we can see ourselves when we take a picture, which stops time, and yet does not contain answers, only fixes mysteries. (1)

We never know the identity of the murderer, the corpse or the girl. We cannot know that the hero will ever see the girl again because she evidently had the substitute film developed and found out that he had misled her. When he returns to his studio after one expedition, he finds that it has been rifled, that all the photographs and negatives of the park episode—except one blurred print—have been stolen. The whole episode is both complete and permanently unfinished. By clicking his camera innocently and at random, he has connected himself for life with a drama of which he can never know more. It can be taken as an epitome of our own personal pilgrimages, clicking along with our eyes every day, gathering up experiences which—in terms of absolutes, of finalities, of understanding—only compound our ignorance.

The photographer-as-hero is more than incidental or convenient. Fashion photograph and the idiotic attitudinizing of models are

---

1. Compare Kauffmann's statement that the film is about photography with Andrew Sarris' view that the film is ". . . a statement of the artist not on life, but on art itself as the consuming passion of an artist's life." *(The Village Voice,* December 29, 1966).

Selections of Stanley Kauffmann's commentary on Antonioni's film, "Blow-Up," from the program produced and broadcast by Channel 13/WNDT, December 26, 1966, as part of its ART OF FILM series. Reprinted by permission of Stanley Kauffmann.

part of the framework, as is the facile success of the young man—so early in life, so frightening because he still has a whole life ahead of him in which either to sustain that success or find other successes. It is fashion photography that makes his fortune—he drives a Rolls-Royce convertible as if it were a Volkswagen—but the rest of the framework is his other photography. He is preparing a book of candid photographs, and it is for this book that he wants his pictures of the lovers in the park. Indeed, when we first meet him he is just coming out of doss-house—a flop-house—where he has spent the night in ragged clothes, with a camera concealed in an old paper bag, taking pictures of the bums and drifters. Like so many who make their livings by being popular idols or by serving popular idolatries, he is justifying himself to himself by other work; and it is this other, serious work that gets him into serious trouble—the immediate difficulty with the girl who wants her pictures back and the longer-lasting trouble, the deepened perplexity about the rationality of existence.

This profession of photography—though it is no longer new in the world—is one that we associate with the young. And Antonioni has used it as an epitome of youth: a profession in which a young man can quickly excel with a quick eye, a quick brain, and brashness, in which experience of life is not necessary for effective art. In fact, this whole film is a paradigm of a young man too soon successful in art who finds himself *deficient* in experience. . . .

To get my other remaining qualifications out of the way: there is in direct contrast with the modernity, one very old-fashioned element. The picture begins with a group of clown-faced masqueraders and revellers, riding about in a jeep. The film ends with a pantomime tennis game played by two of these clown characters and watched by the rest of them and the hero, in the park near the scene of the murder. . . . The effect of these revellers is a combination of Art Nouveau and Jean Cocteau—a film-maker whom Antonioni admires and with whom he once almost worked. The feeling of these clown scenes cuts against both the modernity of Antonioni's atmosphere and the subtlety of his art. As figures, they are old-fashioned; as symbols, they are somewhat heavy-handed.

The only other fault of any consequence, I think, lies in the use of a neighboring couple, an artist and his girl, who live in a house behind the photographer's studio. The quiet warmth of the girl—she is played adequately by Sarah Miles—has a place in the harmonic scheme of the film. Miss Miles makes an agreeable contrast with the much more gorgeous and utterly moronic models who flit through the studio. But her relationship with the hero is insufficiently developed.

As for the color photography in this film, I need only note that it was done by Carlo di Palma, who was the cinematographer of *Red Desert.* Antonioni has not used color as schematically here as in that film, but he has used it exquisitely. If one were to cavil, it would only be to hope—since he says he is only going to make color films from now on—that he will get a bit more used to the fact. But this is to quibble.

The way he uses sound is superb. It is only the second time one sees the film that one can trace the effects in certain scenes to the sound—like the scenes in the park where the wind makes the menace even before anything at all is menacing. . . . (2)

In *Blow-Up* perhaps the most staggering display of virtuoso editing is in the various sequences in which the photographer—absolutely alone in his studio—discovers the secret in the photographs he has taken. The way Antonioni compresses time and engages the eye—using one actor, some photographic equipment and some photographs, and creates a drama out of this material—is cinema mastery, (3) pure and far from simple. . . .

What sustains the film, despite the faults I mentioned, despite the fact that it never truly wrings us profoundly, is a sense that it is the product of a vision of the world: that an artistic intelligence is contemplating, selecting, daring, and disregarding any consequences except the results of its own vision and distillation. In short, behind *Blow-Up* is the mind of an artist—a fine artist at the height of his technical powers and with an appetite for discovery, yet with an articulated style of his own. Thus, whenever an Antonioni film is discussed—and as much as I have said, there is much more that could be said—there is one feeling that remains—very rare in film going experience: and that feeling is gratitude.

---

2. Note how Kauffmann enlarges our aesthetic perceptions here. One would only wish he had offered further examples. "But this is to quibble."
3. What are the criteria here for "cinema mastery"?

Carey Harrison, *SIGHT AND SOUND*
Spring, 1967

Unshaven, red-eyed, dressed in rags, a group of men emerge wearily from a slum dosshouse. It is early morning. A young man separates himself from the group, turns down a side street, and climbs into a limousine. He drives to work: his destination proves to be a fashion photographer's studio. Without changing, the young man grabs his camera and plunges into the routine, bobbing and weaving as he photographs the models, barking at them, shouting. The sweat-stained tramp disguise looks bizarre against the antiseptic chic of the sets. It turns out that Thomas is a fashion photographer who hates his work and despises his subjects; his lives for reportage photography, and the dosshouse sequence is to form a central part of his forthcoming book of Cartier Bresson-style photographs. The first mystery of the film is resolved.

With *Blow-Up* Michelangelo Antonioni has turned to making films in English, and while the film was being shot in London last year, speculation was intense. The film was said to be a devastating exposé of the swinging scene and the lascivious world of fashion photography; the movie became a cult among its expected subjects. But *Blow-Up* is not a study in decadence. His easy life cramps the central character's initiative, and contempt for his own success has upset his values: he regards fashion photography and the fashionable world as utterly unreal, documentary photography and the outside world as completely 'real'. The discrimination is too glib, and the shock is all the more severe when he discovers that the outside world is just as opaque as the sets inside his studio. There is no 'more real' world. The affluent life is the context of this discovery, and not the subject of the film's investigation. Perhaps Antonioni saw, too, that 'swinging London' exists only as a trap for amateur sociologists: the biggest common factor among the 'swinging people' is their anxiety to disown all common factors between them and other 'swinging people'. Their membership card is to have joined no club, which permits each of them to deride the squalid 'scene', and look forward to *Blow-Up's* revelations without feeling exposed.

But Antonioni has not let himself be used. He is not concerned with the fashion photographer as icon of the pop world, nor with the idolatry of the girls who surround him. The hero doesn't need them: he ignores both status and personal relations. As a photographer, he believes he has a consuming, satisfactory relationship with reality, the surface of reality, the subject matter of his art. And the crisis he experiences is with his material, not with the women in his life. By means of the camera he believes himself to be a faithful interpreter of reality, and when his means prove fallible, all his self-confidence is challenged. For the first time in his life, it seems, he realises how deceptive reality can be, that all his life it has been unfaithful to him and his camera. The audience experiences the film as a series of similar discoveries. The opening shot presents a group of tramps, but we are already deceived: one of them is a rich young man in disguise. And like us, Thomas himself is gulled by the properties of the camera, and finally undeceived by it. In the little deceptions of the film, Antonioni invites us to share Thomas' downfall as well as observe it. (1)

Thomas is searching for a lyrical shot to close his new book of photographs, as counterpoint to the squalor of the 'real life' represented on the other pages. Out hunting for some bric-a-brac to decorate his studio, he strolls across a park. The sky is cloudy, the trees disturbed, but the scene is peaceful. Two lovers embrace in a clearing. Thomas skips from one hiding place to another, crouching behind one tree, then the next, taking photographs. He is intoxicated with the activity. But the girl hears a noise and comes over to demand the film. Thomas refuses, and returns to his studio to develop it. When he blows up the prints, he gradually discovers that the scene he was photographing was quite different from the idyllic tableau he thought he had seen: the gentle rapture with which he hoped to close his brutal series of photographs, shots of the old, the poor, the desolate, the photograph that was to be such a contrast to all this, proves to be a document revealing murder in a London park.

This is unfolded in a thrilling sequence, to which the recent scrutiny of photographic evidence in the Kennedy assassination lends an added spice: in increasingly magnified blow-ups of certain

---

1. Does the analysis offered here stand in opposition to those of Kauffmann and Morgenstern? Or is it rather that it is concerned with a different level of interpretation?

prints, a body in the grass and a gunman in the bushes emerge from the apparently innocuous photographs. (2) It is night. In a terrifying stillness, Thomas comes to the clearing in the park. He finds the body. Returning to his studio, he discovers that all the photographs have gone. All have been taken except one, a blurred, inconclusive print which leaves him with no proof of the event at all—apart from the body. He hurries to a friend's house, and urges him to come and witness the corpse. But it is late, a party is in full swing, his friend is drunk, reluctant, and at last Thomas gives up and spends the night there, forgetting his quest. Throughout the day there have been distractions: the girl in the park trailed him to his studio and tried once again to get the film back, but settled for seduction instead; there is a painter who lives in the same studio, and his girl friend makes fruitless passes at Thomas; two aspiring cover girls sue to model clothes, and end by taking theirs off. These are insignificant dalliances, but his surrender to the party proves his undoing: he wakes late and hastens anxiously to the park, but the body has gone.

Thomas is a man who uses language mockingly, disparagingly, with the irony aimed at himself; who contradicts himself, who is content to be confusing, irritating in his words, because he knows he can tell the story of his life in pictures. He believes his photographs tell the truth. But now that the corpse has disappeared, he has no means left of telling this adventure at all. Who will believe him, without the body or the photographs? Not only his mode of expression but his mode of perception is threatened: the fallibility of his perception, made real to him when he discovered what the camera had seen and he had missed, is now endorsed by losing all the evidence of that discovery itself.

In *Deserto Rosso* Giuliana was a neurotic who demanded that her environment protect her, justify her, answer her needs; streets and houses echo her emotions. She had to learn to live with their indifference. (3) Thomas has to learn that he is no more powerful over

---

2. In bringing in the assassination of Kennedy, is Harrison suggesting that the *private association* here enriches the experience?

3. Harrison introduces material from other films of Antonioni. To what end? Is he asking that *Blow-Up* supply the same meanings as *Red Desert* or *Eclipse?* Whatever his purpose, do these references seem helpful?

nature with a camera than without. The final scene is a ritual penitence: as he leaves the park, he comes upon a student rag group, all whited up as clowns. These students are glimpsed at various stages of the film, passing in the street, and we recognize them now. They are miming a game of tennis on the deserted courts. Thomas stops to watch. The ball is struck out of the court, and all the students watch its imaginary flight, in the direction, as it happens, of Thomas. When it lands, and they have mimed watching it bounce, the students gaze hopefully at Thomas. Will he mime the action of throwing it back, and let them continue their imaginary game? He does so, and the Thomas once so sure he could interpret what was real, confesses himself a doubting Thomas, a humble, ignorant Thomas. The last shot seals his loss of faith: we see him in close-up, watching the mime. And on the sound track there begins the noise of a racket striking a ball, then the return, the rally. He concedes he knows nothing: they might be playing a real game, for all he could tell. Thomas has passed, it seems, from one over-simplification to another.

Although the suspense in *Blow-Up,* admirably created but clumsily resolved, is of a murder-thriller kind unfamiliar to Antonioni fans—which is making the film a lot of friends in new quarters—the film's theme is thoroughly familiar. It is a melody already stated in the last 56 shots of *L'Eclisse,* where Antonioni's camera discovers what Thomas does in the course of *Blow-Up*—some of the unsuspected spheres of action contained in apparently familiar events. The closing sequence of *L'Eclisse* is a montage which reviews the lovers' abandoned rendezvous, the place and objects which became the touchstones of the affair: a zebra crossing, a water-butt beside a building site, a water-sprinkler that sprays a nearby park. The climax, announced by a thunderous chord on the organ, is a close-up of the street-lamp bulb that illuminates the whole scene, in the gathering dusk.

The montage stresses two things: the indifference of the objective world whirling about the lovers' own febrile activity, and its energy, like the fan which smugly whirrs behind the exhausted, quarrelling couple in the opening scene. At the end, the zebra crossing which was the prelude to a kiss becomes a trivial stage in the routine walk home of passing businessmen; the water-spray which saw the lovers' first flirtation is casually switched off by a workman; jets pass overhead; other people watch them. The décor, the props of the love affair, prostitute themselves to other actors with less passionate designs, or continue their own activity independent of human behaviour: the twig that Vittoria dropped so poignantly (as she thought) into the water-butt to punctuate a meeting, slips into the gutter as the water flows out of a hole in the butt. The final shot, the mocking energy of electricity, indicts the dissipation of human energy, while the vitality of the objective world continues to expend its energy to scientifically assessable laws.

During the montage passers-by are scrutinised in a series of increasingly magnified close-ups. The gutter and the flowing water are treated with the same intensity. What each blow-up shows is a whole new picture: each pulsing vein in an old man's cheek is allowed autonomy by the intensification of focus; details of clinging mud and leaves form new shapes of microscopic beauty. Vittoria's response to this busy, sometimes mischievous universe is, as far as one can make out, to cope. But Thomas renounces his previous smugness for a worse smugness: the luxury of despair and renunciation of responsibility. (4)

He believed he was wedded to reality by his camera; when he discovers that reality is unfaithful to him, that he has never possessed it completely, he renounces all conjugal rights; all reality, he meekly concedes, is appearance. Although he knows the rag students are miming their tennis match, he invents the sound of racket on ball. The way Antonioni's thesis is presented is inconsistent with both the metaphysical proposition and the physical situation. In the first place, a leap has been made between the proposition that we often settle for over-simplified explanations of an event, and the directive that all explanation is futile. Certainly, Thomas was mistaken in thinking that he had photographed a quiet afternoon; but this is not necessarily metaphysical arrogance: a telephoto lens would have solved the problem at the time, and wedded him to a more complex reality rather more satisfactory than his nothing-is-really-real gesture at the end.

The film seems to be making the paranoiac's leap from the proposition that objective reality is largely indifferent to one's desires, which is an unobjectionable argument, to the proposition that it

---

4. Harrison says, "Thomas renounces his previous smugness for a worse smugness." Is this a judgment the film makes or one passed on the film by the critic?

conspires against one. Anna's disappearance in *L'Avventura* was a mysterious one—but it permitted of certain quite specific speculations: either she drowned; or she ran away, as she had threatened to do. The absence of a conclusive solution didn't lead Sandro and Claudia to see imaginary tennis matches, or to wonder whether Anna ever existed. The same applies to *Blow-Up.* The body disappeared: well, somebody took it away. To rush to the extreme conclusion that nothing is real embraces Pirandellism, and forms a significantly different proposition to the statement that our means of observing and assessing reality are desperately limited.

If this were the gist of *Blow-Up,* there would be no need for Thomas to 'hear' the noises suggested by a student rag mime. He knows as well as we do that there is no tennis match. His camera has just unveiled to him a whole set of circumstances that his senses missed: instead of proclaiming all modes of perception invalid, which he does in the final scene, he of all people—a photographer—should not be surprised at what the camera uncovers. This is the inconsistency in the physical situation: what photographer has this kind of shock in store? (5) As a scientist does, working in a stricter symbology than the artist, a photographer understands what a medium of communication or a mode of perception is: it is a construct, more or less fallible. And when you find it has been fallible, as Thomas does with his senses in *Blow-Up,* you do not kick the mechanism to bits and charge fuming from the laboratory. You acknowledge the error, you discover why it happened, and you set about refiring the machinery with this new information.

This is all Thomas has to do. Because he became involved in a drunken party the night before, when he reached the park the body had gone. This does not mean that the body never existed, and he can no longer trust his memory, or that the mimed tennis match is real, and he can no longer trust his senses. All it means is that he should have extracted himself from the party and pursued his objective. Thomas is blaming on the world a failure of the will. In the

---

5. Note that other critics rejected the tennis match as not quite fitting in with the whole. Harrison rejects it, too, but not so much because it is inconsistent with the film as a whole as because it supplies a meaning which the film would not have had without it and because it is inconsistent with his own *intellectual commitment.*

first place, he has mistaken an event in a public park for something other than it is; in the second place, he has allowed himself so many distractions while investigating it that the search proves fruitless. So he resigns himself to 'hearing' a mimed tennis match: it is the act of a man who avoids the truth, the act of a man who is not prepared to criticise himself.

Which brings us to why Antonioni should move from the intellectual poise of *L'Avventura* to the clumsiness of *Blow-Up,* where he has extrapolated an idea into a story without appreciating that he has changed his area of operations. And the appearance-and-reality proposition of which the film is an embodiment is not merely a tiresome cliché, but a lazy half-truth in narrative form. (6) "All of the other films I did with my stomach, this one I did with my brain," Antonioni said recently in an interview. He used to say bad films were made with the head or the heart, good ones only with the stomach. And we are a far cry from his Chekhovian remark "I never work from an abstraction towards a story." Antonioni claims in different ways, in different interviews (and the interviews themselves are testimony to this), that he has to preserve an area of non-articulate confrontation with his work; that the pressures of film-making make a certain avoidance of analysis essential in preserving this area of spontaneity. (7)

I dislike being asked questions about my work, he has said, because they bring me to a level of ratiocination, whereas I prefer to work on a lower level ('livello inferiore'). Naturally, in every artist the activity must relax down into the subconscious springs of inspiration once the conscious objectives have been defined; or if not the objectives, then the framework of the piece, the broad shapes. But once the area of refusal to criticise grows too large because of arrogance, or grows too intractable because of a constant threat to it, an artist is in danger of settling for the easy choice, for the contrived and the second-rate. He lets things through.

---

6. Wherein does the "clumsiness" of *Blow-Up* lie? Has Harrison discovered an inconsistency in the film or is it that the film's statement is other than he would have it? And if it is the latter, and if the film's "metaphysics" end up as "a tiresome cliché," have we encountered a meaningful criterion for failed excellence?

7. Is Harrison committing an intentional fallacy here?

Blow-up is unconsciously an appeal to the worst kind of intellectual sentimentality. It is a lesson in how to take the easy way out. It could become the handbook of those words-don't-ever-really-communicate and you-can't-ever-really-know-what-I'm-feeling merchants who settle for these half-truths the moment a discussion becomes demanding, in the impermeable conviction that they are bravely confronting a more challenging and subtle reality than you. They use the limitations of perception and communication as a means of avoiding responsibility, as Thomas does in *Blow-Up*. It seems that Antonioni, too, has come to regard these limitations as an excuse rather than a challenge. *Blow-Up* is not merely an intellectual wheelchair for intellectual cripples, it propagates a moral defeatism towards the challenges of living that the film's technical expertise only renders more pernicious.

The craftsmanship is indeed of a very high order. The self-conscious use of colour in *Deserto Rosso* has been left behind as an accessory of Giuliana's neuroticism and an experiment in the neurotic distortion of chromatic values. The art direction is splendid and the camerawork (Carlo Di Palma) relaxed. Antonioni's uniquely meticulous use of sound is in evidence. The rhythm of the film is rather disjointed at times, where scenes have obviously been cut very short, parts expanded, like Vanessa Redgrave's as the girl in the park, or visibly contracted, like Sarah Miles' as the painter's girl friend. The screen is dominated by David Hemmings as Thomas, and the contribution of the other actors is somewhat curtailed by their function in the story, which is to illustrate their insignificance in Thomas' life. Hemmings serves the story extremely well, playing Thomas both expressively and economically, and gaining our sympathy without blinding us to Thomas' indifference to the people around him.

The dialogue, tailored by Edward Bond from the Antonioni-Guerra screenplay, is convincing and unobtrusive; sometimes too unobtrusive—a line tending more to patois than to colloquialism, a delivery more private than intimate. The use of slang can become a restriction of expression, not a freedom; and on these occasions one suspects the director himself is more sinned against than sinning. For a film-maker working in a language other than his own, rhetoric is not the area of dramatic dialogue hardest to assess, but casual chat. In an effort not to betray unfamiliarity, underplaying is left unchecked. (8)

---

8. How do you understand this criticism of the film's dialogue?

But these are rare lapses. Quite apart from its status as a uniquely authoritative debut in a foreign language, the film has a great deal to offer as entertainment, in the narrative, the performances, and the fluency of Antonioni's camera style.

Above all, the story is immensely exciting. Two scenes are unforgettable: the gradual discovery of the murder as the prints are blown up, and the midnight visit to the park. An Antonioni film where the plot is enthralling and the intellectual content banal will come as a shock to a lot of people, but it is deservedly bringing him a wider audience, since the handling of *Blow-Up* as a thriller alone merits it a special place in that genre. (9)

---

9. How does it affect your experience of the film to place it within a genre?

The Blue Angel, Courtesy of *Janus Films*

THE BLUE ANGEL

Mordaunt Hall, *THE NEW YORK TIMES*
December 6, 1930

(1) In a film tragedy titled "The Blue Angel," which was directed by Josef von Sternberg in Berlin for Ufa, that talented German screen player Emil Jannings, who left Hollywood because of the vocalizing of pictures, makes his first appearance in a talking production. Marlene Dietrich, the attractive Teutonic actress who is to be seen at the Rivoli in Mr. Sternberg's "Morocco," shares honors with Mr. Jannings in this foreign work.

The plot of "The Blue Angel" recalls that of "The Way of All Flesh," Mr. Janning's first American silent film, but in this current chronicle, instead of being a bank employee, Mr. Jannings impersonates a professor of English literature in a German boys' high school. The story is cleverly told in most of the sequences, while

---

1. The chief interest here lies in the age of the review. How nice it would be if one could explain away the fact that Mr. Hall does little but evaluate the actors' performances and summarize the plot by pointing to the review's antiquity. Sadly, if we did not know the date of this piece of criticism, we could easily accept it as last Tuesday's review of a new film.

penultimate scenes would be all the better if they were curtailed or modified, as the actual ending is quite impressive.

The fall from grace of an elderly man is a favorite theme with Mr. Jannings, one that has served him in most of his films since the making of "The Last Laugh." As the characters here are different, however, the interest is rekindled and the broken English of the persons involved is accounted for with a certain crafty logic.

As an actor who speaks his lines, Mr. Jannings is perhaps even better than he was in his mute productions, for the speech to a great extent governs his actions and it stays him from his penchant for unnaturally slow movements. There are times here when no words pass the lips of the characters for uncomfortable seconds, but the final analysis is that it is a decidedly interesting picture with exceptionally fine performances contributed by Mr. Jannings and Miss Dietrich, the latter being much more the actress than she is in "Morocco."

Professor Immanuel Rath's (Mr. Jannings) humdrum existence is ably stressed. The landlady where he lives knocks on his door at the same time every morning and announces that his breakfast is served. As the hour of eight rings out from the old clock tower, the professor always is crossing the street or entering the school building. He, for some reason or other, omits the greeting of "good morning" to his pupils, who stand when he enters the classroom and only at his bidding take their seats. As a professor of English he insists on English being spoken. He is a man without a sense of humor, careful about his attire and stolidly opposed to the students betraying any mirth or glee. His curiosity concerning the youngsters who frequent the cabaret, "The Blue Angel," is aroused by finding in his classroom picture postcards of the stellar feminine performer at that gay resort. She is known as Lola Frohlich (Miss Dietrich), who is supposed to be an English singer.

Lola is a rather taciturn creature, but occasionally she reveals subdued enthusiasm, coupled with a dry sense of humor. It is not unfunny to her to have the professor looking for his students in her dressing room, particularly when three or four of them flee after being warned that the pedagogue is in the offing. One evening, however, when the youths are hiding in a cellar, Lola, after the professor has resented the conduct of another man toward her, hears that the police are on the scene and the urbane Rath also takes refuge in the retreat afforded his pupils, who incidentally have lifted the cellar covering and have been watching with keen amusement the professor's admiration of Lola.

Once in the cellar with the young scapegraces, the professor is a target for ridicule and blows. The result is that when he, following a night away from his own abode, arrives late at his classroom, the pupils revolt and the noise they make is heard throughout the building, with the consequence that Professor Emmanuel Rath is asked by the school principal for his resignation.

But all is not lost for the disgraced professor, for Lola becomes his wife. There follow time lapses in which one perceives the professor turned into a clown, wearing a false nose and a ridiculously large collar. This goes on until he eventually becomes insane, imitating the crowing of a rooster, which he had once done for a laugh in his rational days. While the professor is on the stage as the foil for a conjurer, Lola is enjoying the attentions of a lover, and she is observed by her elderly spouse. It is then that his senses leave him, and he eventually staggers over to his old classroom and dies at his desk as the bell in the old clock tower is striking the hour.

Not only is Mr. Janning's and Miss Dietrich's acting excellent, but they are supported by an unusually competent cast.

Having quite a good story, Mr. von Sternberg's direction is infinitely superior to that of "Morocco," and the settings for this film are very effective.

Richard Griffith, *SATURDAY REVIEW*
December 2, 1950

A Petty Bourgeois Tart Revisited

(1) *The Blue Angel* has become a legend, and as such is likely to surprise even those who now see it for the first time. There will be many of these, for, contrary to general belief, the picture was neither successful nor widely shown in this country. Made in Berlin in 1929, it was withheld from release here until Marlene Dietrich's first American film, "Morocco" (1930), had been shown. "Morocco" created a sensation, and audiences were eager to see Marlene Dietrich in the picture for which she had been "discovered." "The Blue Angel" bored them, largely because the dialogue was incomprehensible. Josef von Sternberg had shot an English version simultaneously with the German, but the thick accents of Emil Jannings and Dietrich baffled their hearers. In most U.S. cities where it was shown early in 1931 "The Blue Angel" ran only a few days of its scheduled week. Fortunately, the print now being shown is the original German version, with adequate English titles.

The international success the film achieved elsewhere was due not only to Dietrich but also the character created for her—in film historian Siegfried Kracauer's words, "Lola Lola, a new incarnation of sex. This petty bourgeois tart, with her provocative legs and easy manners, showed an impassivity which incited one to grope for the secret behind her callous egoism and cool insolence. That such a secret existed was also intimated by her veiled voice, which, when she sang about her interest in love-making and nothing else, vibrated with nostalgic reminiscences and smoldering hopes." The impassivity

---

1. It is 1950 and *The Blue Angel* "has become a legend." How does this affect the critic's experience with the film?

couldn't subside in Miss Dietrich's succeeding American films, and what was behind it had to be concealed still further, because our domestic censorship would have balked at the presentation of a "petty bourgeois tart" from Berlin or anywhere else. So she was glamorized into that woman without a country, the *femme fatale,* whose sins are romantic rather than venal, and became more cryptic and stylized until, in her last films under Von Sternberg's direction, she was little more than a talking doll. She might have gone on being a sphinx without a secret forever, had not comedy accidentally rescued her and revealed her best talents. Here we see the real woman before she had been transformed into the puppet, and a shock she will be to some, this plump fraulein. (2) But her reality gives off magnetism in waves, and her famous song, so innocuously translated into English as "Falling in Love Again," knows all there is to know and says it pretty plainly.

Aside from getting acquainted with the original Dietrich, it is hard to decide what the lay public will make of this heavy, skilful drama of a type once popularized by Jannings but now long forgotten. "The Blue Angel" is important in film history because in the first year of sound, when the rest of the world was photographing stage plays, it vigorously resumed the traditions of the silent screen: Sternberg restored the camera's mobility, reduced dialogue to a subsidiary narrative function (the English titles on the present print are hardly necessary), and in his imaginative use of natural sound was ahead not only of his time but, alas, our own. The film is one of the best examples of his impressive if limited talent. The pictorialism which eventually smothered the story values of his later films is here used for a dramatic purpose: to depict a middle-class society in full disintegration. In this portrait of a middle-aged professor led to his downfall by a cafe entertainer objects, buildings, and landscapes take on a life of their own; everything visible and audible accentuates the theme of the helpless and fatal pursuit of pleasure, the draining away of all social values. As Dr. Kracauer says, Lola Lola destroys "not only Jannings himself but his entire environment. A running motif in the film is the old church clock which chimes a popular

---

2. Why is Griffith rejecting the Marlene Dietrich we all love? Is his Dietrich really more "real" than ours? And to what extent does this comic genius he so appreciates depend upon her extraordinary "stylization"?

German tune devoted to the praise of loyalty and honesty *(Ub' immer Treu und Redlichkeit)*—a tune expressive of Jannings's inherited beliefs. In the concluding passage, immediately after Lola Lola's song has faded away, this tune is heard for the last time as the camera shows the dead Jannings. Lola Lola has killed him, and in addition her song has defeated the chimes."

As popular entertainment "The Blue Angel" is out of fashion, but I recommend it as a document for the inspection of anyone interested in the fate of Europe, and particularly to intellectuals given to indiscriminate praise of the esthetic virtues of European films without regard to what they actually say. If we had looked harder at "The Blue Angel" in 1931, we might have had some glimpse of Berlin's future. It is not customary to approach the movies in this spirit, but it might be wise. (3)

---

3. Might it be wise?

Andrew Sarris, *THE FILMS OF JOSEPH VON STERNBERG* (New York: The Museum of Modern Art), 1966

THE BLUE ANGEL occupies a paradoxical if prominent place in Sternberg's career. Emil Jannings reportedly requested Sternberg as the director to guide the silent star past the sound barrier, and Sternberg agreed despite a previous clash of temperament in THE LAST COMMAND. The film was produced simultaneously in German and English language versions for the maximum benefit of the Paramount-UFA combine in world markets, and thus with this one excursion into Europe all the ambiguity of Sternberg's origins reappeared as the "von" in his name was finally vindicated. After THE BLUE ANGEL, Sternberg would once more be treated in retrospect as a European legend corrupted by Hollywood lucre.

"Camp" declared Susan Sontag in the sixties, "is the outrageous estheticism of von Sternberg's six American movies with Dietrich, all six but especially the last, THE DEVIL IS A WOMAN. . . ." Significantly, Miss Sontag pointedly excludes THE BLUE ANGEL from her Camp sight. The snobbery of subtitles aside, THE BLUE ANGEL is undoubtedly the one Sternberg film the director's severest detractors will concede is beyond reproach and ridicule. It is worth noting, if only in passing, that Marlene Dietrich did not appear on American screens in THE BLUE ANGEL until after the release of MOROCCO, actually her second stint with Sternberg.

Although THE BLUE ANGEL may have been admired in some quarters for the wrong reasons, the film stands up today as Sternberg's most efficient achievement both emotionally and expressively. There are no hidden corners, no nagging nuances, no puzzling paradoxes. For once Sternberg is in complete rapport with his audience with a film that is at once his most brutal and least humorous.(1) "In converting the novel into a film which would meet my standards of visual poetry," he recalls, "I introduced the figure of the clown as well as all the episodes and details that led the professor to be confined in a straitjacket."

The ultimately tragic irony of THE BLUE ANGEL is double-edged in a way Sternberg could not have anticipated when he undertook the project. The rise of Lola Lola and the fall of Professor Immanuel Rath in reel life is paralleled in real life by the rise of Marlene Dietrich and the fall of Emil Jannings. When THE BLUE ANGEL was revived in the early fifties, the critical consensus upheld the public on Dietrich's directness over Jannings' detailedness. The tedious ties of elaborately expressionistic acting have long since gone out of style, and there is still a tendency to underrate the Jannings performance. In the context of the screen's cuckolds, however, Jannings surpasses in tragic intensity even Raimu and Ake Groneberg. What he lacks in the style and stature of his Czarist general turned Hollywood extra in THE LAST COMMAND, he more than makes up here with the nakedness of his passion.

Sternberg's sense of tragic dignity in the midst of tawdry downfall is best illustrated at that moment when Jannings hurls himself into a room to wreak vengeance on his wife and her strong-man lover. The camera remains at a discreet angle and distance from the door-

---

1. Is Sarris here presenting some criteria of film excellence?

way through which Dietrich escapes. The men with the straitjacket sweep past her, but we never actually see Jannings subdued by them, only Dietrich looking with ambiguous compassion at the spectacle of subjugation. Jannings has had his moment of masculine beauty on the stage by crowing like a maddened rooster at Dietrich's deception. In that soul-stirring moment Sternberg suggests through Jannings what it is to be a man, and Sternberg will not cheapen that moment by degrading a man who has been defeated.

THE BLUE ANGEL achieves its most electrifying effects through careful grading and construction. When Marlene Dietrich sings "Falling in Love Again" for the first time the delivery is playful, flirtatious, and self-consciously seductive. The final rendition is harsher, colder, and relentlessly remorseless. The difference in delivery is not related to the old stereotype of the vamp finally showing her true colors, but rather to a psychological development in Dietrich's Lola from mere sensual passivity to a more forceful fatalism about the nature of her desires. Lola's first instinct is to accept the Professor's paternal protection and her last is to affirm her natural instincts not as coquettish expedients, but as the very terms by which she expresses her existence. Thus, as the Professor has been defeated by Lola's beauty, Lola has been ennobled by the Professor's jealousy. It is in this complex interplay that THE BLUE ANGEL transcends the trivial genre of bourgeois male corrupted by bohemian female.

The sordid atmosphere with which Sternberg embellishes his drama emphasizes the grossness to be endured in grappling with desire. On one level of characterization, the Professor is a Lazarus resurrected from a dismal fastidiousness of death-like feelings by sniffing his way through Lola's life-drenched garments, *objets d'art* less of a symbolist than a fetishist.

Fortunately, the niggling necessities of economics intervene between the drab décor and any of its frivolously sado-masochistic implications. It is not Lola who forces the Professor to peddle her gamey photos, but rather the financial realities of the situation. The shabbiness eventually engulfs the sensuality, but it is Lola's strength that she has lived with shabbiness long enough to know how to bend without breaking, and the Professor's tragic misfortune to bend first and still to break afterward.

It is not specifically Germany or the German character with which Sternberg is concerned here, but rather the spectacle of a prudent, prudish man blocked off from all means of displaying his manhood except the most animalistic. Sternberg himself has explicitly removed

THE BLUE ANGEL from the socially significant path Siegfried Kracauer has traced *From Caligari to Hitler.*(2) Yet the fact that THE BLUE ANGEL is coincidentally Sternberg's only German-made film and his most violent work may suggest that he felt the conflict between order and nature would be more violent in a German setting than in any other. This supposition, however, does not justify the judgment that Sternberg's deliberately designed drabness reflects realistically observed details of a decadent society. The world of THE BLUE ANGEL is as much a dream world as the world of THE SALVATION HUNTERS, but the illusion of reality is much stronger in THE BLUE ANGEL because the characters are less abstract.

Jean Renoir's LA CHIENNE (1931) and Ingmar Bergman's THE NAKED NIGHT (1953) are more profound examinations of the crisis of cuckoldry in the illusion-shattering life of man, but THE BLUE ANGEL is more successful dramatically. Where Renoir is more realistic and Bergman more literary, Sternberg is more effective in resolving his tragedy within the form he has postulated for it. Renoir arbitrarily ends his film as if it were a stylized spectacle of the Paris streets, but his implication is clear: life goes on, transcending pride, passion, and morality. For Bergman life is a mystery which no amount of thought can solve. Renoir and Bergman are thus concerned with ideas beyond the frames of their films, whereas Sternberg remains within his frames. For the Professor there is only his life with Lola, and deprived of Lola there is nothing but death. There is no life for Lola and the Professor beyond the running time of THE BLUE ANGEL. There is no world beyond the outer limits of the set. Renoir and Bergman appeal to our common sense. Sternberg appeals to our sense of spectacle.(3)

Not that Renoir and Bergman lack mood and mannerism. Far from it. Nor can we single out THE BLUE ANGEL for projecting Sternberg through Jannings.(4) There is a great deal of Renoir in

---

2. What is the plain sense of this? Is Sarris saying that von Sternberg commented on his film? If so, can we then ask if a director can tell us, outside of his film, how we are to interpret that film?

3. Does Sarris convince you that Sternberg is more filmic than Bergman who is "literary" or than Renoir who is "more realistic"?

4. What is Sarris saying here? What is the relationship between *auteur* and actor that is being suggested?

Michel Simon from LA CHIENNE, and a great deal of Bergman in Ake Groneberg from THE NAKED NIGHT. For the most part, however, LA CHIENNE and THE NAKED NIGHT open out on the world, whereas THE BLUE ANGEL turns in on itself. Sternberg's profundity is consequently measured less by the breadth of his vision than by the perfection of his form and by the emotional force of his characters within that form.

How much more painfully poignant, too, is the scene where Jannings helps Dietrich with her stockings than a similar Jannings maneuver with Lya da Putti in Du Pont's VARIETY, where Jannings as the dupe, pure and simple, is treated with amused contempt. By contrast, Dietrich's air of sensual complicity in THE BLUE ANGEL redeems the Jannings character from complete ridiculousness. There is in Sternberg a savoring of sensuality for its own sake that is both more human and more satisfying than Renoir's uncompromising humanism and Bergman's unyielding pessimism.(5) The disassociation of Dietrich's sexuality from normal standards of dramatic psychology becomes more apparent in her later collaborations with Sternberg. In THE BLUE ANGEL, Dietrich is still somewhat submerged in her characterization and not yet completely possessed by her personality. She straddles a chair as she will later straddle a horse in THE SCARLET EMPRESS, imperiously, magisterially, fully the measurer of men in the audience, but yet she is also an organic character who finds a certain kind of maturity in marriage. If "serious" criticism of the cinema were not as puritanical as it is, the experiences of Lola and the Professor would seem more pertinent to the hidden world of domestic sexuality than is now the case. The idea that all eroticism is hopelessly exotic has made Sternbergian cinema seem much stranger than it is.

---

5. Why do you think Sarris has chosen to repeatedly compare Sternberg with Bergman and Renoir? Is he operating on a sort of guilt by association principle? For example, if we speak of Elizabeth Taylor in the same context as Sarah Bernhardt, does this tend to give Miss Taylor added stature? And, more to the point, would such a comparison be appropriate? Is Sarris' comparison appropriate?

BONNIE AND CLYDE

Bosley Crowther, *THE NEW YORK TIMES*
August 14, 1967

Careers of Murderers
Pictured as Farce

A raw and unmitigated campaign of sheer press-agentry has been trying to put across the notion that Warner Brothers' "Bonnie and Clyde" is a faithful representation of the desperado careers of Clyde Barrow and Bonnie Parker, a notorious team of bank robbers and killers who roamed Texas and Oklahoma in the post-Depression years.

It is nothing of the sort. It is a cheap piece of bald-faced slapstick comedy that treats the hideous depredations of that sleazy, moronic pair as though they were as full of fun and frolic as the jazz-age cut-ups in "Thoroughly Modern Millie." And it puts forth Warren Beatty and Faye Dunaway in the leading roles, and Michael J. Pollard as their sidekick, a simpering, nose-picking rube, as though they were striving mightily to be the Beverly Hillbillies of next year. (1)

---

1. One of the central questions raised by Mr. Crowther's review is what has the truth-value, in this case the degree to which the film

---

It has Mr. Beatty clowning broadly as the killer who fondles various types of guns with as much nonchalance and dispassion as he airily twirls a big cigar, and it has Miss Dunaway squirming grossly as his thrill-seeking, sex-starved moll. It is loaded with farcical hold-ups, screaming chases in stolen getaway cars that have the antique appearance and speeded-up movement of the clumsy

---

has been faithful to the actuality from which it derives, to do with artistic worth? It is tempting to answer this question by saying (as does Richard Gilman in a review which follows) that *Bonnie and Clyde* is a fictional construct and thus can neither be true nor false in any meaningful sense. On the other hand, *Bonnie and Clyde* is not a simple fiction, protected by the claim that "any resemblance to actual persons living or dead is purely coincidental"; it is explicitly about actual persons. Another way of perhaps understanding the issue is to consider the difference between our approach to Napoleon and our approach to Prince André in *War and Peace.* André exists only in a work of fiction; Napoleon exists in history as well, and do we then have the right to test the Napoleon of *War and Peace* against the Napoleon of actuality? And if we do not, why has Tolstoy forced us (as indeed he has) to bring to the novel our knowledge of Napoleon? Still another question implied here (which perhaps helps in resolving those posed earlier) is would the issue of truth-value have been avoided or at least substantially modified had the characters been given fictional names? On the other hand, one might argue that unless a film purports to be a documentary it has no obligation to be "true" to anything but the imagination of its creators. It is obvious that our prior experiences of actual people will in some way affect our perceptions of them when they appear in an imaginative work—surely Tolstoy's Napoleon is modified by the image of Napoleon which we bring with us to the novel—but beyond this, does it matter if the source for a work of art is a famous, or infamous, real person or some little-known real person or no particular person at all? The character in an imaginative work has a life of his own in that work regardless of the source from which he springs. The only responsibility that the artist has is to create his work of art so well and so fully that the character *does* manage to exist in that work despite what we might or might not know to be "the truth" about him.

vehicles of the Keystone Cops, and indications of the impotence of Barrow, until Bonnie writes a poem about him to extol his prowess, that are as ludicrous as they are crude.

Such ridiculous, camp-tinctured travesties of the kind of people these desperados were and of the way people lived in the dusty Southwest back in those barren years might be passed off as candidly commercial movie comedy, nothing more, if the film weren't reddened with blotches of violence of the most grisly sort.

Arthur Penn, the aggressive director, has evidently gone out of his way to splash the comedy holdups with smears of vivid blood as astonished people are machine-gunned. And he has staged the terminal scene of the ambuscading and killing of Barrow and Bonnie by a posse of policemen with as much noise and gore as is in the climax of "The St. Valentine's Day Massacre."

This blending of farce with brutal killings is as pointless as it is lacking in taste, since it makes no valid commentary upon the already travestied truth. (2) And it leaves an astonished critic wondering just what purpose Mr. Penn and Mr. Beatty think they serve with this strangely antique, sentimental clap-trap, which opened yesterday at the Forum and the Murray Hill. (3)

This is the film that opened the Montreal International Festival!

---

2. The issue of truth-value appears here in a different guise; that is, in the form of artistic validity. What Crowther seems to be saying at this point is that the meanings implicit in the film (its commentary) are capable of being verified in real life and in this instance emerge as false. Is the test of a work's commentary a violation of its artistic integrity? Is art immune to such verification?

3. Is there an *intellectual commitment* at work here?

Bosley Crowther, *THE NEW YORK TIMES* September 3, 1967

Run, Bonnie and Clyde

(1) Quite as puzzling to me as the production of feelings of empathy and sorrow for a couple of slap-happy killers in the new picture, "Bonnie and Clyde," is the upsurge of passionate expressions of admiration and defense of the film on the order of those from letter-writers that we published in this section last week.

Evidently there are people, including some critics, who feel that this deliberately buffoonized picture of the notorious criminal careers of Clyde Barrow and Bonnie Parker back in the early 1930's achieves some sort of meaningful statement for the times in which we live: something about the confusion of a couple of dumb, thrill-seeking kids who take to armed robbery for a living and are struck by resentment, not remorse, when the consequence of their depredations catches up with them.

I gather that what most of these people feel the picture conveys is a sense of the pathos of youngsters who don't really know what violence is until they are suddenly plunged into it—who recklessly play with fire without a care or a thought of what they're doing until they're fatally burned. The moral would be that violence is an abstract and unconsidered thing in the minds of most careless, flagrant rebels. When it becomes concrete, it's too late.

This might be a respectable reading of the picture, if it actually did what I gather its ardent proponents seem to be confident it does —that is, give a fair conception of the sort of persons its principal characters were and a creditable exposition of the disorder of the

---

1. Consider the ways in which our understanding of Crowther's position is enlarged by this second discussion of *Bonnie and Clyde.*

late Depression years during which Clyde Barrow and Bonnie Parker ran wild through the southwest.

But this, I assure you, it doesn't. The performance that Warren Beatty gives of a light-hearted, show-offish fellow with a talent for stealing cars and holding up banks at gunpoint is mannered play-acting of a hick that bears no more resemblance to Barrow than it does to Jesse James. And the sweet prettified indication of Bonnie that Faye Dunaway conveys is a totally romantic exoneration of that ugly and vicious little dame. Likewise, the scattering of poor people in Texas and thereabouts that Arthur Penn has put forth as grateful recipients of the beneficences of Bonnie and Clyde—including a gauzy, grey-haired image of Bonnie's disapproving old Maw—is a skillful but loaded collection of stereotypes of poverty.

You don't have to take my word for it. This is what a well-acquainted writer for this paper said on the morning after the arrogant desperadoes were killed by lawmen in a planted ambuscade:

"Clyde Barrow was a snake-eyed murderer who killed without giving his victims a chance to draw. He was slight, altogether unheroic in physical appearance. Bonnie Parker was a fit companion for him. She was a hard-faced, sharp-mouthed woman who gave up a waitress job in a Kansas City restaurant to become the mistress of Ray Hamilton, Texas bank robber. Barrow took her away from Hamilton."

And another experienced crime reporter for the New York Daily News described them as two of this country's "most ruthless and kill-crazy outlaws." Said he:

"Not even the more publicized (John) Dillinger and Pretty Boy Floyd, that other veteran terrorist of the southwest, can match the bloody careers of Barrow and his flaming red-haired girl-friend. Dillinger and Floyd, by an occasional act of kindness, have attracted to themselves a certain Robin Hood aura. But Barrow and his desperadoes were bad men through and through. 'A pair of human rats with no more decent traits than any rat would have,' Southwestern peace officers called Barrow and Bonnie, and a glance at their records is enough to prove they deserved the indictment."

Their records, incidentally, are suggested with utterly cavalier distortions all the way through the film. Barrow had run a lengthy and sordid career of crime before he ever met Bonnie, which is inaccurately described by having Barrow first see her nude at a window in her mama's house for the opening of the film. The only historical model for the grinning dirt-kicking bumpkin that the script drags in to be their devoted companion in their subsequent robberies and get-aways is Clyde's former partner, Ray Hamilton, and he was a sniveling punk who, among other things, joined Clyde in killing a sheriff and wounding his deputy just for ordering them not to drink at a dance hall in Atoka, Okla.

Lastly, there is no substantial evidence for the assumption the scriptwriters make that Barrow was impotent with Bonnie, and that the climax of their relationship was when Bonnie wrote a doggrel poem about him which so pleased and exalted him, when it was printed in a Texas newspaper, that he was able to make it with her successfully before they were killed.

This is an indication of the kind of cheating with the bare and ugly truth that Mr. Penn, his writers and Mr. Beatty have done in this garish, grotesque film that makes the crimes of Clyde and Bonnie quite hilarious until the two suddenly are confronted with the grisly slaughter of Clyde's tag-along brother in a blazing shoot-out with the police. After this the film gets very solemn. Clyde and Bonnie are strangely subdued. They make love. Then they are stealthily hunted and finally gunned down in a shattering fire by the police.

No matter how much one reacts to the very skillful fabrication of this film and wants to see something valid in it—a kind of plaintive folk ballad, at least (which is clearly encouraged by the use of rollicking mountain music in the score)—it still is a grossly romantic, sentimental and arbitrary setting up of a collision of comedy and violence, which spews noise and sparks but not much truth. And no matter how much one discovers later that its killers are a bit distorted and absurd, it has built up its sympathy for them. They are not enemies of society. Society is the enemy of them.

Perhaps this is why the picture is getting a favorable response among some compassionate viewers. Society is the antagonist. The Establishment, or the breakdown of it, is responsible for all the woes—for the banks that foreclose on poor farmers, for the greedy storekeepers who don't want to be robbed, for the nasty police, for the illusions and delusions of grandeur of Bonnie and Clyde.

This is certainly a complex thesis to support on evidence as unsubstantial and disreputable as the careers of a couple of fanciful crooks. By this same line of reckoning, one could build up a theme of sympathy and sadness on the thought that the system was the enemy of a character named Lee Harvey Oswald who had a penchant to fire high-powered rifles at moving targets, or that the irony of Hitler's terror was that he was so confused by his early rejection that he didn't realize the awfulness of the violence he caused.

I am sorry to say that "Bonnie and Clyde" does not impress me as a contribution to the thinking of our times or as wholesome entertainment.

Joseph Morgenstern, *NEWSWEEK* August 21, 1967

Two for a Tommy Gun

In BONNIE AND CLYDE, the heroes of which are a pair of 1930s bank robbers, some of the most gruesome carnage since Verdun is accompanied by some of the most gleeful offscreen fiddling since Grand Ole Opry. The effect is ear-catching, to say the least. For those who find killing less than hilarious, the effect is also stomach-turning.

That is the fatal flaw of this otherwise interesting film, directed by Arthur Penn and produced by Warren Beatty, who also plays Clyde. It does not know what to make of its own violence. Were the people in charge of its production actually amused by scores of cops being gunned down or blown up by hand grenades hitting armored cars? Did they feel there was simply no use crying over spilt blood? Or did they use the music as a last-ditch effort to take the curse off their film's essential ugliness? (1)

---

1. What evidence does Morgenstern cite to support his claim that the film is essentially ugly? How many examples does he give of ugliness?

Grace

Whatever the case, the people in charge were not really in charge, and what begins as an engagingly perverse Depression saga, fully equipped with Burma Shave signs, Roosevelt posters, tin Lizzies, rumble seats and a few vignettes derived from "Let Us Now Praise Famous Men," transforms itself, willy-nilly, into a squalid shoot-'em for the moron trade. Try to imagine "In Cold Blood" being played as a William Inge comedy, including an attempt at lyricism consisting of a slow-motion sequence in which the inert bodies of Bonnie and Clyde, being perforated by the law's lead, rise and fall and pitch and turn with something of the same grace that Vittorio Mussolini must have seen in Ethiopia when he compared bomb bursts to rose petals.

Within the ugliness lies some beauty, suggestions of humanity and even some legitimate humor. Bonnie, a West Dallas waitress played well and attractively by Faye Dunaway, strikes up a strange, sexless and yet spirited alliance with Clyde, a back-country bumpkin fresh out of prison. Clyde does what he does in banks because he cannot do what he wants to do in bed. Bonnie, who must have a beautiful soul because she writes clandestine doggerel, keeps telling Clyde not to worry and to let nature take its course, which it finally does in a field with flowers. It is "The Family Way" all over again, except that if the hero had found his potency sooner a hundred lives or more could have been saved.

Joseph Morgenstern, *NEWSWEEK*
August 28, 1967

The Thin Red Line

Last week this magazine said that "Bonnie and Clyde," a tale of two young bank robbers in the 1930s, turns into a "squalid shoot-'em for the moron trade" because it does not know what to make of its own violence. I am sorry to say I consider that review grossly unfair and regrettably inaccurate. I am sorrier to say I wrote it.

Seeing the film a second time and surrounded by an audience no more or less moronic than I, but enjoying itself almost to the point of rapture, I realized that "Bonnie and Clyde" knows perfectly well what to make of its violence, and makes a cogent statement with it—that violence is not necessarily perpetrated by shambling cavemen or quivering psychopaths but may also be the casual, easy expression of only slightly aberrated citizens, of jes' folks. (1)

I had become so surfeited and preoccupied by violence in daily life that my reaction was as excessive as the stimulus. There are indeed a few moments in which the gore goes too far, becomes stock shockery that invites standard revulsion. And yet, precisely because "Bonnie and Clyde" combines these gratuitous crudities with scene after scene of dazzling artistry, (2) precisely because it has the power both to enthrall and appall, it is an ideal laboratory for the study of violence, a subject in which we are all matriculating these days.

Cynicism

Violent movies are an inevitable consequence of violent life. They may also transmit the violence virus, but they do not breed it any more than the Los Angeles television stations caused Watts to riot. Distinctions can and must be made between violent films that pander and violent films that enlighten, between camp, comment and utter cynicism. And there is nothing like the movies for giving us historical perspective on violence we have known, and in many cases loved.

No one but Charlie Chaplin's competitors ever deplored his early comedies, though they served up staggeringly large helpings of mayhem. Cruelty to animals, children and adults was the crucial ingredient in W. C. Fields's social satire. No one ever accused Cagney of excess gentility in "Public Enemy," but people consoled themselves in those days with the notion that violence was the particular

---

1. Is there any evidence in the film to substantiate Morgenstern's view of Bonnie and Clyde as "jes' folks"?
2. What examples of "dazzling artistry" appear in the review?

province of a particular minority, namely the violent. They called the group The Underworld, at least until 1939.

World War II brought back primitivism, which had been on the skids ever since 1918, and its popularity today has not discernibly declined. A fair amount of contemporary movie violence is still conventionally primitive, unadorned by anything but gangrenous nostalgia—"Battle of the Bulge," for instance. Some movie violence is stylishly primitive—"St. Valentine's Day Massacre" pumps slugs into lugs by the thousands, but a few good performances lift the sleazy legend from the sewer to the gutter. Some is pretentiously primitive—"The Chase" was all awash with racial and social symbols, yet seemed most pleased with itself when Marlon Brando's battered face was awash with ketchup. And some is ingeniously primitive—"The Dirty Dozen" spends more than two hours on an outlandishly detailed setup for a half-hour payoff in which the GI demolition squad really demolishes, the charges explode, the Kraut machine guns chatter and the victims (including lots of screaming females) cry themselves a river of blood.

Dollop

Such stuff as this is trash, and at least has the bad grace to give itself away. More serious complications arise when the overlay of comedy or comment is done more artfully. "A Fistful of Dollars" and its sequel, "For a Few Dollars More," were synthetic Westerns made on the cheap in Italy and unmistakably brutal. But their director, Sergio Leone, had done his homework and studied the models he wanted to copy and/or parody. His primary motive clearly was profit, and therefore imitation, but that did not prevent him from adding a pinch of put-on, and a dollop of dubious satire.

Yet violence can serve thoroughly satiric or artistic ends, and not only in Shakespeare, Marlowe, Buñuel, "Marat/Sade" or the coming film version of "In Cold Blood." Violence was downright charming in "The Quiet Man," delightful in "The Crimson Pirate," enthralling in "Psycho" and "The Hill," relevant in "Dutchman." "West Side Story" might well have done with more of it to stiffen its spine, and so might "Up the Down Staircase," which only tiptoed timorously around the crazy chaos of America's slum schools.

There is nothing timorous about "Bonnie and Clyde," in which violence is at once a virtue and a vice. Director Arthur Penn and his colleagues perform poignant and intricate wonders (3) with a Loony Toon gang of outlaws who bumble along from one bank job to another, from one blood bath to another in an inchoate, uncomprehending and foredoomed attempt to fulfill their stunted selves. Both "Bonnie and Clyde" and "St. Valentine's Day Massacre" deal with the same slice of life, yet the characters in the latter are gun racks and the characters in "Bonnie" have a rushing of blood in their veins and a torrent of thought in their minds.

Demeaning

From time to time, however, all artistry falls by the wayside: (4) when a cop trying to stop the getaway car is shot in the face, when a grocer is bludgeoned in a close-up, when a grenade demolishes a police tank, when one outlaw has his skull blown open and another has her eye shot out. These scenes are reprehensible not because they are ugly, or shocking, but because they are familiar, gross and demeaning. When artists are able to bring characters to life and keep them alive, they should not leave death to the special-effects department.

There is, in the depiction of violence, a thin red line between the precisely appropriate and the imprecisely offensive. Sometimes a few too many frames of film may mean the difference between a shot that makes its point concisely and one that lingers slobberingly. These few frames or scenes in "Bonnie and Clyde" will hardly change the course of human events. When we talk about movies, even artistic movies, we are not talking about urban-renewal programs, nuclear nonproliferation treaties or rat-control bills. Art cannot dictate to life and movies cannot transform life, unless we want to retool the entire industry for the production of propaganda. But art can certainly reflect life, clarify and improve life; and since most of humanity teeters on the edge of violence every day, there is no earthly reason why art should not turn violence to its own good ends, showing us what we do and why. The clear danger, of course, is that

---

3. How many examples of "poignant and intricate wonders" do you find in this review?

4. How many examples of "artistry fallen by the wayside" do you find in this review?

violence begets violence in life and engenders confusion in art. It is a potent weapon, but it tends to aim the marksman. (5)

---

5. Does Morgenstern's second review convince you that his first review was "grossly unfair and regrettably inaccurate"? Keep in mind that you are not asked which, if either, of the judgments you agree with.

Richard Gilman, *THE NEW REPUBLIC* November 4, 1967

Gangsters on the Road to Nowhere

"I have a bad memory for facts," Stendhal once wrote, and Flaubert said later that "everything the artist invents is true." I don't mean to imply that Arthur Penn, the director of *Bonnie and Clyde,* or Robert Benton and David Newman, its writers, have anything like that kind of stature, but the principles hold up. Facts are the imagination's pretexts, and the sordid lives of the historical Bonnie Parker and Clyde Barrow—bank-robbers and murderers—have every right to serve as pretexts for an imaginative work that is interested in something other than historical "truth."

Yet if the movie is better than anything Hollywood has done for a good while, it is still a compromise that barely misses being a self-destruction. Its failures, however, aren't due to any infidelity to history or to the American underlife, but to an incomplete loyalty to its own arresting propositions.

Bonnie and Clyde is about violence and crime, and—hopefully, at least—the desire of the ego to define itself, to live in violence and

---

crime if it can't in anything else.(1) To this end it remains properly sympathetic to the characters it has plucked from history, the sympathy being given not to crime (as Bosley Crowther said) but to a process in which crime figures, to the action by which the ego displays itself as the embattled source of everything—crime, love, violence, goodness, error, dream.

What makes it different from the Cagney gangster-hero movies of the thirties or, more subtle creations, those of Humphrey Bogart, is the way it tries to stand apart from its protagonists, its refusal fully to identify with them or to be merely the vehicle of their perversely romantic story. We identified with Cagney and Bogart; in *Bonnie and Clyde,* when it is working honestly and well, we live instead the life of the film, in which the specific destinies of the characters function as the occasion for cinematic art and not as the instrument of a surrogate biography for ourselves.(2)

From its opening moments, during the credits, when a series of slightly blurred family snapshots—those quintessential objects of the ego's quest for definition and permanence—flashes on screen, the movie attempts to fashion a sustaining imaginative attitude toward the tale it is going to relate. On the edge of campiness, but saved from full sneering superiority to its material by the camera's own inventive humility, the first half-hour or so proceeds with as much visual pleasure as anything I've seen this year. The first scenes, wide, relaxed, ironic and cool, hammer in some essential nails: Faye Dunaway, nearly naked in her shabby frame house, yawning with boredom and something more interesting—lack of definition; Warren

---

1. When Gilman talks about "the desire of the ego to define itself," what *intellectual committment* is he expressing? Does he sustain and support his view throughout the discussion? And, does this commitment seem appropriate to the film?

2. What Gilman seems to be suggesting here is that if we do not live the life of Bonnie and Clyde, but "we live instead the life of the film," the moral issue disappears. Do you agree? And is it true that we do not identify with Bonnie and Clyde? If we do not, how do you explain the moral dilemma the film has posed? Is it that so many have not *seen* the film at all? And mightn't the problem then lie in the *actor as barrier?* How do we distance our fantasies from these beautiful people?

Beatty irrupting into our purview as her wide-lapeled, tight-suited, fedoraed young deliverer; the empty small town main street where the pair forges a partnership through a swift, elaborate play of challenge and response—his sly showing of his gun, her dare, the first holdup, the first flight in a stolen, high-backed, chuffing early thirties car.

They move off on this "life of crime," which for a good while will remain picaresque, a peripatetic fling, to the accompaniment of twanging, jittery banjo whose visual counterpart is the bouncing car (first of a series of such rides in which the mad, self-generating life of the automobile in America is given a fertile choreography, Mack Sennett turned half-serious) traveling along roads which seem to imply no destination and through landscapes of dream-like emptiness and deprivation. They steal another car, make a first comic attempt on a bank (it has failed three weeks before), practice shooting ("ain't you something!" Clyde gleefully tells Bonnie when she hits the swinging tire) and add to their gang by enlisting a shuffling, laconic gas station attendant (Michael J. Pollard).

There are more comic or wittily lyric moments, framed widely and moving slowly as the camera acts more as interpreter than historian during which their legend takes shape as exile from a realm larger than that from which crime cuts men off.

One suspects, as the film accumulates, that these are largely set-pieces but they are nevertheless set-pieces around a central act of intelligent imagining. It has been established early, for example, that Clyde is impotent, and the acceptance of this by Bonnie in several understated scenes is exactly the right aesthetic and spiritual movement to reinforce their union as a hunger for support, for mutuality in exile and in the search for a "name" to set before others. In this spirit they alternate between a childlike comradeliness and a bravado donned like a mask before the world. Thus far, the movie is half-mocking, half-sober myth, domiciling its protagonists between the walls of a technique designed to allow them to reveal more than they know by revealing what it knows in its own right.

The first cracks in the wall appear. The film begins to heft its more palpable—and more saleable—materials. Clyde pistol-whips a man who has attacked him during a holdup ("Why'd he try to *kill* me?" he asks Bonnie with bewildered anguish), then shoots another man during a getaway. They are in flight now in earnest, caught up in the great chase, the cops and robbers plot of American popular art. And it is here that the movie begins to lose them as original creations as it more and more takes on the attributes of the gangster movie as we have always known it and makes increasing use of the romantic myth as before, that of doomed young love in an inimical world.

Joined by Clyde's brother and sister-in-law (Gene Hackman and Estelle Parsons), they go through a series of robberies and holings-up, in which the only half-successful attempt is made to constitute them as a beseiged community outside society, sustained by their growing notoriety. The attempt is also made to thicken the film's thematic substance by introducing the Robin Hood motif (Clyde allows a workingman-depositor to keep *his own* money during a bank robbery) and a notion about the vicarious satisfactions "straight" society gets from criminality: a bank guard eagerly tells reporters how he "stared right in the face of death" and smartly arranges his face for the photographers. But there is little time for developments of this kind, or for the more interesting notion that criminal violence has its ground and support in legal violence, the cops maintaining the robbers in flight and existence. For everything converges now on action for its own sake, the kind of thing the American movie purveys best and most self-defeatingly.

From drama to melodrama: the gang shoots its way out of one police trap and then another; bullets fly, blood flows, the brother is killed, his wife blinded. The blood is very red, very real; and this has the momentary effect of shattering both the couples' light-hearted adventure and the cinematic convention of violence as pleasure and romantic game. Yet the very momentum of the film as action yarn swallows up all other subtlety and nuance. When the attempt is made to recover them, to recover a "subject" for the work, the movement is to Scylla from Charybdis. The pair are reconstituted as the fated couple of movie tradition; in a reprehensible aesthetic action Clyde is shown succeeding in the act of love; he isn't impotent after all, and everything can proceed now to the *poignancy* of the denouement. Resting from their wounds, the couple enter an idyllic phase, with life stretching plausibly and hopefully before them. Then they are betrayed and shot down in a storm of bullets.

This last scene does have special virtues. When the police ambush the couple they fire literally hundreds of bullets into their car and their bodies, so that the scene (which in this case is based on fact) mounts up to an image of absolute blind violence on the part of organized society, a violence far surpassing that which it is supposed to be putting down. Beyond this, there is one moment when the entire possibility of the film as new creation is bodied forth with enormous vivacity. As the first salvo hits him Clyde spins, straightens up, then begins to topple to the ground in slow motion through a suddenly unreal air, a great long arc of descent like the very image of the impossibility of his life. As cinema, and not as talk, hint, thematic implication or technicolor virtuosity, this is what *Bonnie and Clyde* is really about.

Caught in their director's tacking and yawing, and with no great resources of their own, Miss Dunaway and Beatty give erratic performances. She is too bland (too blonde, it may be; the camera spends a lot of time on her sumptuous hair). Uneasy with irony, he is too firm-jawed and merely handsome; both seem displaced from more conventional movies. The acting feats are in the lesser roles, in Hackman's and Miss Parsons' energy and wit as the brother and sister-in-law, Pollard's shrewd oafishness as the sidekick, and in a brilliant cameo bit by Gene Wilder as a terrified square the gang kidnaps for a time. That these things are so reinforces one's final opinion of *Bonnie and Clyde* as a hybrid, an ambivalence, an alternation of achievements and collapses, an attempt to have both ways something not clearly enough seen in either. (3)

---

3. Gilman sees *Bonnie and Clyde* as a "hybrid." What in the film does he see as "achievement"? As "collapse"? What criteria of film excellence are revealed in this review?

Breathless, Courtesy of *Contemporary Films/McGraw-Hill*

BREATHLESS

Archer Winsten, *NEW YORK POST*
February 8, 1961

"Breathless" (A Bout du Souffle), at the Fine Arts, brings together the talents of two old New Wavers from France (story by Francois "400 Blows" Truffaut, Supervision by Claude Chabrol), a new New Waver, Jean-Luc Godard, the new acting idol of France, Jean-Paul Belmondo, and the young American, Jean Seberg.

It is a thin story, filled to the brim with extraordinary character of the modern, wild, criminal youth, as exemplified by Belmondo. He's a broken-nosed sloucher who walks gracefully and reminds you, without resemblance, of Brando. He's had a similarly devastating effect on French film audiences. (1)

Jean Seberg the Betrayer

Electricity, magnetism, animal vitality, all that sort of thing in abundance. The way he makes love. The way he curses, flouts conven-

---

1. When Archer Winsten tells us that Belmondo reminds *us* of Brando, and that further, this resemblance is "devastating," are we seeing *private associations* presented as if they were public?

tions, kills a cop when he wants to, runs, hasn't long to live, and dies while running there in the street, all out of breath and dead, right there on the paving stones of Paris, with traffic all around, and the little American girl, salesgirl of the Paris Herald-Tribune, Jean Seberg, his lover and his betrayer, not knowing whether she loves or is through with him, standing above his dead body, her face not knowing.

Tough and Talkative

They move about, these two, in stolen cars. They talk a lot and they talk about love more than seems wise, but eventually they do get to bed. And still they talk, and he always looks tough, and she's always as pretty as she used to be, and, thank goodness, somewhat better as an actress.

He admires Bogart.

He's on the lam in the criminal world. The police are closing in, and it's only a question of time.

It's All Mixed Up

Troublesome questions the script doesn't answer satisfactorily are why Jean Seberg turns him in, why she accepts his love in the first place after so much hesitation, what he's up to, etc. It's all of a piece, crazy, mixed-up, wild, violent, sexy, outspoken, and honest enough if anything is understood. This is one of the popular concepts of modern youth, the kind that's already gone bad and must now either be punished by the law or forgiven and psychoanalyzed.

Art Technique

Artistically the picture stands up extraordinarily well, its camera restlessly in close pursuit of its characters, and they forever running towards an unknown goal which turns out to be tragedy. This new Jean-Luc Godard has directed and screenplay written a very fine piece of work under the guiding hands of his New Wave colleagues, Truffaut and Chabrol.

In the end I doubt if it will amount to much, except as the very clear, virtually poetic expression of this very transient youth phase.(2) But the technique should linger, and so should these talents, here so highly visible and memorable.

---

2. Winsten suggests that the "phase" of youth presented in *Breathless* is a "transient" one. Viewing the film at the present time, do you first, agree with his definition of this phase and second, with his judgment?

TIME

February 17, 1961

Cubistic Crime

Breathless (Films Around the World) is a cubistic thriller that has an audience because half a century of modern art and movies have rigorously educated the public eye. Filmed on the cheap ($90,000) by an obscure, 30-year-old film critic (Jean-Luc Godard) of the French New Wave, *Breathless* would seem to offer little to the average star-struck spectator—it features a Hollywood reject (Jean Seberg) and a yam-nosed anonymity (Jean-Paul Belmondo). What's more, it asks the moviegoer to spend 89 minutes sitting still for a jaggedly abstract piece of visual music that is often about as easy to watch as Schoenberg is to listen to.(1) Then why, in the last year,

---

1. In this opening paragraph, *Time*'s reviewer makes connections between film and music and between film and painting. Can you state precisely, after reading the entire review, what these connections are? Do you find these analogies provide significant insights into your experience of the film? If so, are you in agreement with the opening statement of the review?

has this picture done a sellout business all over France? Belmondo explains some of the excitement. A ferally magnetic young animal, he is now being called "the male Bardot." But more important than Belmondo are the film's heart-stopping energy and its eye-opening originality.

Breathless has no plot in the usual sense of the word. The script of the picture was a three-page memo. Situation, dialogue, locations were improvised every morning and shot off the cuff. By these casual means Godard has achieved a sort of ad-lib epic, a Joycean harangue of images in which the only real continuity is the irrational coherence of nightmare. Yet, like many nightmares, *Breathless* has its crazy humor, its anarchic beauty, its night-mind meaning.

The camera finds the hero (Belmondo) flobbing around Marseille, sucking a cigarette, nothing to do: a portrait of the Frenchman as a young punk. Casually, he steals a car, roars north. Sixty. Seventy. Eighty. Police give chase. Gun in glove compartment. Why not? He kills a policeman, panics, runs. Paris. Meets bedmate, an American girl (Seberg), on the street, makes date, strolls off. Police spot him, give chase. Loses them in subway, goes to a men's room. Man washing hands. Punk slugs him, empties his pockets. Girl goes home, finds him in her bed. "Why did you come?" "To sleep with you." He does. She, with a frown: "I'm pregnant." He: "If these were another man's hands, would you care?" She: "Have you read Dylan Thomas?" To bed again. Out again. Steals a car. Police again. Hides with American girl in borrowed flat. More lovemaking. Later she impulsively calls police, betrays him. He couldn't care less. "I feel like going to jail." Police arrive, shoot him down. Smiles up at her, makes funny faces, murmurs affectionately: "You really are a little bitch." Dies. She: "What does he mean?"(2)

Director Godard obviously means that some people are monsters, but quite possibly the question requires an existentialist answer, too. The hero, though such ideas are far beyond his merely physical preoccupations, behaves like a personification of Gide's *acte gratuit* ("an action motivated by nothing . . . born of itself"), and his story can be seen as an extemporization on the existentialist tenet that life is just one damn thing after another, and death is the thing after that.

---

2. What is distinctive about this synopsis? To what extent does its style reflect the style of the film?

But Godard does not pose his philosophical questions very seriously; he seems chiefly concerned with developing an abstract art of cinema, in which time and space are handled as elements in a four-dimensional collage. Camera and performers, moving at random and simultaneously, create the cubistic sense of evolving relativity. Foregrounds and backgrounds enagage in a characteristically cubistic dialogue of planes. Similarly, noises and images, words and actions conflict or collaborate in amusing, revealing or intentionally meaningless ways. At one point the screen goes black in broad daylight while the characters go on talking—they are really in the dark.

More daringly cubistic is the manner in which Godard has assembled his footage. Every minute or so, sometimes every few seconds, he has chopped a few feet out of the film, patched it together again without transition. The story can still be followed, but at each cut the film jerks ahead with a syncopated impatience that aptly suggests and stresses the compulsive pace of the hero's doomward drive. More subtly, the trick also distorts, rearranges, relativizes time—much as Picasso manipulated space in *Les Demoiselles d'Avignon*. All meaningful continuity is bewildered; the hero lives, like the animal he is, from second to second, kill to kill. A nasty brute. Godard has sent him to hell in style.

Hollis Alpert, *SATURDAY REVIEW*
March 11, 1961

The Conscienceless Hero

I am at the disadvantage of having read several reviews of "Breathless," a French film made by one more in the burgeoning group of New Wave directors, Jean-Luc Godard, and I am close to being brainwashed by certain of our reviewers who have variously called

---

the piece a "masterwork," "an awesome undertaking," and a "cubistic thriller . . . that subtly distorts, rearranges, and relativizes time, much as Picasso manipulated space in 'Les Demoiselles d' Avignon.' " (As though every film did not, to a degree, distort, rearrange, and relativize time!) (1) I suspect that some of those so warmly encouraged to see "Breathless" may have difficulty, however, in recognizing a cubistic thriller when they see one and may also wonder if their limited eyes, ears, and understanding are insufficient to appreciate its masterful qualities fully.

If there are any such, I offer my own membership among them. The only film masterworks I have seen in the last several months have been "Hiroshima, Mon Amour," "Wild Strawberries," and "La Dolce Vita," and I find myself unwilling to place "Breathless" on the same plane. I'll shamelessly admit, too, that I found the picture somewhat distasteful, (2) as well as lacking in the meanings that the French critics (even more than their American brothers) attributed to this largely improvised (3) study of a footloose French thug and one of those pathetic American girls who hawk the Paris edition of the *Herald Tribune* on the Champs-Elysées. (JFK should do something about *that*.)

This is not to deny that the movie is an occasionally interesting experiment in improvisation, (4) that it has original touches, among them a sometimes amusing and sometimes unsettling cutting technique that jumps one sequence into the next, with a resulting jazzy pace that suggests the jerky thought sequences of a young criminal concerned with evading his police pursuers and sleeping with the

---

1. Is this a valid objection to the *Time* reviewer? It is true that all technicolor films are in color but one would still be justified in paying particular attention to the color in, for example, *Red Desert* where the use of color is distinctive and contributes to meaning in a way that color has not in the past. Does the distortion, relativization, and rearrangement of time play a particularly important part in *Breathless?*

2. Does "distasteful" suggest the reviewer may have some *intellectual commitments* which act as barriers in the way of his full experiencing of the film?

3. Does "improvised" mean bad?

4. How does this help you to answer Question 3?

newsgirl.(5) All this is to the good. Godard obviously has ideas about cinematic movement. And he presumably espouses a modish French neo-nihilism. In a nihilistic world (if you wish to posit it as such) why not a conscienceless criminal as hero?

Godard thus whimsically dedicates his movie to Monogram Pictures, a touch that young French intellectuals found delicious. The young French movie enthusiast tends to see something we don't in certain of our lesser pictures. You may remember that an ordinary Rita Hayworth vehicle of the Forties, "Gilda," was taken up in France and more or less enshrined. The French have their own ideas about what truly represents the American mystique. Horace McCoy, a neglected novelist here, had a cult formed around him there.(6) There also existed a Humphrey Bogart cult, more than hinted at in "Breathless." Jean-Paul Belmondo—who plays the thug with a misplaced humor that belies the character's essential psychopathology(7)—is seen fingering his upper lips in Bogart style, and at one point stares fascinatedly at a poster of Bogart, hoping to find a resemblance between himself and the late star. Even more symbolically, a French critic tells us, when the girl joins the criminal in his flight, they escape for a time by entering a movie house!

The way to find meanings in the film, then, is to take it at more than face value, as more than an aimless chronicle of a petty car thief who kills a pursuing policeman in cold blood, filches money from a former girlfriend, mugs a stranger in a washroom, beats up a car dealer, and then, in bed with the American girl, has some long and, I'm afraid, idiotic conversations. Jean Seberg, as the girl, has a

---

5. Here Alpert himself comments on the time distortions and shows that he understands the "jazzy pace" is integral to the film because it "suggests the jerky thought sequences of a young criminal." Isn't Alpert answering his own objections to the *Time* review?

6. Assuming that it is true, as the critic implies, that the French are mistaken in adoring *Gilda* and Horace McCoy, does this necessarily mean that they are mistaken in their appraisal of *Breathless?*

7. Is it possible that the humor is not misplaced? Is it indeed possible that the humor helps the filmgoer to understand that Belmondo is not playing the part of a psychopath, that Belmondo is not simply a French "thug"?

vague, cluttered-up mind; she wants to live in France, to be a reporter, to write a novel, to rid herself of Midwestern scruples about making love, to read Dylan Thomas, to know all about abstract art. The difficulty in all this is to find Godard's intent. (8) Is he parodying these young types? Does he see them as funny, sad, or monstrous? Or is he perhaps merely parodying other movies, with their emphasis on violence and sex?

The "idea" for the story was provided by Francois Truffaut (of "The 400 Blows") and then elaborated in day-to-day improvisation by Godard. Finally the girl (pregnant by now) gets as tired of the moony psychopath as I did and (with relief on my part) telephones the police and tells them how to catch her boyfriend. As he expires in conventional Monogram Pictures style from police bullets in his back he affectionately calls the girl the French equivalent of a bitch. "What did he mean?" she asks bewilderedly. End of cubistic thriller. No old-fashioned moral attitudes or platitudes. All is a washed-up Humphrey Bogart world, a world, of course, that never existed in the first place.

For the knowledgeable, there is also an interview at Orly with an author called Parvulesco, who answers empty questions with empty paradoxes. Hardly hilarious, though. Acting? Pretty much thrown out the window. Miss Seberg is carefully kept a nonactress by her director, who sees to it that both her face and voice remain expressionless. Belmondo, clearly a striking new personality, has an uncommon face and what might be called a "cute" manner. The trouble is, he's all too sympathetic; and he should have been playing someone else.

But Godard, it would seem, has found critical safety in mixing up the real and the unreal, and by eliminating meaning. He has set a clever trap: if nothing is said, (9) what is there to attack? So he has made an intriguing film, but let's face it, not really a good one.

---

8. What does "intent" mean here? Alpert seems to be saying that he has difficulty understanding the movie. Is this synonymous with understanding "intent"?

9. What does "said" mean here? And if "nothing is said," what is it exactly that Alpert has found so "distasteful" in *Breathless?*

Penelope Gilliatt, *THE OBSERVER*, London
July 9, 1961

Journeys to the Interior

In a brilliant piece on "Characters in Fiction," published in *Partisan Review,* Mary McCarthy writes:—

> The fictional experiments of the twentieth century went in two directions: sensibility and sensation. . . . The effect of these two tendencies on the subject matter of the novel was identical . . . both have the effect of abolishing the social. Sensibility, like violent action, annihilates the sense of character.

The film and the novel have always been close siblings, and the same remarks startlingly apply to the new cinema: not only to the American *avant garde,* but also to the sparkling nihilists of the *Cahiers du Cinéma* team and to Resnais, Colpi, Antonioni and our own Peter Brook. What interests film-makers now is not the social and reasonable aspects of behaviour, trimly motivated to finish a plot and build up a "character," but the irrational, asocial bedrock that is common and confusing to us all; and their attempts to drill through to this Stone-Age level lead them in the same two directions that Miss McCarthy discerns among novelists. (1)

The masculine strain of violent sensation, represented by films like "The Connection" and Jean-Luc Godard's *Breathless,* is drawn to

---

1. Miss Gilliatt in this review is addressing our usual expectations concerning characterization in film. What is interesting to consider is whether or not she is supplying us with new expectations here? That is, can we now expect to be put off by the traditional treatment of character in film?

the Beatniks and their world of the *acte gratuit*. The feminine strain of sensibility, represented by films like "L'Avventura" and "Les Amants" and Peter Brook's Moderato Cantabile (Paris Pullman), seems to gravitate towards troubled upper-class woman whose unemployed *cafard* permits a deep study of impulse and caprice. Though both kinds of film characteristically include an act of violence, which sounds a social-enough event, the treatment is always hermetically subjective: in "Moderato Cantabile," for instance, the heroine questions the hero about the motive of the sex-murder they have witnessed not because he knows anything about it, but because his surmises will tell her something about his feelings for herself. The people in "Breathless" and "Moderato Cantabile" exist not as characters in the old sense, like Tom Jones or Becky Sharp, but as what Miss McCarthy calls "palpitant organs," like Mrs. Dalloway or Salinger's Holden Caulfield; we are imprisoned within their own nervous systems.

"Breathless" seems to me the most original, insolently gifted and shattering work the young French directors have yet produced. Set down, the plot goes misleadingly like a routine thriller: a young man steals a car, kills a policeman, runs to Paris, ducks detection for a while by loafing in an American girl-friend's bedroom, is finally betrayed by her and shot down by the cops.

The treatment, however, is far from routine. Jean-Luc Godard makes a film as though no one had ever made one before,(2) and his rude, butting, fitfully attentive style expresses the mode of his characters as accurately as Francois Truffaut's anarchic dialogue.(3) When a sequence bores him, he jump-cuts, much as his hero and heroine will suddenly go to earth in mid-conversation and reappear a mile ahead. Like Belmondo's performance, Raoul Coutard's camera-work is feral and challenging, full of *non sequiturs,* lazy jokes and coldly appraising stares; the niceties of film-making are ignored rather as

---

2. Are we intended to take the remark that "Godard makes a film as if no one had ever made one before" literally? If not, what is its point?

3. While other reviewers tell us the dialogue was improvised, Miss Gilliat implies that Truffaut has scripted the film. In either case, does this have any effect on the filmgoer's experience of *Breathless?*

the characters abjure good manners, feeling perhaps that politeness is a way of keeping life at arm's-length.

The core of the film is a dazzlingly protracted bedroom scene, spiked with private games and small narcissistic cruelties, with Jean Seberg clambering over the bed like a nervy chamois and refusing to let Belmondo make love to her, in an idle spirit that perfectly augurs her final indifferent act of treachery. "You are a bitch," he says as he dies. "What does he mean, a bitch?" she blankly asks the police. I cannot imagine a more freezing expression of the cool generation's ethic. Because Godard nowhere comments on his characters, and because his film has an entertaining surface, it is going to be called light-minded; but "Breathless" is a steadily honest attempt to make a phenomenon comprehensible, which is a good enough definition of seriousness. (4)

---

4. Do you agree that this is a good definition of "seriousness"? If not, can you supply another?

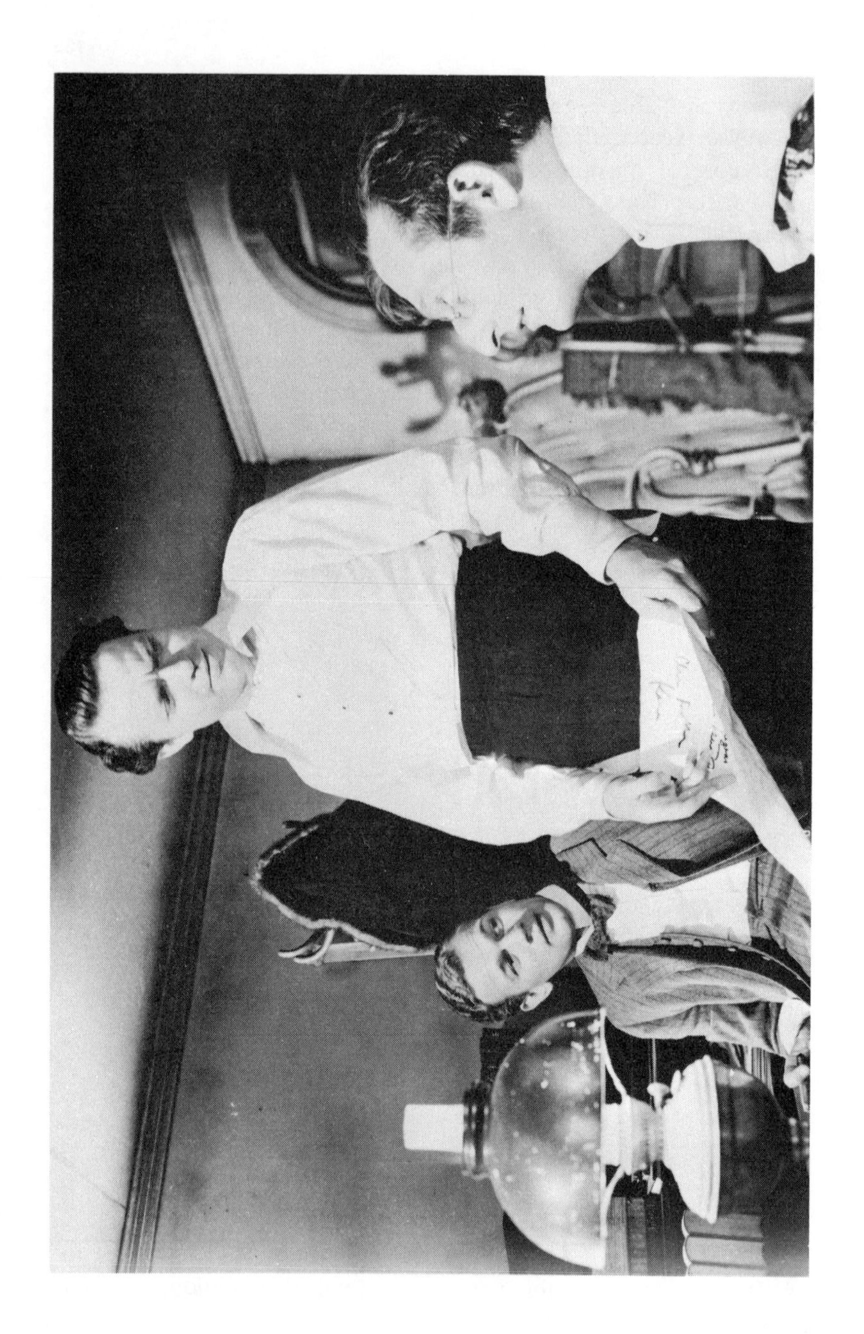

Citizen Kane, Courtesy of *Janus Films*

CITIZEN KANE

NEWSWEEK

January 20, 1941

Hearst vs.
Orson Welles

(1) The varied talents of Orson Welles, No. 1 *enfant terrible* of the theater and radio, bloom at their best in the bright light of controversy and its attendant publicity. He got plenty of both two years ago after his broadcast of a fantastic invasion of the New York area by Martians, and last week it appeared that he was in for a new spanking—this time on the seat of his Hollywood pants.

For months there has been a great to-do over the first film opus of the 25-year-old boy wonder. Titled "Citizen Kane," it credits Welles as author, producer, director, and star. Mystery shrouded the one-man show while it was in production. Although it is an RKO picture, no one on the lot even read the script except George J. Schaefer, RKO president, and the studio's legal staff, who stethescoped it for libel troubles. Actors in the film were given only their own parts, and

---

1. This news item makes clear the extra-aesthetic nature of the controversy raging at the time of *Citizen Kane's* release.

visitors to the set were barred unless given permission by Welles himself.

It now develops that there was ample reason for the secrecy. For the film, depicting the life story of a millionaire's son who creates a publishing empire only to see it partially crumble, who attempts unsuccessfully to build a political career, and who, finally embittered, retires to a fantastic Shangri-La upon a man-made mountain, is a biography startlingly parallel to that of the publisher William Randolph Hearst. Furthermore, it seems Hearst was not consulted—either for approval or disapproval.

Therefore, last week when Louella O. Parsons, movie editor of the Hearst newspapers, saw a preview of the picture—flanked by two grim Hearst lawyers—the remarkable similarity between Citizen Kane and her chief struck the usually overvoluble Miss Parsons completely dumb. But while she said nothing, word quickly got around Hollywood that the publisher had issued an ultimatum: not one word about RKO or its productions was to be printed in any Hearst paper until the studio had agreed to shelve the picture entirely. To prove the point, a big, complimentary review of RKO's "Kitty Foyle," which had appeared in early editions of Hearst's Los Angeles Examiner, was yanked in all further editions—as were other short items about RKO productions.

Faced with all this, Welles said the whole business had him baffled, "but it looks like my throat has been cut." RKO, however, had more on its mind than Welles' well-being, for now the studio stands to face a Hearst boycott or lose an $800,000 investment. There is also the fear that Hearst might start a smear campaign against the entire industry.

John O'Hara, *NEWSWEEK*
March 17, 1941

It is with exceeding regret that your faithful bystander reports that he has just seen a picture which he thinks must be the best picture he ever saw.

With no less regret he reports that he has just seen the best actor in the history of acting.

Name of picture: CITIZEN KANE.

Name of actor: Orson Welles.

Reason for regret: you, my dear, may never see the picture.

(From now on, it's *I*.)

I saw "Citizen Kane" the other night. I am told that my name was crossed off a list of persons who were invited to look at the picture, my name being crossed off because some big shot remembered I had been a newspaperman. So, for the first time in my life, I indignantly denied I was a newspaperman. Nevertheless, I had to be snuck into the showing of "Citizen Kane" under a phony name. That's what's going on about this wonderful picture. Intrigue.

Why intrigue? Well, because. A few obsequious and/or bulbous middle-aged ladies think the picture ought not to be shown, owing to the fact that the picture is rumored to have something to do with a certain publisher, who, for the first time in his life, or maybe the second, shall be nameless. That the nameless publisher might be astute enough to realize that for the first time in his rowdy life he had been made a human being did not worry the loyal ladies. Sycophancy of that kind, like curtseying, is deliberate. The ladies merely wait for a chance to show they can still do it, even if it means cracking a femur. This time I think they may have cracked off more than they can chew. I hope.

The story is that of a publisher, from his whippersnapper to his doting days. His origin is humble, and most likely not acceptable to the quarreling ladies, whose origin is not for a second in question here. A fresh punk out of various colleges, the publisher walks into a newspaper office as a not quite legitimate heir, and thereupon enjoys himself and power. At a rather late date it is shown that his sybaritic pastimes and his power are incomplete, for he can buy or produce everything but love. He doesn't give love; he lacks love. With everything in the world that you and I might expect to bring happiness, the publisher is a lonely, unwanted, feared, tragicomic man. He dies, speaking one mysterious word, a female name. At the end of this wonderful picture you get to know what the name was. You also (later) realize how silly women can be, especially obsequious women.

Look in vain here for any but obscure hints as to the story of "Citizen Kane." My intention is to make you want to see the picture;

if possible, to make you wonder why you are not seeing what I think is as good a picture as was ever made. Up to now I have thought that the very best talking picture ever made was "M." I have seen "M" at least eight times. As a movie writer and press agent I used to have them run off the attack sequence in "The Big Parade," the one in the woods where the boys don't know where the sharpshooter's going to hit next, every time I had a chance. One of my very favorite silents was that beautiful job, "The Great Gatsby." And if you want to settle bets on any phase of "The Birth of a Nation," call me. But "Citizen Kane" is Late 1941. It lacks nothing.

And aside from what it does not lack, "Citizen Kane" has Orson Welles. It is traditional that if you are a great artist, no one gives a damn about you while you're still alive. Welles has had plenty of that. He got a tag put to his name through the Mars thing, just as Scott Fitzgerald, who wrote better than any man in our time, got a Jazz Age tag put to his name. I say, if you plan to have any grandchildren to see and to bore, see Orson Welles so that you can bore your grandchildren with some honesty. There never has been a better actor than Orson Welles. I just got finished saying there never has been a better actor than Orson Welles, and I don't want any of your lip.

Do yourself a favor. Go to your neighborhood exhibitor and ask him why he isn't showing "Citizen Kane." *Then* sue me.(1)

---

1. O'Hara says his "intention is to make you want to see the picture." If you were a contemporary of the reviewer (which means you have been reading many news items similar to the one printed above) would O'Hara have fulfilled his intention? Would you want to see the movie any more now than you did before?

TIME

March 17, 1941

Kane Case

As in some grotesque fable, it appeared last week that Hollywood was about to turn upon and destroy its greatest creation. That creation was *Citizen Kane,* the film which Orson Welles and his Mercury Players had spent more than a year talking and thinking about and 70 days shooting, with $750,000 of Radio-Keith-Orpheum's money.

The film was in the cans. A magazine advertising campaign had begun. But no release was set by R.K.O. for the picture to be shown to the public, and it seemed very likely that none would ever be. Old Mr. William Randolph Hearst, who had only heard reports of the picture through his cinematic eyes, ears, and tongue, Columnist Louella Parsons, thought the life of Kane was too close a parallel to the life of Hearst.

The Picture

The objection of Mr. Hearst, who founded a publishing empire on sensationalism, is ironic. For to most of the several hundred people who have seen the film at private showings *Citizen Kane* is the most sensational product of the U.S. movie industry. It has found important new techniques in picture making and story-telling. Artful and artfully artless,(1) it is not afraid to say the same thing twice if twice-telling reveals a fourfold truth. It is as psychiatrically sound as a fine novel but projected with far greater scope, for instance, than

---

1. Is this merely a play on words or are we being told something about the technique of the film?

Aldous Huxley was inspired to bring to his novel on the same theme. It is a work of art created by grown people for grown people.

The Story begins with the death of Charles Foster Kane (Orson Welles), at one time the world's third richest man, overlord of mines and factories and steamship lines, boss of newspapers, news services and radio chains, possessor of a vast castle in Florida, a staggering agglomeration of art, two wives, millions of enemies. The MARCH OF TIME is running off rushes of its Kane biography in its projection room. But when they are shown, the editor does not think the facts reveal the man. "It might be any rich publisher—Pulitzer, Hearst, or John Doe," he complains. "Get me something that will show it is Kane. Find out his last words. Maybe they meant something."

Kane's last word was "rosebud." Thompson (William Alland), the newsreel reporter, spends two feverish weeks in interviewing five people. Thompson talks to Kane's trollopish second wife (Dorothy Comingore), whom he tried to make a singer, finally established in the castle. There she passed the years assembling jigsaw puzzles until she walked out in boredom. Then, there is Kane's rich guardian (George Coulouris) whom Kane hated; Kane's general manager (Everett Sloan), the sad, loyal, philosophical Jew who stuck by to the end; his former drama editor and best friend (Joseph Cotten) with whom Kane broke after Kane's disastrous try for the Governorship of New York; Kane's butler (Paul Stewart). None know the meaning of "rosebud." But each in his way understood a little of the man: he was not cruel, but he did cruel things; he was not generous, but he did generous things; he was willful, capricious, and he wanted to be loved—on his own terms. The MARCH OF TIME never finds the meaning of "rosebud," nor the key to Kane's frustrations, but almost by accident, the audience does.

So sharply does *Citizen Kane* veer from cinema cliché, it hardly seems like a movie. (2) There are some extraordinary technical novelties through which Welles and wiry, experienced little Photographer Gregg Toland have given the camera a new eloquence—for example, the "stolen" newsreels, the aged and streaked documentary shots. When Susan makes her debut, the camera tells the story by climbing high up among the flies to find two stagehands—one with his hands

---

2. Was it at this point that a new term seemed necessary for filmed entities that weren't movies? Film, perhaps?

pinching his nose in disgust. Always the camera seems to be giving the narrative a special meaning where it will help most: picturing a small bottle beside a tumbler when Susan Kane is lying drugged with an overdose of sedatives, exploring the love nest and the family breakfast table like a pair of prying eyes and ears.

Orson Welles treats the audience like a jury, calling up the witnesses, letting them offer the evidence, injecting no opinions of his own. He merely sees that their stories are told with absorbing clarity. Unforgettable are such scenes as the spanning of Kane's first marriage in a single conversation, the silly immensity of the castle halls which echo the flat whines of Susan.

Hollywood claimed Welles never would make the grade. From the moment he arrived there its citizens resented him and his Martians and his youth and his talent. When he grew a beard for his first film, a sporty press agent sent him a bearded ham for Christmas; while he was dining out one evening, a playful actor cut off his tie with a table knife; columnists dubbed him with nicknames like "Little Orson Annie." At announcements that his first two productions had been called off, the town nodded knowingly. He was just a big bag of publicity.

But whatever Orson Welles did do, Hollywood was pretty sure it would break all the rules. Hollywood was right.(3)

---

3. Does this reviewer make you want to see the film on grounds other than its notoriety? And incidentally, is it one of the functions of a critic to make you want to see a film? If so, why do we so often read critics after the fact?

Peter Bogdanovich, *THE CINEMA OF ORSEN WELLES,* (New York: The Museum of Modern Art, 1961)

Citizen Kane is a criticism of American plutocracy and the power of the popular press, but it transcends these social considerations. It is, as Welles called it, "a portrait of a public man's private life."

Citizen Kane is the story of a search by a man named Thompson, the editor of a news digest (similar to the *March of Time*), for the meaning of Kane's dying words. He hopes they'll give the short the angle it needs. He decides that a man's dying words ought to explain his life. Maybe they do. He never discovers what Kane's mean, but the audience does. His researches take him to five people who knew Kane well—people who liked him or loved him or hated his guts. They tell five different stories, each biased, so that the truth about Kane, like the truth about any man, can only be calculated by the sum of everything that has been said about him.

"Kane, we are told, loved only his mother—only his newspaper—only his second wife—only himself. Maybe he loved all of these, or none. It is for the audience to judge. Kane was selfish and selfless, an idealist, a scoundrel, a very big man and a very little one. It depends on who's talking about. him. He is never judged with the objectivity of an author, and the point of the picture is not so much the solution of the problem as its presentation."

By Welles' own description, one can see the morality-humanity theme clearly developed throughout the movie itself. (1) From the opening shot ("No Trespassing") to the last line ("I don't think any word explains a man's life"), it is evident that Welles has no intention of passing judgment on Kane: "Kane is detestable but he is a

---

1. Although we may be able to see this "morality-humanity theme" (whatever that might be) throughout the film, do we see it because Welles says it is there?

human being." It has been argued that the final shot of the sled is a sentimental oversimplification of Kane's life, but, though it is one of the most successfully surprising and poignant final moments in cinema, it is clear in the script that it was not Welles' intention to make that shot the film's all-encompassing solution: "Maybe Rosebud was something he couldn't get or something he lost, but it wouldn't have explained anything . . . I guess Rosebud is just a piece in a jigsaw puzzle—a missing piece." (2) Though the director supplies that missing piece it serves only as a kind of moving reminder that, in spite of everything, Kane was a man with feeling, passionate and with courage. (3)

Technically, *Citizen Kane* is a treasure chest of the screen-language. With his first film, Welles climaxed the sound cinema; he explored all the possibilities of moviemaking, sharpened old devices, gave new life to tired ones, and brought in some startling new ideas. He thus synthesized what had gone before, foreshadowed what was to come, and made everything seem original and fresh. Perhaps the most valuable innovation in the film was its inventive use of sound, which Welles brought to movies from his years of radio work. The overlapping dialogue (now a Welles trademark) gives the picture a remarkable flow and sense of reality, making most other films seem stage-bound because of their cued delivery: first A talks, then B, then A, then B; but in life A and B are very often talking at the same time, and Welles makes abundant use of that fact. The sound in *Kane* (as in all his subsequent work) is also used for a vivid economy of gesture: when Kane is eight, Thatcher is seen saying, "Merry Christmas . . . " and with that the scene cuts about eighteen years forward to Thatcher saying ". . . and a Happy New Year." With one sharp transition, we have jumped into the story of Kane's adult life. Later, we see Leland campaigning for Kane before a handful of people, announcing that "Kane entered this campaign . . ." and we cut to Kane speaking at the lectern of a huge auditorium ". . . with one purpose only . . ." Again the point has been made directly, briefly, effectively. Or, of course, the famous breakfast-table sequence between Kane and his first wife, where the nine-year deterioration of

---

2. All of this may be clear in the script, but is it clear in the film?
3. Does the image of the sled really tell us all this? Does it inform us most especially of Kane's courage?

a marriage is summed up through one continuing conversation over five flash-pans.

Among the other aspects of *Citizen Kane* which struck the 1941 public with the force of extreme novelty, the "News on the March" sequence is outstanding. A perfectly imitated news digest, it is also, aside from Wolcott Gibbs' profile of Henry Luce, the sharpest of all parodies of "Time-style" ("For forty years appeared in Kane newsprint no public issue on which Kane papers took no stand"). In photography, the most important feature Welles brought to *Kane* (and to all his later movies) was the deep-focus lens developed for him by photographer Gregg Toland, enabling him to keep the entire frame in equally sharp focus, and making for economy of editing: the contract signing scene, for one example, in which within one frame we see the equivalent of a close-up (Bernstein), a medium-shot (Thatcher), and a long-shot (Kane), all equally sharp. This lens made it possible for Welles to compose his frames with maximum depth, and allowed him to use chiaroscuro in a new way. (4)

Beyond all these considerations and their effect on subsequent directors, the script and its significance is all important. It broke with exciting success all the Hollywood cliches of movie construction and brought to the screen an adult, personal style. *Citizen Kane* is the only one of his films made and released exactly as Welles wanted, so it becomes easy to call it his best picture, but we shall see that he developed much further both technically and intellectually. *Kane* remains an extraordinary achievement, (5) important not only for itself, but because it set the theme that haunts all the films of Orson Welles.

---

4. In this paragraph, Bogdanovich uses many technical terms. What is a deep-focus lens? A close-up? A medium-shot? A long-shot? A frame?

5. The larger part of this discussion is devoted to the technique of *Citizen Kane,* and Bogdanovich does convince us that the film is technically an "extraordinary achievement." Does he, however, convince us that it is also an extraordinary intellectual achievement?

Andrew Sarris, *FILM CULTURE* No. 9, 1956

Citizen Kane: The American Baroque

The recent revival of *Citizen Kane* has not elicited the kind of reappraisal the occasion demands. It is too easy to dismiss *Kane* as a great film with the smug confidence that everything that is to be said about it has already been said. If nothing else, the fifteen years that have elapsed since its initial release should provide a new perspective. The fact that *Citizen Kane* still seems to be ahead of its time is as much an indictment of contemporary film-making as it is a vindication of the classic quality of its art. Stripped of its personal and topical sensationalism, the film has risen above the capricious attacks leveled against it fifteen years ago.

A great deal of the hostility aroused by *Kane* back in 1941 was directed at its youthful creator, Orson Welles. Many of his enemies have since been appeased by the simple fact that Welles has joined the mortal herd by getting fifteen years older. Others have come to admire his dogged professionalism in the face of disastrously inadequate financing and even personal injury as demonstrated by his recent performance of *Lear* from a wheelchair. Yet, though tempered by adversity and voluntary exile, the spectacular Welles personality still obscures the more substantial aspects of his genius.

On a less personal level, *Citizen Kane* disappointed many who were caught up in the portentous political atmosphere of 1941. Advance publicity had prepared many liberals for a savage political attack on William Randolph Hearst, one of the most prominent enemies of the New Deal. *The Grapes of Wrath* and *The Great Dictator,* both released in 1940, had made their stands at the barricades. Welles, himself, had recently mounted an anti-fascist interpretation of *Julius Caesar* on the New York stage. The boycott of Welles and *Citizen Kane* by all Hearst publications further heightened the

Reprinted by the permission of the publisher.

suspense of an impending collision between the *enfant terrible* of the left and the grand old man of the right.

When *Kane* finally appeared, it failed to justify all the ideological anticipation. Charles Foster Kane was not William Randolph Hearst in any "significant" sense. Welles and Herman J. Mankiewicz had merely borrowed biographical details, some virtually libelous, to fashion an intricate screenplay that posed a psychological mystery without advancing any cause.(1)

After subtracting the criticism of the Welles personality and the criticism of the lack of ideology, all that is left and all that is relevant is the criticism of *Citizen Kane* as a work of art. To believe, as some do, that *Citizen Kane* is the great American film, it is necessary to produce an interpretation that answers some of the more serious objections to this film.

Citizen Kane has peculiar claims to greatness in that its distinctive merits are related to its alleged flaws. Adverse criticism of *Kane* is based mainly on three propositions: (1) its narrative structure is unduly complicated; (2) its technique calls attention to itself; (3) its intellectual content is superficial.

If any one of these propositions is fully accepted, *Kane* falls far short of greatness. At first glance, all three points have some validity. The narrative zig-zags and backtracks to its conclusion. The technique dazzles the eye and ear. No profound ideas are explicitly developed. A closer examination of the film, however, reveals an inner consistency of theme, structure, and technique. The implications of this consistency are crucial to any effective analysis of what *Citizen Kane* is really about.

Within the maze of its own aesthetic,(2) *Kane* develops two interesting themes: the debasement of the private personality of the public

---

1. If it is true (and surely it is) that all criticism save that of the film itself is irrelevant to a discussion of the film, then why does Sarris devote so much space to personal and ideological attacks? Is it because status is gained from popular unpopularity?

2. Sarris here presents what may well be the insight basic to all discussion of film: a film may establish "its own aesthetic." One might even go so far as to make this a criterion of excellence. A great film will of necessity dictate the particular ways in which it must be viewed and judged.

figure, and the crushing weight of materialism. Taken together, these two themes comprise the bitter irony of an American success story that ends in futile nostalgia, loneliness, and death. The fact that the personal theme is developed verbally while the materialistic theme is developed visually creates a distinctive stylistic counterpoint. Against this counterpoint, the themes unfold within the structure of a mystery story.

Charles Foster Kane dies in a lonely castle. His last word is *"Rosebud."* Who or what is *Rosebud?* This is the mystery of *Citizen Kane.* The detective is a reporter for a news service which produces *March of Time*-like newsreels. The suspects are all the persons and objects Kane encountered in his cluttered life. The clues are planted in the film on three occasions, but, unlike the conventional mystery key, *Rosebud* is the answer to a man's life rather than his death. And since the intangible meanings of life end in the mystery of death, *Rosebud* is not the final solution but only the symbolic summation.

Rosebud is the means through which the past history of Charles Foster Kane is penetrated by the porter-detective and the omniscient camera. Time is thrown back and brought forward in the four major movements of the film, the flashback-recollections respectively of Kane's banker-guardian, his business manager, his best friend, and his second wife. Each major flashback begins at a later point in time than its predecessor, but each flashback overlaps with at least one of the others so that the same event or period is seen from two or three points of view.

There is a fifth flashback—a newsreel of Kane's public career—which establishes the identity of Charles Foster Kane for the first time in the film. There is no transition between the opening scene of a man dying in a lonely castle with *Rosebud* on his lips and the startling appearance of the unframed newsreel. This is the first shock effect in *Citizen Kane,* and it has received undeserved abuse as a spectacularly devious method of narration. What has been generally overlooked is the great economy of this device in establishing the biographical premises of the film without resorting to traditional montages of public reactions and telescoped historical events in the major movements of the story.

By isolating the newsreel from the main body of his film, Welles frees his flashbacks from the constricting demands of exposition, enabling his main characters to provide insights on the external outlines of the Kane biography. After the newsreel, the transitions are worked out very carefully through the logical movements of the reporter-detective. This shadowy, though thoroughly professional, character links the present to the past in an interlocking jigsaw puzzle with one elusive piece—*Rosebud*—appearing only at the very end in the reporter's absence since his services are no longer needed.

The newsreel accomplishes more than a skeletal public biography of Charles Foster Kane. On a narrative level, it introduces Mr. Thatcher, Kane's banker-guardian, whose memoirs will provide the first personal flashback of Kane's life and the first significant clue to *Rosebud.* The newsreel also produces a paradox that previsions the non-political quality of the film. While Thatcher is telling a Committee that Kane is a Communist, a speaker in Union Square attacks Kane as a Fascist. The elderly Kane tells newsreel audiences that he is and always has been an American. This is the first indication that Kane is not really committed to any cause but Kane.

The newsreel fades out; a sudden establishing shot picks up a darkened projection room. The first of the many disembodied voices in the film calls out from the darkness, and the shadow plot of *Citizen Kane* begins. A group of cynical newsmen discuss ways of pepping up the newsreel. The reporter is sent out to find the secret of *Rosebud.* The semi-colloquial dialogue is driven forth with relentless persistence from every direction. There is nothing profound or witty about any of it but it moves quickly and economically.

The reporter begins his search and the major movements of *Citizen Kane begin.* Through a hard, wide-angle lens,(3) the reporter enters a cavernous museum, a dingy nightclub, a solidly upholstered office, a drab hospital ward, the gloomy mansion of Charles Foster Kane. The reporter's world is functional, institutional; an aging, weathered gateway to the life and time of Charles Foster Kane.

The sixth and last flashback of *Citizen Kane* offers the final clue to *Rosebud* and brings the reporter's quest to its unsuccessful conclusion. Interestingly enough, the three clues to *Rosebud* appear at times when Kane is being treated most remotely—in the cryptic death scene at the beginning, in the unfriendly memoirs of his banker-guardian, and in the final flashback narration of a cynical butler. The narrations of his closest acquaintances yield no clues to the symbolic truth of his life. This is the ultimate confirmation of Kane's spiritual loneliness, and it is upon this loneliness that the mystery structure of the film is based.

---

3. What is a wide-angle lens?

The mystery of *Rosebud* is solved in a memorable manner. The reporter and his entourage have departed from the Kane castle. As the cynical butler is directing the disposal of Kane's "junk" into the furnace, a workman picks up a sled in routine haste and dumps it into the flames. The camera closes in on the surface of the sled and the name *Rosebud* as the letters are dissolving in liquid fire. The audience is given the solution with the added knowledge that no one living on the screen will ever know the secret of *Rosebud.*

This solution has been attacked as a trick ending unworthy of its theme. Yet without this particular resolution, the film would remain a jumbled jigsaw puzzle. The burning sled is apt not only as a symbolic summation but as a symbolic revelation. The reporter, the butler, the workman, the friends, the enemies, the acquaintances of Kane never discover *Rosebud* because it is lost amid the "junk" of Kane's materialistic existence.

Kane's tragedy lies in the inability of the props of experience to compensate for the bare emotional stage of his human relationships. Charles Foster Kane collected valuable treasures from all over the world, but his last thoughts were of a sled he used as a boy before great wealth came into his life. At one point in the film, he tells his banker-guardian that he might have been a great man if he had not been so wealthy. *Rosebud* became the focal point of his nostalgia for a different turning point in his life. Kane's view of his own life is deterministic, and Kane's image throughout the film is remarkably consistent with this sense of determinism.

The apparent intellectual superficiality of *Citizen Kane* can be traced to the shallow quality of Kane himself.(4) Even when Kane is seen as a crusading journalist battling for the lower classes, overtones of stiff self-idolatry mar his actions. His clever ironies are more those of the exhibitionist than the crusader. His best friend—a

---

4. What happens if we take the word "apparent" out of this sentence? We have then a fallacious but not infrequently encountered type of critical argument: "It's not that the film is boring; it's that the people it presents to us are boring. So naturally a film about boring people has to seem boring, if we are to understand boredom." The point is, however, that aesthetic achievement lies precisely in presenting these boring people in such a way that the film may be part of an experience about boredom which is not in itself boring.

detached observer functioning as a sublimated conscience—remarks to the reporter that Kane never gave anything away: "he left you a tip." His second wife complained that Kane never gave her anything that was part of him, only material possessions that he might give a dog. His business adviser and life-long admirer expressed the other side of Kane's personality when he observed that Kane wanted something more than money.

In each case, Kane's character is described in materialistic terms. What Kane wanted—love, emotional loyalty, the unspoiled world of his boyhood symbolized by *Rosebud*—he was unable to provide to those about him, or buy for himself. It is therefore fitting that the story of Kane should begin with lonely death and conclude with the immolation of his life symbol.

The technique of Welles and his photographer, Gregg Toland, justifies the narrative structure. Apparently outrageous effects fall into place once the pattern of the film is discernible. *Kane* opens on a solid wire fence with a sign reading "No Trespassing." The camera moves up on a painted castle against a background of dark, brooding clouds. The same shots are repeated in reverse at the very end of the film. This initial and concluding clash of realism and expressionism flanks one of the most stylistically varied of all films. (5)

The opening shots have been attacked as pretentious and the closing shots as anticlimactic. Yet, in a subtle way, the beginning and end of *Citizen Kane* suggests its theme. The intense material reality of the fence dissolves into the fantastic unreality of the castle and, in the end, the mystic pretension of the castle dissolves into the mundane substance of the fence. Matter has come full circle from its original quality to the grotesque baroque of its excess. (6)

As each flashback unfolds, the visual scenario of *Citizen Kane* orchestrates the dialogue. A universe of ceilings dwarfs Kane's personal stature. He becomes the prisoner of his possessions, the ornament of his furnishings, the fiscal instrument of his collections. His booming voice is muffled by walls, carpets, furniture, hallways, stairs, and vast recesses of useless space.

Toland's camera set-ups are designed to frame characters in the oblique angles of light and shadow created by their artificial environ-

---

5. Has Sarris provided sufficient clues to the meanings of "realism" and "expressionism" in this context?

6. Has Sarris successfully defended the opening shots?

ment. There are no luminous close-ups in which faces are detached from their backgrounds. When characters move across rooms, the floors and ceilings move with them, altering the points of reference but never transcending them. This technique draws attention to itself both because it is so unusual and because it tends to dehumanize characters by reducing them to fixed ornaments in a shifting architecture.(7)

Sound montage is used intensively within the flashbacks to denote the interval of time within two related scenes. A character will begin a sentence and complete its weeks, months or years later in a different location. On occasion, one character will begin the sentence and another will complete it in the same manner. This device results in a constriction of time and an elimination of transitional periods of rest and calm. Aside from the aesthetic dividends of pacing and highlighting, *Kane's* sound montage reinforces the unnatural tension of the central character's driving, joyless ambition. In all respects, *Kane's* technique is a reflection and projection of the inhuman quality of its protagonist.

One brilliant use of sound montage that has generally been ignored as a piece of aural gargoyle is the piercing scream of a parakeet that precedes the last appearance of Kane in the film. One flashback and several scenes previously, Kane and his second wife are arguing in a tent surrounded by hundreds of Kane's picnic guests. A shrill scream punctuates the argument with a persistent, sensual rhythm. It is clear that some sexual outrage is being committed. When the parakeet screams at the appearance of Kane, the sound linkage in tone but not in time further dehumanizes Kane's environment. In the baroque world that he has created, Kane is isolated from even the most dubious form of humanity.

Kane's lack of humanity is consistently represented in the performance of Orson Welles, who alters the contours of Kane's rigidity from youth to old age. As a young man, Kane is peculiarly joyless. A gala occasion is recalled in which Kane threw a party for his new writers hired away from a competing newspaper. A group of chorus girls come on the scene. Kane is thrown in the midst and begins cutting up. The scene is heavy with Kane's studied posturing as the life of the party.

---

7. The question here is whether this technique is effective if it draws attention to itself as technique.

The acting in *Kane* emerges as an elaborate arabesque of interrupted conversations, harsh dissonances and awkward physical confrontations. Kane's world peopled by Mercury Players, is tuned to the egocentric performance of Welles. Joseph Cotton, Everett Sloane, and Dorothy Comingore, as Kane's best friend, business adviser, and second wife, respectively, and the main narrators of the film, achieve a strident rapport with the demanding presence of Welles. The intense pitch of the acting charges each line of dialogue with unexpected meanings. The manner of expression often alters the verbal content toward a new level of self-conscious cynicism. In this, the acting evokes the intentional hypocrisy of the few protestations of principle that appear in the script.

Towards the end of his life, Kane reacts to the desertion of his second wife by wrecking the furniture in her room. Again, his violent actions are rigidly controlled by a chilling self-awareness. As he is completing his unduly methodical havoc, he comes upon a crystal paper-weight in which a minute snow storm beats down on a miniature cottage. He speaks the name of *Rosebud* and walks past an array of guests across the path of endless mirrors and endless reflections of his image—mere repetitions of his ego without magnification. This is the final arithmetic of Kane's life, the last material accounting of his greatness.

Citizen Kane presents an intense vision of American life, distorting and amplifying its materialistic elements at the expense of human potentialities. The implied absence of free will in the development of Kane's character is thematically consistent with the moral climate of his environment. Kane's magnitude, unchecked by limiting principles or rooted traditions, becomes the cause of his spiritual ruin. Kane emerges as an extension of the nouveau-riche American seeking a living culture in the dead relics of the past. Striving desperately to transcend his material worth, Kane is victimized by the power his wealth possesses to alter the moral quality of his actions. In the end, everything has been bought and paid for, but nothing has been felt. (8)

---

8. We asked earlier if Bogdanovich convinced you of *Citizen Kane*'s extraordinary technical and intellectual achievement. Now we ask the same question about Sarris. Is Sarris somewhat more convincing? Why?

A scene from the motion picture *Doctor Strangelove* or: *How I Learned to Stop Worrying and Love the Bomb*. Copyright © 1963 Columbia Pictures Industries, Inc. By permission.

DR. STRANGELOVE or: HOW I LEARNED TO STOP WORRYING AND LOVE THE BOMB

F. Anthony Macklin, *FILM COMMENT*
Summer, 1965

Sex and Dr. Strangelove

Regarding his evaluation of DR. STRANGELOVE as sex allegory, Mr. Macklin has received the following note from the film's director, Stanley Kubrick—"I enjoyed reading the piece and I think that you have found a rather engaging way of viewing the film. I would not think of quarreling with your interpretation nor offering any other, as I have found it always the best policy to allow the film to speak for itself."

The most provocative commercial motion picture produced in the United States in 1964 was Stanley Kubrick's DR. STRANGELOVE: OR HOW I LEARNED TO STOP WORRYING AND LOVE THE BOMB. Much has been made of the question of whether or not the

Reprinted from *Film Comment,* Volume 3, Number 3, by the permission of the author and publisher.

film is a satire. Stanley Kauffmann says DR. STRANGELOVE is not satire—it "does not hope to alter men"; he suggests that it is beautiful black comedy. On the other side, Dwight Macdonald says the film is a "barrage of satire," and John Simon also categorizes it as satire. Simon says that DR. STRANGELOVE is *for* something—"it is for humanity." Kubrick has stated that he would like to see the most prominence given to the review written by Robert Brustein in the *New York Review of Books;* Brustein interpreted the effect of the film as purgation.

In all of the varied critical opinion, much has been said about the purposes of DR. STRANGELOVE, but a dominant theme that pervades the film from beginning to end has been ignored. This study will point out how DR. STRANGELOVE is a sex allegory: from foreplay to explosion in the mechanized world.

The picture opens with two planes refueling in the sky in great metal coitus as the sound track croons *Try A Little Tenderness.* The film ends with the mushroom clouds of orgiastic world destruction as the track croons, *We'll Meet Again.* The purgation is thorough and devastating.

When Kubrick began to adapt Peter George's serious novel *Red Alert* into a cutting continuity (pun intended), it is said that several scenes became ludicrous; they had a note of natural humor in them. Kubrick titled his focus and orchestrated these notes into an outrageously comic film on an outrageously serious subject. Part of the comic effect is in the names of the characters. Peter Sellers plays three of these characters—President Muffley, Captain Mandrake, and Dr. Strangelove.

Like Jonathan Swift, who employed Master Bates in *Gulliver's Travels,* the creators of DR. STRANGELOVE (Peter George and Terry Southern assisted Kubrick) gave special significance to names that represent various aspects of sex. General Jack D. Ripper (Sterling Hayden), commander of Burpelson Air Force Base, initiates the attack on the Soviet Union. General Ripper, a sex fiend in his own way, is obsessed by the idea of "bodily fluids" and what is happening to them; he is certain that fluoridation is a Commie plot to destroy the strength of America by undermining her bodily fluids. Ripper's description of the act of love has been described by one woman I know as the sexiest moment in any movie she has seen.

Ripper possesses two objects that are obvious sex symbols. The first is his cigar, which is a dominant fixture. Secondly, there is his pistol. When the President discovers Ripper's attack plan, he orders Ripper's capture. Only Ripper's code can halt the planes heading toward the U.S.S.R. As the army tries to unseat him, Ripper barricades himself in with the unwilling Captain Mandrake, a British exchange officer. While the enemy fights toward him, Ripper enters the bathroom and commits suicide with his pistol. (See Seymour Glass's suicide in J. D. Salinger's *Perfect Day for Bananafish* for an interesting parallel).

General Buck Turgidson (George C. Scott) is also sexually oriented. When the phone call informing him about the attack comes, he is in a bedroom with his secretary. Again, the name has an extra value. Buck, of course, means male with various connotations, and turgid means swollen. Turgidson rushes to the War Room where he cheers his planes on.

After Ripper's suicide, Captain Mandrake tries to get information about the code to the President. The mandrake root resembles the male shape; this gives us a third character with a significant name. Mandrake runs into trouble in the person of Colonel "Bat" Guano (Keenan Wynn), who breaks in on Mandrake as he has worked out the code. In continuing our name pattern we find that guano is manure, particularly that of bats, and is used as fertilizer. Guano holds Mandrake prisoner at gunpoint, but Mandrake finally convinces Guano to allow him to make his call to the President. Still, Guano is uncertain and warns him about any "preversions" in the phone booth. Mandrake is stymied because he doesn't have a coin with which to place the call, and the operator won't heed his pleas without a coin. Finally, Mandrake gets Guano to shoot a cola machine to get the money. The whole scene is reminiscent of Rabbit's golf game (impotence) in John Updike's novel, *Rabbit, Run.*

Meanwhile, the womb-like War Room is the scene of other action. The President, Merkin Muffley, is trying to reach Premier Dmitri Kissoff in Moscow to tell him what is happening. Stanley Kauffmann, in his review in the *New Republic* has called attention to the President's name with the words "erotica students, observe." Merkin means female pudendum (Oxford English Dictionary), which shows the feminity of the President, illustrated by his lack of action. Premier Dmitri is off somewhere with female companionship. Eventually, Muffley gets through and gives Kissoff the news. Although Mandrake relays the code and Kissoff is warned, it is too late. One of the planes has been hit by shell fire, and its code system has been destroyed. The crippled plane is another phallic symbol as it flies on to its destination. As it reaches its target, Major King Kong (Slim Pickens), a Texas ape, mounts the bomb to try to dislodge it from where it is stuck in the plane. He succeeds and rides the bomb down to its climax with an ecstatic yowl.

Meanwhile, back at the War Room, Dr. Strangelove—and this name captures the essence of the film—has made his appearance. The Soviet ambassador reveals that the Soviets have created a Doomsday Machine, an invention that they were preparing to announce. Strangelove verifies the possibility of such a machine. His answer to the problem of nuclear annihilation is for a few men to go under ground. He proposes, with an excited leer, the provision of many women for each man.

The Doomsday Machine, when set off by a bomb, will destroy civilization; but man can come up again after ninety-three years when the radioactivity has lifted.

Strangelove is in a wheel chair, impotent. He is a product of German science, talking in a measured, clipped accent; he is mechanized, his arm snapping at his throat and his crotch in an uncontrollable attack. He is the end result of science. In his final act, his parts take over; and his mechanical arm throws him from the chair. He totters and announces shrilly, *'Mein Führer!* I can walk." And the bomb explodes.

The film concludes with a panorama of beautiful mushroom clouds destroying the world, as Vera Lynn sweetly sings *We'll Meet Again.* Impotence is no more. Warped sex has been eased. Civilization can go back to its beginnings. DR. STRANGELOVE: OR HOW I LEARNED TO STOP WORRYING AND LOVE THE BOMB ends in an orgiastic purgation. Kauffmann says, "This film says . . . 'The real Doomsday Machine is men.' " Actually, the real Doomsday Machine is sex. As King Kong, Buck Turgidson, and Dr. Strangelove himself would chorus, "What a Way to Go!" Love that bomb. (1)

---

1. Repeated in this text is the principle that the best criticism is that which accounts for the most while ignoring the fewest elements in the film. This very amusing piece on *Dr. Strangelove* is a perfect example of the way in which high selectivity can be used to create a very distinctive film. Mr. Macklin's case that *Strangelove* is a sex

allegory rests primarily on name symbolism. One might just as easily (depending on one's cultural associations and *intellectual commitments)* see these same names as revealing an allegory on the comic strip: Bat Guano as Batman; Buck as Buck Rogers; Mandrake as the Magician; M(ervin) M(uffley) as M(ary) M(arvell). From the same angle of vision, Ripper's cigar can suggest *Daily Planet* editor Perry White's, and Strangelove's wheelchair can be seen as an emblem of Billy Batson's crutches. The point is, if we want a film to be our film, we can make it such—depending, of course, on just how committed we are to our particular view.

Robert Brustein, *THE NEW YORK REVIEW OF BOOKS*

February 6, 1964

A Comedy of Disaster

Dr. Strangelove possesses a great many distinctions as a work of the imagination, but I should like to cite it, first and foremost, for valor: I think it may well be the most courageous movie ever made. It is certainly one of the funniest. A nightmare farce which proceeds from horror to horror, culminating in the annihilation of the human race after an American hydrogen bomb has been dropped on Russia, it is, despite its cataclysmic conclusion, a peculiarly heady, exhilarating experience. I can account for this partially by the fact that the

1. Brustein says the film pays "no deference at all to the expectations of its audience." Even so, the film does *make use of* the expectations of its audience. How?

movie pays absolutely no deference at all to the expectations of its audience. (1) Artistic courage always soothes the spirit and makes glad the heart, but when this quality enters as craven a medium as the American film one feels curiously exalted, ineffably happy. Then, too, there is something extraordinarily liberating in the nature of the movie itself. It is the kind of total theater that Antonin Artaud would have admired, with its dark humor, its physical and anarchic dissociation. Dr. Strangelove is a plague experienced in the nerves and the funny bone—a delirium, a conflagration, a social disaster.

What Stanley Kubrick has done is to break completely with all existing traditions of moviemaking, both foreign and domestic. (2) While the European art film seems to be inexorably closing in on the spiritual lassitude of certain melancholy French or Italian aristocrats, *Dr. Strangelove* invests the film medium with a new exuberance, expansiveness, and broadness of vision; compared with the sweep of this masterpiece, (3) the weary meanderings of Resnais, Fellini, and Antonioni seem solipsistic and self-indulgent. Moreover, Kubrick's film is fun—this is its one debt to Hollywood. It is enjoyable for the way it exploits the exciting narrative conventions of the Hollywood war movie—say, *Air Force* or *Thirty Seconds Over Tokyo*—and even more, for the way it turns these conventions upside down, and cruelly scourges them. This is what is arrestingly new about the film: its wry, mordant, destructive, and, at the same time, cheerful, unmoralistic tone. We have heard this sound emanating from our comic novels, cabaret acts, satiric revues, living rooms, and dreams, but, although it rumbled a little bit under the conventional noises of *The Manchurian Candidate,* it has never before fully entered the mass media. With *Dr. Strangelove,* a subterranean vibration becomes a series of earthquakes, shattering cultural platitudes, political pieties, and patriotic ideals with fierce, joyous shocks. If the picture manages to remain open, it will knock the block off every idealogue in the country: even now, I suspect, Sidney Hook is preparing the first of fifteen volumes in rebuttal.

---

2. As you read on, consider in what ways Brustein supports his contention that the film has broken with all previous traditions.

3. What response do we as readers and viewers have to a critic's use of a word such as "masterpiece"?

To avoid a repetition of Mr. Hook's embarrassing performance on behalf of *Fail-Safe,* where he wrote some eighty-odd pages of closely reasoned, technical argumentation to refute the premise of a cheap, best-selling fantasy, let me announce that *Dr. Strangelove* is frankly offered to the audience as a cinematic sick joke, and that it is based less on verifiable facts than on unconscious terrors. The film's source, a prototype for *Fail-Safe,* is Peter George's *Red Alert,* but the film writers have employed the novel very loosely, and the director has imposed on the finished screen play his own style and purpose. This style is Juvenalian satire; this purpose, the evacuation of fear and anger through the acting out of frightful fantasies. (4) Kubrick has flushed a monster from its psychic lair—the universal fear of nuclear accident—and then proceeded to feed and nourish it, letting it perform its worst before your eyes. The consequence of this spectacle is, as the subtitle suggests, a temporary purgation: to witness the end of the world as a comic event is, indeed, to stop worrying and to love the Bomb.

The outline of the film is this: a psychotic right-wing general, convinced that the Communists are poisoning Americans through fluoridation, exercises emergency powers and sends a wing command to bomb the Soviet Union. The President, trying to recall these bombers, learns that the Russians have perfected a deterrent, a Doomsday machine, which is automatically triggered to explode the moment a bomb is dropped on Soviet soil, spreading a shroud of fallout over the earth for a hundred years. After the general's base has been destroyed by American forces, and the recall code has been found, both nations cooperate to bring the bombers back or shoot them down. One damaged plane, however, its radio inoperative, manages to continue on to target. Through the invincible doggedness of the pilot and his crew, a hydrogen bomb is dropped on a Soviet missile complex—and apocalypse follows.

Kubrick handles this external action with ruthless documentary realism. The battle scenes, for example, which show Americans slaughtering Americans, are photographed through a grey morning

---

4. Brustein is, as we know, primarily a critic of drama, and thus he brings to film the vocabulary and theory of the theatre arts. To what extent does his reference to Juvenalian satire seem applicable here?

mist (the same smoky tones so effectively used in Kubrick's *Paths of Glory*) with a hand camera shaken by artillery explosions; and the flight of the bomber over Arctic wastes is a terrifying journey into the frozen unknown. At the same time, however, Kubrick is evoking savage ironies through the conjunction of unexpected images and sounds: the bomber, for example, proceeds to its destination (and to the destruction of the world) over a chorus of male voices humming, "When Johnny Comes Marching Home."(5)

The same blend of farce and nightmare is found in other scenes. During the credits, a B-52 bomber is fueled in the air through a phallic hose, while the sound track plays "Try a Little Tenderness." A looming shot of two monstrous hydrogen bombs, triggered and ready to go, reveals two scrawled messages on them, "Hi There!" and "Dear John." And the epilogue is composed of a series of nuclear explosions (a sequence borrowed, I suspect, from a similar filmed skit used in *The Establishment*), which flower soundlessly while a female voice croons "We'll meet again (don't know where, don't know when)."

What these images suggest is that our heroic postures and patriotic reflexes have become hideously inappropriate to modern weaponry—the same thing is illustrated by the conduct of the crew on the lethal bomber. Kubrick has sardonically included among these crew members the various ethnic stereotypes of Hollywood war movies: a Negro bombardier, a Jewish radio operator, a Texas pilot, etc., all of whom behave, in crisis, according to preconditioned movie patterns—they engage in sexual banter, become comradely, grow steely grim and fighting mad. When the order is received to proceed over enemy territory and drop the bomb, the Texas pilot, Major "King" Kong, takes off his helmet, puts on a ten-gallon hat, assumes an unctuous leader-of-men speaking style, and delivers an

---

5. Note that although Brustein makes clear throughout that he sees *Dr. Strangelove* as an important social document, and one moreover with a point of view to which he has strong *intellectual commitments,* he does not fail in his responsibility as a critic of the total work of art. Here, for example, he shows his understanding of the film aesthetic and of the ways in which this particular film has achieved its effects. Where else in the essay does he reflect such insights?

inspirational lecture to the crew about their duty to "the folks back home," while promising them all decorations, "regardless of your race, color or creed." When the plane is hit by a missile, he keeps it in action, flying low over jutting peaks; and when the bomb doors stick, he courageously climbs into the bomb bay, determined to fix the short circuit and complete his mission.

Kong finally clears the doors, and goes sailing down to target on the back of a bomb, waving his hat and whooping like a rebel. American heroism has become completely identified with American lunacy. So has American know-how—it is almost a structural principle of this film that our technology is wholly mad. Inside the bomber, for example, the camera peeks into complicated equipment and technical apparati—the instrument panel, the radar, the navigator's gear, the auto-destruct mechanism—all efficiently manipulated by this trained crew to create havoc and mass slaughter. The President's War Room, similarly, with its huge locating charts, is a model of gleaming competence and quiet decorum ("You can't fight in here," says the President to two dissidents, "this is the War Room"). Even the telephone works as an obstacle to survival. In one hilarious sequence, a British officer—having discovered the recall code—is trying to phone Washington with only minutes to go; but he lacks the necessary change, and the Pentagon will not accept collect calls.

If our technology is mad, however, then so are the technicians who create, control, and operate it. *Dr. Strangelove* is a satire not only on nuclear war and warriors, but also on scientists, militarists, military intellectuals, diplomats, statesmen—all those in short, whose profession it is to think about the unthinkable. Thus, the movie contains a large number of superb caricatures, all treated either as knaves or fools, but still recognizable as familiar American types.

These include two sharp profiles of General Walker-like military men: General Jack D. Ripper, played by Sterling Hayden in another of his stiff, interesting non-performances—his eyes fanatically narrowed, his teeth clenched on a huge cigar, as he drawls to an aide about how he confines himself to pure alcohol and rain water and refrains from sexual intercourse to protect his natural essences against the Communist conspiracy; and General Buck Turgidson, Air Force Chief of Staff, played by George C. Scott in a fine frenzy of muscle-flexing pugnacity—stuffing his mouth with wads of chewing gum, and flashing an evil smile as he outlines his plan to obliterate the "commie punks" entirely ("I'm not saying we wouldn't get our hair mussed, Mr. President, but I do say not more than ten to twenty million dead depending on the breaks").

Then, there are three magnificent satiric sketches by Peter Sellers: Group Captain Mandrake, Ripper's befuddled British aide; President Merkin Muffley, a bald, bland, liberal Chief Executive, educated and slightly effeminate (a *merkin* according to the OED, is a "female pudendum," while *muffley* is an obsolete word for a pubic wig); and, finally, that eerie figure from the Bland Corporation, the German scientist, Dr. Strangelove.

Strangelove (formerly *Merkwuerdiglchliebe*) is the most masterly character in the film, a composite portrait of Edward Teller, Werner von Braun, and Herman Kahn, played by Sellers with an excess of mischief, and conceived by Kubrick in an excess of fury. Imprisoned in a wheel chair, his mechanical hand gloved in black, his face fixed in a perpetual smile, he stares through dark glasses and sibilates through false teeth, suggesting emotion only through a slight emphasis on certain phrases, the word *human* being particularly distasteful to him. Strangelove is the perfect synthetic man, and he comes to us by courtesy of a Universal horror movie. In his person, the Mad Doctor and the State Scientist merge—Boris Karloff with a computer, calculating the proper use of deterrents and the half-life of cobalt-thorium-G.

This is extravagant enough, but towards the end, Strangelove goes completely haywire. So does the movie, as if Kubrick, having breathed the air of the outer limits for the first time, were suffering from stratospheric drunkenness. The bomb has been dropped; the doomsday shroud is beginning to smother all life on earth; and Strangelove is outlining his plan for preserving "a nucleus of human specimens" at the bottom of mine shafts. His explanation is disarmingly rational but his mechanical hand has gone out of control. It shoots up in a Nazi salute, it punches him on the jaw, it strangles him, and finally it propels him right out of his wheelchair—whereupon he screams at the President, *"Mein Fuehrer,* I can walk!" The lunatic inappropriateness of the remark somehow sums up all the lunatic inappropriateness of the theatrics and celluloid heroics that have preceded it; and it makes the devastation that follows seem singularly fitting and just.

Dr. Strangelove is a work of comic anarchy, fashioned by a totally disaffected and disaffiliated imagination: it is thus the first

American movie to speak truly for our generation. Kubrick has managed to explode the right-wing position without making a single left-wing affirmation: the odor of the Thirties, which clung even to the best work of Chaplin, Weiles, and Huston, has finally been disinfected here. Disinfected, in fact, is the stink of all ideological thinking. For although *Dr. Strangelove* is about a political subject, its only politics is outrage against the malevolence of officialdom. Conservatives will find it subversive, liberals will find it irresponsible, utopians will find it bleak, humanitarians will find it inhuman—*Dr. Strangelove* is all these things.(6) But it also releases, through comic poetry, those feelings of impotence and frustration that are consuming us all; and I can't think of anything more important for an imaginative work to do.

---

6. Assuming that this is true (and the letters to *The New York Times* which follow to a considerable extent force the assumption), does the possibility for so much variation in response make *Dr. Strangelove* a better film or a worse one?

The following letters to the editor are " 'Strangelove' Reactions" from filmgoing readers of *THE NEW YORK TIMES* (March 1, 1964).

To the Screen Editor:

I am glad that you have opened your theatrical pages to a discussion of "Dr. Strangelove." But I note with regret that your critic, Bosley Crowther, after seeing the film for a second time, still does not understand either the point of Stanley Kubrick's satiric method or the soundness of the film's morals.

"Dr. Strangelove" would be a silly, ineffective picture if its purpose were to ridicule the characters of our military and political leaders by showing them as clownish monsters—stupid, psychotic, obsessed. For we know that most of them are in fact intelligent, devoted men, with only a normal proneness to suspicion, pride and error. What has masked the hideous nature of our demoralized strategy of total extermination is just the fact that it has been the work of otherwise well-balanced, responsible men, beginning with Henry L. Stimson.

By presenting the individual components of this strategic system as collossal paranoids and criminal incompetents, Mr. Kubrick has happily found the only way possible to characterize the policy itself. Since in our case the "final solution" of the Communist problem would call for our own country's dreadful mutilation, as well as Soviet Russia's, and might even, if carried on beyond the first day, destroy the human race, there is hardly any method, short of the wildest kind of farce, to describe overt madness on this catastrophic scale. Unless the spectator was purged by laughter he would be paralyzed by the unendurable anxiety this policy, once it were honestly appraised, would produce.

By making "Dr. Strangelove" the central symbol of this scientifically organized nightmare of mass extermination Mr. Kubrick has not merely correctly related it to its first great exponent, Hitler, he has likewise identified the ultimate strategy of nuclear gamesmanship for precisely what it would be: an act of treason against the human race. Those of us who have attacked this policy by reasoned argument have for almost 20 years addressed deaf ears, closed eyes, locked minds: so I salute Mr. Kubrick with admiration for having successfully utilized the only method capable of evading our national censor—relentless but hilarious satire.

What the wacky characters in "Dr. Strangelove" are saying is precisely what needs to be said: this nightmare eventuality that we have concocted for our children is nothing but a crazy fantasy, by nature as horribly crippled and dehumanized as Dr. Strangelove himself. It is not this film that is sick: what is sick is our supposedly moral, democratic country which allowed this policy to be formulated and implemented without even the pretense of open public debate.

This film is the first break in the catatonic cold war trance that has so long held our country in its rigid grip.

Lewis Mumford
Amenia, New York

Anti-American

To the Screen Editor:

"Dr. Strangelove," manifests no reverence for American ideals, American institutions or American political and military leaders. . . . This is not satire. Good satire demands a moral base: the ideal must be present, however subtly or indirectly expressed, and nowhere are we given a glimmer of what the best in American leadership has been and still is.

"Dr. Strangelove" is straight propaganda, and dangerous pacifist propaganda at that. It is an anti-American tract unmatched in invective by even our declared enemies.

Jeanne McQuade
Queens Village, N.Y.

Warped View

To the Screen Editor:

"Dr. Strangelove" indulges in the most insidious and highly dangerous form of public opinion tampering concerning a vital sector of our national life, a sector which needs public funds, public understanding and public support to do its job.

If the Soviets have at best tempered their schedule and route to world domination, and if there is indeed a thaw in East-West tensions, there is only one real reason—the very real and available strategic striking power of the United States, built up and effectively controlled by dedicated Americans in and out of government service for the past two decades.

Those who take this lightly, or who feel that this truth is so distasteful that it needs pictures, are providing no insight to their audiences, only mockery of the very thing which keeps us free enough to mock ourselves. Are we really the warmongers that the Soviets, in their style, and Mr. Kubrick, in his, say we are?

Michael Getler
New York

8½

John Simon, *NEW LEADER*
August 5, 1963

Fellini's 8½¢
Fancy

Things started going wrong with the Steiner episode in *La Dolce Vita.* Fellini was trying to show the problem of the modern intellectual, yet Steiner and his psyche were far from convincing. The devoutest Felliniites donned their most superior faces and informed us that, of course, Steiner was not meant to be the real thing, but an unsuccessful would-be intellectual—look at all those creeps at his party. True, the creeps were creeps all right; but Steiner—witness his trusting altruism, delightful musicianship, appreciation of good painting, modesty, borrowing of books on Sanskrit grammer, exquisite and loving wife and children—is clearly meant to be the genuine article. If he were not, he would be nowise different from Marcello, the hero, on whom he is meant to be a potentially salutary influence. But, here lies the tragedy, the potential savior goes beserk with fear of the future and kills his children and himself. Fellini could not make his motivation very believable, but, luckily, he did not try very hard. (1)

---

1. Does viewing *8½* in relation to the work of Fellini which

Of his third of *Boccaccio 70,* Fellini made a much bigger hash, though the other two thirds were scarcely better. The episode was meant to be ideological—that censorship is a form of prurience, that puritanism is hypocrisy—but the ideas were either too old and obvious or too feebly expressed, and the only thing that registered fully was a more-than-life-size Anita Ekberg, of whom even life-size is too much. (2)

Now comes *8½,* and, despite two or three good scenes, it is a disheartening fiasco. There are several reasons for this. First, it is extremely hard, virtually impossible, to make a good autobiography out of one's present. (3) The present hurts too much. The past is the proper study of autobiography, for it allows of tranquil recollection, self-distancing and perspective. The story of Guido Anselmi, the famous director, successful yet criticized for his recent work, troubled by not knowing what kind of film to make next, torn between Catholicism and Marxism, devoted to his wife and dependent on her yet drawn to all other attractive women and involved with some, attempting to use his film as psychotherapy—all this is humanly understandable and even touching; unfortunately, it makes for bad, because confused, art: The tone is never sure, but falters between irony and self-pity, between shamefaced poeticism and tongue-tied self-mockery. (4)

Confused, also, because ignorant. That is the second failure of *8½:* its ignorance. Art is made out of knowledge—intuitive, partial,

---

preceded it help us in understanding the film? Or does it, in effect, set up the *director* (and his *oeuvre) as barrier?*

2. This is a perfect example of the *actor as barrier.* Simon dislikes Ekberg and apparently cannot even accept her in the service of parody.

3. Simon says 8½ is autobiography; Hatch (see below) suggests it is not. Who is right? You pay your money and you take your choice. Fellini says 8½ is autobiographical; Hatch thinks he's putting us on. But what really matters here is that Simon not only states the film is autobiography but sees in this very non-fact a central cause of the film's failure.

4. To what extent do these judgments that the film exhibits "self-pity . . . shame-faced poeticism and . . . self-mockery" depend on the assumption that the film is autobiography? Can we see self-pity in an anonymous work?

prejudiced, illusory—any kind, but knowledge. *8½* is about floundering, and it is not the flouderer who can give floundering a concrete form. (Floundering, incidentally, should not be confused with doubt, which is the assertion of the self in a negative direction; rather, it is stumbling about in various directions all of which seem, successively or simultaneously, positive.) (5) *8½* piles problem upon problem, which is permissible; but sheds no light, which is not. There is, indeed, a mock resolution tacked on at the end: a kind of dance of life begun by a group of clowns which includes the hero as a boy; and is eventually picked up by all the motley dramatis personae. Yet whereas such a *commedia dell'arte* ending may fit into the style and non-intellectual *Problematik* of a film like *Cabiria,* it is foreign to the matter of *8½,* and remains an inept *deus ex machina.*

Foreignness brings us to the third weakness of the film. In *8½,* Fellini, apparently afraid of becoming a self-repeater with diminishing returns as so many famous Italian directors have become, tries for something new: symbolism, metaphysics, solid intellectual content. Now the sad truth is that he and his fellow-scenarists could not be more unsuited to this kind of art. (6) What made Fellini's early films great—and they, too, tended to be quasi-autobiographical—was their almost total avoidance of intellectualizing, and reliance on character study, accurate local colors, honest and controlled emotionalism, bittersweet humor, an occasional bit of satire, and a simple, lyrical view of the world through a camera that had an eye for the poetic but a stomach for the realistic.

---

5. Who is the "flounderer"? Clearly, Fellini. And how does Simon know he is the "flounderer"? Because he has made a film about floundering. Would Simon come to this conclusion without the assumption that the work is autobiography? Do we see Mike Nichols as a confused young man because he has made a film about a confused young man? Apparently we do not. Is this because Nichols has not told us the film is about himself? And because the young man is not a movie director? And even if Nichols had told us that *The Graduate* was autobiographical, what would we have learned about the film itself?

6. Why does Simon feel that Fellini is "unsuited to this kind of art"?

Already in Fellini's masterpiece, *I Vitelloni,* the one incident that did not quite ring true was the one involving the stolen statue of the angel, where the film was straining for symbolic value. Fellini, after all, is typically and gloriously Italian, with all this implies of a kind of sensuous wisdom, of tragi-comic profundity. That remarkable writer, all too little known here, Vitaliano Brancati, has been aptly called an *"umorista serio,"* and the title sits as well with his kindred spirit, Fellini. A serious humorist, that is what the creator of *The White Sheik, I Vitelloni, La Strada and Cabiria* is; gravely metaphysical or esoterically symbolist films—*trobar clus*—he should leave to more rigorous or recondite minds, to Bergman or Buñuel or Antonioni. In Fellini's hands, this approach is rather like the attempt of a typical Italian composer to forsake *bel canto* for the symphonic; *8½* reminds me of those truly dreary orchestral works of a Respighi, a Casella or a Malipiero.

Wherein does the symbolism consist? The film moves from reality through daydreams into dreams, and one of its main points is that all three states are of equal importance, indeed not readily distinguishable one from the other. Therefore, everything in the film should be equally relevant. But what, for instance, are we to make of the Cardinal's disquisition on the bird called Diomede, because when Diomedes died, these birds, ululating profusely, accompanied him to the grave? What does the satanic young man in the Cardinal's entourage represent? Why are so many of the priests at the seminary manifestly androgynous? Is there a parallel intended between the embalmed saint in a glass case at the seminary and an obviously fake sideshow fakir in a similar case at the thermal resort? (7) And so on.

And the intellectual content? Somewhere or other Fellini must have heard that ambiguity is, or is supposed to be, the hallmark of advanced art. (8) And behold, all the principal characters of *8½* are sublimely dichotomous. There is the protagonist's wife, honest, neglected, touching, yet also a shrew. There is her bosom companion, Rosella, the intelligently muckraking voice of the film, yet she is the very one who goes in for spiritism. There is the sardonic scriptwriter,

---

7. Can you provide answers to any of these questions?

8. How do you respond to the tone of this statement? Why do you think Simon has adopted this tone?

significantly called Daumier, intellectually and artistically intransigent, critical of Anselmi's weakness and compromises, but for all that a prating, negativistic bore. There is the Cardinal, humane yet dogmatic, gently repeating the horrible slogan: *"Extra ecclesiam, nulla salus."*

The same goes for the hero's other women. La Saraghina, the woman-mountain, is a loathsome monolith of flesh, a whore, but also childlike and genuine. Carla, Anselmi's mistress, is nice yet imbecile, devoted wife and perfect slut. Claudia, the beautiful actress (played insipidly by Claudia Cardinale), remains completely bisected by the intellectual chiaroscuro. Only Guido Anselmi is a coherent type—but a type, precisely, not an individual. Though his foibles are recognizable enough, and his childhood neuroses exemplarily Freudian, there is little about him that is specific, interesting, compelling enough to make us care.

The dialogue itself bulges with antinomies; here the intellectual cleavage is given yet more indecent exposure. Thus Daumier is continually citing Stendhal, Mallarmé, Suetonius and what have you, appositely yet unenlighteningly. Claudia is repeatedly described as "young yet old," "a child, yet ancient"; Guido is always characterized in terms of seeking without finding, having nothing to say but wanting to say it anyway, wishing to bury the past but lacking the courage to bury anything.

Worst of all is the systematic undercutting of every utterance. The Cardinal quotes Origen with unassailable finality. But Origen mutilated himself for the sake of the heavenly kingdom; are we to believe such a celestial *castrato?* An effete American journalist (played all too believably by Eugene Walter) mumbles critically, *"Le cinéma n'est pas né comme un jeu intellectuel,"* which would seem to give films like *8½* short shrift; yes, but his character is a ludicrous phoney. Ah, but it is from the mouths of phoneys that the truth comes: It is the absurd American girl, an intellectual flapper, who has written a dissertation on "The Solitude of Modern Man in the Contemporary Theatre"—which Anselmi's life and work demonstrate with a vengeance, if they demonstrate anything at all.

Life is complex and even contradictory; but it is not so simplistically antithetical. Art has every right to subtle ambiguity; but premeditated ambivalence, splitting, hatchet-like, every character, every statement, every hair, is not art. The great masters of ambiguity—Pirandello, Brecht, Proust, Valéry, Eliot—however much they may undercut ideologies, do not chop up the ground on which they stand. (9)

And what of Fellini's metaphysics? It is better to create at all cost, or to admit one's sterility and refrain? Should Anselmi strive for the truth through autobiography or through a film about atomic destruction? Can one say Yea to life without apprehending its quiddity? To all these questions Fellini manages only the already mentioned corybantic answer: a stagey dance of life, even less convincing than the dance of death at the end of *The Seventh Seal,* which undoubtedly suggested it.

There are other obvious echoes—of *Wild Strawberries, Last Year at Marienbad,* Fellini's earlier films (the very score is a reworking of the *Dolce Vita* score), even a broad allusion to Dante's *Inferno* in the steam-bath scene—but the borrowings are not integrated and do not crystallize anything in *8½*. Fellini's intellectualizing is not even like dogs dancing: It is not done well, nor does it amaze us that it is done at all. It merely palls on us and, finally, appalls us. (10)

---

9. Since none of the "masters of ambiguity" that Simon cites are film makers, is Simon implying that "subtle ambiguity" is not achievable in films?

10. For whom is Simon writing? How do you know?

Robert Hatch, *THE NATION*
July 27, 1963

Fellini's *8½* is a work of egotism so striking as to guarantee its notoriety and almost to assure its success. The renowned Italian director (*The White Sheik, La Strada, La Dolce Vita,* etc.), finding himself slack of spirit and unable to fix upon the theme for a new picture, tells us that he decided to film his own desuetude. The

---

impulse is not unlike the schoolboy ruse of writing a paper entitled "Why I have Nothing to Say." Sr. Fellini's doldrums, it seems, were personal as well as professional: his screen alter ego (Marcello Mastroianni) needs to invent a titillating tableau in order to reanimate his interest in a kittenish mistress; meanwhile, he cannot gather himself sufficiently to re-enlist the affection of the wife whom he genuinely loves.

The structure of *8½* is complicated but not notably difficult. (1) The director, after suffering a nervous collapse when the car he is driving is mired deep in traffic, repairs to a fashionable watering place. His work and his life follow him; soon he is surrounded by wife, mistress, producer, co-writer, actors, technicians, friends—the whole cast of his social and artistic identity. He is urged from all sides to take decisions, press forward, acknowledge responsibilities. He does not very much attend these promptings and is forever falling off into memories, dreams and wishful memories. And what action he does take appears, from the hallucinated style of its narration, to be pursued in a mood of severe abstraction. Thus the need to consult with church dignitaries on a point of doctrine embedded in his alleged new production provokes a grotesque pantomime in the spa's steam rooms; prior to that, however, it has recalled an afternoon of his childhood when, with schoolboy companions, he once incited an obese and deranged woman (one who had made a den for herself in a beachhead pillbox left derelict after the war) to perform a lascivious dance; and for which mischief he had been punished with humiliation by his clerical teachers. Thus also, the director, put out of countenance by an encounter between mistress and wife, flees into a daydream in which he is the lord of an adoring harem composed of all the women who are distracting his real life, and where he keeps discipline and earns love by means of a sinister but not evidently brutal whip. Fortunately, the metaphor is not always that blatant. (2)

The co-author appears as an acid chorus; his views are somewhat anomolous. It is his mission to tell the director home truths about his projected work, and his complaints that the script lacks focus, that the incidents are too subjective to be theatrically valid, that the characters are real only to the director's memory, etc., seem to be

---

1. How do we distinguish complexity from notable difficulty?
2. When does a metaphor become "blatant"?

Fellini's sly way of disarming criticisms of *8½*. However, the proposed film which the co-author finds so inadequate, and which at the end he congratulates the director on abandoning (what matter the cost to the producer), concerns a flight to the moon, and the objections raised are not relevant to it. I think Fellini is engaged here in some kind of *nouvelle vague* cuteness, but that does not detract from the grand irony of the immense rocket scaffoldings that are erected by the distracted producer before his genius of a director has cast the picture or indeed come to terms with its scenario.

The imagery and comment of *8½* are presented with an infectious grin; not every episode explains itself and characters appear in the action by reasons of association that are not always supplied. However, we understand that the director's brain is sparking with the unpredictability of a damp battery, and the unexplained bits and pieces fall easily enough into the flow of the picture: Fellini's ability to make a film flow with the sparkle, surprise and occasional peril of a quick stream is the key to his distinction among contemporary directors.

How much autobiography is there in all this? Not, I should think, a great deal. The picture may have been conceived in the manner Fellini would have us believe, but once under way it looks to have been spun like a taffy from an inventive and irreverent mind. What may have begun as confession and therapy soon must have turned into the shrewdest entertainment—a game not to be taken seriously. At least, I cannot seriously believe that Fellini is so plain-souled that he could throw off melancholy by reminding himself that a man must be taken for what he is, not what others would have him be; or that the value of one's life is to be measured by the people with whom one shares it. The finale, for which everyone in the huge cast joins hands in a giant ring-around-a-rosie, to the music of a clown band, is visually most engaging, but I doubt that it epitomizes Fellini's philosophy, or stands for anything more than a good camera shot. Deception in the theatre is never more cunning than when we are told that the masks are down and the illusions stored. (3)

---

3. This is Hatch's second explicit reference to Fellini's "cunning." Does this suggest the way in which Hatch can deal with Fellini's claims that the film is autobiography without allowing these claims to interfere significantly with his experience of the film?

Hollis Alpert, *SATURDAY REVIEW*
June 29, 1963

The Testament of Federico Fellini

Having explored his immediate environment and its moral climate with stunning brilliance in *La Dolce Vita,* Federico Fellini has now turned inward and explored in his new film, *8½,* an individual much like himself. (1) The subject this time is an Italian motion picture director, artistic, capable, and not uncommercial. The man, if not nervously exhausted, has reached a point of needing a rest cure. Thermal baths are prescribed. He has bad dreams, of being caught in a traffic jam in a tunnel, for instance. His producer will not wait for him to take his own good time about working out his next film project, and is already building sets, while the director searches for the film he may or may not have in him.

The setting is one of those bath resorts, with a turn-of-the-century hotel in the grand style, grounds with benches for the guest-patients, cavernous steam rooms, and massage parlors. Fellini makes marvelous use of the place, with characteristic strongly defined images, faces that emerge from halos of steam, from patterns of sunshine and shade, to face the camera eye—or the eyes of Guido Anselmi, the film director. (2) This man, who wears a floppy hat indoors and out, who sometimes forgets to shave, who wonders if he is all or only part

---

1. Notice how Alpert avoids embroiling himself in the question of autobiography by making a simple, irrefutable statement: the protagonist in *8½* is "an individual much like" Fellini.

2. Is Alpert here resolving the ambiguities other critics have seen in the film or is he merely taking sensuous pleasure in his experience?

fraud, who searches for the sources of his previous strength, is played by Marcello Mastroianni, a film actor of sensitivity, subtlety, and precision.

The film is a mingling of reality, dream, and fantasy. The reality is that the director has come to the resort to recuperate. Following him like pack rats are his producer, production manager, a cynical writing collaborator, and people hoping to play parts in his film. They set up a production office at the hotel, they build a monstrous set on the nearby beach, they take over a local theatre and show screen tests, begging the director to make up his mind and choose.

His dreams take the form of curious recollections. Overwhelmingly poignant is one of his dead mother and father greeting him gently in their village cemetery. A haunting sequence in itself is that involving Saraghina, a fat, gross prostitute, who rolls her hips on a forlorn stretch of beach for the enjoyment and edification of schoolboys.

His mistress joins Guido at the resort and attempts to revive his passion for her. His wife arrives, and with her some of his other relatives. Their seeming tolerance of his frailties plunges him into self-critical brooding, and he escapes into another fantasy, this time of a harem in which he is lord and master, and in which his wife gladly cooks and scrubs for his handmaidens.

But the film's demands must be met, the inevitable press-conference must be held, and escaping from it all by a symbolic suicide, the director is at last free to see the truth. The people he has been attempting to fit into a form are real, and the artist (he now knows he is one) must express the reality he feels and sees. Dream and reality merge in one love-filled final scene. The people of his life becomes his performers, the performers become his people, and he joins them. The director, the artist, has made his peace with himself, and he may proceed.

Fellini has taken a personal and most difficult subject, treated it with all this imagination he is capable of, and fashioned a film of the highest distinction. (3) He has been unafraid to confess weaknesses and reveal his privacy. His actors quiver with feeling and provide his testament with a living, breathing quality. Again, as in *La Dolce Vita,* it is hard to pick the best, because they are all so

---

3. Is Alpert saying here that Fellini did as good a job as he was capable of doing?

amazingly good: Anouk Aimée as the wife, Guido Alberti as the producer, Sandro Milo as the mistress, Edra Gale as Saraghina. But there are many more. Fellini is blessed with more than a touch of genius. So is his new film.

THE GRADUATE

Adelaide Comerford, *FILMS IN REVIEW*
January, 1968

The Graduate is a genuinely funny comedy which succeeds in being so despite an uninteresting and untalented actor in the title role.

The actor: Dustin Hoffman. The role: a college graduate, totally ignorant of life, being introduced to some of its more "affluent" aspects.

These "affluent aspects" include seduction by the mother of the girl with whom he ultimately falls in love. The seduction is played, in bed, by Anne Bancroft with a feminine realism that is a joy to watch. Her performance will do much to reverse the waning trend of her reputation as an actress. The seduction scene would have been even funnier had Mr. Hoffman been able to achieve more than one facial expression, one voice tone, one halting mannerism. (1)

---

1. This judgment of Hoffman makes dramatically clear the enormous difficulties encountered in any attempt to be objective about film. Hoffman either turns you on or turns you off—and this has little if anything to do with his talent. For, finally, is talent—acting talent, especially—an easily measurable quality, if measurable at all?

Reprinted with permission from the January '68 issue of Films in Review.

The girl who becomes his fiancée is played by Katharine Ross, and although she is not yet able to vary her facial expressions with art, or, indeed, to vary them at all, her face is so attractive you forgive her. The rest of the cast, which includes William Daniel, Murray Hamilton, Elizabeth Wilson and Brian Avery, all help the comedy. (2)

Mike Nichols directed, from a screenplay by Calder Willingham and Buck Henry, and Nichols' far from orthodox mind created some novel situations. Certainly what he puts on the screen does not resemble American life as we know it. But Nichols' distortions never get so broad they are self-defeating.

The color-photography in this film, by Robert Surtees, is an outstanding example of how much cinematography can do to enhance a moving picture which otherwise would seem ordinary. His camera placements, and the color purity of his individual shots, give *The Graduate* distinction. (3)

---

2. In this review, the focus is pretty much on the actors. Does the film, itself, invite this response in any way?

3. To what degree might the director be credited here as well as the cameraman? It is not only the cinematographer of *Red Desert* and *Blow-Up* who is praised for the use of color in these films, but also (if not primarily) Antonioni.

Stephen Farber and Estelle Changas, *FILM QUARTERLY* Spring, 1968

Mike Nichols's name is so magical today that even if *The Graduate* had been the worst movie of the year, people would be buzzing reverently about it. As it is, *The Graduate* is only the most cleverly fashionable and confused movie of the year—and the responses, from critics and customers alike, have been ecstatic. We expected a lot—we're young, and so is Nichols; in addition to youth, he has money, talent, intelligence, irreverence. And after lots of quickie exploitation films about teenyboppers and acidheads, *The Graduate* might have been the first movie about today's youth to tell it like it is. But Nichols has too much at stake to risk involving us. He's adored because he's hip and safe at the same time; his audiences know that he won't go too far. (1)

The Graduate opens promisingly enough. Ben, a successful young Eastern college graduate, is returning home to Los Angeles, and Nichols immediately and effectively conveys his isolation by focusing exclusively on Dustin Hoffman's apprehensive face moving through the crowded LA airport. Nichols has said that he chose the thirty-year-old Hoffman (a talented comedian—to get that out of the way) to play his callow young hero because he had a face that suggested suffering. Hoffman himself thought there was something strange about the choice; he felt he wasn't suited to the part, which he described as "a young, conventional squarejawed *Time* Magazine Man of the Year type." Hoffman was right of course. We soon learn that Ben, for all of his credentials and in spite of his vulnerable face, is clean-cut and stupid. He's supposed to be a champion college debater, but he can hardly form a sentence. In the first scenes he's thrown into his rich parents' cocktail and poolside parties; it's easy enough to caricature suburban phoniness, and we see quickly—Nichols provides a slick, superficial summary of anti-bourgeois satire of the last decade—everything that's wrong with LA society. But what does Ben see? He gapes a lot, but he never looks more than bewildered by what's going on. He certainly can't articulate any sort of protest. All he knows is that he wants his future to be "well . . . different. . . ." He really sweats to get that word out, but he doesn't seem capable of going further. When he's troubled, he stares into his bedroom aquarium.

Of course we're supposed to like Ben because he's victimized by all of those nasty, aging country clubbers. (2) In the face of their

---

1. What are Farber and Changas suggesting here?

2. If this is true, Nichols is clearly making use of *culturally induced associations.* The issue is: do we feel we are being manipulated when we see the film?

boozing and their twaddle, he has a chunky innocence that is to endear him to us. Nothing is going on in his head, but because he's "mixed up," as he says at one point, and abused by his parents, audiences cluck over him and rush to give him credit for understanding anxieties that are actually beyond his grasp.

Nichols does use a few fine Simon and Garfunkel songs (written long before the film was conceived) to pump poetic and intellectual content into *The Graduate.* Because the songs, especially "The Sounds of Silence," are so concise, lyrical, eloquent, we're tempted to believe that the film contains their insights and that Ben understands them. We're supposed to assume that Ben shares Paul Simon's perceptions of "people talking without speaking, people hearing without listening" in a world whose "words of the prophet are written on the subway walls," but in truth Ben couldn't *begin* putting the world in that kind of order. He's only a beer-drinking *Time* magazine type, as Hoffman recognized, rather harmlessly stupid and awkward, but tricked up with a suffering face and an *Angst*-ridden song intent on persuading us that he's an alienated generational hero. And audiences eager to believe that all young people are sensitive and alienated and that all old people are sell-outs or monsters gratefully permit Hoffman's mannerisms and Paul Simon's poetry to convince them of a depth in Ben that the part, as written, simply does not contain. (3)

The film's best scenes are the early ones in which Ben is seduced by the wife of his father's partner (superbly played by Anne Bancroft—her performance is reason enough to see the film). Bancroft, a young man's deliciously provocative sexual fantasy come to life, makes us aware that there *is* something to be said for women over thirty. When she's on, Ben might just as well roll over and play dead. Bancroft is engagingly wicked as Mrs. Robinson; she is at once supremely confident of her sexual power and mercilessly casual in the face of Ben's adolescent fear of her. Alone with him in her house, she takes calm delight in exposing her legs, while he ejaculates moral misgivings. Her sophistication enables her to see through his repeated protests: "You *want* me to seduce you, is that what you're trying to tell me, Benjamin?" she chants in poker-faced style. And finally, having trapped him in her daughter's bedroom, she remains utterly

---

3. Is this an instance of the *reverberating heart string?*

cool, while her daring flirtatious assault, comically caught by rapid cuts from bare bosom to Ben's anguished face, leaves him helplessly gasping, "Jesus Christ, Mrs. Robinson!"

Unfortunately, this is about the only scene which allows us to see that Ben is sexually attracted to Mrs. Robinson. Most of the time Nichols insists that Mrs. Robinson is repulsive because she is sexual and Benjamin lovable because he is not. Sheer boredom, Ben confesses, is the only thing which brings him to her time after time. And later he explains that bedding down with Mrs. Robinson meant nothing; it was "just another thing that happened to me . . . just like shaking hands." Apparently we are to believe, as Stanley Kauffman has written, that Ben "sees the older woman's advances as a syndrome of a suspect society," and that he deserves congratulations for his indifference; what seems an astonishing blindness to Mrs. Robinson's very real sexiness is to be taken as a moral victory. (4)

Ben's voice of morality, though, is rather unpleasantly self-righteous: "Do you think I'm proud that I spend my time with a broken-down alcoholic?" The scene in which he tries to liven up their evenings by getting Mrs. Robinson to *talk* to him has been much praised, and it *is* an interesting scene, though not for the reasons given, but because it presents Mrs. Robinson with more complexity than usual. When, in the middle of their abortive conversation, she orders Ben not to take out her daughter, the only reason he can guess for the command is that she thinks he isn't good enough for Elaine, and he announces angrily that he considers this liaison "sick and perverted." Bancroft's face, marvelously expressive of deeply rooted social and personal discontents, makes clear to us that this is *not* Mrs. Robinson's reason, that her reasons are much more intense and tortured than Ben suspects—mostly, presumably, an envy of youth and a fear of being cast off for her daughter—and deserve his sympathy, not his moralistic outrage. Ben is too insensitive to see that when she seems to acknowledge that she thinks her daughter too good for him, it's only out of desperation and confusion; she has feelings more intricate and disturbed than she knows how to

---

4. Is "sexiness" a measurable quantity? And furthermore, is Ben really indifferent? Or is he merely exercising control? Or does the movie fail to provide an answer to these questions? And if so, does this constitute a failing in the film?

explain to him. His rejection of her at this moment may look moral, but given the depth and the anguish of her emotional experience, it's a pretty ugly, unfeeling response. Mrs. Robinson's answer to Ben's plea that she talk to him—"I don't think we have much to say to each other"—proves to be quite accurate, but it doesn't expose her shallowness, as Nichols seems to have intended, it exposes *Ben's*. She has so much more self-awareness than he, and so many more real problems, why *should* she talk to him? Anne Bancroft is really too interesting for Nichol's sentimentalities about the generational gap; (5) so he treats her characterization with no respect; after this scene, he turns her into a hideous witch, an evil Furie maniacally insistent on keeping Ben and her daughter apart. This goes along with the current urge to see the generational conflict as a coloring-book morality play—the young in white, the old in black—but it's a cheap dramatic trick. (6)

What really wins the young audience to Ben is his compulsive pursuit of Mrs. Robinson's daughter Elaine in the second half of the film. His single-minded dedication to securing the girl he pines after may be the oldest staple of movie romance, but it is also manna to today's Love Generation. Elaine, though, is a problem. She's gorgeous, all right, she's earnest, and she smiles nicely, but what Ben sees in her beyond her lovely face is kept a secret from us. She does seem to be as clean-cut and stupid as he is. But since she wears her hair long and uncombed and goes to Berkeley (another put-on, much like Hoffman's suffering face), we're to assume that she's an extraordinary catch. Doesn't the fact that she dates and almost marries a smooth, starched medical student confirm the opposite? (7)

---

5. Why is the film's view of the generation gap judged to be sentimental? Does the review provide a defense of its position?

6. The review suggests that the hysteria of Mrs. Robinson in the face of her earlier control and complexity is a "cheap dramatic trick"? Are you convinced that this is true? Although Mrs. Robinson's circumstances change, the critics still distrust the change in her responses. Why?

7. How is the medical student characterized in the film? That is, how do we know what kind of a guy he is? Do you agree that the use of the medical student serves as a revelation of Katherine's character?

Ben, incidentally, doesn't even admit her physical attractiveness; his excuse for wanting her so desperately is that at last he has found someone he can talk to. What two such uninteresting people could talk about is a real stumper; and Nichols must have thought so too, for he bars us from one of their few conversations, placing them behind the windshield of Ben's convertible. Perhaps if Nichols were a more experienced film director, he could have convinced us of the vitality of Ben's and Elaine's love with some pungent, seductive visuals; but he relies only on modish out-of-focus shots of flowers and foliage (shots that looked a lot prettier in *Two for the Road* anyway).

All that does express their love is an old-fashioned Hollywood Kiss. (8) On their first date, after treating her quite wretchedly, Ben tries to get her to stop crying and kisses her. And that does it. She forgets her humiliation and smiles. It's love at first sight, just like in the movies, but because the actors look casual and sensitive and alienated, audiences think their instant jello of a romance is "real." A little later Elaine learns of Ben's affair with her mother and flees back to Berkeley; he follows her there, and she comes to his room at night to ask why. But first she asks him to kiss her once more, and when he does, she's satisfied; her doubts are erased, and she's ready to marry him. It's all very reminiscent of Betty Grable cheerleader movies. And it's interesting that there seems to be no real sexual attraction between Ben and Elaine. Even their two or three kisses are awfully restrained. After receiving her second kiss, which looks about as exciting as a late-night cup of hot chocolate, Elaine darts quickly out of Ben's door. The movie is rather offensively prudish in splitting sex and love, (9) implying that sexual relationships are sick and perverted, but that in a healthful Young Love relationship—why, sex is the furthest thing from the kids' minds. In this respect the film fits nicely with the flower talk about love, which for all of the bubbles and incense and the boast of promiscuity, is equally insipid, passionless, ultimately quite as sexless.

---

8. In this film, what is the purpose of the "old-fashioned" kiss? How does it contrast with the sexual behavior of Mrs. Robinson and Benjamin? Is it merely, as the critics suggest, another touch of sentimentality?

9. What *intellectual commitment* is suggested by the words "offensively prudish"?

How bizarre it is that the vacuous Elaine, who has been so easily conned into marrying the fraternity's ace make-out king, can cause such a cataclysmic change in Ben. He throws off his lethargy, chases after her and breaks up her wedding at the last minute, bellowing an anguished "Elaine" as he beats against the glass that separates him from the congregation. A minute later, when Ben punches Elaine's father in the stomach, when he beats off the suburbanites with a giant cross and locks the door with it, the audience cheers vigorously—and to give Nichols his due, it's a pleasing, outrageous image. But it's much too glib to turn Ben suddenly into a rebel hero—this same Ben who's spent most of the film staring blankly into his aquarium and lounging by his pool, transformed by a kiss from a sweet litle coed into a fighter for his generation. The motivation may be phony, but we can all laugh at how the old folks get theirs in the end.

The Graduate, like Nichol's film of *Virginia Woolf,* has been applauded for its boldness—never before in an American movie, it is said, could a hero have slept with a woman and married her daughter. The premise *is* arresting, but it's interesting how Nichols blunts it, makes it as easy as possible for his audiences to accept the outrageous. By minimizing Ben's participation in the affair with Mrs. Robinson, by suggesting that it's boring and unpleasant to him, and then by leaving sex out of the relationship with Elaine altogether, the film scampers away from a situation that would be truly challenging and compelling—a young man with strong sexual desire for mother and daughter. (10) Ben doesn't have any sexual desires, apparently, and his unwilling involvement in the affair with Mrs. Robinson lets us off too comfortably. And at a time of much irrelevant nudity and bedroom talk in the movies, this is one film that's entirely too fastidious; the absence of sex in *The Graduate* is a real failure (as it was in *The Family Way*) because the film is, to a large extent, *about* sexuality. But the urgency of Ben's triangular predicament is lost because we don't know much about what goes on in the bedroom, or even in Ben's fantasies. The incestuous longings that lie beneath the surface of the relationships are too uneasily

---

10. The critics seem here to be clarifying what was meant earlier in the review when they characterized Nichols as "hip and safe at the same time."

sketched to carry much force. Any development of the oedipal rivalry between mother and daughter is also skimped. This hostility must be behind Mrs. Robinson's command that Ben not see Elaine, and if Elaine is human, she would have certain feelings of jealousy toward her mother. By making her outrage at Ben's affair *purely moral,* by ignoring its psychological content, the film misses an opportunity to explore its potentially explosive situation with depth and humanity—just as it cheated earlier by defining Ben's response to Mrs. Robinson in purely moral terms. Nichols titillates us with an intrigue that we haven't seen before in a movie, but he never gets close to feelings that would upset us. He knows how to startle, but he also knows how to please.

The movie as a whole is a Youth-grooving movie for old people. Nichol's young people have senile virtues—they're clean, innocent, upright, and cute too. Tired rich audiences can relax and say, "So *that's* what this youthful rebellion is all about; the kids want just what you and I want, Daddy—a happy marriage, a nice home, and they're really so well-behaved." Nichols doesn't risk showing young people who are doing truly daring, irreverent things, or even young people intelligent enough to seriously challenge the way old people live. All that ennobles Ben, after four years of college, is his virginity. He and Elaine are very bland, and that suits the old folks just fine; bankers and dowagers know that it's "in" to celebrate the young, and in *The Graduate* they can join the celebration with a minimum of fret or identification. The film is actually an insult to the young who aren't so goody-goody—young people who have complicated conflicts of loyalty and affection and who aren't able to make such a decisive moral rejection before they marry the most beautiful sweetheart of Sigma Chi.

Yet young people are falling for the film along with the old people, because it satisfies their most infantile fantasies of alienation and purity in a hostile world, their most simplistic notions of the generational gap, and their mushiest daydreams about the saving power of love. The movie swings on their side, though from a safe, rather patronizing position, and bleats that even when the middle-aged degenerates are cruelest, all you need is a closed-mouth kiss.

As for Nichols's film sense, he does seem to be learning. He still holds shots much too long or dresses them up much too self-consciously—as in the scuba-diving episode, a good idea ruined by clumsy direction. His images are mostly clichéd—not just blurs of flowers and sunrippled water and car headlights reflecting on his lens, but even monkeys in the San Francisco zoo. He's good when you feel he's enjoying an unpretentiously silly, charming comic touch for its own sake, and he shows a nice eye for good-natured satiric detail (he's hardly a caustic talent)—Mrs. Robinson watching *The Newlywed Game* on TV, a daffy, myopic lady organist at Elaine's wedding. And perhaps it's not fair to give the impression that the film fails because of expediency and calculated compromise; it may be that Nichols actually did not know what he was doing. He has stated recently, in an interview, that Ben and Elaine are not to be envied at [the] film's conclusion, and that Ben will end up exactly like his parents—which suggests attempts at a more harshly sardonic point of view than the film manages to convey. (11) Why do people cheer so exuberantly and walk out so happily if the film means to criticize Ben? Have they all missed the point? Whatever Nichol's intentions, *The Graduate* never really seems to be attacking the young people; all that can be said is that it celebrates them with a strange lack of conviction, which may once have been meant as savage irony, but comes across only as particularly hollow and ineffective film-making. Along with his handling of actors, Nichols' only real success in the movie is with the same sort of lighthearted, inconsequential farce routines he's provided for Neil Simon's comedies on Broadway; there's no point in encouraging him to believe that he's the seriocomic prophet of the plastic generation. Maybe Nichols does have the talent to do something more important—so far he has the energy and the ambition—but we're not giving to find out as long as an evasive gimmicky hoax like *The Graduate* is trumpeted as a milestone in American film history.

---

11. Note the sophistication which the critics bring to bear on the question of intention. They remind us that it is not the director's intention which is important, but rather the director's accomplishment—the film—which must stand by itself.

Jan Dawson, *SIGHT AND SOUND* Summer, 1968

The structure of Mike Nichols' second feature inevitably reminds one of those brilliant gramophone records on which he and Elaine May, in a series of four or five minute dialogues, worked their way through a succession of characterisations and situations—two Feif-ferish characters, never so distorted as to be unrecognisable, each of them determined to have the last word.

But if the ability to assume several different personalities in as many minutes is a positive attribute in a revue artist, it can be a definite handicap to actors having to establish themselves as credible characters in a coherent narrative. And while *The Graduate* (United Artists) contains several dialogues which are both hilarious and pain-ful, they remain essentially separate—stock situations that involve not distinct individuals but recognisable types: the middle-class father (William Daniels) trying to communicate with his mixed-up son; the dissatisfied older woman (Anne Bancroft) trying to seduce the virgin graduate by alternating threats, cajolery and commands; the younger man trying to get closer to his detached mistress by starting a discussion about Art in the middle of the night; the young lover assuring the outraged husband that it's his daughter (Katharine Ross), not his wife, whom he's really interested in.

Each sequence is faultlessly played in itself, but the connections between them are more formal than plausible. The characters change without really developing. Anne Bancroft, who has some wonderful Jeanne Moreau-style moments, (1) is required to pass from the role of knowing and sardonic seductress to a jealous Fury bent on forcing her daughter into an unhappy marriage. Dustin Hoffman, the passive and essentially conventional graduate, is supposedly galvanised by a

---

1. Does this really tell us anything about Miss Bancroft's perfor-mance? And notice the reviewer's reliance on our sharing his per-ception of Jeanne Moreau.

kiss from a pretty co-ed into acts of revolt and even sacrilege. In a final sequence that owes a lot to *Morgan,* he whisks the bride away from the alter *after* she has pronounced her vows and wards off her relatives by using the cross as a club.

The Graduate's titles unfold against the musical background of Paul Simon's beautiful song "The Sounds of Silence" ("... people talking without speaking/people hearing without listening ...") and this theme, of a desire to communicate matched only by an inability to do so, does serve in part to unify the different episodes. Almost every empty conversation (and it's interesting that Nichols seldom attempts to confront more than two of his characters at the same time) is preluded by one of those painfully earnest pleas in the American vocative ("Ben, can I talk to you for a minute?"). Perhaps it's significant that when the hero finally runs off with the one person he claims he can talk to, they sit together side by side in silence.

Ironically though, it's the hint of serious themes—incest, alienation, the generation gap, the *déjà vu* critique of suburban society—that prevents one enjoying *The Graduate* as the first class entertainment comedy it basically is. The film somehow gets hoist with the petard of its own pretensions, and Nichols ends up like his characters, wanting to communicate something he can't quite get across. (2)

---

2. This seems to be a case of putting down a film because it isn't what it isn't. If the film "hints" at "serious themes"—and incidentally, does it merely hint?—then perhaps it isn't really "basically" an "entertainment comedy."

Renata Adler, *THE NEW YORK TIMES*
February 11, 1968

A Brilliant Breakdown

Seeing "The Graduate" is a bit like having one's most brilliant friend to dinner, watching him become more witty and animated with every moment, and then suddenly becoming aware that what one may really be witnessing is the onset of a nervous breakdown. (1) After a perfect start and in spite of keeping every minor touch and detail perfect all evening long, the movie suddenly begins to exercise a series of basic, totally implausible options. As though the screenplay itself had lost its mind.

The script is quite faithful to the novel of the same title by Charles Webb. The difference is that the book is written quite clearly from the viewpoint of the Graduate, his perspective, his distortions, his caricatures of his elders and of himself. One can adjust to that perspective, make allowances for it, figure out more or less automatically what the reality was. What, in particular, the seduction meant to Mrs. Robinson, why she subsequently behaved as she did, what was really going on. Readers can project from the information there is.

Movies are a more autocratic form; (2) and when "The Graduate," after beginning as a straight, beautifully made Mike Nichols satire, takes on almost imperceptibly the viewpoint of its major character—becomes afraid with him, for example, of Anne Bancroft and begins

---

1. Renata Adler organizes her review about the central metaphor—an informing metaphor if you like—of the dinner guest who has a nervous breakdown. Does this metaphor seem appropriate to the film under discussion?

2. What does Miss Adler mean when she says, "Movies are a more autocratic form"?

to see her as a villainess in a melodrama—it is, in conventional movie terms, very puzzling. Particularly since the acting is so good. Everyone becomes as the Graduate sees him, and only people who share his view of the world can really be completely satisfied with the film after that. Or people who are so delighted with sheer professionalism that they don't care too much about messages. Those who expect the movie to maintain the clear external focus with which it began become exasperated, do not understand the claims that are made for it, and suspect the film—for quite a long interval—of cracking up.

The breakdown, such as it is, knocks a few times before it occurs in force. The first intimation is when we are asked to believe that Dustin Hoffman is a track star named Benjamin Braddock. That is what the script says. But it is implausible. It is not the part Dustin Hoffman plays, or the one Mike Nichols directs him in, or the person the movie is about. Hoffman's whole situation in the movie, his whole interest really, is as a shy, inhibited intellectual (probably Jewish) who has never played on any team in his life. (3) That is clear from the first. The beginning of the movie, however, inspires confidence in so many other ways—Hoffman and his suitcase advancing through the credits along an airport conveyor belt, the cocktail party, the man who has the single word, plastics, to say to him—that one is willing for a time to believe almost anything. Hoffman himself, with his stare and his nervous bipping noise, acts his real part so well that one forgets his nominal part for a while, in absolute trust.

The second knocking comes when Anne Bancroft throws his car keys to him and they land in the fishbowl. It is off key. It is broader than anything that has gone before. Such great things are continually done, however, with shots of water throughout the film—Hoffman's agonized face photographed through the fishbowl, his descent into the pool in his diving gear, his floating on the pool all summer, and the wonderful cut of his leaping onto a raft in the pool and being borne along by Anne Bancroft in bed—that we forget this, too. Perhaps it is necessary, perhaps his hand plunging in after the keys is symbolic. Anyway, it is funny.

---

3. What do you make of the critic's contention that Benjamin "really" is a "shy, inhibited intellectual (probably Jewish)"?

But in the Robinsons' house, it knocks again. Why is she coming on like such a monster? Why is he behaving like such a buffoon? Well, it is all right: some of the movie's frequent uses of words like "upset," "neurotic," and "mixed up" occur here and they seem to explain a lot. The humor has become too broad and Mrs. Robinson is too grotesque. The whole movie has begun to share his fear of her, and to complicate matters she seems for a moment (with a Jewish inflection on, "Now if you won't do me a simple favor I don't know what") to be sharing the film's ethnic schizophrenia. But the arrival of Mr. Robinson, the perfect dialogue, and his strong acting soothe Benjamin and stabilize the movie again.

There follows a completely reassuring, very funny, absolutely controlled run of film. In the book, Benjamin calls Mrs. Robinson only after he has been on the road for a few weeks, fighting fires, hitching rides, sleeping with prostitutes in cow pastures. This is clearly not the movie Benjamin's sort of thing. It is wisely left out.(4) The first hotel scenes are wonderful, the reception, the bar, the lobby, the phone calls, his hand on the room clerk's bell, brushing his teeth, her rubbing the spot from her dress. When he kisses Anne Bancroft in the bedroom before she has time to exhale her cigarette, it is one of the most hilarious moments on film. The seduction is right because this is how it was, or the way it might happen to anybody. They are both still human at this point.

It is in the bedroom scene where they argue that trouble starts in earnest and the movie's early symptoms return. Benjamin, whom the film had earlier alternately mocked and treated kindly, becomes cruel, boorish and stupid. He begins baiting Mrs. Robinson. In terms of the book's track star, this makes a certain amount of sense. He is a lout. He is not aware. But Benjamin in the movie has been, until this point, sometimes a jerk but essentially a sensitive young man. Even the alienation and sense of guilt he is supposed to be acting from would not make him behave as he does. Suddenly, everything about him seems wrong. His still calling Anne Bancroft Mrs. Robinson seems a tired joke in the script. His flat stubborn baby voice and the relentless stupidity of his remarks throughout the film force themselves upon one's attention. It becomes clear that he has never

---

4. Do you think it is pertinent to compare the novel and the film? Does it help the filmgoer in experiencing the film?

been a very interesting character, and that, unless this scene is being shot entirely from his own self-mocking, awry perspective, he is unreal.

And the options chosen for Anne Bancroft are really strange. There are, after all, some reasonable objections she might have to permitting the young man she has been sleeping with to take her daughter out. But from this moment on, Benjamin and the script choose to regard her objections as purely venomous and insane. She makes no further sense. Even the photography collaborates: none of the older people make a plausible move or are ever photographed as other than really ugly again.

Suddenly, her whole previous behavior is cast in doubt. It was presumably out of kindness, or desire, or affection, or some human thing that she slept with Benjamin in the first place; and it might be human for her to regard his dating her daughter as obscene. (And she is given one tragic-looking moment under Benjamin's interrogation in bed, as though the film were about to relent and make her plausible.) But it isn't treated that way and for a while, she and Benjamin and the entire "Graduate" go haywire.

The business of the dancer with the separately rotating breasts is too strong, mother and lover would not race to confide the affair to Mrs. Robinson's daughter, jokes like Benjamin's dialogue about his intention to marry (Father: that sounds to me like a half baked idea. Benjamin: Oh, no. It's completely baked.) simply emphasize the wavering focus upon him, and the "How could you rape my mother?" fiction simply makes Elaine Robinson unreal for a moment, too. It is almost all that way in the book and—literal truth or not—it doesn't work there either. It is not realism, or absurdism, or satire. It is out of control.

But the movie continues to surround everything with details of immense intelligence, competence and care (Mrs. Robinson and Ben's mother looking so much alike. Benjamin's new smoking habit, all the comedy routines that work) that watching the film for a while is like observing a loved and meticulous lunatic.

As soon as Elaine comes to his boarding house, though, to kiss him, everything becomes right again. This scene is so convincing and well done that a whole new reservoir of trust is established, and all the succeeding absurdist touches (including another conclusive demonstration that Benjamin could not possibly have been a track star) seem simply fine absurdist touches. That is all. The movie reasserts control just about the time Benjamin begins taking initiatives, and by the time his car is racing across the Golden Gate Bridge, with the familiar Simon and Garfunkel song, "Here's to you, Mrs. Robinson. Jesus loves you more than you can know," the film is at top speed again. The perspective makes no further demands upon one's preconceptions about old and young. (5) And one is certainly in the hands of the most brilliant, if rather unstable, movie in quite some time.

---

5. Miss Adler's point is similar to that made by Farber and Changas. Notice that she shares their assumption that the film should not, to use Miss Adler's words, "make demands upon one's preconceptions." Is this always true?

HIGH NOON

NEWSWEEK

July 14, 1952

High Noon (United Artists). Judged on action and suspense alone, (1) this story of a few morning hours in the frontier town of Hadleyville would be a must for Western fans. Add a string of plausible characterizations (2) and an excellent performance by Gary Cooper as a former town marshal, and "High Noon" moves up into the class of absorbing drama.

The sun is high when three riders of the disbanded Miller gang lope into town and take up an enigmatic vigil at the dinky railroad depot. At 10:40 a.m. a telegram brings the news that their leader, Frank Miller—supposedly tucked away for life on a murder conviction—has been unaccountably pardoned. In less than no time, all Hadleyville knows who will be on the noon train and that the man Miller will be gunning for is Will Kane (Cooper), the marshal who broke up the gang five years earlier.

---

1. In this review, is the film ever judged on any other grounds than "action and suspense"?
2. What makes for "plausible" characterization?

When the telegram arrives, Kane is about to move on with the Quaker bride (Grace Kelly) who had persuaded him to turn in his tin star and reject a life of violence. Urged by his wife and friends, the ex-marshal does make the start, but a few miles out of danger he turns back, knowing that some day, in some future town, he will have to outdraw the vengeful Miller in a showdown.

Part of Carl Foreman's screenplay is a cynical, discouraging report on Hadleyville's desire for law and order without the courage to contribute to the effort. Long before noon the good citizens are safely indoors; the coffinmaker is working overtime in the back of his shop, and the saloonkeeper is stacking up for a holiday night at his pub. Here and there a few Hadleyites respond to Kane's attempt at mustering a posse—a reluctant family man, a hero-worshipping boy —but in the end the man with the badge is left alone in the deserted streets when the noon train chugs in.

Director Fred Zinnemann has staged this one-sided climax in the great Western tradition, and he is just as effective in dissecting the nervous tremors of the beleaguered town, and in reflecting the white, slanting heat of its sun-parched streets. Katy Jurado, a newcomer from Mexico, adds pressure as Kane's discarded sweetheart, and minor digressions from the main action are helped by Thomas Mitchell, Lloyd Bridges, Otto Kruger, and James Millican. Very much part of the Stanley Kramer production is the Dimitri Tiomkin score that includes the ballad "High Noon," sung effectively by Tex Ritter. (3)

---

3. We are offered in these paragraphs Kane's explicit motivations, together with the literal story line of the film. Is there any suggestion that, below this surface, implicit meanings may be found which extend beyond the events of Hadleyville and its brave ex-sheriff? And if we see such significance, are we reading into the film?

Bosley Crowther, *THE NEW YORK TIMES*
August 3, 1952

A Western Legend

There isn't the slightest reason why anyone need apologize or feel embarrassed about the Western—as a type of movie, that is. (1) It is certainly the most indigenous and perhaps the most potential genre we have, not only for pictorial demonstrations but for the stating of strong, heroic themes. This is said in complete recognition of the many crimes committed in the name of the Western and the utter desecration that has occurred from its overwork. But it is also said in remembrance of the many great Westerns that have been made and the every-so-often reassurance that there are more great ones yet to come.

Since the days of the Robin Hood adventures of Bronco Billy and William S. Hart, the legends of frontier heroics have been grist for the movie-makers' mills. James Cruze's "The Covered Wagon" and John Ford's "The Iron Horse" expanded the horizons of the genre to embrace brave deeds of national enterprise. Mr. Ford's

---

1. Does the establishment of a genre sometimes arm us with a particularly rigid set of *aesthetic presuppositions* which act as a barrier to the experiencing of films which seem to be part of that genre? To what extent does this happen with *High Noon* and thus prevent us from experiencing the film as a single and particular work of art? And what makes for a genre, anyway? Is every film set in the West a Western? Is *The Misfits,* for example, a Western? Conversely, can a Western take place in the East? Is *West Side Story,* which uses many of the conventions of the Western, actually better understood as part of that genre? And, incidentally, does seeing *High Noon* as an original within a genre perhaps inflate its value?

subsequent "Stagecoach" brought the subtle play of character within its range and William Wellman's "The Ox-Bow Incident" pitched social drama within the Western's frame. Now we have Stanley Kramer's brilliant and electric production, "High Noon," to manifest further the achievement of mature dramatic expression in the genre.

Moral Courage

For "High Noon," directed by Fred Zinnemann from a dandy Carl Foreman script, is as honest and pertinent a drama as we've had on the screen this year—a drama of moral courage in the face of bullying threats, a drama of one man's basic bravery in the midst of a townful of cowards. It is a story that bears a close relation to things that are happening in the world today, where people are being terrorized by bullies and surrendering their freedoms out of senselessness and fear. (2)

In substance, it is simply the story of how the marshal in a Western town, on the day of his wedding and retirement, elects to stick around and face up to a vengeful killer who is returning from prison, rather than cut and run; how he bears the disheartening desertion of his wife and the townsfolk, one by one, as the magnitude of the peril and the zero hour draw nigh; and then how he steps forth from his office, empty and alone, to shoot it out with the killer and his henchmen when noon strikes and the train arrives.

That is the outline of the story, and in every respect it reveals its straight and legitimate descendance in the line of Western legend films. The forces of law and order are confronted with wickedness, and the good man and the bad man are finally brought face to face. But, in two strong respects, this presentation rises far above the gun of Western fare; the drama is beautifully written and it is brilliantly presented and played.

Mr. Foreman has not dangled puppets, he has truly and artfully conceived real characters whose motives and dispositions are clear and credible. The marshal, played by Gary Cooper, is not the usual

---

2. In this paragraph Crowther makes clear what constitutes excellence in his critical lexicon. Is it possible that the complexities of contemporary life makes it possible for us to find pertinence in any fictional (or, for that matter, historical) account of the past?

square-jawed, stalwart sort; (3) he is a tired and unglamorous sheriff who would gladly crawl off in a hole if he thought that would mean an avoidance of a showdown—but he knows it won't. He is a man with the sense to meet a challenge, not duck in the hope it will go away. This marshal can give a fine lesson to the people in Hollywood today.

Realistic

And others are equally realistic (4)—Lloyd Bridges as a brash young deputy who, in the showdown, withholds his assistance because he is sore at not having been given the sheriff's job; Thomas Mitchell as a prudent townsman who thinks of commerce rather than right; Otto Kruger as a judge who packs his law books, folds up his American flag and quietly steals away. Grace Kelly and Katy Jurado are also true as the wife and an old flame.

But it is also Mr. Zinnemann's direction that gives this picture magnitude and class. He has constructed a real pictorial ballad with imagination and skill—a ballad of poetic rhythm (5) that flows from realistic images paced to the strolling-minstrel measures of a fine Dimitri Tiomkin musical score.

Mr. Zinnemann has so made his picture that you get the dusty feel of a western town, the lean and stolid nature of its people, the loneliness of the plains and the terrible tension of waiting for violence and death in the afternoon. This is no story-book western; this seems a replica of actuality. It is a picture that does honor to the western and elevates the medium of films.

---

3. Is Crowther implying that there is a positive value in the mere violation of convention? Can there be constructive use of film convention?

4. Is Crowther here offering us insight into his reasons for admiring the avoidance of convention? And is he also implying that mere violation of convention makes for realism?

5. It is useful to examine Mr. Crowther's metaphors. What is he seeing when he perceives *High Noon* as a "pictorial ballad"? Or as a "ballad of poetic rhythm?"

Alan Stanbrook, *FILMS AND FILMING*
May, 1967

A Man for all Movies: the Films of Fred Zinnemann

Fred Zinnemann's works encompass a western, a musical, a religious picture and assorted dramas and melodramas, but this versatility merely diverts attention from the underlying coherence of his films. Pervading them is a single, unifying concept, but it is hydra-headed and sometimes obscured by a multiplicity of aspect. (1) At the heart of Zinnemann's films lies a preoccupation with identity and individuality. He is concerned with the uniqueness of the human personality and has little sympathy with a purely mechanistic attitude to man. Any system which herds people together and demands uniformity of behaviour is abhorrent to him. For Zinnemann, man's salvation lies in recognising his duty to be and to prove himself at all times. Inevitably Zinnemann's heroes are figures apart, for they cannot fulfill themselves as cogs in a wheel; even if they are married they must resolve their problems themselves. (2)

The intense isolation of Zinnemann's characters was embodied in its most quintessential form in *High Noon.* Will Kane, the hero, is fully aware of his identity and duty. Tempted to leave Hadleyville with his new bride, he knows that if he does not stay and face Frank Miller he will 'lie a coward in his grave'. Though he has technically relinquished the post of marshal, his successor is not due till the next day and he realises that the delay could give Miller

---

1. Stanbrook claims that all of Zinnemann's films (as disparate as they are) have an "underlying coherence . . . a single, unifying concept." Is this an illustration of the *director as barrier* fostered by the *auteur* theory?
2. Is a *private association* at work here?

and his desperadoes time to re-establish Hadleyville as 'just another wide open town'.

Set against Will's resolute conviction is the venality of the township itself. Many of the inhabitants—the bar tenders and hotel clerks—miss the bad old days when trade was booming and resent the law and order brought by Kane. And even those who are grateful are not prepared to form a posse to prevent a recurrence of lawlessness. It is the political parable—the suggestion that fascism thrives on collective inertia—that is uppermost in Carl Foreman's script. But Zinnemann sees the story differently as a variant on his theme of the importance of the individual and his compulsion to realise himself to the full. (3)

The director's artistic credo here achieves its richest and most lucid expression. Curiously, however, scant attention has been paid to the film's technical skill, even the chronometric structure having been widely misrepresented. The film runs eighty four minutes, little short of the ninety minutes between the wedding scene at 10.30 and the arrival of the noon train. But the assumption that real time and film time follow an identical course would be quite inaccurate. Clocks are strategically placed throughout the film—in the court room, in the marshal's office, at the rail-road depot—but the hands on the clock faces have little connection with those on the cinema clock as the film unrolls. Time is often artificially prolonged: in two scenes between Lloyd Bridges and Katy Jurado, separated by ten minutes of real time, the clock in her room has advanced by only a few minutes. Time elapses very much faster early in the film, so that the subsequent slowing down increases the tension in the moments before the train arrives. Fifteen minutes on the cinema clock absorb thirty minutes of screen time and there is a constant sense of time running out at an accelerated rate. In Katy Jurado's room there are two clocks so that from every camera angle we are aware of the time and when Kane comes down the stairs after leaving her, the hotel clerk is standing in the well moving the hands on the grandfather clock forward.

After the initial rapid consumption of time, reflecting Kane's panic at the thought of Miller's return, the pace eases, seventy minutes of

---

3. Stanbrook distinguishes here between the meaning of the script and the meaning of the film. On what grounds is this distinction made?

film time taking fifty-five on the clock. The chronometric and psychological measurements of time are still out of alignment but a brake has been applied. Immediately before noon the process is dramatically reversed and three minutes of the story are spun out for five of real time, building up a powerful atmosphere of tension. Finally the closing stages of the story (taking place after noon) are compressed into the last fifteen minutes, whereas in reality they would have occupied double this time, giving a concentrated impression of rapid and violent action. (4)

Symbolism is constantly invoked to underline the significance of the action but there is no gratuitous striving after effect, the symbols emerging rather from properties belonging naturally to the locality. The tin star, the marshal's badge of office, plays a dual role as a symbol of law and order and of the violence which Kane hopes to abandon. As the ex-marshal says, 'in the end you wind up dying all alone on some dusty street. For what? For nothing—for a tin star'. The speech is recalled with added force later when Kane's wife drives past him on her way to the depot and Zinnemann's camera cranes up to frame the lone figure walking down the dusty street to his rendezvous with Frank Miller. The scene is matched in the last sequence, where Kane is seen standing with his wife over the dead body of Frank Miller. Gradually the townsfolk crowd back onto the deserted street and as a final gesture of fulfilment and disgust, Kane drops the tin star in the dust.

But this is only one of the many symbols. (5) When Kane seeks to enlist the aid of the judge in forming a posse, the latter is discovered removing the American flag and the scales of justice from the courtroom prior to flight. The depot itself, like the film's obsession with clocks, becomes a motif periodically interjected as a reminder of Kane's destiny. And, significantly, in the rhythmic cutting of the final seconds before noon, the montage ends with a track towards

---

4. Stanbrook does not merely say that Zinnemann manipulates time, but shows us how it is done.

5. Is Stanbrook failing to distinguish between ready-made symbols (conventional signs with immediately recognizable meanings such as the sheriff's badge or the flag) and symbols whose value and significance must be established by the particular context in which they appear?

the chair in which Miller had vowed vengeance, followed by a cut to the depot as the train pulls in. (6) The movements of the camera and the train are in head-on collision, symbolising the conflict about to be played out. (7)

One of the most arresting symbols is the choice of clothes for the central characters. Kane is dressed in black, emphasising the sign of death hanging over him. But so is Helen, his ex-mistress, in direct contrast to the white wedding gown of his wife. Yet it is Helen who is the more sympathetic character—the traditional values attached to black and white are purposely reversed.

The idea of death is kept continually before the audience. As Kane enters a barber's shop he is disturbed by a sound of hammering from the funeral parlour at the rear. Searching for help, he collides with a group of children already dramatising the imminent gunfight—'Bang, you're dead Kane'—and the agonising moments before the first whistle announces the noon train are filled with a scene showing Kane writing his will. He is alone, as the ex-marshal had said, and the only people prepared to back him are a boy and a man with one eye—'in the country of the blind. . . .'

Zinnemann's greatest success lies in the establishment of attitudes and relationships, seen at its best in the opening sequence. Nothing is spoken, but as the three horsemen converge at the crossroad we already suspect from their resolute glances that they are bent on some desperate action, confirmed by the shot of a woman crossing herself as they ride by. The reactions of the inhabitants are minutely particularised, the fear of the stable lad, who backs away as the camera tracks past, and the contented smiles of the men in the saloon. A sudden tilt up to the marshal's sign and the first line of dialogue ('You in a hurry?') discloses the purpose of the ride into town—to murder the marshal. The scene is intercut with the wedding scene between the marshal and the Quaker girl in the judge's office so that in one short scene the exposition has been deftly despatched.

---

6. What is rhythmic cutting? Montage? A track?

7. Has the meaning of "symbol" shifted here? Is everything that has more than a literal meaning to be called a symbol? And, if so, is it a useful word? And would Stanbrook's insightful commentary have been more convincing and useful had he been more precise in his application of this highly connotative and elusive term?

It remains only to identify the other characters and their respective reactions. Kane is rapidly sent on his honeymoon to avoid bloodshed and, as the carriage rolls past, Zinnemann cuts to a shot of his deputy gazing down in amusement from the hotel window. A slight pan to the left reveals the presence of his mistress, the Mexican saloon owner, Helen Ramirez. Already it is apparent that he has his own reasons for wishing Kane to leave.

Amy, Kane's wife, is opposed to violence on principle and refuses to go back with her husband. Her attitude is conveyed by a careful timing of the theme song ('Do not forsake me, oh my darling') to coincide with her decision to leave on the noon train. She goes to the depot to buy her ticket and a long shot of the three gunmen eyeing her foreshadows her fate if Kane is killed.

Glances rather than words are the key to Zinnemann's revelation of relationships. When Kane's deputy kisses her, Helen turns away in boredom. In a later scene, when she decides to sell the saloon on generous terms, her partner exclaims 'You know, my wife . . .' and Helen immediately freezes in resentment of the implied antipathy of the town matrons. Helen, in a sense, unites the various groups of the story. She has been Miller's mistress, to judge from her haughty gaze as she encounters him at the station. She has even been Kane's mistress, as we gather from the hotel clerk's cynical remark 'Think you can find it all right?' as he goes upstairs to see her.

The director's feel for the correct camera position is infallible. A high angle shot as Kane enters and leaves the church meeting accentuates the timidity of the congregation and Kane's isolation. But Zinnemann really comes into his own in the precise geography of the closing gunfight. As Kane walks towards the camera, a ninety-degree pan reveals Miller and his men advancing down the side street. Similarly when Kane takes shelter in the hay loft, the camera is placed in the roof beside the aperture so that we can see the respective positions of Kane and the gunman stalking him from below at all times. It is finally this care in the planning of the slightest detail that makes *High Noon* Zinnemann's most controlled and successful film. (8)

---

8. Has Stanbrook helped us to understand the difference between a novel and a film?

Jules and Jim, Courtesy of *Janus Films*

JULES AND JIM

Stanley Kauffmann, *THE NEW REPUBLIC*
May 7, 1962

No Design for Living

Love has its risks; and the risk of loving art as much as the French do is that one can become so interested in invention and refinement of technique, so immersed in the atmosphere of art, that one loses sight of purposes. It is a confusion of the sheer happiness of being in the studio (paint or film) with the reason for being there. (1)

Jules and Jim, the new film by Francois Truffaut who made *The 400 Blows,* is an instance. No viewer can be unmoved by its joy in imagination, by the way Truffaut runs *to* the film form to experiment and dare, by his pure reveling in the powers and possibilities of the

---

1. What is Kauffmann implying here about the purposes of art? There are those who would say that art is for art's sake. (R.I.P. Walter Pater, et al.) Must art have a purpose beyond itself—beyond its own creation? Is there an *intellectual commitment* at work in Kauffmann's remark?

medium. Nor is this to patronize the picture as a mere attempt; there is very much in it that is beautiful.

The story is about a triangle which is at first isosceles and ends up virtually equilateral. Jules and Jim are two young writer-friends in 1912 Paris, the former a German, the latter a Frenchman (who insists on the English nickname). Together they explore art, sport, love of women. Jules falls in love with Catherine, a French girl, who eventually marries him. Jim loves her, too, but says nothing, contenting himself with another girl who loves him but whom he declines to marry. The war separates the two men. Afterwards, Jim visits Jules and Catherine and their daughter in the Rhineland and discovers that Jules is unhappy because he is no longer truly Catherine's husband; she has lovers. Still, Jules is satisfied as long as she will live with him. Jim and Catherine become lovers (with Jules' knowledge), then she tires of him because he cannot give her a child. Jules and Catherine move to France, near Paris. There is an attempt by Catherine to renew the affair with Jim which ends when she threatens to shoot him. He runs away. Some time later the three meet amiably in a film theater and go to a country restaurant. While Jules watches, she invites Jim for a drive and plunges the car into a lake. Both Catherine and Jim are drowned; cremated; Jules sees the ashes interred and walks away through the cemetery.

The disjointed effect of this synopsis is not unfair to the film. It begins as a light-hearted *vie boheme* comedy of Toulouse-Lautrec Paris (with charming music by George Delerue). The war intervenes —at too great a length for its importance to the story.(2) Then the triangle resumes with a changed tone: Strindberg's goddess-gutter view of women combined with the Emancipated Neurotic of the twenties. The shift would be interesting if it were a true modulation: time finding the bones beneath the flesh-bloom of youth. But the

---

2. Since the war does go on for a long time, is Kauffmann merely making a nonsense statement when he says the war intrudes for too long a time? In the story, admittedly, the war is long. Would the film have been *better* with a shorter war, or merely different? And, given the long war, it would seem that the critic has the responsibility of trying to discover the reason for its length. We must first establish that the long war serves no purpose before we can decide that it *intrudes* in the story. It *is* the story.

structure seems haphazard, full of irrelevancies, almost cantankerous. What starts as a rueful-happy Gallic *Design for Living* tilts sideways to become a semi-pathological study—to no perceptible character or thematic point. Besides, in this script by Truffaut and Jean Gruault (from a novel by Henri-Pierre Roché), there is a growing disparity between what is said and what we see. Jules says he puts up with Catherine's behavior because her presence blesses him to whatever degree she remains in his life. Jim worships her on more or less the same ground. But where is this warm beneficent woman? We see a self-indulgent sensualist, self-consciously sensitive, full of whims and impatience, who never really does anything for anybody and who—because she is finally rejected by Jim—kills him and herself in front of her husband. And even this seems pettish caprice; she and Jules were again living together pleasantly and just happened to meet Jim at the movies. (3)

Goethe's *Elective Affinities* is quoted in the film, and there is a hint that a parallel is intended. Although Goethe's novel deals with a quadrangle, it has certain resemblances in story and idea. But can the deaths of Catherine and Jim have been contrived for the same reason as those of Ottilie and Edward? Goethe said: "Either morality triumphs or is defeated. . . . Ottilie and Edward had to perish after they had given free rein to their inclinations. Therein consists the triumph of the moral principle." Can this heavy sentimentality have been Truffaut's goal?

The patchwork effect of the script is reflected in Truffaut's direction, which returns us to the matter of art for artmaking's sake. The film is such a fireworks display of cinematic techniques and devices that our first impression is that we are in the hands of a master. Soon, however, we feel that we are only in the hands of an imaginative enthusiast. The film is filled with intense close-ups, lovely lighting effects, swift cuts, investigations of texture. There are freezes and resumptions of movement in mid-scene as the camera is arbi-

---

3. There are two points to note here. First, *is* there a "disparity"? Does Jules say that he is blessed by Catherine's warmth or beneficence? Or is it possible that it is her very sensuality, her sensitivity, her whims which he worships? Second, even if there is disparity, might this not be one of the points of the film? We all know, after all, that love is blind. Are we seeing a *private association* or a *culturally induced association* or neither at work here?

trarily stopped for a moment; there are sequences in which the camera is hand-held for no apparent reason; there are trick fade-ins. (On a black screen the upper right corner of the next shot is seen, then it spreads out to fill the screen.) Some of the newsreel shots of the war are distended to fill the wide screen, some are used in their original 35 mm. width.

Shot by shot, almost all of the film is visually exquisite. (4) (For one example, the shot in which the three shutters of the white beach house are thrown open in the brilliant morning sunshine.) But there is no controlling sense of style or of pertinence, only a coltish enjoyment of the camera's potentialities. What is the point of the scene in which Catherine's nightgown catches fire and Jim extinguishes it? Why the long silence when the trio sit down to their first meeting after the war? Why the long song she sings with her lover Albert? (5) Because Truffaut enjoyed these scenes in themselves; that seems to be the only reason. They are all well done but are unrelated to the whole, thus despite their excellence of execution—in fact, because of it—make the film ultimately disappointing.

As Jules, Oskar Werner has a sweet, tousled quality, full of canine patience. As Jim, Henri Serre presents a handsome Gaugin-like face but does little more. It is Jeanne Moreau, as Catherine, who gives not only the pivotal but the best performance: mercurial, egocentric, tyrannical, appealing. Whether she is kidding her own femininity in newsboy's cap and painted moustache or sitting as *hausfrau* in steel-rimmed spectacles and high shoes or embracing a lover, she is supplying a better performance than the part can support. Her Catherine is a character in search of an author.

Truffaut said in a recent interview:

> My films are circus shows . . . After the elephant comes the conjuror; after the conjuror, the bear. I even arrange an interval round about the sixth reel because people may be getting a bit tired. At the seventh reel I take them in hand again and try to end up with the best thing in the show.

---

4. Is there some contradiction between seeing Truffaut as "only . . . an imaginative enthusiast" and at the same time as the creator of a "visually exquisite" film?
5. Can you provide answers to these questions?

When Diaghileff commissioned Cocteau to work for his ballet company, he said, *"Jean, étonne-moi."* This seems to be Truffaut's principal esthetic. There is a lot less here than meets the eye, (6) but what does meet the eye is frequently astonishing.

---

6. While this is an amusing play on words, can there ever be less than meets the eye? Isn't Kauffmann here offering us a clue to his resistance to the film? Hasn't he dismissed much of what has met his eye? Has he really tried to answer his own questions?

R. M. Franchi, *N.Y. FILM BULLETIN: AMERICA'S FILM MONTHLY* III, 3, issue 44

JULES AND JIM . . . Even the title conjurs to baffle, for this film is about neither Jules nor Jim. It is about Katherine and the actress who brilliantly plays her, Jeanne Moreau.

Truffaut, in his third feature film, shows us the major weakness of his "Politique"—granted it is a weakness readily self-admitted. (1) One can dismiss Michael Curtiz—a career of banality. But one cannot dismiss CASABLANCA. It can be explained away as "Actor's Cinema", but that too is inadequate, for CASABLANCA exists and, as long as it does, we must recognize it as a masterpiece of its own genre. It is much the same with JULES AND JIM.

---

1. Who is Franchi's audience? Do you think that not knowing what "Politique" is is *not being with it?*

Truffaut proved himself a major director with THE 400 BLOWS and SHOOT THE PIANO PLAYER, but if JULES AND JIM were the only film to arise out of a career filled with atrocities, it would still command respect. Not so with the two earlier films, for only with a liberal soaking in Truffaut's background can they be appreciated for the major works that they are. The compromises of THE 400 BLOWS and the extravagances of SHOOT THE PIANO PLAYER are not detriments to a critical appreciation for those who understand Truffaut. JULES AND JIM needs no such pre-knowledge in order to exist as a great work. (2)

JULES AND JIM, the growing mystique of Truffaut's career to date, the whole application of the "Politique" to its creator, the habitual proclivity of "in" cinematic references—all these elements are neatly tied into a telephone call I received a few months ago from a friend recently returned from Europe. Upon being asked if he had seen anything interesting, the friend replies, "I saw a great new Renoir film." I answer, "Oh, I didn't know LE CAPORAL EPINGLE was finished." "No it isn't—I meant JULES AND JIM".

If THE 400 BLOWS is Jean Vigo, if SHOOT THE PIANO PLAYER is Hitchcock cum Walsh, etc., then JULES AND JIM is Renoir *pur sang*. But more specifically it is about the ideal of woman in the films of Renoir (vide PICNIC ON THE GRASS). It is again, about Jeanne Moreau—the totally modern, totally liberated free spirit who wanders the "boughed halls of arcadie" concerned only with absolutes, unburdened with moral responses ("This is vitrol for lying eyes".) (3) It is exactly this overblown phraseology which best pinpoints the elusive quality of the personality projected by Moreau through Truffaut's ever directorial eye.

And perhaps it is this over-self consciousness which separates Truffaut from any other director working today, with the possible

---

2. If *Jules and Jim* needs no such "pre-knowledge to exist as a great work," why does Franchi find it necessary to make so many references to directors, films, and ideas which in fact constitute such "preknowledge"? What would seem then to be the relationship of all this knowledge to the experience of the film?

3. Note that Franchi sees this as a film about Jeanne Moreau and not about Katherine who is played by Jeanne Moreau.

exception of Welles, for JULES AND JIM is a film about two things: people and cinema.(4)

Truffaut has never relented in his role as a critic—an ingrown incentive without which the film would become a dull piece of work for the director. Does it matter if no one realizes that the scene of Jim's sawing wood during the German idyll is a reference to Murnau's SUNRISE? It didn't realize until I was informed and it didn't detract at all from enjoyment of the film. But if Truffaut had been denied this oblique reference, it would most certainly have detracted from his pleasure.

For all this, what we have to work with is simple enough. Stated frankly: a *ménage à trois*. An ideal situation for an unconventional film. An even more ideal situation for a "pure" exploitation film. Instead we are handed a soaring, lyrical full salute to freedom. Not "free love". Not even necessarily "moral freedom", but rather that freedom which grows from a relationship that is completely honest and innocent. What we have is Truffaut directing Moreau in a role which recreates the entire character of a generation. Truffaut himself has created the standard: a good film can be summarized in one word. The word for JULES AND JIM is: bohemianism.

The devaluation of the bohemian ideal, its inevitable replacement by the beat gospel, has left the word and the concept with little currency today. That a creature like Katherine could exist and, as she does for the first part of the film, thrive, is more a comment on our times than a comment on the turn-of-the-century reality which Truffaut recreates so vividly. The key to the disintegration of the *vie bohème* is in the newsreel footage which is interpolated throughout the film, ending with the book-burnings of Isherwood's Germany in the early thirties. As Truffaut stated in an interview: when they started burning books it was the end of the era of the Jules' and Jims (and Katherines).

As sexual freedom has "grown" over the past fifty years, as the Victorian restrictions and pruderies have been eliminated from our moral code, ironically we have been losing personal liberty—for any

---

4. Kauffmann has implied that *Jules and Jim* is art for art's sake. Franchi suggests, when he says the film is about "cinema," that it is art about art. Are these critics really making two different points? Is there a difference between art for art and art about art?

non-conventional behavior now seems to be as codified as the restrictions once were. The currency of freedom has been debased by inflation.

In keeping with this theory of diminishing returns, it is Katherine who suffers most. The swift emancipation of women has also tended to lead them into more restricted paths—at least those who were free to begin with. Her suicide (immolation) is inevitable as the last action of a free spirit who has been trapped. Irony is ever the keynote, for her exit is accomplished with a car, one of the great levelling factors of the years of liberation, one more technological advance (among many) which changed the moral tone of our time. There is little in this film which does not correspond to this inexorable thematic progression. All the elements point in one tragic direction. Coutard's photography, which at the opening is fluid, almost wild in its rule-breaking, becomes increasingly quiet and conventional towards the end—taking a more tack, moving back to cease commenting on the action. Delerue's music with its early ecstatic extravagances, especially during the seashore visit, seems to grow moodily somber as disaster approaches, but deceptively so since Truffaut's chiaroscuro mood changes are once more introduced via ebullient outbursts of tuneful melodies in the midst of near-tragedy. Truffaut has controlled all these elements—even, of course, to the pace of editing to make his point and it is well taken.

Technique never was and never will be Truffaut's forte. His eclecticism tends to defeat him, but most of all, the very aspect which makes him a great director, his fierce interest in people, is the most damaging. Renoir, Apollinaire, Lubitsch, Murnau, Vigo, Hitchcock, etc. are strange bedfellows as common physical elements of a film, but no stranger than Jules and Jim and Katherine as the common personal elements. JULES AND JIM teaches us a lesson: always expect something different from Truffaut, on the surface.

With THE 400 BLOWS, he gave us the definitive first film: an artful work, one made with a calculating commercial eye. SHOOT THE PIANO PLAYER is the definitive second film: an off-beat, funny, very personal joy ride, taking full advantage of the freedom granted by the first. With JULES AND JIM, Truffaut once more creates a new standard, a new category and gives the "Third Film"—a film in which the director finally, with a long sigh, finds his stride.

James Breen, *THE OBSERVER*, London May 20, 1962

Love and the Life-Force

Right from the credit-titles, with their rip-roaring musical accompaniment and their silent-film knockabout images, the nervous spontaneity of Francois Truffaut's latest film, Jules et Jim (Cameo-Poly), is apparent. (1)

Truffaut's aim (2) is to explore individual human relationships, not to wrap up a carefully patterned tract for Our Time. A narrator's voice comes between us and the screen and remains throughout the film: telling us the story of the three-sided love-affair between Jules, an Austrian, Jim, a Frenchman, and Catherine, the woman they both love.

The film almost has the quality of romantic legend. Catherine is described as "a vision for all men, not a woman for one"; despite the passage of 20-odd years, the heroes and heroine do not age and, throughout, they are all exclusively preoccupied with their personal relationships. (3)

It is no accident that Jules is an Austrian, Jim a Frenchman. We see them in the trenches, fighting on opposite sides, but still thinking in personal terms—hoping only that neither will have occasion to

---

1. It is worth considering the aesthetic principles embedded in this paragraph.

2. Breen speaks of "Truffaut's aim," but he does not fall into the trap common to so many critics of replacing the movie he has seen with a construct external to the film. The "aim" for Breen is synonymous with what he sees in the finished film.

3. Does the accumulation of detail here serve to convince you that "the film almost has the quality of romantic legend"?

kill the other. The war, in short, is an irrelevant triviality; (4) what matters is their love for each other.

Again, Catherine never loses her romantic intensity: at the end of the film she has not "settled"; she is still the curious improviser, never satisfied, anxious always to expand, to roam, to be the full woman—loving, loved, dominant, fertile. In a sense, the camera takes its cue from her: it quests and invents ceaselessly, shooting from a variety of unexpected angles, now high, now low, now swirling round and round the characters, now giving itself up to the landscape. There are wonderful images of happiness: especially in the countryside, when the composition of meadow and tree and mountain and Georges Delerue's sweetly pretty music underline the lovers' innocence and togetherness and natural joy. Oskar Werner and Henri Serre fit together like a musical duo; we hardly need their embraces, nor even their sudden shared jokes, to feel their oneness.

But, as one of the characters says, "Happiness fades without anyone noticing it," and the happiness goes out of this extraordinary triangle. Jules and Jim remain close, but Catherine goes from one to the other, needing total love; the mother of Jules's child, she wants to bear Jim's also; not particularly beautiful or intelligent, but with the life-force strong within her, she takes other lovers, endlessly seeking new experiences, in order, as Jules thinks, to acquire wisdom, until finally she destroys the pattern.

Beautifully scripted by Truffaut and Jean Gruault (after the novel by Henri-Pierre Roche) this profoundly rewarding film has only one miscalculation—the casting of Jeanne Moreau as Catherine.

Mlle Moreau plays the part brilliantly, as you might expect; but she is a Cassius of an actress—she thinks too much, she is too aware, too odd and intense to convey the instinctive, maternal naturalness of this character. Nevertheless, she is, as always, stupendously worth seeing. (5)

---

4. Kauffmann has said the war goes on too long; Breen sees it as irrevant. What is the difference between what these two critics are saying?

5. Examine carefully Breen's grounds for feeling Miss Moreau miscast. What is his source for seeing Catherine as maternal and instinctive if Miss Moreau does not convey these qualities to him? Is the critical problem here similar to that identified in Kauffmann's response to Miss Moreau? Or is it here rather a question of the *actor as barrier?* If it is, is it Jeanne Moreau's earlier roles that interfere?

THE LADY VANISHES

Howard Barnes, *NEW YORK HERALD TRIBUNE*
December 26, 1938

Even in so synthetic a medium as the screen, it is possible to recognize the work of a master craftsman. "The Lady Vanishes," at the Globe, is the product of individual imagination and artistry quite as much as a Cezanne canvas or a Stravinsky score. (1) It is an extraordinarily exciting and powerful melodrama because it has been staged by Alfred Hitchcock, who is one of the greatest directors in motion pictures. With consummate skill, he has taken a none-too-novel spy story and wrought it into a brilliant and tensely absorbing photoplay. He has kept it every inch a show, but he has stamped it with the authority of his peculiar genius to make it a memorable screen drama. It boasts superb acting and the sort of dialogue which advances rather than impedes the plot, but these are minor blessings compared with Mr. Hitchcock's contribution.

Those who had the good fortune to see "The Man Who Knew Too Much," "Thirty-nine Steps" or the curiously neglected "The Woman Alone" know the Hitchcock technique. Here they will see it at its best. He does not rely on obvious cliches to build up suspense, terror and dramatic climax, but prefers to interweave situations and char-

---

1. Note this foreshadowing of the *auteur* theory.

acters in a complex visual pattern.(2) While he approaches scenes obliquely and juxtaposes them startingly, he rarely calls on mere tricks to give them impact. The result is a film which is fluent, cumulatively entertaining and always a true film. Mr. Hitchcock is a great story teller who talks eloquently in cinematic terms.

The tale of "The Lady Vanishes" is melodramatically substantial in any case, but it is the treatment which makes it the best film of its kind of the year. Although most of the action takes place on a trans-European express train, Mr. Hitchcock has conjured up terror and excitement with every click of the camera, until the suspense grows almost intolerable. A nice, tweedy old Englishwoman disappears from her compartment, and the young girl who wants to know why is driven frantic when every one tells her that there never had been such a person. A famous brain surgeon diagnoses her ailment as hallucination and it is only when an insolent young man aids her that a crisscross puzzle of espionage, counterespionage and attempted assassination is solved. It would inevitably spoil your pleasure to tell more of the plot, except that a pitched battle between the kidnapped occupants of a dining car and foreign agents is no more exciting than the repeated image of two brandy glasses on a table. It is scenes such as the latter which give a true key to Mr. Hitchcock's enormous film gifts.

The acting, as I think I already mentioned, is magnificent. Margaret Lockwood and Michael Redgrave make a plausible and engaging pair as they try to find out if there ever had been a lady and how and why she vanished. Dame May Whitty is superb as the woman who disappears and Paul Lukas and Philip Leaver are particularly sinister villains. Moreover, there are vastly humorous and credible portrayals of two cricket-loving Englishmen by Naughton Wayne and Basil Radford which would have made any film worth seeing by themselves. The script, incidentally, is well written and well plotted and gives Mr. Hitchcock the benefit of fine dialogue throughout. Superlative direction has made "The Lady Vanishes" a top-notch screen melodrama, to be recommended with absolutely no qualifications.

---

2. Barnes is very perceptive, we think. Would detailed evidence help us to know?

Archer Winsten, *NEW YORK POST* December 24, 1938

In the field of mystery melodrama the directorial work of Alfred Hitchcock is in a class by itself, which is why "The Lady Vanishes" at the Globe Theatre is the best thing of its kind seen this year.

If you strip this film down to its plot essentials, spy stuff and attempted murder somewhere in Europe, it is quite ordinary. But when you see how these essentials have been transformed by Hitchcock, his writers, Sidney Gilliat, Frank Launder and Alma Revelle, and the cast into a tense and characterful thriller with extraordinarily humorous asides, it's time to raise a cheer for art.

I should say that it has more suspense and thrill to it than the best murder mystery drama of the year. At the same time it can match the best of the comedies with its subtle characterization of the two cricket-loving Englishmen.

Students of film technique have long been praising the work of Alfred Hitchcock. This reviewer, while recognizing his brilliance, has not always agreed with them. Too often his studied effects have given an impression of wilful eccentricity which hindered any straight-forward story telling. He seemed to be all technique and no substance.

But this time his method is perfectly suited. At no time does it distract you from the rapid unfolding of his mysterious tale.(1) Moreover, the satirical portrait of the two cricket-followers, is a work of such perfection that if the picture had nothing else, it would be a "must."

"The Lady Vanishes" is hereby recommended to every one, but especially to those whom the happy spirit of Christmas has filled to the point of surfeit. Here is another world of violence, humor and menace, miraculously wrought out of base ingredients. Mr.

---

1. Does Hitchcock's "method" merely not "distract" from "the rapid unfolding of his . . . tale"? Or, does it in fact help? Or, are the two even synonymous?

Hitchcock should be hailed as the wizard who has discovered the secret of making silk purses out of sow's ears. (2)

---

2. What is the process by which a "sow's ear" is made into a "silk purse"? And how does this help us answer our first question?

John Mosher, *THE NEW YORKER* December 24, 1938

Christmas List

If you happen to be murder-minded on Christmas Eve, you can run over to the Globe and take in Alfred Hitchcock's latest mystery. It's called "The Lady Vanishes," has nothing whatever to do with Christmas, and is as full of surprises, horrors, thrills, even humor, as the other Hitchcock productions. In this case, the story begins somewhere in the Balkans, in a village inn crowded with tourists of all sorts, and moves quickly to one of those trans-European trains which are always such delectable settings for drama and scheming. Although the leading figure in the general excitement is a little bespectacled spinster, far beyond her first youth (Dame May Whitty), I think there is even more scuffling, shooting, and fisticuffing in this particular Hitchcock than in the others, which isn't the reason for my admiration of it. It's the neat polish given each detail that really counts. In fact, after the film has finished, you may look upon the mystery and its solution and realize it's one of the oldest mystery themes going, a realization which won't occur to you, however, while the film is on the screen. The rich English girl in the inn (Margaret Lockwood) has the airy way of her species before she is singled out for plot exigencies. The various travellers, who are there just for atmosphere, are each so entertaining that you might almost think no plot necessary at all and that a mere Hitchcock sketch of an ordinary trip with the lot of them would be instructive enough. When the accessories are so good that the plot seems superfluous, you can really relax and forget all. (1)

---

1. Christmas or not—echoes of Scrooge—is there an attitude toward film revealed in this review?

Alan Stanbrook, *FILMS AND FILMING* July, 1963

Few Hitchcock films have had such a unanimously enthusiastic press as *The Lady Vanishes.* Even Claude Chabrol, a staunch defender of his transatlantic work, (1) admits: *'C'est un excellent film anglais, un excellent film d'Hitchcock'*. C.A. Lejeune, writing in *The Observer* of October 9, 1938, declared: 'Hitchcock has done it again. This master of screen melodrama has reached the point when every new film of his can be regarded as a blind date for connoisseurs of mystery fiction—something we can go to as safely as we would ask for a new Ellery Queen, a new Margery Allingham, or a new H.C. Bailey from the library. (2)

---

1. Stanbrook is referring to Chabrol's usual preference for Hitchcock's American films as opposed to his English films.

2. LeJeune and Chabrol would seem to have very different reasons for admiring this film. Chabrol regards Hitchcock as a master technician while LeJeune sees him as an entertainer. In point of fact, are these two separate phenomena? Truffaut may be providing an answer when he says of *The Lady Vanishes:*

> They show it very often in Paris; sometimes I see it twice in one week. Since I know it by heart, I tell myself each time that I'm going to ignore the plot,

to examine the train and see if it's moving, or to look at the transparencies, or to study the camera movements inside the compartments. But each time I become so absorbed by the characters and the story that I've yet to figure out the mechanics of that film.—Francois Truffaut and Helen Scott, *Hitchcock* (New York: Simon and Schuster), 1967, p. 83.

'*The Lady Vanishes* is possibly the best, almost certainly the most successful of all his pictures. Adapted rather cunningly from Ethel Lina White's first rate thriller, *The Wheel Spins,* it tells the story of a drab middle-aged music teacher who suddenly disappears from a trans-continental express under curious circumstances . . . The device has been used before in mystery tales but it is still effective. Hitchcock plays up to the full the chill and panic of the situation—the girl's doubts, her growing obstinacy, the increasing tension of the atmosphere. Like W. S. Van Dyke, he has his fun, too, and nobody who sees the picture will forget the grim couple of English sportsmen determined, at all hazards, to get home for the last day of the Test Match.'

On the same day, Sydney W. Carroll, *The Sunday Times* film correspondent, wrote: 'Alfred Hitchcock is the Prince of English thrill-makers. His latest exploit, *The Lady Vanishes,* is to my mind easily the best constructed, the most ingenious and the most entertaining. Based upon a popular novel, *The Wheel Spins,* it concerns in effect a mysterious old lady whose disappearance forms the central incident in a string of adventures that never for an instant bore or fatigue but keep one guessing till the finish.

'The cast is excellent in every detail, including that magnificent young English actor Michael Redgrave, Margaret Lockwood, Paul Lukas, Naunton Wayne, Basil Radford, Cecil Parker and Mary Clare. As for Dame May Whitty, who is the vanishing lady of the picture, her characterisation is delightful throughout with not one flaw in the playing. *The Lady Vanishes* is the finest British thriller I can remember and one of the most vigorous I have ever seen.'

The following Saturday, October 15, William Whitebait in *The New Statesman* said: 'Max Beerbohm is said to "like his niche" and it is clear that Mr. Hitchcock likes his. For a long time he has confined himself to suspense and comedy thrillers, but they get better and better, and his latest, *The Lady Vanishes,* is perhaps the best of all—a capital sample of his highly individual style. He has exploited to the full his particular sense of the sinister and the bizarre and built up the tension by a masterly use of detail—the heavy panting, for example, of a powerful locomotive brought to a standstill on a side line.' Whitebait had reservations, though, about the dialogue given the hero and heroine, maintaining that 'the English should leave amorous wisecracking to the nation which invented and alone understands that art.' But he praised the acting of Lockwood and Redgrave and concluded, 'to complete our pleasure, the film contains a number of lines rendered almost embarrassingly topical by the events of the past few weeks.'

Revaluation

The Lady Vanishes is, in Michael Redgrave's phrase, 'quintessential Hitchcock' and enjoys the reputation of being his most accomplished British production. If personal preference leans towards the extravagance of *The Thirty Nine Steps,* there is no gainsaying that Hitch's vanishing lady act is a formidable display of *legerdemain.* It is certainly his most homogeneous and completely successful film of the pre-war years. The preoccupation with spies and international intrigue, which Hitchcock so assiduously borrowed from Fritz Lang, has always been his most fruitful field and the result is a cunningly fashioned and superior entertainment.

The plot is, of course, fantastic, involving a nun in high heels, a mysterious doctor, a dear old lady who proves to be an arch spy and a gun battle in a besieged railway coach 'somewhere in Europe'. This deliberate repudiation of realism in favour of *Boys' Own Paper* heroics is entirely typical of the director at his best. It recalls the world of *The Spiders, The Spy* and the *Mabuse* films and shares with them a naïve innocence which seems largely to have deserted their directors in recent years. The Hitchcock of *Psycho* and the Lang of *While The City Sleeps* are more sophisticated, more knowing, but one sometimes longs for the pristine vigour of those early gems.

Characteristic, too, of *The Lady Vanishes* are the two Englishmen whose life revolves around the Test Match score. As imperturbably played by Basil Radford and Naunton Wayne they constitute a great part of the film's humour. And the film is extraordinarily funny, thanks to a witty script by Frank Launder and Sidney Gilliat.(3)

---

3. Is the critic ignoring visual humor when he says that the film is funny because of the script-writers?

Everything, and especially everything British, is fuel for their barbed satire. Stranded in a decrepit, Central European inn, Charters and Caldicott insist on donning dinner jackets before eating their bread and cheese. Compelled to share a room with the maid, they attribute her lascivious winks to the workings of 'a rather primitive form of humour'. Charters primly bars the maid's view of Caldicott's exposed chest, only to be caught a second later without his trousers.

The Test Match mystique provides a constant source of ironic mirth as does the rivalry between dark blue and light blue. The Army Officer, who holds the passengers at gun point, assures them that they will be unharmed because he went to Oxford; Redgrave clubs him from behind with the admission, 'but I went to Cambridge'. Adding especial irony to the work, bearing in mind its production date, is the portrait of a pacifist, whose morality is depicted as self-interested and who dies ignobly with a bullet in the chest. This is satirically contrasted with Basil Radford's look of faint outrage when shot in the hand. Launder and Gilliat's contribution has in fact been underestimated. The dialogue has a sharp, acid tone and frequently contains innuendos of remarkable audacity for 1938. Thus: 'My father said "never desert a lady in trouble"—he even carried it as far as marrying mother'.

There is nothing novel, of course, in the film's architecture, which is built upon the oldest and most solid foundation—a varied assortment of companions, united by a common danger. It has provided the groundwork of many a subsequent film, such as Ford's *Stagecoach* and Clair's *Ten Little Niggers*. But the exposition is effected with admirable economy by the device of making the characters register at the inn, and the authors always have a surprise in hand when the course seems too predictable.

Hitchcock's direction is at all times smoothly brilliant. Pace is sustained throughout and repeated cut-in shots of the train rounding a bend, of speeding rails and telegraph wires add impetus to the narrative. When detail would impede the action, Hitchcock summarily curtails it and indicates a cross channel voyage by a simple dissolve from a steamer to a shot of Victoria station. But when he wishes to emphasise a point he carefully isolates it in close up. He once wrote: 'The point is to draw the audience right inside the situation instead of leaving them to watch it from outside, from a distance. And you can do this only by breaking the action up into details and cutting from one to the other, so that each detail is forced in turn on the attention of the audience and reveals its psychological meaning'. Thus in *The Lady Vanishes* we see the label of Harriman's Herbal Tea momentarily adhering to the window before the train's speed whisks it off, and a close up of sinister hands silhouetted against a wall as they strangle an innocent ballad singer, followed by a close-up of the uncollected coin tossed down by Miss Froy from her window.

Part of the fun for contemporary Hitchcock admirers lies in the recognition of old tricks, which the director has successfully revived in his later productions. No less than John Ford, Hitchcock is self-eclectic in the best sense. The supposedly drugged glasses are placed judiciously in the camera mouth to give a foreshortened emphasis in much the same way as the poisoned coffee cup of *Notorious* or the open razor of *Spellbound.* Similarly Miss Froy's little gasp following a gun shot proves to be a red herring, prompted by an entirely different cause: one recalls the same hoax in reverse from *North By Northwest* when a United Nations official gasps at the sight of a photograph and promptly pitches forward with a knife in his back. Again the shock cut to a fiendishly grinning, life size poster of the Vanishing Lady showman has much the same force as the shrieking entry of Mrs. Bates in *Psycho.*

If Hitchcock's direction has faults they lie principally in the opening scenes with their paste board evocation of an Alpine setting. (4) The first shot is particularly unpromising with its model railway station, puppet figures and dinky car. All Hitchcock's elaborate camera movement cannot disguise the artifice. Nor is the assassination of the ballad singer satisfactorily explained. These early scenes, in which the director lacks the budget for the locations they demand, are clearly of little interest to him and, like Renoir in *La Bête Humaine,* he cannot wait 'to play trains'.

Hitchcock has recently admitted to a nostalgia for the swifter narrative pace of silent films. Certainly his own style has remained essentially visual, with suitable aids from the sound track, like the train whistle which prevents the heroine hearing Miss Froy's name.

---

4. Is Stanbrook raising a question about direction, about budget, or about taste? Incidentally, in *Marnie,* Hitchcock uses a painted drop to simulate the sky when clearly his budget for this film gave him the further options of location shooting or process shots.

Its corollary, the etching of the name on the window pane, links sound and visual into an organic unity. Hitchcock has never been much given to optical trickery (5) and when he dabbles in it the effects are sometimes grotesque, like the Dali dream of *Spellbound*. Here he limits such excesses to a multiple image of waving hands at the station to indicate Iris' giddiness following the blow on the head. His strength lies in other directions—the innocuous pan to the right around the train compartment which aptly assumes a sinister quality when repeated in the opposite direction after Miss Froy's disappearance, or the tiny, revealing detail, like Todhunter's care to close the window when his mistress raises her voice.

A master of the cinematic confidence trick, Hitchcock will fill the frame with the form of a woman dressed in Miss Froy's tweeds only to reveal that it is not Miss Froy as she turns her head. He will adjust the focal length of the lens to bring Dr. Hartz's profile into prominence as Iris drinks the doctored whiskey or satirise English prudery by making Charters and Caldicott gallantly face the wall as the maid disrobes. (6) Hitchcock has a finely developed sense of fun of the Billy Bunter variety. It is infantile but everyone has a spiffing time. Nothing could be more amusing, for example, than the spectacle of Redgrave earnestly jotting down the creaking clog dance of two aged inn servants or the sound of a nun launching into a Cockney diatribe in reply to Paul Lukas' cloquent Ruritanian. *The Lady Vanishes* is not for your supercilious man of the world, but it is as good a Hitchcock as any on which to cut your teeth.

---

5. Would Stanbrook classify some of the shots in *The Birds* as "optical trickery"? And if so, what would his assessment of the film be? Curiously, Hitchcock is famous for his use of elaborate devices to achieve special effects. Is Stanbrook, then, using the term "optical trickery" in a very special sense? Or is this a *failure in aesthetic perception?*

6. While it would be very difficult on stage to effect the surprise that one has at the turning of the bogus Miss Froy's head, Charters and Caldicott could face the wall and elicit the same laugh in another medium. Are these tricks, then, all "cinematic" ones?

LAST YEAR AT MARIENBAD

The following program was distributed at the premier engagement of *Last Year at Marienbad* in New York City. How would reading it before seeing the film direct your experience with the film?

The film you are about to see will, in all probability, upset every normal viewing habit you have formed.

The events, as they are revealed to you, are not only portrayed by the actors as they happened, but, also, as the characters would have liked them to happen. The past is fused with the present and the future, real scenes with the imaginary.

While viewing this film of rare visual beauty, you will want to give a meaning to what you see, and most certainly you will find one; but your neighbor will perhaps find an entirely different one. This is because the meaning is not imposed upon you, but rather, with a respect for your intelligence that is uncommon in the cinema, your collaboration is required to complete your personal understanding. Listen to the voice that, throughout the film, relates this unusual love story that is, perhaps a dream of love. Allow it to guide you without fear of losing yourself.

The Story

Three people, two men and a beautiful woman, are involved in the simple, basic story of the film. The central event, as with all triangles through the centuries, is the crisis which arises between the three characters, and its consequences.

The actual events that occur in this unusual love story could be told, or happen, in the space of no more than five minutes; the manner in which it is told places it out of the ordinary.

The narration, in fact, is not based on a series of events, but on what happens beneath them, in the incessant flow of the emotions, of the mind and of the unconscious in each of us.

The story takes place in a large hotel, a kind of international palace, immense, baroque, of opulent but icy decor, a universe of marble columns, stucco floral designs, gilded paneling, statues and stiff-backed servants. An anonymous, polite, idle, unmistakably rich group of guests observes seriously but without passion the strict rules of society games, dances, empty chatter of pistol practice. Within this closed, suffocating world men and things both seem victims of some spell, as in those dreams where one feels led along by a fate which it would be as vain to try to alter as to try to escape.

An unknown man wanders from room to room—rooms at times filled with formal crowds, at times completely deserted—he passes through doors, walks down interminable corridors. He picks up fragments of conversation. His eye passes from nameless face to nameless face. But he continually returns to the face of a young woman, a beautiful prisoner who is perhaps still alive in this gilded cage. He offers her what seems to be the impossible in this place where time has been abolished. He offers her a past, and a future of liberty. He tells her that they have already met, a year ago, and that they loved one another; he claims that he is now at a rendezvous which she herself arranged, and that he wants to take her away with him.

Is this unknown figure a common seducer? Is he a madman? Or is he just confusing her with someone else? The girl, in any case, begins by taking the whole thing as a game, meant to amuse. But the man is not joking. Obstinate, serious and sure of this story of the past which he is slowly unfolding, he is insistent, he shows proof . . . and the girl, little by little, hesitatingly gives ground. Then she becomes frightened. She does not want to leave this false world which is hers, to which she is accustomed, represented for her by another man, tender, distant and disillusioned, who watches over her and who is, perhaps, her husband. But the story the stranger tells her becomes more and more real. The present, the past, become confused while the agonizing tension among the three protagonists creates in the heroine's mind phantoms of tragedy: rape, murder, suicide. . . .

Then, suddenly, she is about to yield—she already surrendered, in fact, a long time ago. After a final attempt to escape, a last opportunity she gives her guardian to win her back, she seems to accept being what the stranger expects her to be, and she goes away with him toward the unknown hazards and adventures of the future.

ASTOR PICTURES
presents
"LAST YEAR AT MARIENBAD"
Directed by ALAIN RESNAIS
Original script and Dialogue by ALAIN ROBBE-GRILLET

Cast

Woman . . . . DELPHINE SEYRIG
Stranger . . . . Giorgio Albertazzi
Husband (perhaps) . . . . Sacha Pitoeff

Others In The Cast

Francoise Bertin
Luce Garcia-Ville
Helena Kornel
Francoise Spira
Karin Toeche-Mittler
Pierre Barbaud
Wilhelm von Deek
Jean Lanier
Gerard Lorin
Davide Montemuri
Gilles Queant
Gabriel Werner

CREDITS

Producers . . . . Pierre Courau (Preceitel)
Raymond Froment (Terrafilm)
Director . . . . Alain Resnais
Assistant Director . . . . Jean Leon
Director of Photography . . . . Sacha Vierny
Cameraman . . . . Phillippe Brun
Stage Settings by . . . . Jacques Saulnier
Sound Effects . . . . Guy Villette
Film Editors . . . . Henri Colpi
Jasmine Chasney
Music . . . . Francis Seyrig

Settings	Environs and natural settings in Munich (chateaux of Nymphenburg, Schleissheim, etc.)
Gowns for Mlle Seyrig	Chanel
Costumes	Bernard Evein
English Titles by	Noelle Gillmor

French-Italian co-production Terra Films, Societe Nouvelle des Films Cormoran, Preceitel, Como-Films, Argos-Films, Les Films Tamara, Cinetel, Silver-Films, Cineriz (Rome).

RUNNING TIME: 93 MINUTES

Brendan Gill, *THE NEW YORKER* March 10, 1962

Dreamers

The French film "Last Year at Marienbad" arrives here already famous for having stirred violent feelings pro and con in Paris and London, and local pride would seem to require that we in New York respond to it with equal violence, but for once my gift for chauvinism fails me; I simply and uncombatively like the picture very much. (1) An experiment with no air of the experimental about

1. Earlier, we suggested that a statement such as "This is a fine film" is frequently little more than a rephrased "I like it." How would our responses have been altered had Gill opened his review with "This is a highly successful work of art," rather than with "I liked this picture very much." Does Gill's opening remark set the tone for the rest of his review? How so?

it, a novelty without a trace of the crudely new, it flows past one's eyes with the suavity and never-to-be-questioned illogic of a dream, and indeed it may be that we are intended to perceive that its story is a sort of dream within a dream. Watching it, I was unexpectedly reminded of another work of art based on the world of sleep—the nightlong, lifelong tossing and pitching called "Finnegans Wake." (2) Radically unlike as they are, the movie and the novel have it in common that they are successful forays into unmapped country and that their success has nothing tempting about it. No one has tried following Shem the Penman through his thickets of groanery-raillery prosody, and I doubt if "Last Year at Marienbad" will be paid the compliment of being imitated, even by its makers.

The author of the screenplay is Alain Robbe-Grillet, a member of the school of so-called anti-novelists now staring hard at things in France (I'm told no member of the school admits that it exists, anti-novelists being quite naturally anti-school); the director of the picture is Alain Resnais, who gave us "Hiroshima, Mon Amour." M. Robbe-Grillet's literary specialty is strict attention to objects rather than thoughts about them, and for this purpose the camera is a far more useful instrument than words. To prove the point once and for all, M. Resnais has provided an innumerable host of beautiful and curious things for his camera's incessantly wandering eye to light upon, always as if by chance—*"par hasard"* is a key phrase in the picture—and with a dispassion that defies us to diminish ourselves by taking them for metaphors. (3) The settings are largely the palaces and gardens of Nymphenburg and Schleissheim, in Munich, and their baroque splendor perfectly sets off the bleak little melodrama of love at first or second sight that may or may not be taking place entirely in someone's mind. (4)

---

2. Is Gill introducing an irrelevancy, or is he instead attempting to recreate and examine his response to the film?

3. How do you understand this statement?

4. Brendan Gill strongly implies here that ambiguity is the chief virtue of this film. Alton Cook suggests that this same ambiguity is its chief defect. The question here is not so much who is right as it is whether or not ambiguity can be considered a standard of success in a film. Further, is it possible that a work of art can itself introduce new criteria of excellence?

I call the melodrama bleak (5) because in essence it consists of a young woman and two men obsessively encountering each other in the rooms and grounds of a vast hotel full of wealthy people embalmed in boredom. These encounters are either head-on collisions or sudden, total turnings-aside and, being human, are never complete; they are splinters of an uncreated whole, and their poignancy is the contrast between them and the stony assurance of the statuary, the geometric precision of the gardens, the easy, infinitely repeated duplicity of a hundred mirrored walls. The poor trio have very little to say, and that little is interesting only because it is mysterious. The young woman appears to be married to one of the men. The other man wishes her to run away with him and assures her that he became her lover a year ago, at Marienbad, and that she had then begged him to allow her one more year of her accustomed life. At first the young woman claims to remember nothing about Marienbad, but the man is strong and sure of himself; we sense that she is breaking down and that whether she had actually been at Marienbad is less important than his being able to convince her that she had been. As for him, does he really believe that they were lovers, or is this merely a device for bringing the relationship about? And what of the supposed husband? How much is that wily party taking in? (Most of his time is devoted to triumphantly outwitting opponents at the match game. "I can lose," he says, "but I always win.") These are only a few of the dozens of questions that one asks in the course of the picture, and I wouldn't think of telling you the answers, in part because, as with any good mystery story, it wouldn't be fair, and in part because I don't know. I don't even know for certain how the picture ends; I just sort of agreeably, hazily *hope* I know.

Delphine Seyrig is downright ravishing as the young woman, and the two men are played with solemn effectiveness by Giorgio Albertazzi and Sacha Pitoëff. Praise should also be given to Sacha Vierny, the Director of Photography, and to Chanel, who has dressed Mlle. Seyrig to the nines.

---

5. What does Gill mean by "bleak"? Do we have to guess?

Alton Cook, *NEW YORK WORLD-TELEGRAM AND SUN*

March 8, 1962

"Last Year at Marienbad" is a weird exercise in confusion, narrated as though clarity would be the ultimate humiliation for a movie. This strange experiment from France is at the Carnegie Hall Cinema.

The picture is built around a wisp of episode that contains no more than a few details. During a holiday at an old-style luxury hotel, a man and married woman fell abruptly and helplessly in love.

Hesitantly, she asked the man to wait a year before she finally faced her wrenching decision. When they were reunited after the year, she still was frightened and he repeated his wooing.

Cling to Fragments

Director Alain Resnais and his scenarist, Alain Robbe-Grillet, cling persistently to these fragments, depicting them over and over, as they really occurred and as they might have been in the wishful dreams of various participants.

The camera flits capriciously among these versions, seldom bothering to make clear which attitude is being expressed. Abrupt switch from flashback to present adds to the perplexing obscurity.

The narrative device has been used in many a movie, of course, notably in the Japanese "Rashomon." The bewildering style of execution is the flaw of the new picture. Also, the ideas hardly seem substantial enough to bear such prolonged and repetitive examination.

Radiates Evil

The cast works in stylized immobility that might almost have been done behind masks. The most successful of these is Sacha Pitoeff, whose face even in repose radiates sinister evil and menace. The erring wife is Delphine Seyrig, a stately beauty allowed more range of expression, even some laughter.

The supporting players are used mainly to give composition and movements to backgrounds. Those latter, incidentally are stunning, a constant exploration of the lavish expanses of an old palace and its gardens.

"Last Year at Marienbad" is one of the most intellectually ambitious movies of the season. There is genuine regret here in a report it falters. (1)

---

1. How do Cook's commitments to *technical consistency* control his response to *Marienbad?*

Jonas Mekas, *THE VILLAGE VOICE* March 15, 1962

Alain Resnais' "LAST YEAR AT MARIENBAD" is many things. But it is neither a great nor a revolutionary film. (1) It is a very well made film, a most beautiful piece of craftsmanship. It effectively uses many devices introduced by the experimental cinema. One could discuss at length many successful techniques which Resnais employs. To me, however, the main importance of "Marienbad" is that it provides the missing link between the commercial dramatic film and the experimental, poetic cinema. One might say that Cocteau provided it long ago. But that is not exactly true. Cocteau was never

---

1. Mekas shares his concern—is *Last Year at Marienbad* revolutionary?—with many other critics (see, for example, Eric Rhode below). It is clear that for Mekas, at least, its failure to be revolutionary is a failure in aesthetics. If it's new, must it be good? If it's old, must it be bad? Are we discovering here a current meaning for the put-down "derivative"?

commercial when he was good; he was commercial only when he was bad. Resnais is commercial when he is good. (2)

Little Revolutionary

For the critics and movie-goers not familiar with the experimental cinema, "Marienbad" is the "furthest out" cinema. This shows how little our critics know about what is going on in modern cinema. Had they known Maya Deren's "Ritual in Transfigured Time" or "Meshes of the Afternoon"—both made 15 years ago—they would have found little that is revolutionary in "Marienbad." Not to mention "Ten Days That Shook the World." And you can see Resnais' famous short flashback used best in "The Raven," a picture made in 1916. I am by far not a purist, and my interest in history is limited. I believe that once a certain technique is discovered, it can be used and perfected by others—like a new word in a vocabulary. But I become uneasy when the "newness" of Resnais is blown out of proportion. Resnais himself has modestly stated that "Marienbad" is "an old film," and that is much closer to the truth.

"Who is further out than Resnais?" you will ask. I have a surprise: Stanley Brakhage, Marie Menken, Robert Breer. In Brakhage's films ("Anticipation of the Night," "The Dead," "Prelude") we find not only a more subtle cinematic form but also a more advanced cinematic technique. I was told by my spies that Resnais saw "Anticipation of the Night" at Brussels four years ago, and was much taken by it. It is in "Anticipation" that we find the most perfect fusion of past and present, the constantly flowing, moving camera, brushing past objects and faces—which makes up the main beauty of "Marienbad." When you watch "Anticipation" or Menkens' "Arabesque," you can hear Robbe-Grillet's lines: "I walk again through these corridors, through these gardens. . . ." The big difference is that there is not a word pronounced in those films, no Robbe-Grillet. Whereas, as in few other films, "Marienbad"

---

2. "Commercial" is another common put-down. What are we really saying when we say a film is "commercial"? Are we saying that all movies that are popular share something in common (aside from their popularity)? And are we saying (considering the connotations of the term) that mass taste is suspect?

begins and ends in the brain of Alain Robbe-Grillet, who wrote the script.

New Theme

One of "Marienbad's" virtues is its theme. It is new, it is thought-provoking. It is a sort of horror film on persuasion. And that's how it should be taken. I don't think Resnais wanted anything else. He was only trying to tell his strange story. No doubt there are various symbolic meanings which one could read into it. But what theme, what idea, what thought could survive long in the pages of Vogue, in that chic and frozen world which is the world of "Marienbad"? It soon ends up as an abstract, decorative pose. At best, "Marienbad" could be called "poetic" in terms of its being bad prose. I believe it was Robbe-Grillet himself who did worst to the film: he sentimentalized it with his commentary. There is plenty of false psychology in it. Which means that for Robbe-Grillet "Marienbad" is a step back into the morass of "bourgeois" psychologism—just the thing he is avoiding so successfully in his writings.

I can see the historical importance of "Marienbad" as a forerunner of a commercial experimental film. But that's all. Bergman forced the critics and audiences to think. Antonioni took the plot away from them. Resnais breaks away from the realist tradition, goes into the subconscious. And that is his greatest contribution to the contemporary dramatic film. The next step is the experimental poetic cinema.

Pure Poets

As it is now, I still prefer the pure experimental poets like Kenneth Anger, Stan Brakhage, Marie Menken, Robert Breer to the commercial-experimental cinema of Resnais. Their work makes me see the world and myself in a new way,(3) and the beauty of it sends me into ecstasy. This is modern cinema, and it is a cinema that is human in the most essential way. "Marienbad," in comparison, is a frozen, pretentious ornament, full of postures, declamations. Its forced intellectualism is sick. When I watch it I feel as if I am being

---

3. Is Mekas providing us with a workable basis for the criticism of film?

pulled back into the abstract, impersonal hell which is the end product of Western Civilization and from which my generation is making a desperate and perhaps last attempt to escape. That's why, to me—and I risk the making of many enemies this time—"Marienbad" is only a beautiful piece of craftsmanship gone awry. It is not a blueprint for the future, not a beginning; it is an end, a stone in the cemeteries of the dead.

Eric Rhode, *THE LISTENER AND BBC TELEVISION REVIEW*
March 8, 1962

Back to Byzantium

Alain Resnais' film *L'Année dernière à Marienbad* has aroused much controversy wherever it has been shown, and this is not surprising. For example, consider what has been said of it by its script-writer, Alain Robbe-Grillet: 'I would like anyone who sees it to interpret it in terms of its meaning to him'. This remark appears to be as good an excuse for critical anarchy as one could imagine. How can a coherent film—and *L'Année dernière* is coherent—be so ambiguous? (1) And yet, though Robbe-Grillet may be guilty of stating a half-truth, I do not think he intends to mislead. It is clearly difficult to make more than a subjective judgment about a film whose plot no one seems able to define.

Imprudently, one might say that this plot is created out of a simple anecdote. In a vast, baroque hotel a man, curtly named X, ap-

1. Here again is a reference to the aesthetic value of the ambiguity of *Marienbad*. Does Rhode provide a solution to the problem?

proaches a woman named A and reminds her of their meeting, a year before, at Marienbad. She denies this completely: says she has never met him before, never been to Marienbad. And yet, eventually, the man persuades her to leave the hotel with him. This anecdote is the closest one can get to a strict definition of the story. At the same time, by assuming motives and connections which the plot does not try to describe, this anecdote, like any other attempt to tell the story, simply will not do. (2)

A Revolutionary Film?

For no other reason than this, then, is *L'Année dernière* a revolutionary film? Only, I suggest, in the sense that revolutions, as the word implies, often have the peculiar habit of taking us back to the point from which we started. Most of our difficulties disappear if we can place this film in a historical context, if we can see it as having returned to a position taken up by much nineteenth-century art under the pressure of a familiar crisis.

During the past 200 years many writers have been perplexed: should they associate themselves with the truths of science? Or should they subscribe to the truths of the imagination? Since these two modes of apprehension are incompatible—you cannot see reality both as mechanized nature and as a revelation of eternal realities—they were in a dilemma. They knew that the two opposing doctrines arising out of this situation—naturalism and symbolism—were insufficient when isolated from each other. Both represent a splitting of the world; and this partiality is, in effect, a denial of the human element. While naturalism turns men into machines, symbolism turns them into images. (3)

Since the two doctrines cannot, apparently, be reconciled, these writers were forced to make a choice between one or the other, and to develop as well as they could within their chosen field. But such

---

2. What is Rhode saying here about our expectations of plot?

3. In this section of his discussion, Rhode attempts to categorize the film as either symbolist or naturalist. He finally concludes that, taken to their extremes, symbolism and naturalism are identical. What, then, do you think is the value of this discussion? And further, is it useful to have this kind of label for a film?

a development did not release them from their dilemma. As a matter of fact, their dilemma became more acute. Both naturalism and symbolism, when developed, lead to a dead end: they both become meaningless. There is little difference, I suggest, between an art of esoteric symbols and an art of haphazardly accumulated objects; and so, when taken to an extreme, these two doctrines become identical; and the vision of a total world which combines the public and the private, the world of humanity in fact, remains uncaptured.

I would argue that *L'Année dernière à Marienbad* is a symbolist film, whose symbolism is sufficiently developed for it to have many of the characteristics of naturalism. And this is what confuses the critic. Is he to apply symbolist or naturalistic criteria to this film? Or if both, how does he strike a balance?

If we look at Robbe-Grillet's third novel, *La Jalousie,* a work which has close affinities to *L'Année dernière,* we begin, I think, to untangle this problem. At first reading, this novel appears to be naturalistic. The narrator—the cuckold in a commonplace love triangle—never comments on the action. He merely records the world as if he were, literally, the passive eye of a camera. When he describes his wife in her day-to-day life he uses the same terms as when he describes her photograph, so that the distinction between an event and a photograph of an event is broken down. Life becomes a series of photographs, an endless listing of whose inventory parodies the naturalistic accumulation of objects. Through this series of minutely described stills, the relationship of lover and wife is evoked. Though this may be a triumph of technique, the novelty lies not in this but in the way the stills are presented without any sort of chronology. Sometimes the same one is repeated twice, sometimes we return to an earlier one, sometimes we leap forward to one which, in terms of time, is quite out of order. As these same flat descriptions recur in growing confusion, we see that they are emblems representing the disorder of a mind sick with jealousy.

Dimension beyond Time

In this we realize how Robbe-Grillet departs from the doctrine of naturalism in two important ways. One is that, by eliminating our sense of time, Robbe-Grillet creates a world which exists in eternity —that is, in a dimension beyond time. This concept of eternity is hard to conceive of for minds bred on chronology and action. Angrily we are tempted to ask 'Do the events of *La Jalousie* take place in a few seconds as they flash through the narrator's mind? Or do they take place over a period, say, of a week? Or do they, indeed, ever take place at all?' In eternity, of course, these questions are meaningless; and Robbe-Grillet makes much fun of this incongruity in his second novel, *Le Voyeur,* in which his commercial traveller, Mathias, tries to sell watches to people living in this curious dimension.

The other way in which Robbe-Grillet diverges from naturalism is that his heroes, like the symbolist poets, live in isolation. And like the symbolist poets, they are forced to dream some terrible vision in order to fulfill themselves. Yet one would be wrong to look for a psychological motive behind this obsession. *La Jalousie* is not primarily about jealousy, nor *Le Voyeur* about a man troubled by the thought that he might have committed rape; the motive in each case, as for the symbolists, is a need for revelation. And this motivation is true for *L'Année dernière*. Robbe-Grillet has described this film as 'the story of a conviction: it has to do with the reality which the hero creates out of his own words and vision'. This hero, treading ceaselessly the thick-carpeted corridors of a palatial hotel, is the latest of a long line of romantic phantoms trying to break out of the mirror world of their isolation into a world which is real—into a public world in which the total human being may exist.

Symbolist Imagery

Despite this groping towards symbolist expression, the script of *L'Année dernière,* like Robbe-Grillet's novels, is not symbolist. The objects described in it lack that synthesis between life-in-death and death-in-life which is at the heart of the symbolist image—that image which (at a terrible cost to the poet) reconciles all opposites into a Unity of Being. Yet, thanks to the direction of Alain Resnais, *L'Année dernière* can be considered a symbolist film. I think we can show this by one example alone: the lengthy garden scene centred on a statue. In Robbe-Grillet's script this statue is no more than a piece of stone into which the characters read their fantasies, much as we might read all sorts of memories into a faded snapshot. In the film, Resnais transforms this statue into an image by superb interplay between camera movement and sound, so that, like the symbolists' image of the dancer, it embodies life-in-death and death-in-life to the point that it almost speaks.

In this single example one has a typical demonstration of how the talents of Robbe-Grillet and Resnais complement each other. Though Robbe-Grillet may be a naturalist by temperament, Resnais, on the contrary, is a symbolist who is trying to create a cinema of pure form. Significantly, his first work as a director was to make a series of documentaries on the work of various abstract painters. As an artist, Resnais' indifference to the world borders on the inhuman. In *Hiroshima Mon Amour,* for instance, he used the bombing of Hiroshima as no more than a stylistic device. As far as he is concerned, it seems, almost any script will do; his values are purely aesthetic, and these he supplies himself. He can make a film out of a novelette by Marguerite Duras or from newsreels taken of Auschwitz, and the result is always the same: an essay in pure cinema. And so, though Resnais, through indifference, retains the characteristic features of Robbe-Grillet's script—the romantic dream, the obsessive counting of objects, and the ironical play on our assumptions about time—he does, simultaneously, transform them into a symbolist exercise.

In the light of this, we find that most of our critical problems resolve themselves if we read *L'Année dernière* as if it were, primarily, a symbolist poem. Take, for instance, Robbe-Grillet's statement that we can interpret this film in any way we wish. This is his way of saying that the film, like a symbolist poem, is in its totality, an image that will not disclose itself to a Cartesian explanation—that it is an enigma which we should apprehend sensuously as we would apprehend, say, a piece of music. To ask what *L'Année dernière* may mean is to ask to be teased, much as Proust was when he tried to elucidate that haunting phrase in Vinteuil's sonata.

In a discursive sense, the meaning of the film is both everything and nothing. Its action, like the action of a symbolist poem, consists of images playing one against the other as do the *leitmotifs* in a Wagnerian opera. As one might expect, this type of action opens up an ample range of abiguities—a range which is further extended, for images transcend the truth tables of formal logic. To enter the world of the imagination is to enter the realm of possibility. One can say of an image that it is possible; one cannot say that it is true or false. For instance, in *L'Année dernière* the principal images are associated with various zones in the hotel and its adjoining gardens, and these images stand for a number of alternatives.

The woman's bedroom is the place where love, murder, or rape might take place—together, singly, or not at all! Parts of the garden represent the possible meeting of the man X and the woman A during the previous year. The salons, where the recurring match-stick games are played, is the zone where X perhaps challenges his double, M, the man 'who might be A's husband'. The most important of these images, however, the total one of the hotel and its surrounding estates, is not equivocal, since it represents an absolute—the ideal of the imagination itself. And this absolute is synonymous with another absolute—the ideal of the perfect work of art. In his poem, 'Sailing to Byzantium', W. B. Yeats described this perfection as 'the artifice of eternity', and identified it with Byzantium itself.

It is in this sense I suggest that *L'Année dernière* is revolutionary. For it brings us back, whatever its makers may say, to the *fin-de-siècle* cult of the Byzantine, both in taste and style. The late Romantics were fascinated by this empire, primarily because they saw in its mosaics the perfection of the image. According to Frank Kermode, 'The image has nothing to do with organic life, though it may appear to have; its purity of outline is only possible in a sphere far removed from that in which humanity constantly obtrudes its preoccupations'. The late Romantics believed that Byzantine provided this sphere. In the hieratic courts of Justinian and of Theodora the human element, allegedly, was excluded. All was ritual and ceremony—a perfection of form. And all was unnatural. As Yeats wrote:

> A starlit or a moonlit dome disdains
> All that man is,
> All mere complexities,
> The fury and the mire of human veins.

When symbolism is taken to an extreme it becomes, through its denial of the human, identical with extreme naturalism. So it is not surprising to find that the late Romantics were attracted to another, less savoury, aspect of Byzantium which is as much naturalistic as symbolist. 'Décor is everything in these works', claims Mario Praz, 'but it must be noted that the value of the décor isn't scholarly. The meticulous catalogues of trappings, of objects, of acts, don't merely aim at giving an atmosphere. The ferment of impure, violent deeds which these décors have witnessed underlies the description of them'. And the pathological strain in naturalism reveals itself in the symbolists' fascination with the unnatural in Byzantium—in a taste for the androgyne and the perverse, in a childish pleasure of relishing the knowledge that behind the mask of courtly indolence lurks hysteria.

L'Année dernière is a typical example of such a sensibility. In the glittering hotel with its overbearing baroque décor, bejewelled guests group stiffly round card-table and staircase like mosaic emperors. These nameless, enigmatic priests of a hieratic society, who are forced to act out a ritual ten times higher than the highest mass, yet bleed beneath the copes and mitres of decorum. For this formality exists in order to conceal hysteria and destructiveness. These poor wretches know they are caught in the eternal recurrence of the symbolist world. Rightly they doubt whether they will ever be able to escape. *L'Année dernière* is Byzantine not only in its sensibility, but also in its formal perfection. In it every detail plays a part; from the sustained rhythm of its images down to the beautiful convolutions of its dialogue. Truly this film is an 'artifice of eternity'.

And yet, how important is it all? Not as important, I am afraid, as many of its admirers have made out. In having failed to reconcile the doctrines of symbolism and naturalism, *L'Année dernière* has failed to make a significant step forward. It is a work of art, but of a minor order. Like most symbolist poetry it is obscure, hermetic, and precious. Its dream world denies the use of reason, of moral obligation, of all that is, in the last resort, human. (4) At the same time, *L'Année dernière* does have the force of symbolist poetry at its best. It awakens in us a sense not of the mystification but of the mystery of life, which is something, I suggest, naturalistic art cannot do. And the struggle of X and A to break out of a mirror world into true life fascinates. It fascinates because we are all, to some degree, involved in this struggle ourselves.

Robert Graves once wrote a poem about a ghost compelled to visit over and over again a pier-glass in whose reflection she was captured. This ghost, who desperately wanted to break free and did not know how, is closely related to Robbe-Grillet's characters. Her horror is theirs as she describes her fate:

> And gliding steadfast down your corridor
> I come by nightly custom to this room,

---

4. What is Rhode's implicit definition of "human" in art? Would he consider a surrealist work "human"?

And even on sultry afternoons I come
Drawn by the thread of time-sunk memory. (5)

---

5. Having read this essay, do you believe that a filmgoer unfamiliar with Robbe-Grillet's literary work, unfamiliar with Yeats, unfamiliar with the *"fin-de-siécle* cult of Byzantine," could have a valid experience with *Last Year at Marienbad?*

THE TIMES LITERARY SUPPLEMENT
February 9, 1962

L'Année dernière à Marienbad is in some ways less of a film than an intellectual trap. Certainly it is a trap if the spectator goes at it with the intellect, wanting to know what it means and determined to work out one explanation which will fit all the facts (if they are facts) the film offers, or at least enable him to distinguish the fact from the fiction. It will no doubt provoke here, as it has already provoked in France, a reaction of outraged puritanism in which critics announce brusquely that of course the film is only a confidence trick and they, for their part, are not going to be taken in by it. But if a confidence trick is involved at all, it is a trick which the spectator persists, in spite of all warnings to the contrary, in playing on himself: both the author, M. Alain Robbe-Grillet, and the director, M. Alain Resnais, give him no reason, either explicitly, in their statements on the film, or implicitly, in the film itself, to suppose that it does all "mean" anything, and if nevertheless he goes on rationalizing and worrying when he fails to rationalize, he has no one to blame but himself.

Having got that out of the way perhaps we may venture to fall into this very trap ourselves (knowingly) by asking, with the script before us, what exactly the film is about. Well, it is about a persuasion. A man meets a woman in a large, luxurious, overpoweringly gloomy hotel and puts it to her that they met last year at Marienbad, that they had, or nearly had, an affair there and were on the brink of going away together when (perhaps) something dramatic happened, but in any case she asked for a year's grace before they should meet again. At first she denies everything, then little by little accepts what he says, and finally they leave together (or appear to do so). So much is as certain as anything in the ambiguous world the film conjures up.

But from here on we are out on our own. The first question which must strike the would-be explorer is, which of them is right? Did they or did they not meet last year? The film's creators are no help at all here. M. Robbe-Grillet says that of course they did not: it is the story of a battle of wills and personalities which X (the man) wins, forcing A (the woman) to accept his account. M. Resnais, perhaps in sheer perversity (one remembers a similar disagreement between him and Mme. Duras over what happens at the end of *Hiroshima Mon Amour*), says that he believes they did meet before and that he made the film on this assumption. There is also the third possibility, offered by M. Resnais in an interview with *Les Cahiers du Cinéma* a couple of months back, that they are both right, and the film shows the working of some semi-Ouspenskian spiral of time.

At this stage various other strands of meaning (or possible meaning) make themselves felt. For instance, is the hotel really an hotel? According to one way of looking at it it might actually be a luxurious mental home. X would be a psychiatrist, amateur or professional, and his job would be to resolve some sort of trauma inflicting A.

Or again, the hotel might be Hell (shades of *Huis Clos*) or at least Purgatory. Near the beginning there is a reference, obviously applicable to the immediate surroundings, to "cet hôtel, lui-même, avec ses salles désormais désertes, ses domestiques immobiles, muets, morts depuis longtemps sans doute, qui montent encore la garde à l'angle des couloirs", and the whole joyless death-in-life of the hotel society suggests some sort of "city of dreadful night" which no one can escape (in another casual exchange a man says to a young woman, "C'est un drôle d'endroit", and when she answers "Vous voulez dire: pour être libre?" he replies, "Pour être libre, oui, en particulier"). Moreover, the grounds are suggestive (deliberately?) of a graveyard, with no grass or foliage but only stones—something frequently insisted on in the dialogue—and when we see the main walk of the French garden inhabited for once by guests they are all standing immobile, like monumental statuary (an eerie effect deliberately achieved by giving them painted shadows on a dull, otherwise shadowless day).

Or again, X could himself be Death, pursuing an unwilling A like some hound of heaven (consider the overtones of his last words to her, as they leave.... "vous étiez maintenant déjà en peine de vous perdre, pour toujours, dans la nuit tranquille, seule avec moi"). Or the whole thing could be a metaphysical commentary on the last two reels of *Vertigo* and the "Hitchcock silhouette" by the lift early in the film could be a deliberate cryptogrammatic pointer. And so on and so on.

So, then, it means many things partly but means nothing when it is all put together? Yes and no. It all depends—to hedge tiresomely—what you mean by "mean".(1) Noticeably, nearly all the parallels one picks up are from romantic poetry—*The City of Dreadful Night, The Hound of Heaven* and the rest—and clearly the Symbolists could yield many more. And as in Romantic or Symbolist poetry, we are dealing with symbols, properly speaking, not allegories. There is no simple, complete equivalence for anything, and yet meanings hover in a cloud and each object presented to our attention—the hotel, the garden, even the curiously depersonalized characters—gradually accumulates significances which our minds hold simultaneously in suspension. And right down the middle of the film is a conflict which assumes various guises—present against past (real or imagined), freedom against convention, life against death—but remains appreciably the Romantic Agony at its last gasp.

And this, finally, is what the film is "about" (whatever that means): it is a series of variations on a romantic theme disguised as a film for film's sake, depending in the end on its power to enrapture us into suspending intellectual judgment. It is a film to give in to in the first five minutes or put aside altogether. It is, anyway, a film not to talk about or even to read, but to see.(2)

---

1. When the critic here says "it all depends" on "what you mean by 'mean'," he is pointing to a very basic problem in film criticism. What do you mean by "mean"?

2. Does this discussion help us to understand the difference between the experience of seeing the film and reading its script?

THE MAGNIFICENT SEVEN OR THE SEVEN SAMURAI

Tony Richardson, *SIGHT AND SOUND*
Spring, 1959

Akira Kurosawa's brilliant new film is a long episodic reconstruction of an incident in 16th century Japan. A peasant village is harried by brigands; in despair the villagers decide to hire professional soldiers to defend them; after recruiting difficulties, seven are collected; they organise the village's defence and succeed in wiping out the bandits completely. This basically simple plot Kurosawa elaborates in two ways. He introduces a profusion of incidents and subplots—the youngest samurai falling in love with a village girl disguised by her mistrustful father as a boy, the attempts of a wandering, humorous braggart to be accepted by the others as a samurai; and he gives to each of the many characters an intensely differentiated individual personality—the mature, kindly, selfless leader, the unassuming but obsessive professional swordsman, the traditional braggadochio.

In *The Seven Samurai* (Films de France), and in the light it throws back on *Rashomon,* Kurosawa's method and personality emerge clearly. He is, above everything else, an exact psychological observer, a keen analyst of behaviour—in a fundamentally detached

Reprinted by the permission of the publisher.

way. His handling of the young lovers is typical of this. He notes and traces with precision and truth their first, half-terrified awareness of each other sexually, the growth of mutual attraction, the boy's *gauche* admiration, the girl's aching and almost frantic abandonment; what he fails to do is to convey any feeling for, or identification with, the individuals themselves. (1) He strives for this, he uses other images to heighten their scenes—the flower-covered hillside, the sun filtering through the tops of trees (an echo of its more successful use as an orgasm metaphor in *Rashomon*), the dappled light swarming like insects over them as they lie together in a bamboo hut—but somehow these remain perfunctory, a little cold, lacking in real poetry. (2)

In this it is not unrewarding to compare Kurosawa with Ford—by whom, report has it, he claims to have been influenced. There are many superficial resemblances—the reliance on traditional values, the use of folk ceremonies and rituals, the comic horseplay—to Ford in particular and to the Western in general. The fast, vivid handling of the action sequences, the staccato cutting, the variety of angles, the shooting up through horses rearing in the mud, are all reminiscent of recent films in this genre. But the difference is more revealing. The funeral of the first samurai, killed in a preliminary skirmish, is exactly the sort of scene to which Ford responds, with all his reverence and honour for times past and the community of beliefs and feelings which they embodied. Kurosawa uses the scene in two ways, first as a further observation of the character of the "crazy samurai"—who, in a defiant attempt to satisfy his own feelings of frustration and impotence, raises the flag the dead man had sewn—and secondly, as an effective incident for heightening the narrative tension: the bandits launch their first onslaught during the funeral. One of the love scenes is used in a similar way, and in both cases one feels an ultimate shying-away from any direct, committed emotion—except anger.

Of course, to say Kurosawa is not Ford is critically meaningless; the comparison has value only in so far as it is a way of gauging the

---

1. Richardson tells us what he means by "personality" and indicates that it informs the film. But is it really helpful to see the detachment implicit in the film's point of view as an element of Kurosawa's personality?

2. What is "real poetry"?

film's intentions, and its realisation of them. (3) What made *Rashomon* so unique and impressive was that everything, the subject, the formal structure, the playing, even perhaps the period, allowed for this exterior approach to behaviour. In *The Seven Samurai* Kurosawa is striving for something different, a re-creation, a bringing to life of the past and the people whose story he is telling. Here, for all the surface conviction of period, the perceptive observation, the raging vitality and the magnificent visual style, the film doesn't quite succeed. All the elements are there except the depth and the generosity of life. One feels that each incident is too carefully worked into the texture as a whole. The Donskoi of the *Gorki* trilogy is a much simpler and, in many ways, more ordinary personality; but he achieved, almost without realising it, what Kurosawa labours for. Life itself seems to have taken over from Donskoi, carrying him along on its great stream, but Kurosawa has engineered a stunning aqueduct along which it must flow. Only in his handling of the "crazy samurai" does it occasionally overflow. Toshiro Mifune, gibing at the samurai, waving, in mocking triumph, a fish caught in a stream, and —another Falstaff—bullying his hopeless recruits, brings to his portrayal a reckless and at moments out-of-hand gusto. It is a splendid performance, losing no opportunity, and it only fails to integrate a gratuitously introduced class motivation—he is really a peasant wanting to be a samurai. (The fault here lies with the script rather than the performer.) This is perhaps a momentary and rather glib contemporary analogy out of keeping with the rest.

These ultimate reservations should not, however, prevent us from recognising the film's astonishing qualities. Incident after incident is created with biting precision for the whole 2½ hour length (the exported version, incidentally, is an hour shorter than the original)— the villagers shunning the samurai on their arrival only to tumble towards them in panic as the alarm is sounded, the capture of a thief and, brilliantly suspended in slow motion, his death, a brief and wonderful sketch of a farmer's wife abducted by the brigands stirring, guilty but sated, in her sleep. On a different level, Kurosawa is a virtuoso exponent of every technique of suspense, surprise, ex-

---

3. Has the comparison with Ford proved "not unrewarding"? And how does the comparison with Ford help us to gauge Kurosawa's "intentions"?

citement, and in this he gives nothing to his Western masters. Only in his handling of the series of battles is there a hint of monotony. He knows exactly when to hold a silence; how to punch home an extraordinary fact with maximum effect; and his use of the camera is devastating—dazzling closeups as the village deputation, overawed and desperate in their quest for samurai, scan the crowded street, or wild tracking shots as the drunken Mifune stumbles after his assailant. Visually the film makes a tremendous impression. Kurosawa can combine formal grace with dramatic accuracy, and many scenes create a startling pictorial impact. The raid on the bandits' hideout, when their slaughtered bodies are hurled, naked and haphazard, into the muddied pools outside their burning hut, is not unworthy of the Goya of *Los Desastres*. The final effect, indeed, of *The Seven Samurai* is not unlike that of "Salammbo," a triumph of rage and artifice; and one's final acknowledgment is not of the intrinsic fascination of the material but the wrested skill of the artificer. (4)

---

4. Is Richardson here making explicit a criterion of excellence which explains his previously expressed reservations about the film?

Donald Richie, *THE FILMS OF AKIRA KUROSAWA* (Berkeley and Los Angeles: University of California Press, 1965)

Like the Russians (Eisenstein, Dovshenko) to whose epics *Seven Samurai* has often been compared, Kurosawa—here perhaps more than in any other single film—insisted that the motion-picture be composed of *motion*. The film opens with fast pans of the bandits riding over hills, and ends with the chaos of the battle itself, motion so swift we can almost not see it at all. There is no shot that does not have motion, either in the object photographed, or in the movement of the camera itself. The motion may be small (the quivering nostrils in the long-held image of the village elder) or it may be great (the huge, sweeping frescoes of the charges) but it is always there.

At the same time, another kind of motion is present. Kurosawa, always an economical film-maker, uses a number of short-cuts which hasten the pace of the story itself. When the farmer first approaches Shimura the continuity is:

> *Farmer, face down in the dirt, Shimura looking / cut / new location, an inn, and Shimura is saying to the farmer: "It's impossible."*

All obvious retelling is left out, all obvious continuity linkage (the two of them walking to the inn, for example) (1) is rigorously excluded. Again, Inaba (sensing that Kimura is waiting with the stick just inside the door) stops outside.

> *He says: "Oh, come now. No jokes," / cut / inside the inn, he and Shimizu are sitting down and he is saying: "Well, it sounds interesting."*

Sometimes scenes are telescoped and put into one. There is a beautiful example of this during the funeral of Chiaki. All are gathered around the mound and Mifune dashes back to get their banner (which Chiaki had made) and climbs a roof to put it on the ridgepole—a gesture of defiance. He suddenly looks at the hills and there, as though in answer (a marvelous image), come wave after wave of bandits, riding down on the village, heralding the first of the major battles. As Mifune looks, there is a wide pan which moves

---

1. This is Richie's first explicit use of the word "example," although he has already given us several of them. Richie will use the word often and, more significantly, will offer us many examples to illustrate his generalizations. In this sense, this excerpt from his book-length treatment of Kurosawa's films can serve as an excellent model of critical method. The point here is not so much whether Richie's observations are or are not valid, but rather that we know clearly with what we are agreeing or disagreeing.

from village to hills. At the same time the sounds of weeping turn to cries of alarm from the villagers, to cries of exultation from the samurai—who now want to fight. Within this single scene not only has action been carried forward but—as though the pan had caused it which, in a way it did—the entire mood has been changed, in just two seconds, from abject sorrow to the most fierce joy.

Another means of telescoping is through the interlinking of very short (usually funny) scenes, connected with wipes,(2) that Kurosawa has used from *They Who Step on the Tiger's Tail* onward. It is seen at its funniest both here and in *Sanjuro*. The samurai are being taken to the village, and their journey is seen in a mosaic of tiny scenes the point of which is that they are being followed by Mifune who, taciturn, apparently stupid, wants to join them, and at the same time cannot bring himself to. The entire sequence (covering a seemingly enormous journey) takes just three minutes and at the end Mifune, looking down at the village, utters his ironic and prophetic remark which (in retrospect at any rate) makes him appear much more human, much less of the clown: "Whew—what a dung pile. I'd certainly hate to die in a place like that."

All of these short-cuts and telescopings, all of this motion on the screen, means that the picture moves very fast indeed. It is so swift that Kurosawa has availed himself of at least several devices to insure that he does not lose his audience. The first of these is the banner and, at the same time, a list which Shimura draws up in which the number of circles indicates the number of bandits. Like the bullets in *Stray Dog*, like the money in *One Wonderful Sunday*, the viewer keeps score, as it were, by seeing how many down, how many to go. Each scratched circle means one less bandit.

Another way in which Kurosawa keeps his audience up to the pace he has set is by a full explication of the visual surroundings. In the original version of the picture, this is even stronger, but even in the cut version (which is all that other countries ever see of this picture) this explication is very strong. He begins with a map (as he does in *Stray Dog*, in *The Hidden Fortress*, and in *High and Low*)—a map which Shimura has drawn and which is a bird's-eye view of the village. Kurosawa loves bird's-eye views, and he is particularly fond of anything which will show all the ingredients of a certain

---

2. What are wipes?

situation, which will allow you to spread them all out before you and try to put them together. It is like the watchmaker's interest, the cook's interest—the finished thing is all very well but how it got finished is the most interesting thing. Consequently we learn all about the various sections of the village and (as with the room in *The Lower Depths*) we get to know it extremely well, better perhaps than most places we actually visit. In the same way we watch the samurai, first hear of their plans, and then see them in action (much as we, fascinated, watch the police force in *High and Low*) and then judge the results. As always, Kurosawa is particularly careful to shows us *how* a thing happens.

Finally, in the last reel, we are shown how a battle occurs. It resembles what we have been prepared for, but at the same time it is entirely different. Shimura speaking in measured tones and pointing to his map is one thing; this inferno of men and horses, rain and mud, is quite another thing. Reality is very different from illusion.

Even on a technical level, quite removed from the context which gives it its final meaning, this last reel is one of the greatest of cinematic accomplishments. It is chaotic but never chaos; disordered but orderly in its disorder. The rain pours down; bandits dash in; horses neigh and rear; Shimura poses, bow ready; Mifune slashes; an arrow thuds home and we glimpse it only for the fraction of a second necessary; riderless horses rear in terror; a samurai slips; Mifune grabs another sword. All of these images and literally hundreds more are crowded into a final reel which galvanizes the screen. (Having already given us plenty of excitement in the earlier battles, here Kurosawa does himself one better and uses telephoto lenses—a rarity in 1954—to bring the action directly into the laps of the audience. The first of these telescopic shots is a horse-fall which seems to occur directly where the camera is and rarely fails to evoke a gasp from the audience.)

At the same time, in the final reel, we again see that what keeps this film (and all of Kurosawa's films) so completely vital is, after all, the cutting, and consequently the tempo. We have had indication of this before in the film. In the hunting-for-the-samurai section, a set piece like the journey-to-the-village which follows, Kurosawa shows us the four farmers in two pairs, each searching through the same town. In between each image of a pair of farmers looking from right to left, or left to right, their eyes following the samurai, sweeping pans (3) of the samurai themselves are intercut. Thus the sweeping pans are answered by sweeping movements of the eyes of the peasants. The delight of this sequence (4) (the delight of the hunt, of the unknown, accompanied on the sound track by music unmistakably of that intent) lies in the very brevity of each shot. Each is no longer than two seconds. Thus, even in a simple sequence such as this, expectation and excitement are generated through the cutting.

Mifune's fine scene with the armour is another example of Kurosawa's editing. It plays so very well and is so powerful that it is only on re-seeing that one notices, first, that Mifune acts directly into the camera—which is one of the reasons for the power (as in the final close-up in *The Lower Depths*) and second, that each shot of Mifune is a bit shorter than the one which went before. The tempo is accelerated by the cutting, and these long scenes become shorter. The next to last (Shimura) and last (Mifune) are the conventional one-two shots, each lasting for a conventional amount of time.

Another example of creative cutting is the raid on the bandits' fort. There is a broad downward pan. First we see mountains, then below it the road along which the three horsemen are galloping. The pan does not turn sidewise with the horsemen, however, nor does it stop (as one might expect)—rather, it continues on down, leaving the road (and the action) behind. At the same time, as the road disappears at the top of the frame, a slow lateral wipe (left to right) begins. This is the waterfall scene, and the samurai are already at their destination. The effect on the screen is, oddly, diagonal. Two essentially unrelated scenes have been perfectly connected, and we accept cause and effect though there is actually a great and purposeful lapse in the continuity. This fine effect of continuous movement is achieved entirely in the editing, since it would be impossible to obtain it photographically.

Sometimes sound enforces the cut. On the first day of the battle, there is a good example:

> *The samurai, all asleep / cut / enormous close-ups of horses running, the bandits approaching, hoofs thundering on the sound track / cut / all asleep, but the swordsman*

---

3. What is a pan?
4. What is a sequence? And how is it distinguished from a scene?

has heard (though we hear nothing) and stands up / cut / racing and hoofbeats / cut / all the samurai are standing and waiting; we hear hoofs very faintly and then, in the far distance see the dust raised by the horses.

These are only four shots and each is slightly shorter than the other. By the time the battle begins, we are quite prepared for it, and the editing has done it.

Besides technique, however, there is something else about this film (and about most of Kurosawa's pictures) that defies analysis because there are no words to describe the effect. (5) What I mean might be called the irrational rightness of an apparently gratuitous image in its proper place, and the image that I always think of is that wonderful and mysterious scene in *Zéro de conduite* where it is apparently Sunday, Papa is reading the paper, and the boy's little sister moves the fishbowl (hanging on a chain from its stand) so that when her brother removes his blindfold he can see the sun touching it. The scene moves me to tears and I have no idea why. It was not economical of Vigo to have included it, it "means" nothing—and it is beautiful beyond words. (6)

Part of the beauty of such scenes (actually rather common in all sorts of films, good, bad, and indifferent) is just that they are "thrown away" as it were, that they have no place, that they do not ostensibly contribute, that they even constitute what has been called

---

5. Here Richie treads on dangerous ground. What does he mean when he says "there are no words to describe the effect"? To employ elementary (but nonetheless valid) logic, if there are no words, how then can Richie write two paragraphs on the effect?

6. Richie seems to use "means" here as if he believed that scenes in films which do not contribute to the advancement of story are without meaning. (Would you agree with him?) Here we begin to understand, then, just what it is that Richie sees as defying analysis—and, in this context at least, as "beautiful beyond words." But couldn't one say that it is the obligation of the critic to find words with which to describe film experiences? Isn't Richie merely suggesting that some experiences are so powerful that we would prefer to accept them as mysterious phenomena rather than subject ourselves to the rigors—and possibly to the resultant pain—of the analysis of our own responses?

bad film-making. It is not the beauty of these images, however, that captivates (plenty of films, particularly Japanese films, are filled with irrelevant and beautiful scenes which completely fail to move) but their mystery. They *must* remain unexplained. It has been said that after a film is over all that remains are a few scattered images, and if they remain then the film was memorable. That is true so far as it goes but one must add that if the images remain, it means only that the images were for some reason or other memorable. Further, if one remembers carefully one finds that it is only the uneconomical, mysterious images which remain.

Kurosawa's films are filled with them, and if I have not spoken of them before it is because I have been trying to make certain similarities among the films clear, to trace a general family likeness among them. Actually, these isolated images are his most beautiful, and (because so mysterious) his most profound.

For example, in *Drunken Angel* there is a scene where Mifune lies ill in the room of his mistress. Shimura comes in and does not wake him but sits by the bed. He opens the girl's powder-box. It has a music-box inside and plays a Chinese tune. While it is playing, he notices a Javanese shadow-puppet hanging on the wall. While looking benevolently at the sleeping Mifune (and this is the first time he has been nice to him—when he is asleep and cannot know it), he begins to move the puppet this way and that, observing its large shadow over the sleeping gangster. While one might be able to read something into the scene, it is so beautiful, so perfect, and so mysterious that even the critical faculty must hesitate, then back away.

Its beauty, certainly, is partly that in the closely reasoned philosophical argument which is this film, it is a luxury—take it away and it would never be missed. It gives no information about plot or characters. (7) Kurosawa's films are so rigorous and, at the same time, so closely reasoned, that little scenes such as this appeal with the direct simplicity of water in the desert. There are many more (a mysterious shot of the tinker in *The Lower Depths* all alone, outside, huddled up on the ground, devouring a piece of candy; a

---

7. At this point, Richie makes explicit an attitude which earlier was only implied. It *is* advancement of plot and character which "means."

completely unmotivated scene of Mifune in *Scandal* roaring his motorcycle—only the motorcycle is in his studio, where he brings it for the night, and it is up on a stand, going no place; etc.) but in no other single film are there as many as in *Seven Samurai.*

What one remembers best from this superbly economical film then are those scenes which seem most uneconomical—that is, those which apparently add nothing to it. There is a short cut during the burning of the bandit's fort where we watch a woman awake, see the fire, and yet refuse to warn the others. (She is the wife of one of the farmers, raped and carried away by the bandits.) The scene is beautiful enough, this hopeless farm woman, clothed in stolen silk, half obscured by the wisps of smoke—but Kurosawa renders it utterly mysterious (and completely right) by inserting beneath it the sound of the Noh flute with unearthly effect—a trick he later repeated, less gratuitously, in *The Throne of Blood* and *The Hidden Fortress.* Again, there is the short scene where a prisoner has been caught, and the oldest woman in the village—she who has lost all of her sons—is called to come and murder him. She marches slowly forward, a hoe in her hand, terribly old, terribly bent, a crone. And though we sympathize, the image is one of horror—it is death itself because we have seen, and will see, men killed and think little of it, but here is death itself with a hoe, mysterious, unwilled. Or, those several shots of the avenue of cryptomerias, and two bonfires, one far and one near. This is where the bandits will come but we do not yet know this. Instead, the trees, the fires, the night—all are mysterious, memorable. Or, that magnificent image which we see after Mifune has rescued the baby and burst into tears. The mill is burning and Mifune is sitting in the stream, looking at the child and crying. The next scene is a simple shot of the water-wheel turning, as it always has. But the wheel is on fire. Or, that curiously long close-up of the dead Mifune. He has stolen some armor but his bottom is unprotected. Now he lies on a narrow bridge, on his face, and the rain is washing away the dirt from his buttocks. He lies there like a child—all men with bare bottoms look like children—yet he is dead, and faintly ridiculous in death, and yet he was our friend for we have come to love him. All of this we must think as we sit through the seconds of this simple, unnecessary, and unforgettable scene.

Or, my favorite among all of these magical images, that following Shimura's saying that the bandits are all dead, and Kimura's sinking, weeping, into the mud. The screen slowly darkens. It is as though the end has come, and one hopes it has not, because this, somehow, is not enough and because, even more strongly, we do not want to leave these men yet. The screen gets darker and darker. They are lost in the gloom. We sit in the darkness and then we hear music. It is the music of the farmers, and the screen lightens to reveal one of the most delightful and heart-breaking of sequences: the rice-planting.

It is seen as dance, which indeed rice-planting is in Japan. A small orchestra (flute, drums, bells, singer) accompanies the girls as they plunge the new shoots into the wet earth, all in unison. Since this is the way rice is actually planted, we accept it as real. At the same time, after the uproar, pain, horror, grief of the final battle, we had not expected a divertissement. Strictly speaking, the entire rice-planting sequence is unnecessary to the film; not speaking strictly at all, it is vital—perhaps because it relaxes, with its very beauty and its anticlimax. Nerves have been played upon and wrought up to an extent completely unusual in an action-picture, and suddenly—childlike beauty. When tears flow in *Seven Samurai,* they flow here. (8)

Then comes the great final scene with its reminiscence of the opening scene, followed by Shimura's profoundly ironic remark, and the picture ends on the splendid image of the high grave-hill with four naked swords stuck into the top, and three mere men standing below. And, under this, the child-like music of the peasants fades and is replaced by the music associated with the samurai.

Kurosawa has given us beauty in the midst of knowledge, a kind of reassurance while questioning all reassurances. At the same time that he questions deeds, hopes, thoughts, he has purposely played upon our emotions and we, too, have become open and child-like. More, in this profoundly subtle and mysterious final sequence (samurai and peasants; fighting and rice-planting; silence and music; darkness and light), he has indicated hope. We are all, after all, human; we all feel the same—we are all peasants at heart.

---

8. Finally, Richie comes to terms with one of those mysterious and magical moments of beauty. There are sequences in films which are not "strictly speaking" necessary but which are still "vital." Is Richie beginning to question his own criteria of plot and character advancement?

Robert Hatch, *THE NATION* December 8, 1956

The new Japanese film, *The Magnificent Seven,* is also in the fashionable new length—two and a half hours, approximately. It was directed by Akira Kurosawa, who was responsible for *Rashomon,* but it is much more easily accepted by Western audiences than was the earlier film, or for that matter any of the major Japanese films that have been shown here. (1)

It is being defined as an Oriental Western, which I think is about as helpful as calling a bullfight a Latin rodeo. It doesn't need to be defined—it can very easily be described. (2) Some five hundred years ago (I take this in the sense of "once upon a time") a remote Japanese village, grown desperate from repeated plunder by a robber band living in the nearby hills, determines to hire some samurai (professional warriors) to destroy this plague. Samurai are expensive and normally work for princes, but by persistent search the agents from the village are able to find seven who, from temporary poverty, interest in a new kind of fight, or appreciation of the villagers' misery, are willing to accept the job.

The picture, then, is the story of how these professionals prepare to defend a defenseless position against improbable odds, the relationship between the elegant, sophisticated warriors and their almost savage employers, and finally the battle itself which takes the form of repeated onslaughts, each more desperate and deadly than its predecessor. This is melodrama, romance, knight errantry—universal material. (3) In this particular picture it is excellent because the

---

1. Does Hatch tell us what it is about this film that allows it to be "more easily accepted by Western audiences"?

2. Hatch makes an important distinction between "definition" and "description." What is the difference between these terms?

3. What Hatch is saying here is that the patterns which emerge from this film can be found in all cultures. Everybody can respond

---

characters are admirably differentiated and thoroughly interesting and because the details working up to the decisive encounter are engrossing and skilfully timed to pull the tension tight. I am not persuaded that samurai as a class were as amiable, high-minded, inventive or entertaining as this group (one of the seven, a pseudo-samurai, is even a brilliantly athletic clown), but Kurosawa and his cast share an image of chivalry that is exceedingly winning. (4) Beyond that, the picture is beautifully photographed: the village, the enticing, dangerous woodlands, the bandits' stronghold, meticulous details of defense and drill, horses in wild flight, close-order battle and quiet scenes of mourning, even a lightly-sketched love affair, are all photographed with a direct, uncluttered vision that shows a delight in the clarity and flexibility of the camera. It is not remarkable camera work, except that it is remarkably good. And *The Magnificent Seven,* for all it will be shown in art houses, is not an arty or even a remarkable film. (5) Except that good story-telling is always worth remarking. (6)

---

to romance, melodrama, knight errantry. Despite their universality, however, "melodrama, romance, knight errantry" are usually critical pejoratives. Why? Does Hatch in the sentence that follows provide a sufficient answer? And does he further help us to understand what is meant by these terms?

4. Is Hatch raising a question about the truth-value of art?
5. What does "arty" mean when applied to film?
6. Is a criterion of excellence being presented here?

NEWSWEEK
December 10, 1956

The first brief script outline may have gone something like this: A little mountain town has become completely demoralized by the imminence of an attack by a gang of roving bandits. There seems to be only one solution: The town must hire some professional fighters of its own. It finds them, hungry ones, poor ones. They all settle down and wait for the raid. Finally, it comes in mighty rushes on horseback, and the slaughter in the street is gory and excessive. The town is saved, but the hired fighters (three survive out of seven) hit the lonesome road again, rootless and melancholy.

Connoisseurs of Westerns will immediately recognize this as one of the basic plots. They should find considerable interest in the current variation, since it was made in Japan by the director of "Rashomon" and deals with the siege of a Japanese village in the late sixteenth century. People who are not connoisseurs of Westerns will also find it absorbing much of the time, despite its length—two hours and 38 minutes. Most of the hired fighters are memorable individuals; the picture glows from time to time with affection and humor; it gathers great momentum, and all along the way from its leisurely beginning to its wildly clangorous ending it is full of small fascinations for Americans, of unaccustomed acting styles, from virtual immobility through well-nigh hysterical gasping to compulsive hopping.

Summing Up: Fine Eastern Western.(1)

---

1. Hatch has suggested that calling this film an "eastern western" is as useless as "calling a bullfight a Latin rodeo." Does this review prove his point?

THE NIGHT or LA NOTTE

TIME

February 23, 1962

The Body of This Death

The Night (Lopert) begins at noon. In brilliant sunshine, silently, from the summit of a glittering skyscraper, from the zenith of man's pride and material achievement, the camera descends relentlessly into the convenient hell of a meaningless marriage, into a dark and joyless night of the contemporary soul imagined with monstrous art by Michelangelo Antonioni, the somber master of cinema who made *L'Avventura* (TIME, April 7).(1)

In the first scene of the movie, a well-known Italian writer (Marcello Mastroianni) and his wife (Jeanne Moreau) arrive at a hospital in Milan to visit a dying friend (Bernhard Wicki). Leaving the friend's room some minutes later than his wife, the writer is accosted

---

1. In this first paragraph, the reviewer refers to the camera. Note the context. Is he using the term in a technical sense? If so, what information are we being given about the workings of the camera; that is, what shot or device is being pointed to?

in the hall by a mental patient, a nymphomaniac. Impulsively, he enters her room.

The incident is revolting and revealing. The writer, frightened by the presence of death, snatches at sex for reassurance. But a man who cannot die cannot live: the writer is a moral cadaver. Since he cannot face his condition, his wife has to face it for him. On the way home he confesses somewhat too readily what has happened—if she forgives, he can forget. (2)

Night falls. Man and wife are restless and preoccupied—easier to go out than to be alone together. They drift off to an all-night brawl at a millionaire's mausoleal residence. "They're all dead here," the wife sighs as they enter the house. Antonioni's point is unmistakable: his hero, like Orpheus, has entered Hades, (3) the contemporary hell of unmeaning materialism—will he find there the love, the soul, the vital core of meaning he has lost? He finds the daughter of the millionaire (Monica Vitti), a dark-haired charmer whom he fiercely pursues, only to find her as empty and desperate as he is. "At heart," she tells him with a vacant smile, "I'm just a girl who likes golf." Dimly he begins to understand that something is dreadfully wrong with him. (4)

---

2. To what extent is the reviewer at this point offering us insight into what actually happens on the screen? To what extent does he assume the universality of his own moral views?

3. There are several things to consider in this sentence. It is clear that at least in this context the reviewer subscribes to the *auteur* theory of film. This film is the creation of Antonioni. And indeed the whole review seems to be a preparation for the concluding paragraph, which is devoted to Antonioni's life-view. The question that must be answered here is this: to what exent is the reviewer discussing the film and to what extent is he discussing Antonioni? Are the two synonymous?

Further, from the construction of the sentence, it would seem that this metaphor is Antonioni's. We know from our experience of the film, however, that such a metaphor is clearly not made explicit. Where else in the review does this confusion of the reviewer's metaphors with those of the film occur?

4. Again in this paragraph, the reviewer has assumed that his view as to what choices people should make is a generally accepted one. Where has this been revealed?

Morning sheds a cold, clear light on the subject. The writer and his wife wander through the expensive desolation of the millionaire's golf course. She explains to him calmly, without bitterness, that he simply does not exist—he has never lived, he has only written. She adds that she no longer loves him, but she has too little strength to make a break, to start a new life; and he has even less. Death, the dread of his own unbeing, frightens him once again into the arms of the nearest woman—ironically, the woman is his wife. He begins to make passionate, terrified love to her at the edge of a sand trap. "But I don't love you any more," she protests wearily. "Be quiet," he mutters hoarsely, tugging at her skirt. (5)

The Night, made a year later than *L'Avventura,* is its sequel in spirit. It examines the same diseases of leisure: anxiety, despair, loss of soul, and the degenerate eroticism that serves as a soul substitute. (6) It employs the same radically original methods: the deliberate, contemplative, novelistic pace of the narration ("I write with a camera; I make visual novels"), the lifelike lack of any point-to-point correspondence between what a character is doing and what he is thinking, the inspired sense for the importance of unimportance, for what is happening when nothing is happening.

In *The Night,* as in *L'Avventura,* these methods have produced a picture that, for all the fascination of its photography and performances, moves too slowly, lasts too long (two hours) and demands too much intellectual attention to command a mass audience. (7)

---

5. What indications do you find in the preceding five paragraphs that this is a review of a film rather than a novel or a play?

6. Here, the reviewer ostensibly begins to talk about technique. He notes the "novelistic pace of the narration" and in parenthesis, quotes Antonioni to clarify the "method." What is your understanding of "novelistic pace"? And how relevant is Antonioni's own view of his work? Is Antonioni more qualified to "explain" his film than is the reviewer? Note, too, the reviewer's inclusion of "the lifelike lack of . . . correspondence between what a character is doing and what he is thinking" and "inspired sense for the importance of unimportance" under the category of cinematic "method." Are these *methods* and are they *cinematic?*

7. The reviewer now explicitly evaluates the film. Pace and length are traditional kinds of judgments, whether or not they seem

Even moviegoers who liked *L'Avventura* will probably find *The Night* black and cold; it has a basilisk intensity that turns the heart to stone. Nevertheless, at the heart of Antonioni's plutonic pessimism lives a blazing mote of hope. Though he confesses no faith, he is essentially a religious artist. (8) He believes that a spirit inhabits human beings, and in every film he proclaims his creed: to obey that spirit is to live, to deny it is to perish. In every film his heroes, though in humbler phrases, cry as St. Paul once cried aloud: "O wretched man that I am! Who shall deliver me from the body of this death?" And Antonioni always pities them. He attacks the weakness, not the man. He takes no pleasure in human suffering. He forces himself to examine it as a doctor would examine it. (9) He is a pathologist of morals, an Italian Chekhov. (10)

---

appropriately applied here. His third point, however, is that the film "demands too much intellectual attention to command a mass audience." What are the implications of this remark?

8. In what sense does the reviewer's dismissal of Antonioni's profession of "no faith" contradict his earlier use of Antonioni's own comments regarding his film technique?

9. To what extent have hope and despair become aesthetic criteria in these statements?

10. For whom is this film recommended?

Pauline Kael, *THE MASSACHUSETTS REVIEW* IV, 2, Winter, 1963

The Come-Dressed-as-the-Sick-Soul-of-Europe Parties: La Notte, Last Year at Marienbad, La Dolce Vita

. . . In *La Notte* the wife goes back to where she and her husband *used* to go, reads him a letter to remind him how he *used* to *feel.* Like the nagging hypochondriacs who enjoy poor health, she has nothing to do but savor the dregs of old experience as she wanders aimlessly in her melancholy. Well, what has defeated them all? (1) I don't want to sound like a Doris Day character—the All-American middle-aged girl—but when I put the coffee on in the morning and let the dogs out, I don't think I feel more alienated than people who did the same things a hundred years ago. (2)

I have heard that at the graduate-school level Antonioni's endings are said to be very beautiful, even inspiring, that the "shared hope-

---

1. As indicated, the passage presented here is part of a longer essay in which *La Notte* is only one of several films discussed. Thus in the question, "What has defeated them all?", *them* refers not only to the husband and wife of *La Notte* but to characters in the other films as well. Still, it is interesting to consider whether or not *La Notte* provides an answer to the question, at least in so far as Lidia and Giovanni are concerned. And more significantly, does the film have a responsibility to do so?

2. How relevant are Mrs. Kael's feelings of alienation to an informed evaluation of the film? And what is implied in her comparison between present feelings and those of the past? What does she expect of a film?

lessness" indicates that modern human experience need not be altogether downhill, that you must make the best of a bad world, and that there is nobility and beauty in resigning yourself to the futility of life. Surely this is the last gasp of depleted academia.(3) In *La Notte* Antonioni has intentionally created a ghastly spectacle: two people sharing an empty life.(4) The problem of interpretation is simply whether we can accept the meanings and overtones with which he surrounds this dead marriage; is it so central and so symbolic that all these ornaments and icicles can be hung from it?

I reject the terms of the film on commonplace grounds: why the devil do they stay together, why doesn't she leave him if this is how she feels? What has made this a world in which there are no alternatives, no hope? And what is so shocking about a married couple, after ten years or so, no longer being in love or having anything to say to each other? What is so dreadful about their looking for other people to whom they can feel some response? Why are they shown as so withered away, destroyed, dead because they are weary of each other? And if they have no other interests, why should we care about them?(5)

And isn't it rather adolescent to treat the failure of love with such solemnity? For whom does love last? Why try to make so much spiritual desolation out of the transient nature of what we all know to be transient, as if this transiency somehow defined our time and place? If it is the sickness of our time that married people get fed-up with each other, when was the world healthy? I thought it was the health of our culture that when married people have had it, they are free and sufficiently independent to separate. (Perhaps the

---

3. What is the function of the phrase "graduate-school level"? Similarly, "the last gasp of depleted academia"?

4. How does Mrs. Kael know what Antonioni *intended* to create?

5. Pauline Kael calls *La Notte* a "ghastly spectacle." She then asks a series of questions, including "And what is so shocking about a married couple . . . no longer being in love . . . ?" Is there a contradiction here? Or is Mrs. Kael pointing to a disproportion in the film between what might be called the stimulus (the loveless marriage) and the response (a sense of hopelessness—the creation of a "ghastly spectacle")? And if the latter, have we hit upon (if inversely) a criterion of excellence?

marriage in *La Notte* just lasted too long; I don't know anybody who has stayed married for ten years—nobody except relatives.) (6) Surely there are some institutions, like magazines, to which we must apply criteria, other than durability: we do not, for example, call Dwight Macdonald's *Politics* a failure because it ceased publication or the *Saturday Review of Literature* a success because it is interminable.

---

6. To what extent has Mrs. Kael replaced aesthetic considerations of the film with her own judgments about what is important and what is trivial in life? How relevant is the marital experience of Mrs. Kael's friends to an evaluation of the film? Note that this kind of criticism raises significant questions about the relationship of art to reality, by no means a concern special to film. What is it we mean when we say a film is true-to-life? Do we mean it's true to my life or your life? Must it be true to our friends' lives or only our relatives'? Or do we allow for the possibility that it can inform us of aspects of life that we are unfamiliar with and whose truth factor remains at best untestable?

Stanley Kauffmann, *THE NEW REPUBLIC* February 26, 1962

An Artist for an Age

Michelangelo Antonioni's new film *The Night* is so perfectly congruent with our concerns, so piercingly honest, that it is close to a personal experience. Such an acutely subjective reaction is not always the purpose of art, but it is his purpose and he achieved it.

The story is spare. In Milan live Giovanni and Lidia, a novelist and his wife, childless, in their thirties, married some years, affectionate with each other but no longer in love. The film covers about 18 hours in their lives: a visit to a dying friend in a hospital; a publication-day party for Giovanni's new book (which he fears may be his last); a long lonely walk by Lidia through the city; their visit to a night club where they see an erotic balancing act; an all-night party at a millionaire's villa where each of them meets someone who —temporarily, at least—attracts him. At dawn they cross the huge lawn together, the tired dance-band still playing. Behind some trees they sit. She reads to him a tender love-letter, addressed to her. He asks her who wrote it. "You did," she replies. Stung with anguish for his lost self and love, he seizes her. At first she denies him, saying she doesn't love him any more. He persists and she gradually acquiesces. The film ends with the couple making love on the grass. Whether they will be able to *re*-make their love is undecided. (1)

The film has no plot. It is a series of events given their dynamics by the depth of character of the two people passing through them: (2) a man and a woman, once in love, who still live with and like each other but who have floated apart out of finger-tip's reach. Seen through their eyes, vibrated through their nervous systems, the incidents in the film—sometimes unremarkable in themselves—take on the proportions of a pilgrimage. (3) This is because their relationship

---

1. Note Kauffmann's extensive summary of the events of the film in place of the more conventional selective summary. This foreshadows Kauffmann's general approach to the film; he ignores nothing in it and regards all aspects of the film as contributing to its effect.

2. Kauffmann tells us there is "no plot" in *The Night.* There is, however, he says, "a series of events." What does he mean by "dynamics" and how does this provide an important clue to the distinction between a plot and "a series of events"? Consider here the role of cause and effect in traditional concepts of plot.

3. When Kauffmann comments on the fact that the film is seen through the eyes of the characters, he is of course making reference to point of view. In what ways is point of view established in film when it is not simply that of the camera—the physical relation of the camera, that is, to what it is photographing?

is not sexual *ennui* or a stage in marital intrigue; it is the result of their being perceptive people in a world inimical to confidence, therefore inimical to lasting love. With no sense of strain whatever, this pair step forward as protagonists of the age's love tragedy: the lack of a whole, oriented self to give in love.

I must make it clear that this is not just one more European film about "the moral collapse of our time"—the label that every lurid French or Italian film carries to justify its luridness. *The Night* is certainly concerned with the theme of Yeats' *Second Coming*; the best *do* lack all conviction, while the worst *are* full of passionate intensity. (See the millionaire host.) (4) The film exists in an ambience that is post-Hitler, post-Stalin, post-Bomb, in a society caught between the far-reaching but iron-lined avenues of Marxism and, on the other hand, a creeping corpulence fed extensively by military preparations to deter that Marxism. (5)

But Antonioni is no glib, self-scratching Jeremiah. He is not merely past outmoded hope, he is past despair. He looks at this new environment as his home and, having decided not to die, lives. His characters are in their habitat and know it; they face the task of imagining a viable future. As for their marriage, we see them discovering the geography of the island on which they have been cast, recognizing that other lovers are at best excursions that will only take them to other islands, that in the fact of mutual compassion there is justification for compassion, that they can stay together because they are somewhat consecrated by knowledge of each other's weaknesses and by the time they have passed together. The film finishes without rosiness but with the cleanliness of scouring candor, a sense that the worst is known.

"I know what to write," says Giovanni, "but I don't know how to write it." Like every artist in history, he sees more than he is capable of expressing, but, unlike them, he has no relevant framework within which to strive. He no longer knows how to speak or the point in speaking. "A writer is an anachronism," he says, "doing something that can't be done yet by machines." The horrible moment for him

---

4. What is the function of Kauffmann's parenthetical remark in this context?

5. Who is Kauffmann's audience? In what ways does he make his concept of audience clear?

comes when his industrialist-host offers to take him out of his anachronism with a job as corporation historian and publicity director; an offer made with all the lubricity of the materialist ego that knows how to re-enforce itself with the quasi-idealistic. The horror of the offer is that Giovanni realizes its aptness. The job would at least fill a gap in him, even though he knows it would be one long, plump suicide. But the real purification by this horror comes near the end when he tells Lidia of the offer and she says, "Why not?" When she who knows him and has admired him can say that, it is rock-bottom for him. Her bland acceptance is the shock that may reawaken him and connect him with a revised world.

As for Lidia, the death of their friend Tommaso is the end of her last link with selfless love. Tommaso, who was never physically her lover, worshipped her, and almost convinced her (she says) that she was intelligent. Giovanni spoke to her only of himself "and I loved it"; but now all that is left of Giovanni for her is an ego that doubts itself. The loss of Tommaso's love—the only one without ego—is like losing parents a second time. She is reconciled to loneliness, even to her husband's quest for illusions of refreshment in other women, both because she is no longer jealous and because she wishes him well. But at the end, if she is not convinced that he is again capable of his former love, she at least knows that he realizes this and is ashamed of it, instead of accepting it; and in that shame is a possible seed.

Marcello Mastroianni, as Giovanni, brings to full flower the wide range of talents he has always shown. It is a performance of utter comprehension and delicacy that *begins* by being true and then goes on to harrow us. Jeanne Moreau, who plays Lidia, has seemed to me until now a film actress in the least complimentary sense, a woman whose performances were for the most part albums of varyingly interesting photographs. Under Antonioni's hand, what was semblance has become vitalized. "The director," he says, "must know how to demand," and he has certainly demanded well of her. She moves through this film like a sad suite of airs. Her face, elegiac and passionate, seems to brood over this film, even when she is absent.

Monica Vitti, brunette in this film, has a less complex role as the millionaire's daughter, but gives it waywardness without coyness and sex with sensibility. Bernhard Wicki (the director of *The Bridge*) endows his brief appearance as Tommaso with the clarity of the dying and the pride of a man who has faced his limitations—all this so sharply that the later news of his death make us feel a loss. (6)

As for Antonioni himself: I have now seen *The Night* three times and I speak carefully when I say that I think he is making a new art-form. In this film, even more strikingly than in his *L'Avventura,* he is forging a new language apposite to a changed world. For a society theistically based and teleologically organized, the concepts of drama that derived substantially from Aristotle have sufficed for centuries. The film was born to that inheritance and, out of it, still produces fine works (although with a perceptibly increasing tinge of nostalgia). Antonioni has seen the dwindling force of this inheritance and is finding means to supplement it. He is achieving what many contemporary artists in his and other fields are seeking and not often with his success: renewal of his art rather than repetition.

Jackson Pollock, Hans Hofmann, and their kin are exponents of dissatisfaction rather than re-creation. The anti-novelists, in their frustration with the limits of the conventional novel, ask readers to share their professional problems rather than to be affected as readers. Brecht jostled the traditional drama healthily, but his theater is didactic, aimed towards a different god-head—a temporal one that now seems sterile to many. The so-called Theater of the Absurd faces reality rigorously and poetically, but a theater of images and no characters is limited to disembodied effects—and each author seems to have one reiterated effect. Who needs to see another play by Beckett or Ionesco or Pinter? In films, too, the avant-garde—Cocteau and many others—have tried to find new methods; but they, too, have so concentrated on the attempt that they have neglected to communicate much content. A more conventional artist, Ingmar Bergman feels present spiritual hungers as keenly as anyone, but his films so far, for all their superb qualities, exemplify Mulligan's line to Dedalus: "You have the cursed jesuit strain in you, only it's injected the wrong way."

Antonioni, however, seems to be making the miracle: finding a way to speak to us about ourselves today without crankily throwing away all that went before and without being bound by it. He is reshaping the idea of the content of film drama, discarding ancient and

---

6. What are Kauffmann's criteria for excellence in film acting?

less ancient concepts, re-directing traditional audience expectations towards immersion in character rather than conflict of character. (7) He is re-shaping time itself in his films, taking it out of its customary synoptic form, wringing intensity out of its distention, daring to ask us to "live through" experiences with less distillation, deriving his drama from the very texture of such experiences and their juxtaposition, rather than from formal clash and climax and resolution. Fundamentally, he gives us characters whose drama consists in facing life minute after minute rather than in moving through organized plots with articulated obstacles; who have no well-marked cosmos to use as a tennis-player uses a court; who live and die without the implication of a divine eye that sees their virtues (whether men do or not) and cherishes them. (8)

John Grierson once said that when a director dies, he becomes a photographer; but Antonioni gets emotional utility—in a film about *people*—out of surfaces and compositions. He uses photography for enrichment, not for salon gasps: for example, the scene where Lidia goes for a ride in the rain with a man and the downpour seems to put the car in danger of dissolution. (9)

The sequence that best represents Antonioni's style, is the one in which Lidia slips away from the publisher's party and wanders through the streets. Conditioned as we are, (10) we *expect* something; we think she is off to meet a lover, or to kill herself, or to get involved in an accident. But nothing happens; and everything happens. She strolls past a bus conductor eating a sandwich and is fascinated by his

---

7. What distinction is Kauffmann making here when he suggests that *The Night* directs the audience's attention toward "immersion in character" rather than "conflict in character"? Can you find evidence in the film to support or refute this contention?

8. What elements does Kauffmann cite to support his earlier statement that Antonioni is creating "a new art form"?

9. What criteria does Kauffmann imply as regards photography when he uses such phrases as "salon gasps" and in his reference to Grierson's remark?

10. Is Kauffmann right when he speaks of the motion picture audience as *conditioned*? And, if so, in what ways does this conditioning provide obstacles to the enjoyment of *The Night.*

existence and his appetite in the same universe with her; she passes two men laughing uproariously at a joke and she smiles, too, although she has not heard it, anxious to join them, to be one of the human race; she encounters a crying child and kneels briefly and unsuccessfully to comfort it; she tears a flake of rust off a corroding wall; she sees two young men punching each other ferociously, watches horrified, then screams for them to stop. (The victor thinks she must be attracted to him and starts to pursue her, and so Antonioni touches another old tribal nerve.) Then, in the suburbs she watches some boys shooting off rockets.

She finds she is in a neighborhood where she and Giovanni used to come years before. She telephones him and he drives out to pick her up. (11)

By drama-school definition, it is not a cumulative dramatic sequence. It is a miniature recapitulation, deftly done, of the possibilities of life: a child and an old woman, a man eating and a man punching, sunlight on a fountain and a greasy lewd stall-keeper. Antonioni holds it all together with something like the surface tension of liquids and, by not commenting, comments. It is essentially as drastic a revolution as abstract expressionist painting or Beckett's litany-like dialogue, but Antonioni has not estranged us in order to speak to us about loneliness; he has not sacrificed the link of recognition to make new images; he has not had to use absurdity to convey the absurd.

Of every directorial technique he is an easy master. I specify only two. His use of sound: the low-pitched conversation in the hospital is interrupted by the passage of a helicopter like a pause in music so that the hushed key will not become tedious. His symbolism (which is unobtrusive); the mushroom cloud of smoke that envelops the boy who fires the rocket, and the fact that Giovanni meets Lidia after her walk in front of a long-abandoned church.

For me, Antonioni has made in *The Night* and in *L'Avventura* the most subtly truthful theatrical works about the relation of the sexes since Joyce's *Exiles*. But he has done more. In *The Night* he has used a vitiated marriage as a metaphor of the crisis of faith in our age, the faith within which profoundest love and pettiest whim

---

11. What constitutes "style" for Kauffmann?

have always been contained. (12) He has used his camera as a hound of non-heaven ranging through the streets of Milan to find the beauty in necessity, the assurance in knowing that one can live without assurances. This film leaves us less deceived; thus with the truth in us less encumbered.

---

12. Does Kauffmann convince you that the metaphor he identifies is Antonioni's?

A NIGHT AT THE OPERA

Joseph Alsop Jr., *NEW YORK HERALD TRIBUNE*
December 15, 1935

Surrealism Beaten at Its Own Game

The first thoroughly successful example of surrealist art has arrived in town, with a surprising absence of acclaim by the critics of the avant-garde. You will not find in it a single slit eyeball, or even one ant crawling out of a hole in a woman's hand, but then, there are the Marx brothers, and they are quite sufficient. (1)

The truth is that Jean Cocteau, Salvador Dali, the gentlemen of "transition" and their friends and admirers may just as well forget about the whole business now, for those hardened left-bankers,

---

1. Is Alsop serious when he describes *A Night at the Opera* as "surrealist art"? Although Alsop may have *intended* to make a joke, does that preclude the possibility that his insight is a useful one, deserving serious consideration? And similarly, assuming that the Marx brothers did not *intend* to make a surrealistic film, does it follow necessarily that they did not make one?

Groucho, Harpo and Chico, have produced the ultimate in the surrealist line. Its name happens to be "A Night at the Opera," and it is one of the most generously amusing comic pictures on view in these parts for a considerable period.

Surrealism, should you happen to be unacquainted with the writings, paintings and photoplays of M. Cocteau, M. Dali and their none too cheerful companions, is a sort of dream art. There is more than a trace of Freud in it, and more than a trace of a strange lunatic humor. The artist is expected to set down images which occur, as it were automatically, inside his head. With M. Dali it takes the form of melted watches, stout women sitting on grisly shores with the silhouette of a night table cut from the center of their bodies, and "Le Chien Andalou," in which ants crawled and eyeballs were slit. With M. Cocteau, besides his cinematic adventures, it breaks out in such things as "Les Maries de la Tour Eiffel," with its celebrated end man and Mr. Bones, Phonograph No. 1 and Phonograph No. 2.

As a matter of fact the bloody sun seemed to be setting on surrealism's little but definitely hectic day until the Marx brothers came along with "A Night at the Opera." As you can imagine, since surrealism is a dream art, one of its most marked features has always been surprising transitions. The characters in the surrealist drama never know quite where they are at. Neither do the Marxes, or at least they seem not to know or care, which is better still. A Marx brothers picture has a good deal of the flavor of that unconsciously surrealist masterwork in verse, in which:

> He thought he saw an Albatross
> That fluttered round the lamp;
> He looked again, and found it was
> A Penny-Postage-Stamp.
> "You'd best be getting home," he said;
> "The nights are very damp."

There is one incident in a "Night at the Opera" which is probably surrealism's shining peak. It is quite useless to recount the plot of the show, for, like all good surrealist drama, its plot is not very important, although it does not imitate most of its predecessors in being also pretty bad to repeat in mixed company. Anyway, it is all about how the Marxes brought a young couple together, and placed them both, warbling madly, on the stage of the Metropolitan Opera House.

In the course of the proceedings the sinister Harpo has occasion to assault one of the menaces with a big mallet. The menace falls prostrate to the floor, there to remain prone for a while. Groucho and Chico dash up and place their right feet upon the unconscious menace with a subtle indication that he is not a dead rhinoceros, but a barroom rail.

"Two beers please," says Groucho, in his best saloon manner.

"Two beers for me, too," says Chico impressively.

And then the action dissolves into something else. It begins, continues and ends in a strange, wonderfully laughable dream; a dream happily different from most funny dreams recounted at the breakfast table in having had the services of George S. Kaufman, Morrie Ryskind, the Marxes, and the great gagman, Al Boasberg, to improve it here and there. They have conferred on it such wild moments as that when the Marx family and a score or so of more innocent people find themselves in a fairly confined ship's stateroom with a good number of mops, brushes and other household implements, and several trays of food cascading here and there almost as dangerously as Harpo himself.

Then there is another splendid period, when the tenor not favored by the Marxes has got upon the Metropolitan stage. Harpo, Groucho and Chico all become seriously entangled in the machinery of operatic production and Harpo out-Weissmullers Weissmuller, using the ropes which move the scenery for the lianas in his private jungle. The unfortunate singer finds himself working away behind a number of rather peculiar backgrounds, and then, suddenly, he is snatched up by the Marxes, into a peculiar, Marxian ape-nest in the higher reaches of the scene-shifting apparatus. The Marx favorite tenor pinch-hits, and all is well.

These devices alone are sufficient to make the Marx brothers the world's leading surrealists. They are agreeably unconscious of their distinction. Groucho and Chico are in Hollywood, too far away for questioning, but Harpo has joined Mrs. George S. Kaufman in purchasing a bit of "Hell Freezes Over," a drama about the hazards of exploring at one of the poles, and the other day he was found in rooms at the Waldorf, ready to supervise production at the drop of a hat. When he was discovered he was taking a delicate breakfast of green peas and stewed fruit at 2:30 p. m. A large, appropriately golden harp stood by the breakfast table. He does not travel with his harp, but the thoughtful harp-makers lend him a complimentary one when he comes to New York. They know he likes to play before breakfast, just after he gets his teeth done.

Without his wig and his leer, with his harp not really in hand, he was a smallish, unsurprising-looking man, who left the self-assertive note to be struck by his maroon silk pyjamas. At the suggestion that he and his brothers might be great surrealist artists he failed to coruscate with comment, but he was exceedingly interesting on how the Marx brand of lunatic wit was evolved, and how a Marx brothers show is made. Since this is a piece about surrealism and the Marxes, the following information may be regarded as a few hints to M. Cocteau and M. Dali on how to go about it. All Harpo himself would say on surrealism was:

"I don't know much about that."

Surrealism, it seems from Mr. Marx, was born long before its Parisian practitioners have usually thought, some twenty-two years ago, when Groucho, Chico, Harpo and Zeppo were appearing on vaudeville stages around Chicago and the West as four childish nightingales. This period lasted a couple of years. Then their voices began to lose their steady soprano, and vaudeville managers showed signs of reluctance to book the nightingales. Under the guidance of their indomitable mother they stopped being nightingales and began to be a school act. Already in that distant era the Marxian roles were set. Groucho was a domineering, older fellow, the teacher in fact, while Chico was an Italian and Harpo was a wild, red-headed creature. He still talked then.

The school act came to birth on a one-night stand in Texas, where the manager insisted on new material. It was run up overnight, and it lasted for some time, until it was at last replaced by "Mr. Green's Reception." It was in this masterpiece that Harpo took a Trappist vow for his appearances on the boards. He had a bit where he kicked a policeman, and he found the audiences laughed harder at it when he stuck to pure pantomime. It was thus by a process of trial and error, that their comic characters, so moonstruck but so energetic, came to be worked out in detail. About this time Harpo learned to play the harp because his grandmother had been a harpist, and his mother wanted a harpist in the family.

"We bought an old harp for $45 on time," said Harpo. "With us everything was on time in those days. Ludwig Baumann was a household name. We were so used to collectors that all you had to do was say Ludwig Baumann and we'd all jump up and lock all the doors and windows. I learned to play the harp all by myself, and the biggest laugh I ever got was when I tried my first solo in the act."

From the earlier acts better ones were evolved, until the Marxes were doing very nicely in vaudeville. Then they quarreled with B. F. Keith and they were up against it. Fortunately a Philadelphian coal baron turned up, with an itch to put on a summer show in his native city. He could have had all four Marxes (they are now only three, for Zeppo has deserted the fold) or one comedian from the legitimate stage for $250 a week. He chose the Marxes, "figuring," remarked Harpo, "that four would be better than one any day for the same money." The show he put on was "I'll Say She Is" and, in spite of a production which later led Robert Benchley to remark that the costume numbers were the funniest things he had seen on any stage, the show was a hit. After a year of profitable touring the Marxes managed to get the coal baron to send the show into New York, where it ran forty weeks.

"After that things were sort of easier," said Harpo, with a grin. "Now I guess we're pretty well settled in Hollywood, but, of course, I'm a New York producer now, so you can't tell where it'll end."

In Hollywood they build their mad comedies by the same process of accretion and selection which produced their comic other selves. After the script of "A Night at the Opera" was written by Messrs. Kaufman and Ryskind, the Marxes and Al Boasberg set to work rehearsing it, filling in business, casting out and substituting lines, changing the pace and sprinkling laughs liberally about. Then the script received a final retouching from its authors, and a sort of cut-down stage version of it was taken on the road, to Salt Lake City and elsewhere, in the four-a-day. Thus laughs were tested at a hundred or so performances, and finally the nascent cinema was taken back to Hollywood and filmed.

"Sometimes we just think of laughs by accident, and sometimes we think of them when we're trying," said Harpo simply. "Of course we had a wonderful script from George Kaufman and Morrie Ryskind, and Al Boasberg thought of a lot of good gags. You just can't tell how a gag'll come, and I guess you can't tell why it's good or why it's bad. It just is."

These rather discouraging remarks ended the conversation on the subject of the art of the Marx brothers. So probably, after all, M. Cocteau and M. Dali will never know how to regain the places in the hearts of their admirers where the Marx brothers have superseded them. Harpo did not seem to care very much. A wild gleam had appeared in his small brown eyes, and he was muttering something about a church. It soon appeared that he was trying to remember a church's name. He spoke with great sadness.

"I just can't remember it," he said, "and it's really pretty important. This church asked me to play my harp, and I said I would if they'd let me wear my red wig, so they said I could, and now I expect to play my harp in church. But I just can't remember its name. I want to remember it, because I want to play the harp in it. Also I want to play cribbage."

C. A. Lejeune, *THE OBSERVER,* London November 19, 1944

All fanciers of the Marx Brothers, whether they belong to the group that upholds the Brothers' early, primitive school, or to the class that prefers their later, more florid manner, will join with me in rejoicing that "A Night at the Opera" is to be reissued tomorrow.

To my mind, "A Night at the Opera" contains the funniest sequence the Marx Brothers ever invented—the scene in the steamer cabin, where every living thing within reach, human and animal, is grabbed and pushed into that tiny set. But it would be enough for me if it only contained the Marx Brothers, such is my delight at seeing clowning that is real clowning again. These boys knew what they were about. They had style, a virtue notably lacking on the modern screen.(1) The cold, clear illogic of their fooling was as mathematically precise as the nonsense of Lewis Carroll. They were grotesques in costume and make-up, and yet there was about them a kind of awful solemnity. Their teamwork was brilliant but imperceptible,

---

1. In this paragraph, does Miss Lejeune make clear what she means by "style"?

and no one will ever be able to discover, I fancy, quite how much Harpo's dumbness owed to Groucho's gabble, or Groucho's urgency derived from Harpo's pantomime. Above all, they knew the difference between a joke that was funny, and a joke that merely should have been funny. They made it their business to know.

Since the Marx Brothers stopped operating on the screen, there has only been one comedy as sane as the nonsense they used to produce, and that was "Hellzapoppin." The Brothers were zanies and merry-andrews; they were buffoons and clowns; but they were never crazy. Nowadays it is the fashion for everything to be crazy. The film people treat "crazy" as though it were a word for progress; a recommendation really; hinting at the four freedoms with just a touch of lovable aberration. Have they ever referred to the dictionary, I wonder? Probably they have and discovered that "to craze" may mean "to produce small cracks on pottery." Rushing off with whoops of joy to smash up the furniture, they possibly omitted to read the subsequent definition of "crazy"; which means dilapidated, unsound, shaky, sickly, insane, mad. (2)

The great screen comedians of the past, such as Chaplin and the Marx Brothers, Harold Lloyd, Buster Keaton, Laurel and Hardy in their best days, may have been crackpots in the literal sense, but they were certainly not mad, insane, sickly, shaky, unsound, or dilapidated. They were extremely shrewd and efficient craftsmen, with a sober sense of responsibility, who liked to work out their own comic situations and perfect them to the final detail. I do not say that the comedians of to-day may not have the same impulses, but they certainly have not the same opportunities. The best a modern funny man can hope for is to crack a joke here and there among the serious business of the song hits; and to speak his given lines in such a way that they appear to have been written by someone who is at least half-witted. (3)

---

2. Is the critic's discussion of "crazy" helpful to the reader? What does "crazy" mean here?
3. What are this critic's criteria for good comedy?

Joe Bigelow, *VARIETY*
December 11, 1935

The punch of the Marx lads' latest, as with their previous pictures, is an ability to belt the customers with solid laughs on a high frequency basis for an hour and a half. That gags fall on top of each other makes no difference. The total score can't help but be uncommonly high. The comedy material is always good and sometimes brilliant. Box office reaction should be solid. (1)

While the story this time is a bit more involved the book isn't too much to the fore. The comedy dominates, which is certainly the best procedure for the Marxes.

There are two or three comedy situations which give cards and spades to most of the present day picture comedy writing. Particularly hilarious, and an ideal type of material for the Marx boys, is a crowded stateroom—at which nobody will fail to laugh. It arrives early and tends somewhat to take the edge off the following antics, but paradoxically sets a pace for the comedians so that most everything they do, or say, thereafter sounds and looks funny.

Story is a rather serious grand opera satire in which the comics conspire to get a pair of Italian singers a break over here. For their foils the Marxes have Walter King (Woolf) and Siegfried Rumann

---

1. What criterion of excellence is operative in this paragraph? Considering that *Variety* is a theatrical trade paper, is this surprising? The larger question here is to what extent all critics write for their audiences. The vocabulary and interests of the readers of this review are so special that we have no difficulty in seeing that the critic takes for granted a body of shared assumptions among his readers. But how widespread is this phenomenon among critics in general? Does, for example, Kauffmann writing in *The New Republic,* or Arthur Knight writing in *Saturday Review,* assume that his audience shares a body of common knowledge and assumptions about film and even life?

as heavies, Robert Emmett O'Connor as a pursuing flatfoot, and Margaret Dumont to absorb the regulation brand of Julius Marx (Groucho) insults. This quartet makes as clear a target for gags as any comedian could want.

Although King also doubles on the vocals, Kitty Carlisle and Alan Jones do most of the singing as the love interest. Miss Carlisle has never looked better, but she doesn't receive the best of it from the recording, especially in the higher register. Jones obtains more favorable mechanical aid, hence stands out in the singing department.

Groucho and Chico in a contract-tearing bit, the Marxes with O'Connor in a bed-switching idea, and a chase finale in the opera house are other dynamite comedy sequences, along with the aforementioned stateroom situation plus a corking build-up by Groucho while riding to his room on a trunk. The backstage finish, with Harpo doing a Tarzan on the ropes, contains more action than the Marxes usually go in for, but it relieves the strictly verbal comedy and provides a sock exit.

Chico and Harpo slip in their piano-harp routines during one of the picture's two production numbers. Both of these flashes are well done, but not too lavish. The scenic overhead seems to be mostly in the opera house.

Two songs are 'Alone,' ballad, and 'Cosi-Cosa,' novelty number, both okay. But songs in a Marx picture are generally at a disadvantage because they're more or less interruptions, the customers awaiting the next laugh.

Dialogs and gags, written for Groucho, are set-ups for him, and spotted where they'll do the most good. But the impossibility of timing gags for the screen to perfection was shown at the Capitol where, on two different shows, the audience responded in a different manner. In the stateroom the physical business is so good that the laughs shut out most of the talk. The verbal material, too, shows the influence of the new brand of radio writing, as exemplified in one gag of a type that Groucho wouldn't have attempted in a picture a couple of years ago:

'Do you rumba?' asks Groucho. 'Then take a rumba from one to 10.'

Stately Margaret Dumont is on the receiving end of that one and many others, and her dignified Stonewall Jacksoning throughout is no small help. This is also the picture for which the Marxes went into the western film houses to try out material prior to starting at the studio.

Allen Eyles, *FILMS AND FILMING*
February, 1965

Revaluation

In *A Night at the Opera,* the Marx Brothers allowed their humour to be contained by a plot and polished by the MGM gloss which sparkled on all that studio's top products even into the fifties. The blending is so smooth that the film ranks as an entertainment masterpiece (and surely, therefore, as art); (1) it is as secure today as ever it can have been once the dated nature of its romantic asides between Allan Jones and Kitty Carlisle has been acknowledged. But if it is a master product of the Hollywood assembly line, it is also a vehicle for the highly distinctive personalities of the three Marx Brothers. This is at some cost to the screen image that the team had previously developed. It certainly increased their popularity and led to their artistic decline, but whether the change lessens or enhances *A Night at the Opera* itself is a matter of personal preference.

The best scenes in any case are only basically derived from the plot. There's the opening in the restaurant in which Groucho abandons an attractive companion to go and pacify a stood-up Margaret Dumont with the words: 'This bill is an outrage: if I were you, I wouldn't pay it!' There's the sequence back-stage in which Groucho and Chico negotiate the contract tearing off strips they don't like. There's the celebrated sequence with half the ship's complement crushed into one cabin so that, if it hasn't got the person sought, Groucho can declare 'We probably have someone just as good.' And

---

1. This implied definition of art is of particular interest in that distinctions are so frequently drawn between mere entertainment and fine art.

Reprinted by the permission of the author. Subsequently revised and expanded for *The Marx Brothers: Their World of Comedy,* New Jersey: A. S. Barnes, 1966, 1969.

there's the search of Groucho's apartment by the plain-clothes man, Henderson ('You look more like an old-clothes man to me'), with the unseen Harpo and Chico moving out the furniture behind his back and Groucho verbally chiselling into his wavering composure. And there's that final imbroglio on the opening night at the opera house, quite possibly suggested by Clair's *Le Million* but extended with dazzling inventiveness.

In these scenes we find the Marxes as they always were—absurd in themselves (Groucho's moustache, Chico's accent, Harpo's wig)—but treated with solemnity. This is the world's initial mistake for the Marx Brothers lead an unending crusade against ceremony in any form.

The most basic is conversation, the ludicrous spectacle of people making noises at one another. The sounds may have generally accepted meanings, but their severe limitations result in the semantic confusions of any Marx picture. Even though Harpo doesn't speak (but is infinitely eloquent in gesture and expression), his inventive miming of messages (not seen in *A Night at the Opera*) plays on double meanings and the sound of parts of words; and he can certainly hear: 'Cut the cards,' says a gambler in *Horse Feathers* and a passing Harpo obliges with his axe. Chico's guise as an Italian gives him the excuse to perpetrate outrageous puns. These are more a feature of earlier films, but there's an echo of them when Groucho's attempting to discuss the sanity clause in a contract: 'Hey, you can't-a fool me, there ain't no such thing as Sanity Claus.' But Chico's misunderstanding of words tends to fall flat very often because they are so far-fetched even though they thereby reinforce the idea of Chico as an obvious phoney.

Groucho exhibits the most diverse methods of stopping the progression of any line of argument or thought. Communication most often collapses by Groucho taking an expression literally as, when he familiarly calls Margaret Dumont 'my good woman' and she rebuffs him with 'I am *not* your "good woman," he generously declares 'I don't care what your past has been.' Later, he offers his hotel bill as an insurance policy with a line of sales talk that includes 'You lose a leg, we help you look for it.'

Besides being wily and aggressive, Groucho can be ingenious and irrelevant. 'Have you got any stewed prunes?' he asks the waiter. 'Give them some coffee—that'll sober them up.' Groucho gazes intently at Lassparri's costume while the latter sounds off at him, and asks with scholarly meekness 'How can you sleep on your stomach with such large buttons?' Or he'll qualify a remark, thereby reducing it to the bathetic, as when he threatens not only to resume his raucous singing if Margaret Dumont doesn't visit his cabin but also to put on his squeaky shoes. And besides rolling out clichés like 'Very few of us will be coming out of this alive' or 'Hold on, the cavalry are coming!' in a tight corner, but the wrong kind of picture, he'll introduce by a casual comment some ridiculous but just tenable analogy to a scene that gives it an extra dimension and sets the mind reeling: for instance, Lassparri is twice knocked out by Harpo letting a weight drop on his head and Groucho remarks 'How early the fruit is falling this season.'

This is also done visually in the same scene when Groucho and Chico each put a foot on the prostrate body of Lassparri which is transformed into a bar-rail by Groucho's 'Two beers, bartender!'. But this is particularly Harpo's field, and there are such visual incongruities as his silencing an alarm clock with a mallet or the sublime glimpse of a puffed Harpo wearing a tea cosy and rocking in an armchair made of Chico covered by a blanket, all of which fools Henderson into thinking he's drifted into the wrong room in his search for them. The opera continuing with the performers set against changing back-cloths such as a battleship (and even being separated by one) is an extension of this principle.

Since words are largely the basis of our culture and sum total of knowledge, this imposing edifice is a target for the Marx team. Even with music, the Marxes' sympathy lies not with the opera but is given to the simplicity of the harp, to Chico's crude but effective style of piano playing, to the folk-dancing on ship, or the Negro song and dance in *A Day at the Races* and *At the Circus.* (In the latter film, an orchestra is brought from Paris to play on a specially built floating platform: they drift out on to the ocean playing Wagner to the seagulls while the intended audience relishes a circus instead.) Thus Groucho can materialise in the aisle at the Opera House calling 'Peanuts! Peanuts!' and Harpo rip the dress off a passing dancer while hiding out on stage.

The Marxes' common purpose unites their differences of technique. Chico also resolves the difference between the apparent simplicity of Harpo and the apparent worldly wisdom of Groucho. Chico and Harpo are often cast as friends or brothers, and there's a rather charming little scene in *A Night at the Opera* where they rush to greet one another, Harpo delays their embrace by circling round a fire escape, and the two turn out to have brought each other identical presents. Between Chico and Groucho there is a sort of mutual admiration expressed in a scene where one tries to take advantage of the other, here in the contract scene, and in *A Day at the Races* the classic bit with Chico selling his tootsie-frootsie ice-cream.

It's sometimes said that the Marxes' satire is limited by its concentration on upper-class targets, ignoring that these are obviously more fruitful, or indeed that *Horse Feathers* ridiculed speakeasies and college football, both of which were pretty wide targets. Furthermore, their attack on the Opera is a response to provocation, specifically by Gottlieb and Lassparri. However, there is an added element in that the Marxes have adopted a purpose, that of helping the heroine. Never before would Groucho have run messages between the lovers or have been so captivated by a rewarding kiss.

But a more fundamental change is the way in which the Marxes undergo humiliation, from Harpo being whipped for wearing Lassparri's costumes (pleading childlike for a truce) to Groucho being fired from the Opera House. The latter sequence is particularly elaborate with everyone conspiring to welcome him on his way in and later helping to boot him out. Even the water fountain dries up on him in the park, and he has only to remark 'Well, nothing more can happen to me now' for a keeper to order him off the grass.

These changes have the effect of making the Marx Brothers vulnerable to sentiment and misfortune. It's easy to see why. Mary McCarthy quotes a woman's criticism of Jimmy Porter in *Look Back in Anger:* 'He wouldn't let me pity him.' The Marx Brothers were largely unsuccessful in drawing women to see them until their pictures made them a little sympathetic and lovable.

Also, it is obviously good plot construction to have them reduced to near despair so that their subsequent triumph is the greater, as is the pleasure of the audience from siding with them. Perhaps a more orderly form is necessary to sustain them over the greater running length of this picture, but it does have the effect of subduing the team by fitting them in predictable routines and letting them fulfill the anticipations of the audience.

Previously, they had been unpredictable (their actions often seeming improvised, as perhaps they were); they were not misfits being pushed around in a hostile world but charter members of Wilde's 'state republican where everyman's a king.' Unlike other comedians, they were never on the defensive. They were quite happy in themselves, but once disturbed they took to the attack, their ultimate aim being to regain peace and quiet. We can still see this in *A Night at the Opera,* but it is innovatory for their supreme confidence to be faced with even momentary defeat. It's true that in Groucho's character there are signs of persecution mania (including a readiness to read insult into the most innocent remark) and that he is often cast as a parasite on society, but he invariably reserves his independence. His sagacity is always superficial ('They threw apples at me' complains Lassparri; 'Well, watermelons are out of season' comments Groucho), and he is basically as innocent as Harpo. His practised routines of seduction are a means of support and never lead him to any commitment, just as Harpo never caught those women he used to pursue with such vigour and in *A Night at the Opera* kisses *everyone* goodbye.

Even though the characters of the Marx Brothers may be diminished in *A Night at the Opera,* they still offer a sense of liberation, pushing no ideas or proverbial truths at us but freeing us from the rigours of logical thought and orderly behaviour. The film itself does offer the contradiction of displaying form and organisation, but for many this brings the humour of the Marx Brothers to the point of being acceptable. (2) It is unflaggingly inventive; the Marx Brothers are never left at a loose end. On its own terms, the film is extremely rewarding.

The Marx Brothers merely saw themselves as eccentric comedians, a product of traditional comedy from vaudeville. The techniques which they came by, however, were merged by their writers (particularly S. J. Perelman) to greater ends, as their influence on the Surrealist movement (Dali wrote an unfilmed screenplay for them) and the present-day Theatre of the Absurd (Ionesco claims them to have been the greatest influence on his work) makes clear. (3) They are the cinema's representatives of a school of humour that arose in

---

2. What is Eyles suggesting about expectations of *technical consistency*?

3. Alsop has perhaps jokingly suggested that the Marx Brothers were surrealists. Here Eyles cites evidence—albeit of the it-takes-one-to-know-one variety—to demonstrate that they are unconscious surrealists. Are you now convinced?

the late 'twenties in New York, and included Perelman, Robert Benchley, Ring Lardner, Dorothy Parker and many more; in fact, the Marx Brothers were discovered by Alexander Woollcott, almost the chairman of the group. (4) It was cynical, mocking high living, and aloof from the Depression.

Thus *A Night at the Opera* has a vigour and independence of spirit that is refreshing and seemingly impossible in modern times when everyone is oppressed—even a figure like M. Hulot by the time of *Mon Oncle*—and there are no comic heroes. Perhaps their value was best expressed by H. L. Mencken, that veteran cynic of their time, when he remarked in a volume of his *Prejudices:* 'The liberation of the human mind has never been furthered by . . . dunderheads; it has been furthered by gay fellows who heaved dead cats into sanctuaries and then went roistering down the highways of the world, proving to all men that doubt, after all, was safe . . . One horse laugh is worth ten thousand syllogisms. It is not only more effective; it is also vastly more intelligent.'

---

4. Does the critic treat this film as film or merely as a performance by the Marx Brothers which happens to be on film? And if the latter is true, to what extent is Eyles justified in taking this stance?

A scene from the motion picture *On the Waterfront*. Copyright © 1954 Columbia Pictures Industries, Inc. By permission.

ON THE WATERFRONT

A. H. Weiler, *THE NEW YORK TIMES*
August 1, 1954

Dockside Violence: "On the Waterfront" Is an Arresting Use of the Motion Picture Medium

The faint whisper some five years ago that the story of the crimes against the workmen of our wharves was to be filmed, gradually grew to what amounted to a tumult of tub-thumping and was climaxed last week by the opening of "On the Waterfront." Most of the great expectations were realized. This drama of the docksides was the most violent, graphic and technically brilliant job of moviemaking to be unveiled this year. And the performances of the principals, headed by Marlon Brando's superb characterization of a troubled tough guy, left little to be desired.

But an observer, who, in all honesty, could find little fault with the acting; or Elia Kazan's expert direction which kept this explosive saga moving with the speed and shocking effect of a sudden left hook; or with the hard but natural vernacular provided by Budd Schulberg, the scenarist, could not allay the uneasy feeling that they might, perhaps, have delved deeper into the terrible truths from which this dramatization stemmed. (1)

Disturbing Aspects

The thought persists that ship-owners, who also were involved in these sordid matters, are just barely mentioned in a line or two of dialogue. Despite the validity of dramatic license, (2) one can't help thinking that the character Karl Malden forcefully portrays—a priest who is a prime mover in upsetting the labor boss' ruthless rule—is accorded a mite too much emphasis. And a viewer can be disturbed by some of the plotting which is somewhat standard and pat and an ending which is strangely rosy and happy considering the murderous events which precede it. (3)

Those are facets, however, which do not vitiate the smashing power of the melodrama or the artistry of the professionals who fashioned it. Although this brutal tale was inspired by the more incisive and revealing facts previously presented in newspapers and television, Elia Kazan's predilection for effectively using the faces of the crowd, as well as principals, gives this fiction an uncommon impact.

Plot

They are enacting the grim story of Terry Malloy (Marlon Brando) a not-too-bright and contented tool of a venal longshoremen's union

---

1. Is Weiler, in this passage, pointing to a sensation derived from the film, itself—a superficiality, perhaps, that characterizes the material; or is he expressing a form of *intellectual commitment?* Is he, in other words, asking the film to be a different film or a better film?

2. Poetic license, we all know, generally means the right to alter spellings and grammatical constructions for the sake of sound and rhythm. Does "dramatic license" similarly point to freedom in formal adjustment for the sake of cinematic art? Or does it mean the right to alter reality for dramatic effect? And if the latter, is this a right or an inevitability? Does the context here tell us which of these meanings is intended?

3. Do you feel the ending of *On the Waterfront* is "strangely rosy"?

boss, who is not averse to wresting large tithes from his subjects, both dock workers and ship owners. He is tough enough to have his goons dispatch anyone who dares to "sing" to a crime commission investigating waterfront racketeering. And, it is the macabre tale of the killing of one of these fearless men; Brando's meeting and romance with the dead man's sister; his growing awareness of the evils around him; the slaying of his brother (the labor chief's right hand man) and Brando's testimony which leads to the deposing of the racketeer in a bloody finale. (4)

It is Brando's portrayal of the inarticulate but colorful hero which is the film's outstanding attribute. Although he knows the hired assassins with whom he is involved, he is basically apathetic to their baseness until the older brother, who has made his life easy, is murdered because the younger man would not listen to the racketeer's warning to keep quiet. The groping for words, the pugilist's walk and language, the inner torment of this young man in a vicious world he can't quite understand, are made pitifully clear when he agonizingly says to his brother, "I could have been a contender instead of a bum."

Cast

In Lee J. Cobb, the drama has the services of an unmerciful racketeer and in Tami Mauriello, Tony Galento and Abe Simon, authentic, erstwhile heavyweight contenders, it has goons to the manner born. More importantly, Kazan's choice of Eva Marie Saint, as Brando's romantic vis-a-vis, is inspired. She is sweet, intelligent and appealing in the role, and one scene, in which the pair passionately embrace, is poignant, tender and moving.

Above all, however, this tight team had the good sense to film these proceedings entirely in Hoboken's sleazy tenements and docks

---

4. Weiler's use of the name of the actor rather than that of the protagonist is characteristic of the ways in which we all talk about movies. Although this practice may simply be a convenience for the critic (a way of keeping the character straight for those of his readers who have not seen the film), it does point to the ease with which we can allow the actor to interfere with our experience of the character he portrays.

and streets hard by the harbor, which lend some of the vivid tones of a documentary to this harsh account. Its glaring spotlight on thugs preying on harried men whose code demands silence in the face of injustices, and its unrelenting violence are frightening and impressive. But it is not violence which, as Hazlitt once observed, "defeats its own ends." It is a stark, swift, sharply etched and arresting use of the techniques of the movie medium.(5) Its rewards are ample and exciting.

---

5. Weiler refers to the technical brilliance of this film more than once (look, for example, at the critic's headline). In what specific techniques does he suggest its brilliance lies?

Lee Rogow, *SATURDAY REVIEW*
July 24, 1954

Brando on the Waterfront

Let me say right off that "On the Waterfront" (*Columbia*) is one of the most exciting films ever made in the United States. Later on I will qualify that statement,(1) but I want to report at the outset that there is a tremendous picture around, a film absolutely explosive in its impact on the emotions and on the motion picture as a form.

In the past several years there have been two things happening in the movies. On the one hand, Hollywood has been developing its capacity to bedazzle. The new aspect ratios and the ultimate-weapon

---

1. How *is* this statement qualified later on?

budgets are the latest means by which the Technicolor Tintorettos have turned film into the mightiest canvas the world has ever seen. At the same time, a number of earnest toilers in the business have been aware that the Europeans made us look like popcorn peddlers when it came to showing life problems of working-class persons in their own homes and on their own streets. The other half of the Hollywood story has been a conscious effort to make contact with the living plainness of the European film image. That effort was a vain one—until now. No matter how many camera crews were sent on location to Brooklyn or New York's East Side, there was usually a synthetic flavor to the material, principally because such settings were used for manufactured stories in which violence was a major titillation.

Now Elia Kazan has moved his cameras onto the Hoboken docks and has broken through the subtle filter which has previously shielded American lenses from the harsh light of reality. And if "On the Waterfront" were not an event for this reason, it would be one because of the performance of Marlon Brando, one of the finest things any man has done on the screen.

"Waterfront" is the story of an ex-prizefighter who is the errand boy for a crooked labor leader. Johnny Friendly, union boss, has turned the docks into his personal fief, the longshoremen into his serfs. He clips their pay envelopes, lends them money at Shylock rates, orders them out on flash strikes when he sees the chance to shake down a shipper with a dockful of perishable fruit, brutally snuffs out the life of anyone who plays stool pigeon for the crime commission investigating conditions on the waterfront. The background facts for Budd Schulberg's screenplay were supplied by Malcolm Johnson's prize-winning articles, and the film documents a story of peonage enforced by thugs with the acquiescence of the shippers.

In the midst of these assassins, Terry, the prizefighter, is little more than a mascot, tolerated because his educated brother is counsel for the union boss. Brando's performance in this role is a piece of genuine artistry. With half-sentences finished by body shrugs and fish gestures of the hands, with a drawn-brow groping for words, with a street arab's laugh or quick insult, with an ex-athlete's bounce to his walk, Brando projects a wonderfully absorbing portrait of a semi-stupid, stubborn, inner-sweet young man.

Terry is not particularly troubled by his role as coffee-runner and messenger boy for the mob until one of his errands helps set up the sudden death of a neighborhood pigeon fancier who had given a statement to the crime commission. The murder becomes the occasion for the formation of a rump organization spearheaded by a militant priest and the sister of the murdered boy. The prizefighter meets the sister, takes her to a saloon, buys the parochial schoolgirl her first glass of beer, and falls in love with her in a scene that is inexpressibly sweet.

The fighter is subpoenaed by the crime commission. Johnny Friendly sends the lawyer brother to stop his mouth. The brothers have an unforgettable scene as they ride together in a taxi toward the execution headquarters. "It was you made me a bum, Charlie," says the prizefighter, and Brando's reading of this line is matchless. "I coulda had class. I coulda been a contender." The lawyer, ashamed, lets his brother escape, and is murdered by the mob in his stead.

The prizefighter testifies before the crime commission and then returns to the docks, where the labor racketeer's hold over the men is eventually broken in a blood bath finale.

Kazan has served himself well in casting the film. Lee J. Cobb is effective as the labor boss. Eva Marie Saint, a television actress making her first movie appearance, is appealing as the girl, and Karl Mauldin makes a forceful priest. Rod Stieger displays a brilliant understanding of the weak, easy-money, easy-power attorney who stands at the labor boss's side.

"On the Waterfront" will undoubtedly create a storm of excitement because of its use of the screen and because of Brando's vitalizing performance. I suspect that among the viewers there will be many who will find the ending somewhat pat and preachy and the plotting a bit slick. The word "slick," I am aware, is an abused word in the critic business, for slickness is part of our delight in many plays, motion pictures, and stories. But there are times when a certain easiness, a certain plot maneuvering, debases the currency of the work. This is probably the reason why "On the Waterfront" is more an electric piece of journalism than it is a drama of the first rank. (2) But despite "Waterfront's" shortcomings, there is no doubt that a landmark in American movie-making has been established by this documentary of the docks.

---

2. What distinction does Rogow see between journalism and drama?

Penelope Houston, *SIGHT AND SOUND* October-December, 1954

Elia Kazan's *On the Waterfront* (Columbia) is a significant, almost a definitive, example of a type of film which traditionally finds Hollywood at its most expert: the melodrama with a stiffening of serious ideas, the journalistic exposé of crime and corruption. Its subject harks back to the racket-smashing thrillers of the 'thirties; its style—location shooting, conscientious concern with surface realism—belongs to the present decade; its pretensions, the attempt to build authentic drama out of an investigation of waterfront gangsterism, are characteristic not only of the director but of a whole school of Hollywood thought.

The film's central character, Terry Malloy (Marlon Brando), is a young man in his late twenties, once a boxer, now an aimless hanger-on in the retinue of Johnny Friendly (Lee J. Cobb), the corrupt union boss who imposes gangster law on the New York waterfront. Terry is involved in the murder of a recalcitrant docker who has threatened to speak out against Friendly; he falls in love with the victim's sister; a Catholic priest works, deliberately, on his slowly awakened conscience; the murder of his brother, Friendly's lieutenant, gives him a motive of personal revenge, and he agrees to testify before the Crime Commission. The sequel to this action is a savage beating up and an almost symbolic conclusion, as the dockers wait for Terry—his face smashed in, his walk a blind, lurching shamble—to lead them back to work. Taking his background material from Malcolm Johnson's Pulitzer Prize winning articles, Budd Schulberg has written a script which is vigorous, credible, at times (in the scenes between Terry and the girl) authentically touching, and which, though it has its over-conventional elements in the characterisation of Friendly and of the priest, never falls into the familiar, specious habit of "dignifying" its working-class characters by making them speak in pseudo-Biblical language.

The script, in fact, contains the basis for a sharply observed journalistic investigation of a man's slow realisation of the truth about his environment, and Marlon Brando's playing gives the film the opportunity to become something rather more than this. This is a strong, confident performance, wholly contemporary in feeling and taking us right away from the old, chip on the shoulder thug-hero on the Hemingway model. The battered prize fighter's face, the slouching walk, the shoulder-shrugging gestures completing half-spoken sentences, the cocksure, gum-chewing arrogance and the gentle, uncertain half-smile are all used to unerring effect; as he walks in the park with the girl, aimlessly pulling on her glove while they talk, or makes it clear to his brother (admirably played by Rod Steiger) that his betrayal of the gang is irrevocable, relationships are crystallised, situations exist, as it were, outside their screen context. Although the playing otherwise is less satisfactory—Eva Marie Saint is gauche and adequately appealing as the wanly courageous heroine, but Karl Malden gives a strident, unrelaxed performance as the priest, and Lee J. Cobb's blustering gang leader is a conventionally overdrawn figure—Brando's performance gives the film a wonderfully firm centre.

Kazan, however, not content to let the story develop its own impetus, tends to over-inflate the simplest situation, to build up an atmosphere of artificial tension and urgency. Abetted by Leonard Bernstein's score, which undoubtedly contributes forcefully to the mood of the film, he has gone all out for the raucous, aggressive, showy effect. The virtuosity of Kazan's handling, the skill with which he sets a scene of violence, are not in doubt; one does, however, question the validity of his methods and of his approach. This seems to derive directly from the Group Theatre tradition (it is worth recording, incidentally, that Kazan, Karl Malden and Lee J. Cobb all appeared in the Theatre's 1937 production of *Golden Boy*), from the depression period of the 'thirties when the New York stage discovered "realism" and playwrights such as Odets created the man-in-the-street hero, semi-articulate, inevitably victimised, reaching vaguely for higher and gentler things. (The Golden Boy had his violin; Terry, the reluctant thug, keeps pigeons.) The influence, now more than a little jaded, persists in the attitude to character, in the insistence that ordinary people are remarkable and must somehow be made to appear so, in the sentimentalising of the tough guy (Schulberg, too, has always a soft spot for the broken-down boxer).(1)

---

1. Miss Houston makes very clear what she sees as the influence of the Group Theatre on Kazan's approach. Does she present with

During recent years, Hollywood "realism" has developed its own immediately recognisable conventions and attitudes.(2) A now familiar technique of handling actors demands those mannerisms—Karl Malden's check in mid-speech, for instance—always just a little too studied for naturalism. There is the cunningly employed understatement, so that a scene of violence and tension ends with the priest demonstrating the human touch by ordering a glass of beer. And it seems symptomatic that, as in the Hollywood-influenced *Terminal Station,* location shooting no longer guarantees an appearance of actuality. In spite of Boris Kaufman's beautifully atmospheric camerawork, recording the pale, cold early morning light on the docks, the depressed back streets and dismal little parks, the scenes are so carefully set, the characters so deliberately grouped (as in the saloon interior, with the two comatose down-and-outs propped picturesquely against the staircase), that we seem to have reached a point halfway between the studio and the real.(3) It is a long way from the rougher idioms of *The Naked City,* though perhaps Kazan's own *Panic in the Streets* was already moving in this direction.

Primarily, however, one distrusts this sort of convention because, in making it too easy to create a plausible seeming surface, a set of characters who will be accepted for their familiarity, it inevitably encourages evasion. In *On the Waterfront,* there is a scene in which Terry has to tell the girl of his part in her brother's murder: as they speak, their voices are drowned by a bellowing ship's siren. If the picture were presented as no more than melodrama, the trick would seem acceptable enough; but in building up his subject as he has, Kazan has foregone his right to evade so crucial a stage in this particular relationship. In a sense, the incident may be taken to sum

---

equal clarity her argument with his "method"? Or is method to be seen as implicit in approach?

2. Other critics in other contexts have implied a connection between convention and cliché. Is Miss Houston suggesting that once convention is "immediately recognizable" (and can it be convention if not so to at least some viewers), it has the effect of cliché? And if this is true, are the terms "convention" and "cliché" to all intents and purposes synonymous?

3. Does Miss Houston convince you that the scenes are too "carefully set"? Does a single shot serve as sufficient evidence?

Open City, Courtesy of *Contemporary Films/McGraw-Hill*

OPEN CITY

Rachael Low, *RECORDS OF THE FILM* No. 8 (London: British Film Institute)

Here is a film of the underground movement which has the ring of authenticity, by the side of which the British and American imaginings to which we became accustomed during the war seem insubstantial and mock-heroic. Filmed largely in the actual neighbourhood where the story is supposed to take place, by people who were themselves familiar with life under the Nazis, the Resistance is conceived not as a central mystery but as an all-pervading atmosphere, danger not as an exciting adventure but as an accepted and inescapable element in ordinary life. The film itself was planned in secret by Rosselini and his colleagues while the Germans still held Rome, and production was not started until after the entry of the Allies. Stories are told about the making of the film, of secret meetings in mountain caves, cameras stolen from the Germans, production in an old ballroom and difficulties overcome in obtaining film stock and electricity.

The theme, courageous resistance to a tyrannical occupation, is a noble one and the people who made the film comprehended it from the inside. But the film has virtues far greater than that of mere authenticity. (1) Story, direction, and acting which in several cases is magnificent, all combine to give it epic qualities which place it in an altogether higher category artistically than, for example, the equally sincere Czech resistance film *Men Without Wings.* (2) The nerve-wracking reality of occupation by the Nazis is illustrated by the lives of a group of people made so intensely real, so familiar, that their suffering is emotionally overwhelming. The story is of a group of workers and a local priest in the Rome of 1943, when the Nazis had declared it an "open city" and were ruling it with the ruthless technique of a tyranny perfected in the occupied countries. Underground leader Manfredi finds refuge from the Gestapo in the home of his colleague Francesco, a block of workers' dwellings where poverty and hunger, bombing and fear are part of daily life and children play at sabotage in horrifying earnest. The building is raided by the Gestapo. Francesco is driven away before the eyes of Pina, the woman who is to marry him and who already bears his child. Running after the lorry in an agony of desperation Pina is shot like an animal. Francesco, escaping with Manfredi, hides in the apartment of Manfredi's mistress, an actress who by prostitution and by friendship with a Gestapo woman agent has not merely survived German rule, but prospered. For drugs and a fur coat she betrays Manfredi, who is arrested with Don Pietro, the priest who is helping him. Manfredi dies under torture without betraying information of the resistance movement, and Don Pietro, refusing to use any influence over Manfredi, is shot as an "enemy of the Reich."

In this relatively simple story not only director but to a notable extent writers and players have found the elements not merely of a powerful resistance film, but of a tragedy transcending the immediate

---

1. Note the criterion at work here. Authenticity is apparently a virtue, but in itself a minor one. Is the writer assuming that authenticity is a function of pointing one's camera at a reality with which one is familiar? Is this the way authenticity is achieved in a film?

2. How is the word "epic" being used here? Is it "epic" as a technical literary term (e.g.: epic poem, epic theatre)? Or is it "epic" as it might appear on a movie marquee (e.g.: See the great epic of the Civil War—*Gone With the Wind*)? Or is Miss Low simply using the word as a synonym for "large"?

time and place. (3) It epitomises the universal theme of heroic resistance to foreign tyranny. For the resistance is essentially patriotic rather than democratic and there is no anomaly in this, the greatest of the resistance films, coming from a country which submitted so long to a dictatorship.

The principal characters as conceived by S. Amidei and F. Fellini, and acted by some of the principal stage and screen stars of Italy, have an even balance of heroism and humility, whether in the sombre purpose of the resistance leader, the acquiescent courage of Pina, or the kindness and simple dignity of Don Pietro—a dignity which is all the more poignant because the final voice of denunciation comes from that same grave little priest who trots about the playground with the local children, the football bouncing on his head, to his mild surprise. Much is undoubtedly due to the restraint with which Aldo Fabrizi plays Don Pietro; much also to the warmth and dignity of Anna Magnani as the ungainly, untidy Pina, fighting for bread when the bakery is raided, scolding her little boy, weeping with exhaustion on the stairs in the evening, repentent in her confession to the priest but proud that Francesco should have chosen her when he could have had a younger, prettier woman. Gesticulating, shrugging, arguing, apologising for the quality of the coffee she struggles with the unromantic difficulties which are the concrete expression of the insecurity of life.

The treatment of her brutal death in the road and the brief shot of Don Pietro as he squats beside her, as well as the business-like sadism at the Gestapo headquarters, are as unsentimental as a newsreel. (4) Unstressed facts are eloquent—the huddle of tenants in the street as the Gestapo search the building; the constant presence of children —the future citizens—in a lawless world, and the final image of small boys walking slowly home after watching the execution of their priest. It is perhaps significant that slight exaggeration appears only in the characterisation of the Gestapo chief and his agent, a distortion which in itself might be regarded as a mark of the sincerity with

---

3. The same questions as were asked of "epic" may be asked of "tragedy." What does the term mean in this context?

4. When Miss Low says a newsreel is "unsentimental," she is offering us an interesting definition of sentimentality. Is she making a valid point?

which the film reflects the viewpoint from which it was made. But sentiment is permitted only for Don Pietro, the apotheosis of a tolerant but fighting Christianity, the fat little priest who dies for the same cause as the atheist worker because all who fight for the truth, fight for God. The final passionate assertion of resistance which is the climax of the film, the emotional crisis to which unemotional film reporting have led us, is the priest's malediction after the death of Manfredi. The ultimate appeal to our pity is his small black-coated figure tied to a chair, waiting for death as the children he had taught whistle a resistance song to comfort him.

Open City, a prize-winning film, is one of the most famous of a series of Italian films which may be said to portend a post-war rennaissance of the Italian cinema. Its director, Rosselini, is perhaps the most gifted of the new school (his films include the equally well-known *Paisa*) and, trained in the production of documentary films, has all the realism and simplicity characteristic of the present break with Italian traditions of film making. The cruel force of *Open City* is in its matter-of-fact assumption of death and fear. There is no morbid central display of futile pain, but a bleaker cruelty incidental to its theme. The theme itself, however, is essentially a positive one, a statement of the nobility of human suffering in a great cause. It is in a theme of such magnitude, rather than in a display of technical virtuosity, that the main significance of the film lies. (5) It is more than a faithful record of what life under a Gestapo is like. It is a record of rare dramatic and emotional power.

---

5. Is a criterion of excellence implied here? If so, what?

James Agee, *THE NATION*
April 13, 1946

Open City is a story of underground resistance during the late phases of the German occupation of Rome. The heroes are an underground leader; a co-worker and friend of his who hopes to marry a widow, pregnant by him; a priest who, generally at great risk to himself, is eager to help all of them. The villains are an epicene Gestapo officer; his Lesbian assistant; and a rudderless young Italian girl, misled by dope, sex, poverty, and easy money into betraying the patriots. The widow is shot down in the street. The leader dies under torture, without denouncing his comrades. The priest, who has to witness the torture, does so without pleading with the victim to give in and without ceasing to pray for his courage; then he is executed. The widow's lover survives; so does her eight-year-old son, who is active, with other children, in an effective underground of their own.

I have no doubt that plenty of priests, in Italy and elsewhere, behaved as bravely as this one. Nor do I doubt that they and plenty of nonreligious leftists, working with them in grave danger, respected each other as thoroughly as is shown here. I see little that is incompatible between the best that is in leftism and in religion—far too little to measure against the profound incompatibility between them and the rest of the world. But I cannot help doubting that the basic and ultimate practicing motives of institutional Christianity and leftism can be adequately represented by the most magnanimous individuals of each kind; and in that degree I am afraid that both the religious and the leftist audiences—and more particularly the religio-leftists, who must be the key mass in Italy—are being sold something of a bill of goods. I keep telling myself that the people who made the film were still moved to reproduce recent experience and were in no state of mind and under no obligation to complicate what they had been through; I recognize with great pleasure how thoroughly both the priest and the partisans are made to keep their distinct integrities; and the fire and spirit of the film continually make me suspicious of my own suspicions. Nevertheless, they persist; so I feel

---

1. Agee raises several issues which are central in critical practice. First, he suggests that *Open City* may not be true to life in that its chief characters may be unrepresentative of the majority of priests and leftists. Let us suppose they are idealizations. Does this necessarily make for a failure in aesthetics? And to what extent are all heroic types idealizations? Second, Agee suspects the film makers of exploiting the *reverberating heart-strings* and *intellectual commitments* of the film's audience. Assuming this is true, is the film maker (as Agee implies with his repeated use of the term "suspicion")

it is my business to say so.(1) If I am right, as I hope I am not, institutions of both kinds are here, as so often before, exploiting all that is best in individuals for the sake of all that least honors the individual, in institutions.(2)

One further qualifier, which I mentioned a few weeks ago, no longer applies; some especially close details of torture have been cut, with no loss I feel, considering the amount of backstairs sadism any audience is tainted with. I have another mild qualifier: *Open City* lacks the depth of characterization, thought, and feeling which might have made it a definitively great film.(3)

From there on out I have nothing but admiration for it. Even these failures in depth and complexity are sacrifices to virtues just as great: you will seldom see as pure freshness and vitality in a film,(4) or as little unreality and affectation among the players; one feels that everything was done too fast and with too fierce a sincerity to run the risk of bogging down in mere artistry or meditativeness—far less the

---

somehow dishonest? Is it possible for the creators of a film not to use the viewer's responses? And is there a meaningful distinction between "use" and "exploitation" in this context? Indeed, would it be possible to say that the best film makers are those who best understand and most fully control the responses of their audiences? We have said that the film exists as a function of the celluloid strip and the filmgoer's experience of that strip. If the creator is insensitive to the possibilities of interpretation embodied within what is given and within its audience, has he created art or has he merely produced a cinematic Rorschach? Third, Agee raises the issue of aesthetic distance. He suggests that the film makers may be too close to their material to make sound aesthetic decisions. Must art, if it is to be good art (and is there such a thing as bad art?), always be "emotion recollected in tranquility"?

2. Is Agee at this point replacing the film with his own *intellectual commitment?*

3. Note the criteria of excellence Agee establishes here. It is worth considering just what constitutes "depth of character," how the film maker achieves it, and how the audience comprehends it. The same questions might be applied (if less fruitfully) to "depth of thought" and "depth of feeling."

4. Are these measurable quantities?

WPA-mural sentimentality and utter inability to know, love, or honor people to which American leftists are liable. The film's finest over-all quality, which could rarely be matched so spectacularly, is this immediacy. (5) Everything in it had been recently lived through; much of it is straight reenactment on or near the actual spot; its whole spirit is still, scarcely cooled at all, the exalted spirit of the actual experience. For that kind of spirit there has been little to compare with it since the terrific libertarian jubilation of excitement under which it was all but inevitable that men like Einstein and Dovzhenko and Pudovkin should make some of the greatest works of art of this century.

Roberto Rossellini, who directed this film, and Sergio Amadei, author and script writer, are apparently not men of that order of talent; but they are much more than adequate to that spirit and to their chance. They understand the magnificence of their setting—the whole harrowed city of Rome—as well as the best artist might and perhaps better, for though their film bristles with aesthetic appreciation and eloquence, these are never dwelt on for their own sake; the urgency of human beings always dominates this architectural poetry; nor are the human beings or their actions dwelt on in any overcalculated way. The raid on the bakery, the arrest of the priest and the partisan leader, the rescue of partisan captives, and a sequence during which all the inhabitants of a tenement are hauled down into a courtyard by a German searching party are as shatteringly uninvented-looking as if they had been shot by invisible newsreel cameras.

The scene which shows the violent death of the widow and the violent reaction of her son—in cassock and cotta—has this same reality, plus a shammed operatic fury of design which in no way turns it false. There are quieter scenes which I admire fully as much —a family quarrel, an apartment scene involving two men and two women, and a casual little scene between the underground leader and the widow in which anyone of even my limited acquaintance with

---

5. Here Agee favorably responds to the "immediacy" of *Open City.* He seems to be suggesting that the immediacy emerges because of the proximity in time and space of *Open City* to the actual experiences which inspired the film. Is it possible for a film to have both aesthetic distance and immediacy?

underground activity will recognize the oxygen-sharp, otherwise unattainable atmosphere, almost a smell, of freedom. The performances of most of the Romans, especially of a magnificent woman named Anna Magnani, who plays the widow, somewhere near perfectly define the poetic-realistic root of attitude from which the grand trunk of movies at their best would have to grow; (6) and the imitations of Germans seem better than our best imitations because they are more strongly felt and more poetically stylized. The picture is full of kinds of understanding which most films entirely lack, or reduce to theatricality. I think especially of the sizing-up look and the tone and gesture with which the Gestapo officer opens his interview with the newly captured, doomed partisan leader. In art only Malraux and Silone, so far as I know, can equal that in experienced, unemphatic astuteness.

Open City was made during the distracted months just after the Allies took Rome over. It was made on a good deal less than a shoestring; mainly without sets or studio lighting; on varying qualities of black-market film. All sound, including dialogue, was applied later. The author and director had a good deal of movie experience; nearly the whole cast was amateur. The result is worthless to those who think very highly of so-called production valyahs [sic] and plenty of people in Hollywood and elsewhere will doubtless use that fact twice daily, like Mothersills. Others may find this one of the most heartening pictures in years, as well as one of the best. Not that anything it proves will come to them as a revelation. The Hollywood cameraman Karl Brown made his excellent pitiful title *Stark Love,* a story of Southern mountaineers, about twenty years ago, on about $5,000. And most of the great Russian films used amateur players—and surroundings—on budgets which would probably not pay for an American singing Western today. But plenty of people realize a point that

---

6. Agee is stating what seems to be his fundamental criterion for greatness. While his metaphor would suggest a concern with origins, it is significant that he deduces the origins from the film and, in practice, it is the finished product rather than its origins which occupies his attention. Notice how, then, Agee has neatly sidestepped committing the "intentional fallacy." But a question still remains. Using Agee's full statement together with our own experience of the film, how are we to define "poetic-realistic"?

many others will never understand and that there is no use laboring: some professional experience is exceedingly useful and perhaps indispensable, but most of the best movies could be made on very little money and with little professional experience. Judging by *Open City* they can be made a great deal better that way.

John T. McManus, *PM*
February 26, 1946

The Open City strikes me as the first sure-bet film classic of the war. This is said with full recognition of the historic greatness and collective effort which have distinguished such Soviet war films as *The Rainbow* and *No Greater Love,* the only war films which up to now have impressed me as of classic proportions.

The Open City has the qualities of these films and more. It has behind it neither the urgency of steeling national morale behind a war effort nor that of maintaining a studio production schedule, as has been the case with most films of the war which we have seen.

Instead it represents the determination of a long-suppressed but finally liberated spirit of a freedom movement to record its story while the memory of the fight, with its heart-breaking setbacks, the unspeakable tortures of reprisal, the glowing heroism and fortitude of its martyrs, are still white-hot memories.

It is the story, as told in pictures in PM's Picture News two weeks ago, of the last days of Rome under the Nazi occupation and the scourge of terror and brutality and degradation visited by the Gestapo and the collaborating Fascist police against the people of Rome and the resistance forces among them.

It is a living record, re-enacted by the people themselves in the very locales of their struggle, of the catholicity and unswerving purpose of resistance in the very birthplace of fascism.(1) Its principal

---

1. Can we say that all films are living records? And can we say that films are time-binding in that Charlie Chaplin in 1914 can be seen in 1970? Incidentally, if films are time-binding, does this add to their aesthetic value?

characters, and ultimately martyrs together, are an Italian partisan—a leader of the Committee of National Liberation—and a Roman Catholic priest, known as the Partisan Priest and a vital link between the partisan groups outside the city and their supporters in Rome.

The story is involved only as the turbulent cross currents of life among the people of the story complicate it. Otherwise it is simple and straightaway: Manfredi, the partisan leader, has come to Rome to get money for the underground. Don Pietro, the priest, undertakes to deliver the money to a secret rendezvous.

Meanwhile an intensive manhunt is in progress after Manfredi, whose presence in Rome has been reported to the Gestapo. The dragnet misses him narrowly twice but eventually he is caught, along with the priest, on information acquired for the Nazis by a woman Gestapo agent who plies Manfredi's actress sweetheart with lavish attentions and drugs.

The running sequence which follows, between the Gestapo chief, Bergmann, the partisan leader and the priest, is perhaps the most significant in the film. Manfredi, despite excruciating tortures, has refused to yield any information about the underground movement. The Gestapo chief leaves the torture chamber to appeal to the priest. The priest professes to know no more about the man than that he is a man "in need of my modest help."

"Then I will tell you who this man is," the Nazi Bergmann hisses. "He is subversive. He is a man who fought with the Reds in Spain. He is a man who dedicated his life to fighting society, religion! An atheist! . . . Your enemy!"

The priest folds his hands quietly and bows his head before answering. Then he speaks.

"I am a Catholic priest," he says. "And I believe that he who fights for justice and truth walks in the paths of the Lord—and the paths of the Lord are infinite . . ."

Then, of the chances of Manfredi talking, the priest promises confidently: "He will not talk. I will pray for him."

At last Manfredi dies under the torture without telling his captors any information. The priest witnesses the death.

"You have not talked," he says softly over the dead man. "Now it is over." Then, turning to the Nazi captors, he speaks in a voice freighted for the first time with anger:

"You wanted to kill his soul and you have only succeeded in killing his body. . . . Malediction upon you!

"You will be trampled in the dust like worms!" (2)

Then, again the humble people's priest, he turns his face to God and asks forgiveness for saying these things. Next day he dies, too, before a firing squad, while the small boys of his parish watch heartbroken through a distant wire barrier, gamely whistling phrases of the Partisans' rendezvous melody to let him know of their presence at the end.

More must be said at another time of the many incandescent excellences of *Open City* (3)—of the fine performance of an Italian journalist in his first film role as Manfredi; of the human understanding of Aldo Fabrizi, normally a film comedian, as Don Pietro; of the lusty portrayal by Anna Magnani, a Rome cafe singer, as a stalwart woman in the story and of the stout-hearted lad who plays her son and who is a Roman shoe-shine boy in ordinary life.

There are some of the things which make *Open City* a true people's picture, these and the intensity and realness with which these people play their parts again in a drama through which they all have lived once before.

The film will bear much more talking about, but meanwhile, get in line at the World Theater. *Open City* will be there for many moons, I am sure, but the World has only 300 seats and they should be at a premium at every showing.

---

2. It is very rare to see the dialogue of a film quoted so extensively. Certainly this technique has narrative interest, but has it any other effect? Does it suggest an attitude towards the film experience?

3. What excellences are cited in this review? Which are "incandescent"?

PATHER PANCHALI

Eric Rhode, *SIGHT AND SOUND*
Summer, 1961

Satyajit Ray: A Study

In general, Satyajit Ray's films embarrass the critics. Admirers go impressionistic, talk airily of Human Values, and look offended when asked to be more precise. Detractors are no less vague. Some of them call his work charming, in a tone which could hardly carry more weight of suspicion and distrust, or say they are not interested in the problems of the Indian peasantry. Only M. Truffaut, in describing *Pather Panchali* as Europeanised and insipid, has firmly placed himself in the opposition. This mustn't have taken him much trouble, since he apparently walked out of the film after the first two reels. Those who stayed on to the end, however, had every reason to be more hesitant; for the supposed simplicity of this work—and indeed of all Ray's films—disarms the critic. Only after close scrutiny do most of them turn out to be artefacts of the most subtle sort. It is a case of art concealing art, brought about by Ray's precise construction of plot—so that craftsmanship seldom shows—and by his ability while shooting to improvise against this structure in a way which gives his work a continual spontaneity.

I have heard some of Ray's admirers say that analysis of any kind can only destroy this spontaneity, and therefore distort one of the most important qualities of these films. But to believe this surely is to fall into an old trap. The myth of the Natural Genius, piping his native wood-notes wild, dies hard in certain quarters; and Ray it seems is to be the latest victim sacrificed upon its altars. (1) He can only be made to play this part, however, if one ignores his robust plots and the density of his symbolism. Not that his best work is mannered, as this might suggest. His symbolism is not like that of Bergman and Pabst (say), who are usually considered symbolist directors. All art in a sense is symbolic, and the success of symbolism lies in it being unobtrusive. This is not so with Bergman and Pabst, who, in trying to conceal the thinness of their material, let symbols sprout out of their feeble plots like straw out of a scarecrow. They fail because they are unable to construct suitable

---

1. Since the film has no mode of existence within itself but can only come into being as the product of both the strip of celluloid *and* the viewer, isn't the viewer who objects to analysis of the film really objecting to analysis of his own responses? An even more pertinent question here, though, is based on the observation that there are certain kinds of films which tend to elicit this sort of response more frequently than other kinds. Why? It is easy to say that they are films with which we identify deeply. Yet with films such as those of Satyajit Ray which have so frequently brought forth the anti-analytic response, such identification is unlikely. Rhode points to *Pather Panchali*'s apparent spontaneity (the impression it gives that art has imposed itself minimally upon nature) as the source of this attitude. But even if this will serve as a satisfactory explanation, there are many problems which remain unresolved—problems that arise from assuming such an impressionistic attitude toward art. First, are there works of art distinguished from other works of art in that they defy analysis? Second, if there are, are such works better art for that fact? And finally, could one say that films which crumble under analysis reveal themselves to be poor works of art: works which contribute little to the dialogue between celluloid and viewer, allowing merely the construction of elaborate fantasy?

plots, which in turn is a failure properly to explore their material. (2) In the best of Ray's films, on the other hand, the integration of symbol and action is so assured that we are hardly aware of the technical problems involved in such a feat. Yet Ray's continuing success has not been bought cheaply. After shooting *Pather Panchali* he went through a period—at about the time he was filming *Aparajito* and *Parash Pathar* (*The Philosopher's Stone*)—when he had great difficulty in making plots. It is part of his talent's strength that he managed to break through this sterile passage into the lucid and rich world of *Apur Sansar*.

What is so interesting about this talent is the limited means by which it has reached such richness. Ray's vision so far has been a narrow one. In his films there is no portrayal of evil (in the Christian sense), nor is there any sign of violence. The staple ingredients of the Occidental film—lust, murder and rape—play no part in his work. Most of his central characters are sensitive, often idealised people, usually scholars or rich men who have been dispossessed and therefore made vulnerable to poverty and suffering. (The trilogy could as well have been called *The Unprotected* as *The Unvanquished*.) Though this range is highly limited, I don't think it counts against him; for within it Ray has managed to deploy the old tragic conflicts with remarkable ease. What he has in fact done is to describe the relationship between art and life, duty and the emotions, free will and destiny, in very personal terms. And this he has brought off, I believe, by showing us how, in a most vivid way, these conflicts tie up to his major, almost obsessive, theme.

"In what way," asks Ray, "can man control the world, and what is the price he must pay for trying to do so . . .?" This, as I would see it, is the Promethean theme behind all his films. Why it should be this one rather than any other is a debatable point; but I would surmise that Ray is haunted in this case by the most traumatic event in recent Indian history: the granting of Independence in 1947. With this event India was born into responsibility. Besides her foreign problems she had to handle the problem of industrialisation; of modernising the agricultural techniques of backward settlements; and of coping with the underfed and the under-privileged. Though the scope of such a task may have been invigorating, there was

---

2. Rhode has here offered us two explicit criteria for the assessment of art: one concerning symbolism, the other plot.

always a heavy price to be paid. Independence brought with it the most terrible of border massacres, and mechanisation involved the destruction of ancient pieties. Inevitably, the India of Science was against the India of Myths. (3)

Though Ray is clearly troubled by this situation, and is indeed involved in it, his feelings remain ambivalent; (4) and from this ambivalence arises a tension which gives his work its force. In *Jalsaghar,* the protagonist is an ageing nobleman who, finding himself out of place in the modern world, tries to escape from it into the world of music. He fails. The sound of trucks passing to a factory owned by his *nouveau riche* neighbour echoes through his hollow palace and shatters the necessary silence. Unable to continue his traditions into the modern world, he destroys himself. Though this nobleman is little more than an old panjandrum, he becomes for us an oddly moving figure; for he is shown as the last representative of a civilisation Ray admires, a civilisation in which the mandarin virtues of ceremony and folly are prized and in which love of the arts takes a central place.

Ray's feelings may be divided about this nobleman, but they aren't half as complex as are his feelings about the characters of the trilogy. Though Ray's sympathies are primarily with the new men (like Apu) as they break away from superstition and ignorance, he is at the same time aware of the price they must pay for this liberation. The power involved in trying to control the world requires ruthlessness. It may also imply an evasion of life. So Apu betrays his mother's affection by leaving her to die alone in a remote village; and later, as a man of learning, begins to lose touch with life—with Mother Earth, as he puts it—to his natural detriment.

One would never call Ray a reactionary—too obviously is he one of the new men himself. This doesn't stop him feeling great tenderness for those who have lost out, for those who have been unable to control the world, at least in part. Most of *Pather Panchali,* for instance, is taken up with describing the hopelessness of such people —a hopelessness which, as Ray makes clear, is in no way a matter of despair. He shows us that they are fatalists who yet manage to enjoy

---

3. Rhode's guesses are presented clearly as guesses. Why though should he introduce them? And how relevant is the social and political history of India to our experience of the film?

4. How does Rhode know what Ray's feelings are?

the world. This mood is established from the opening moments of the film, as a child ineffectually sweeps a sun-baked courtyard while kittens frolic in the shade. This is life lived at its most primitive, biological level. Food is the primary pre-occupation: the mother continually crushes harsh roots; the children steal fruit or yearn for sweets they can't afford; the grandmother quietly gobbles in a corner. At no point does the family stop eating its scraps of rice, its rotting guavas, or its pieces of raw sugar-cane.

At first these biological processes seem to be the only defence against a destructive universe, in which the impending jungle creeps through a broken wall, and the monsoon beats down the house. Even amongst the villagers there seems to be no defence. Neighbours are rapacious, and education at the hands of the local grocer seems as futile a preparation for life as is primitive medicine a guard against death. (Death with Ray, though regular, is always unexpected. Not surprisingly he wishes to film *A Passage to India.*) The world is uncontrollable and the family, each in his own way, is its victim. The father, a gentle, distracted egoist, dreams about his ancestors' greatness but is unable to make a living. His neighbours cheat him and he writes plays no one wants. The mother, as the inarticulate conscience of the family, is the only one close to achieving some control over her life; but her failure is evident in her continual scrubbing and scraping, and in the nagging which alienates those about her. Above all there is the grandmother, who never despairs though she has the least hope. It is not in gloom but with wry joy that she says, "I am old and I have nowhere to go." Unlike Gorki's grandmother, who is an earth-goddess embodying (as one of the revolutionaries says) the best of Old Russia, she is never more than irresponsible and childlike. All she can offer is love.

From the difference between these two women one can deduce a significant difference between the Gorki and the Ray trilogy. Gorki is concerned with the drama of Revolution and with showing how his characters, even at second-hand, react to this. Ray is not interested primarily in such a drama. In developing his characters he is more concerned with understanding the world than with changing it—though to understand *is* to change it. His comment on social progress remains, often aggravatingly, ambiguous. The difference between these two trilogies is not necessarily antagonistic: it is the difference one might say between the zestful Russia of the late Twenties and present day neutralist India.

Anyway, even if they wanted to be, the characters of *Pather Panchali* could never be revolutionaries. Unable to control their lives in any way, they are never more than childlike. Though it may be a brilliant touch to have all the characters like children in a film which purports to be about a child, and therefore to relate a primitive agricultural society to the limitations of this age group, it does induce a certain ambiguity of vision. (5) Are we or are we not looking at the world through the eyes of a child? Ray never makes this clear. But he does deal effectively with another problem arising from this situation. Though similar, the characters never become monotonous; for the scenes in which they are involved are always epic, and therefore embody the differing strands of the various themes. (6)

There is the pivotal moment, for instance, when Apu sees a train for the first time and begins to understand the nature of man's power. (Trains are a recurring motif in the trilogy, and this scene takes on a particular force when we realise how later in Calcutta Apu is to try to commit suicide by throwing himself beneath one.) Though the sequence is a short one, it does—by its build-up—dominate the film. We see Apu and his sister move through the wilderness of a cotton field. As they listen to the eery humming of telegraph wires, seeds drift from white plumes. Then the train chatters past. Its smoke, like a feather, obliterates the sky. For us, all quite unimportant perhaps: but for Apu a mechanical Messiah has been born. Just as typical of Ray's art is an earlier, more complex sequence which in its unstressed interplay of moods reminds us of Chekov. It is evening, and the house is in darkness. The grandmother tries to thread a needle but is too proud to admit failure. Near her the mother fusses alone. The father stops trying to write a play and, holding up a moth-eaten bundle of manuscript, says gently, "Things have come to a pretty pass." Beside him Apu is learning to write. The father smiles at the success of his work. A passing train whistles. "Now," says the father, "write the word for wealth."

Through such a mosaic of action Ray establishes his major themes. In an uncontrolled world the comic travelling theatre, the father's

---

5. Is "ambiguity of vision" necessarily a fault in film? Or does an individual film dictate the degree to which ambiguity succeeds or fails?

6. Has Rhode made clear what he means by "epic"?

escapism, and the folklore of the grandmother appear incongruous. The mother, in trying to control a dwindling budget, goes out and sells the family silver; and the price she pays is to rob Apu of his patrimony and to destroy the lingering remains of a family tradition. This theme of control and its cost is, as I have written, the central one of Ray's work; but it does have an almost mystical extension which is to play a large part later in *Apur Sansar*. It is to be found even in such a simple scene as the grandmother rocking the newborn Apu in his cradle. Though she fears for his future she yet looks at him with hope. This mingled regard reveals her knowledge and her strength; for the old woman knows that ultimately the power of life itself transcends the suffering of people caught in an uncontrolled universe.

In the last resort, the destructive force is negated by the force of continuing life. Though the fetid lake may swallow the last trace of the sister's existence, and the jungle obliterate the house, it is the images of the passing bands and kickshaws, of children running through sunlit glades, and of trains, especially trains, with their hope of work in Benares and their promise of a new and better society, which remain burnt into the mind. Aptly does the English for *Pather Panchali* mean *On the Road*; for it is above all the activity of life that counts. As one of the villagers sagely remarks, "it's staying in one place that makes you mean."

And now the growing Apu begins to control the world. Premonitions of this in the pivotal scene of *Pather Panchali,* when he first saw the train, are confirmed by the pivotal moment in *Aparajito* when a shot of the boy triumphantly holding a small globe is followed by a shot of his home-made sundial. Time and space have begun to be conquered. (7)

---

7. Rhode moves on, at this point, to a discussion of *Aparajito.* Later, he will discuss *Apur Sansar (The World of Apu).* Is the implication here that the trilogy must be considered as a totality, that each of the three works can neither be fully experienced nor adequately discussed separately? And what is it we mean by a trilogy? Do *From Russia with Love, Dr. No,* and *Goldfinger* constitute a trilogy? Apparently not. What then distinguishes the relationship of these works to one another from that which exists between *Pather Panchali, The World of Apu and Aparajito?* Are they distinctions which provide an understanding of the concept of trilogy and if not, does this concept have meaning in the context of film?

Aparajito is an uncertain film. There is no plot to it, only a series of episodes related to each other by the most tenuous of connections. Symptomatic of this is the restless shifting of location: Benares and the father's death, Dejaphur, a village, Calcutta, and another village —it is all very fragmentary, and Ray tries to obscure this by overplaying the train motif, by sensationalist cutting, and by a symbolism which is too often of the Bergman and Pabst sort. Even the pathetic fallacy, of all things, is dragged in at one moment. As the father dies, pigeons scatter over the city.

The problem in making a sequel to a well-plotted film is that of finding another plot for the same characters in which they can, without strain, be put to a different use. In *Aparajito* Apu has become the protagonist, but has neither the personality of a child nor the character of an adult to sustain the role. The kind of adolescent problems which could interest us are beyond the range of Ray's fastidious talent, and the character is seen in middle distance.(8) The mother, too, doesn't fulfil the new demands made on her as a central character. In *Pather Panchali* she was never more than a form of conscience, nagging away like an aching tooth. There was no need for her to be more than this. Naturally such a character can never develop into a major role. The consequence of this is that her part in *Aparajito* becomes an increasing embarrassment to Ray, until finally—she is so much at cross-purposes with the action—he forces disastrously the pathos of her death. To enact this scene expressionistic technique runs riot. The camera veers over the walls and lingers on ominous flames. It is all very embarrassing. Unfortunately it is not the only confusion here: we never learn if we are looking at the world through her hallucinatory vision or not; nor is it explained why this sick woman, chatelaine of a large house, is allowed to die alone.

These failures are a matter of more than one film. They relate to an overt self-consciousness in Ray himself, which manifests itself in the mannered facetiousness of his next film (*Parash Pathar,* 1958/59) and in the obtrusive symbolism of *Jalsaghar.* The latter is a curious piece (imagine *Rosmersholm* rewritten by W. B. Yeats), but through being consistent it does work; and because of this such symbolism as the chandelier, representing the Tree of Life, is made plausible.

---

8. Is Rhode suggesting that if Ray were not so "fastidious," he would become involved with sex and thereby interest us?

But in *Aparajito* no such convention is sustained. The film is neither realistic nor symbolic: it is merely awkward. There is a sense of hiatus about it which only just manages not to be a sense of void. It is saved, in fact, by a number of typical Ray vignettes, such as the school inspector who admires Apu's work and so bestows on him a benign smile, or the bed-sitter bachelor who lends the boy a box of matches and then makes a pass at the mother. On the lesser level it is helped by a magnificent evocation of Benares with its lively ghats. It would be wrong therefore to describe *Aparajito* as a failure. It manages (just) to hold our interest between the earlier masterpiece of *Pather Panchali* and the later, probably finer, masterpiece of *Apur Sansar*.

At this point, Ray conquered his self-consciousness by finding a way in which he could develop the themes of *Pather Panchali* into a new unity. By making Apu give up his study of science in order to become a writer, Ray puts him into a position which also tells us much about his own preoccupations with art at that time. Apu's failure as a novelist reflects on Ray's most serious problem: that of transforming the dialectic of his themes into a direct sensation of life. (9) "He doesn't make it," says Apu to his friend Pulu, speaking of a character in his novel but referring unknowingly to himself. "He doesn't make it, but he doesn't turn away from life. He faces up to reality." Ray wants to do better than this. He wants both to face up to reality *and* to make a work of art that conveys such an apprehension. In showing why Apu fails as a novelist, and how he comes to terms with life, Ray has I believe succeeded in doing this.

Apu fails because his art is wilful. In trying to control the world he has gone too far, and so cut himself off from the sources of life. Ray brings this out vividly. From a shot of Pulu inviting Apu to a wedding and telling him in an affectionately mocking tone of the Olde World village where it is to take place, Ray cuts immediately to a panning shot of Apu walking along an embankment, chanting a poem which ironically reflects on his own predicament. "Let me return to thy lap, O Earth! . . . Free me from the prison of my mind . . ." This is in fact what has happened to Apu: he is caught in the prison of his mind. Inevitably divorced from the industrial

---

9. Does Rhode assume that the work of art has a one-to-one correspondence with the concerns of its creator?

society around him, Apu is locked away in his garret room with his onanistic flute-playing and with his (of all things) autobiographical novel. People enter his room as if they had come from some foreign land.

But this deadening sense of control is jolted by his unexpected marriage—by quite extraordinary circumstances he is forced into this, and so initiated into the happiest period of his life—before being finally destroyed by his wife's death. What the universe giveth it taketh away . . . or so at first it seems to Apu. Reality becomes incomprehensible to him, uncontrollable in a way he had never envisaged. He thought he had achieved some sort of order—in one of his books he kept a dead fern leaf—and that he had somehow categorised the world. But now, as he moves grief-stricken through a forest, he comes across a bunch of ferns growing by a tree and is shocked by their mysterious otherness. His novel, he sees, is inadequate: he has misunderstood everything. Unable to carry on as a creative being, he withdraws from life. It is only later, in his first encounter with his five-year-old son, that he realises how wrong he has been. The boy, by his very presence, acts as a criticism of Apu and makes him aware of how he has failed to face up to life. (Life here is understood to relate inextricably to a sense of duty and obligation.) It is through the boy, in his uniqueness and his unselfconscious vitality, that Apu begins to return to sanity.

It is not difficult to see behind this final scene the kind of criticism Ray must have been making of his own past work: how art without life leads to a kind of death, and how the artist should neither have a total control over his material nor be entirely controlled by it, but must in some way transcend this situation. One of the reasons why I think *Apur Sansar* is the best film of the trilogy is that in it Ray has managed to see how this can be done. He has brought it off, I believe, by raising his subject to a mythopoeic level without at any point destroying its realism.

As he sails with Pulu down a river to the Olde World village, Apu sings: "Where are you taking us, O Fair One?" The boatman, thinking he is being referred to, smiles. But this humour masks a profound irony, for Apu is unaware that the fair river is leading him directly to his yet unknown wife. The river in fact is the central symbol, linking together both the realistic and the mythopoeic levels of the work. It represents both the arbitrariness of nature and the regenerating power of water. It is by a river that Apu theatrically decides to marry; it is by a river—now shrunken to a stream—that Pulu tries to pull him back to life after four years of mourning; and it is by a river finally that he and his son are reconciled.

On a mythopoeic level the film tells of a god's death and resurrection. The point is stressed that Apu is an avatar of Krishna, the flute-playing god. Krishna, you will remember, was allowed for a brief time to love a milkmaid named Radha; and so for a brief time is Apu allowed to love Aparna, his wife. But only for a brief time. After Aparna's death Apu descends into the underworld, where he is imprisoned with his own echo in a landscape of salt. (Though he is like some holy man, going with mat and shawl into the wilderness, his sacredness is sick. Ray—and this is an unexpected belief for an Indian—shows little sympathy for those who seek spiritual contemplation at the expense of duty.) Apu's resurrection into the world through his son is a clearer, more enacted statement of the theme of regeneration which we found in *Pather Panchali* (see the grandmother rocking Apu in his cradle). Ray's touch, however, is here more sure; and the two characters, without losing their definition as human beings, take on the firm lines of allegory. The feeling of eternal recurrence in this scene—Apu in a symbolical sense returns to the village where he was born and confronts his childhood self—gives the whole trilogy the cyclic form proper to myth.

Quite a number of people have criticised the way Ray idealises his characters; and certainly to see Apu as an avatar of Krishna may be thought presumptuous. Ray reassures us, however, through his use of Pulu, Apu's friend, who laughs at Apu for his self-regard and yet admires him to the point of idealisation. On this point the myth works for us, because we are conditioned by Pulu's critical approach. Where it does falter perhaps is during the wedding scene. As one of the guests says that the curse has become a blessing, the music on the sound track implies that Ray takes such a magical suggestion seriously. This is never made clear. Again, symbolism is forced when Apu throws his novel away and the sheets fall gently over the forest. But these are minor points. In general the myth works beautifully. It ties together themes, illuminates details, and brings an immediate sense of life to the machinery of plot.

This account of Ray's films has so far neglected his originality as a director: his ability to apprehend experience in cinematic terms. There is his sense of cutting, for instance, which has developed from the clumsy opening sequences of *Pather Panchali,* where the figures often appear to be caught in the frame, into an unusual, implicatory style. This style falls somewhere between Eisenstein's anti-narrative montage and Hollywood's story-telling techniques. (10) The success of Ray's symbolism, his ability to compress densely, is in part brought about by this style (see, for instance, Apu's attempted suicide, or his search for a job). Too often, though, Ray's diffidence in committing himself is helped by this implicatory—and therefore illogical—technique. We never learn, for example, if the nobleman in *Jalsaghar* has lost his fortune because of an obsessive interest in music, or because he has abandoned himself to mourning after the death of his family.

Ray's handling of actors is also exceptional. Like De Sica he knows how to winkle performances out of children, and how to create relationships in a quick though not a glib way through the use of the striking glance or the precisely right gesture. Unlike De Sica though, whose characters must always be up and doing something, he has (and I think this is an unique achievement) a sense of the inner poise of his characters, of a stillness which is never static. His frequently sustained shots of the *Jalsaghar* nobleman, as he sits meditating, do not bore us.

These accomplishments are technical, and as much the work of Ray's excellent and permanent team of collaborators (Mitra, the cameraman, Ravi Shankar, the composer) as of Ray himself. What first concerns us is the single-minded way in which he has grown as an artist. His achievement, for me anyway, has been that he has managed to find a rich connection between his own personal problems and the problems of a society. In coming to terms with his own creative powers, in other words, he has found it easier to understand the world about him. The duel between life and death, between manic control and hopeless abandonment, relates closely—if one can use Melanie Klein's psychological terms—to the artist's need to pass through the depressive (or mourning) phase in order to recreate his destroyed inner world. In discovering this in his own terms, Ray has temporarily managed to resolve the conflicts within himself and the conflicts between his various themes. (11)

Under western eyes Ray's diffidence—his unnecessary ambiguities

---

10. At least four key technical terms appear in this paragraph: cutting, sequence, frame, montage.

11. Does Rhode subscribe to the *auteur* theory?

of vision and statement—is often infuriating. Yet in the last resort his achievement is so positive that we forget this. In his hands the most unusual of occurrences, like the *ad hoc* wedding or the first encounter of a father and his five-year-old son, become representative of our deepest feelings, of our most normative of day to day experiences. This golden touch should be more than respected. Indeed, for my own part, I believe that what a Bengali doctor once said to Yeats about Tagore could as well apply to Ray: "He has spoken out of life itself, and that is why we give him our love."

Frank Morriss, *THE TORONTO GLOBE AND MAIL,* Toronto, Canada

March 18, 1960

Indian Movie Displays Authentic Touch of Genius

Everything about Pather Panchali, which opened at the International Cinema yesterday, points to the beautiful life of the human spirit. (1) This Indian film, which has won almost countless prizes and acclaim, (2) moves with the quiet tempo of its peasant characters, revealing their inward thoughts, recording their heartbreaks and laughter and their capacity to penetrate the web of beauty. It has been written for the screen, and directed by Satyajit Ray with the authentic touch of genius and it has been acted with truth and dignity by its small cast.

Pather Panchali is a film for the discerning filmgoer who is willing

---

1. What is "the beautiful life of the human spirit"?
2. How does the knowledge that Pather Panchali "has won almost countless prizes and acclaim" affect our experience of the film?

to accept its unhurried and probing pace and is not looking for artificially created climaxes. (3) It flows with quietness but there is never a moment in which you are not aware of quickening turbulence which is just below the surface. This mood, once accepted, will encompass you and you will leave the theatre the richer in human experience. (4)

Pather Panchali is the first of a trilogy, based on a popular novel by Bibhuti Banerji. The others are Apparajito and The World of Apu, but the opening movie stands on its own with a completeness that is wholly satisfying.

With the encouragement of Jean Renoir, who was in India at the time making The River, Director-Scenarist Ray made the film largely with unpaid amateurs and when the production stalled for lack of funds, the Indian Government supplied the money to finish it.

What it sets out to do, (5) and what it accomplishes with such heartwarming effect, is to give you the lives of one peasant family. The mother, laden with care, must realize with bitterness that her husband, a priest, is a dreamer who is going to rely on optimism rather than effort, to keep the family from starving. The aged grandmother has her fretful life among them and the children are accepting, but disturbed about, the uncertainty of it all.

This, in the telling, may sound drab and hopeless, but with his eye for the pity, as well as the humor of things, Mr. Ray has illuminated it with touches that quicken the imagination and warm the senses.

Time and time again, it takes wing . . . as, for instance, in those moments in which the camera records the elemental forces of nature, or stops to examine the slight rustle of the wind as it creates patterns on a patch of water lilies.

There is no more rewarding moment than the one in which the two children, Durga and Apu, find their way to the railway line which runs through the primitive country. The hum of the wind on the telegraph wires, the distant sound of the train, increasing in volume, is the beginning of one of those screen experiences that come

---

3. What is Morriss saying about our expectations of *technical consistency*?

4. Can you think of a film experience which will not make you "richer in human experience"?

5. How does Morriss know what the film "sets out to do"?

seldom in a lifetime. You know, then, that changes are coming in India, that so-called civilization is going to take them and shape them. It is all done with marvelous subtlety.

This, however, is only one great scene in a film which abounds in them.

The performances are in keeping with the stature of the movie. They are not of the flashy virtuoso type. They become part of the canvas as a whole and when Mr. Ray wants to bring out their depths, he illuminates them with character traits.

The core of the acting, however, goes to Karuna Banerji as the mother. This is the one on whom the family depends. She is a person of depth, and the capacity to suffer and accept. Only occasionally does bitterness come to the surface.

Miss Banerji's performance is all-encompassing in its ability to give you the fullness of this woman's life and bitterness. Karuna Banerji plays her husband with gentle optimism. The children are played by Subir Banerji Uma Das Gupta.

There is a remarkable delineation of the grandmother by Chunibal Devi, an 85-year-old actress who was coaxed out of retirement by Mr. Ray, and the rest of the cast is excellent.

Although Pather Panchali started out as the work of a man who had never made a film before, Mr. Ray was fortunate in the encouragement he got during its production. Jean Renoir was of help, and so was Director John Huston. Mr. Huston happened to be in Calcutta and Mr. Ray showed him the rough cut.

Mr. Huston recommended it to Monroe Wheeler, director of exhibitions for New York's Museum of Modern Art. The film had its world premiere at the museum.

And now Toronto filmgoers have a chance to see it in a commercial house. It deserves the kind of success that will result in the other two parts of the trilogy being shown to the general public here.

Bosley Crowther, *THE NEW YORK TIMES* September 28, 1958

Film from India: 'Pather Panchali,' Odd and Lovely Bit of Art

It is good that a generous disposition prevails among serious movie fans to go all out in touting unusual and exotic films that do possess uncommon merits, though perhaps not as many as the touting implies. For otherwise such a fragile picture as the subtle and sensitive Indian film, "Pather Panchali" ("Song of the Road"), which arrived at the Fifth Avenue Cinema the other day, would never have made it all the distance from Bengal to lower Fifth Avenue.

Initial credit for the attention that ultimately propelled it this way must be given to John Huston, the American director, who first saw the unfinished film while it was being produced by an absolute novice, Satyajit Ray, in India four years ago. Mr. Huston was so impressed by it that he recommended it be acquired for showing in an Indian exhibition to be held at New York's Museum of Modern Art.

This started the ball to rolling. Money for Mr. Ray to finish the film was advanced, on the museum's recommendation to the Indian Embassy, by the West Bengal Government. It was shipped to New York and shown at the Indian exhibition three years ago. There it was seen and applauded by a number of serious movie fans, whose educated endorsement made it a natural for the international film festivals. It won the grand prize at Cannes in 1956 and picked up other palms and laurels at festivals around the world. And with that kind of approval, it has finally got a commercial release in New York.

Thank the Fans

So, you see, we can thank the serious film fans and the juries of festivals for generating the momentum that has got us this tender foreign film, as we can thank them for touting such other treasures as Arne Sucksdorf's "The Great Adventure" and the Japanese "Rashomon."

But, again, as we say, the implications of such kudos may possibly lead to expectations of capital merits that the pictures may not possess, at least, to the extent indicated.(1) And that's something to beware of in the case of this Indian film.

For "Pather Panchali" is a low-key and often exquisite little thing that still lacks certain characteristics that would make it more acceptable to the average Western taste. Little, did we say? Well, the fact is it takes nigh onto two hours to develop a formless story of the effects of poverty upon a middle-class family in the great Indian state of Bengal. And that length of time and the random nature of the continuity are among the picture's flaws.

You might call it a cinema mosaic, done by an inexperienced man whose priceless assets are integrity, compassion and a great feeling for pictorial imagery. In little scenes and graphic implications, he loosely assembles this humble, human tale of a mother harassed by a shiftless husband (who is cheerful and well meaning, withal), by mischievous but wondrous children and by an aging aunt, whose demands upon the meager family larder are secretly encouraged by the little girl.

Impressionistic

It is largely impressionistic. Out of the little scenes emerge the subtle stimulations that create an emotional pattern for the viewer.

For instance, the most exciting experience for the two kids is a run through the woods and across a flax field, bursting in delicate bloom, to a distant point where they can watch a steam train, with puffing engine and rattling cars, roll by, and where the lad can put his ear against the framework of an electric transmission tower and hear the magical hum of the outside world. As the camera encompasses this experience in an unhurried and affectionate way, the emotional afflatus of it quietly comes to you and sinks in.

Plainly, it is the creation of an artist, which Mr. Ray was before

---

1. Crowther here provides us with some answers to the second question posed of Morriss above.

he took to picture-making,(2) and plainly it betrays his lack of skill at cinema construction, especially in its earlier reels. But the spirit is there and it is breathed forth by a remarkably graphic native cast, so that one feels at the end of this experience an intimate contact with a phase of Indian life.

This is a picture of India of a sort we have not yet had—not even in Jean Renoir's "The River" nor in Robert Flaherty's "Elephant Boy." This is a communication of human experience out of the heart and fiber of Bengal. It is a universal experience, appropriate to the screens of the world.

---

2. How is Ray's former occupation "plainly" revealed in this film?

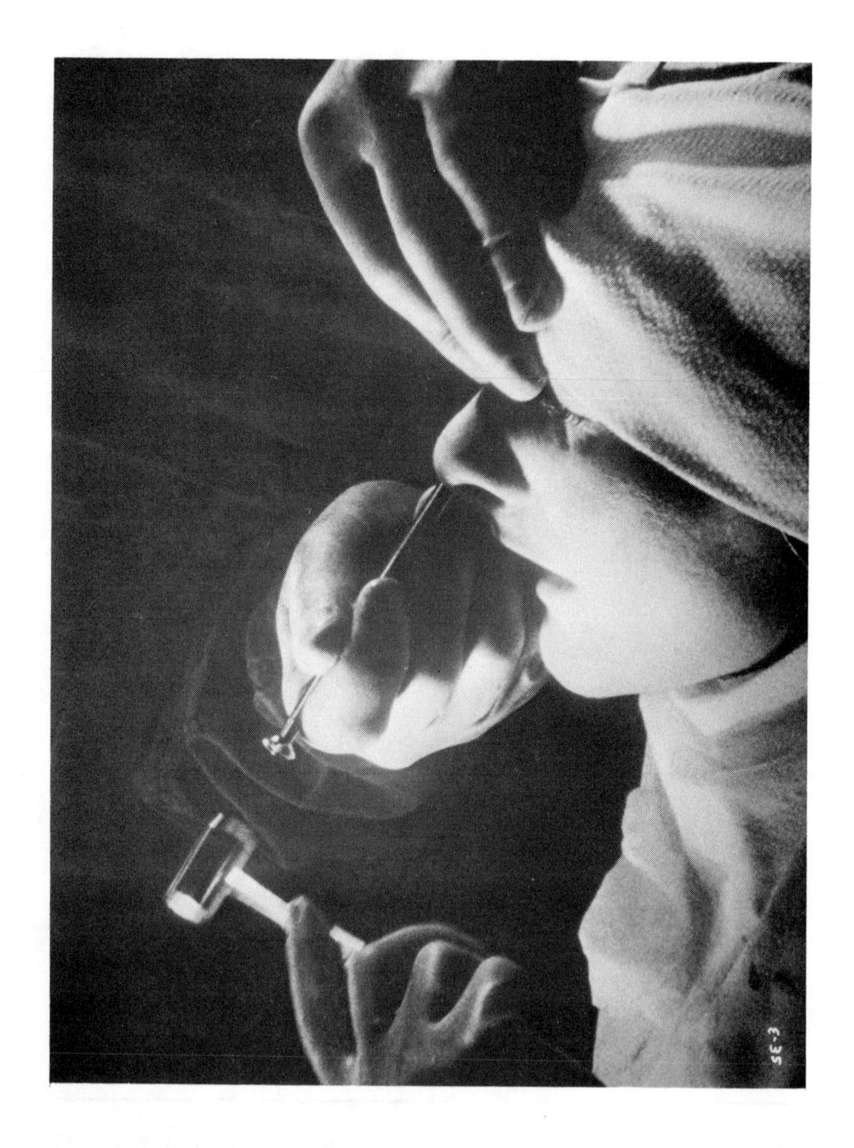

The Savage Eye, Courtesy of *Brandon Films*

THE SAVAGE EYE

John McCarten, *THE NEW YORKER*
June 18, 1960

No Rose-Colored Glasses

Three capable film-makers and five expert cameramen spent four years and sixty-five thousand dollars, give or take, to create "The Savage Eye."(1) I mention the cash outlay merely to point up the possibility that when all the papier-mâché walls of Hollywood—so expensively molded into nice and profitable conformity—come tumbling down, this small economy semi-documentary structure will be regarded as a repository of some of the facts about our time.(2) They

---

1. If a film costs $65,000, we tend to be more generous toward it than to its two million dollar big brother. Should we be?

2. Is the film as "repository" a criterion of excellence? Aren't all films with contemporary locales repositories of facts of our times? Is McCarten suggesting that this film's historical interest is greater than its aesthetic interest or that its historical interest is part of its aesthetic interest?

are not pretty facts, and while the film was shot in Los Angeles, where an old friend is somebody you met a week ago Friday, it does not pertain only to the denizens of that peculiar and widespread community, several of whom are shown on the screen along with the professional actors. For as written by Ben Maddow, who also wrote the screenplays for "The Asphalt Jungle," "Intruder in the Dust," and "The Unforgiven," and as co-directed and co-produced by Mr. Maddow; Sidney Meyers, who had a hand in "The Quiet One;" and Joseph Strick, who is another director of some merit, "The Savage Eye" adds up to a general indictment of the foolishness of the lives of people—not only there but here—who have to find some stimulation in watching wrestlers fake a fall, transvestites trying to look like wet nurses, drunks agape with a spurious glee, and so on and so on. Admittedly, this is shocking stuff that is rendered by the cameramen —Jack Couffer, Helen Levitt, Haskell Wexler, Sy Wexler, and Joel Coleman—but there is not a scene that does not indicate the awful consequences of an empty life until toward the end, when the heroine of the drama, after being almost killed in a traffic accident, decides that, having had blood transfusions from all kinds of volunteers, it is her duty to find love in everyone. (3)

In his screenplay, Mr. Maddow has largely dismissed any ordinary exchange of dialogue among the various characters introduced and has trusted to a kind of interior chat between his heroine and her off-screen guardian angel, or conscience, to get most of his points across. The heroine, it seems, is a newly divorced woman who comes to Los Angeles, Heaven help her, to calm herself down after the

---

3. Earlier McCarten says this is a "semi-documentary." Why "semi"? Because it combines the use of actors and a fictionalized narrative with a record of real people engaged in real life activities? Or because it expresses a clear point of view towards its material—whether that material is actual or fictional? The real point is to what extent we see the documentary film as a record of reality, or rather of what is sometimes called objective reality. But what if we can never be objective, if the camera can never operate without selectivity and thus point of view, and if finally the very presence of the camera inevitably alters the reality which it records? Can there ever be such a thing then as full documentary in the sense of a work which shows us the world as it really is?

wrench of breaking up nine years of marriage. Her experiences are horrendous, and they include a dreadful affair with a married man, which she describes with alarming candor to her inquisitive guardian angel. But it is when Mr. Maddow and his associates explore a bout of faith healing looked in on by the lonesome heroine—and in this picture women without men are as lonely as any human beings on earth—that all the frustration and foolishness of people who just have to believe in something is sharply brought into focus. I don't quite know how most of "The Savage Eye" was accomplished, particularly getting some of the characters on view in precise camera range, but I can assure you that they are all described in precise documentary style. (4)

Among the actors—the professional ones, that is—we have Barbara Baxley, who plays most ingeniously the divorcée who sees and participates in so much of the depressing activities, and Herschel Bernardi, as the married man who invades her lodgings. By way of the invisible guardian angel, or conscience, we have Gary Merrill, whose prose is delivered in a rather high-flown fashion, but after all, he didn't write it. Apart from a couple of other actors—Jean Hidey, who plays a naked lady, and Elizabeth Zemach, who plays a nurse—the cast consists of people roaming aimlessly about Los Angeles. There but for the grace of God . . .

---

4. We would all agree that there is such a thing as documentary style. How might it be defined?

C. A. Lejeune, *THE OBSERVER*, London November 15, 1959

Mud in Your Eye

One thing can be said with certainty about The Savage Eye, the new feature at the Curzon, it will provoke argument. Possibly it will provoke more argument than any film since "Citizen Kane."

It is a piece of very free free cinema,(1) which won the Roy Thomson Award at the last Edinburgh Festival. Responsible for it are three Americans, Ben Maddow, Sidney Meyers and Joseph Strick. Mr. Maddow, we are told, is screenwriter, director, poet, novelist. Mr. Meyers is chief editor Office of War Information, screenwriter, director. Mr. Strick is simply a director. Although, in view of all the circumstances, "simply" is not quite perhaps the apposite word.

Unlike some of its fellows in free cinema, "The Savage Eye" has a faint thread of story. The narratious heroine—the "I" of the Eye, if I may so put it—is a woman called Judith McGuire, who has just divorced her husband. Seeking consolation for her loss, she goes out on a round of pleasure. Everything she sees disgusts her. So she turns to the world of people without pleasure—the sick, the poor, the lonely—and finds it equally contemptible. So she drives her car carelessly until she crashes, and comes round, in hospital after a blood transfusion, to find the life-giving poison of the people she detested coursing through her veins.

There is a certain notion here, you'll agree. It combines the potentialities of "Ministering Children" with the opportunities of "The

---

1. What is meant here by "free free cinema"? Is Miss Lejeune pointing to an effect in the completed film, or to a process in the making of the film which may or may not be evident in the finished work?

Hands of Orlac." It could be treated in a lot of ways; clinically, morally, psychoanalytically, sociologically or with the grisly relish of full-blooded melodrama. The producers have elected to treat it poetically. (2)

The result is mainly a speechless film, with words added. A collection of hundreds of candid camera shots, some of them brilliant, most of them dispiriting, interpreted by voices on the soundtrack. There are two voices. One of them belongs to the heroine, the unhappy Mrs. McGuire, who is shown moving silently through her field of mouthing ghosts. The other, a male voice, is that of her *alter ego,* her spiritually good companion; described by Synopsis as The Poet, but what variety would probably call The Feed. His job is to prod her along with questions to which she can provide the carefully written answers. "Arthritis of the soul! Signals to nowhere!" "You're sad? No, I turned off the key in my head. It was all mechanical. I was a thousand years old. Nothing. Zero. Zero." Even when he is forced to relinquish her in hospital she still responds to his unspeaking presence. "Drowning up in waves of blood" (if I remember the phrase rightly), she manages to elocute the undying words, "I love you, poet and paranoid."

I am well aware that persons with taller brows than mine will tell me that "The Savage Eye" is a wonderful picture. It may be so, and I'm always glad to hear that the cinema has given cause for satisfaction. Experiment is interesting, and its good to know that Hollywood has caught up with the sort of thing that Cocteau, Vigo, and Germaine Dulac were trying to do in the 1920s. But in my poor view this is a pretentious effort, which says nothing, or nothing very memorably, and doesn't really come off as a film at all. (3)

---

2. Is the statement that the material is approached "poetically" presented as a fact or a judgment? In either case, what evidence does Miss Lejeune provide?

3. Does Miss Lejeune's final assessment of the film as a pretention which "says nothing" and which "doesn't really come off as a film at all" follow from what has been said earlier?

Jonas Mekas, *THE VILLAGE VOICE*
June 23, 1960

This is only an imaginary movie made by imaginary film-makers. (1)

The background of the film-makers: 30 years ago they were socially-minded men who wanted to improve the world. By now they have given that idea up. Now they look at the world with cynicism and disgust. Like most of the generation of the 30's, they have understood the change of man only as an outward manifestation. If by now they have familiarized themselves with Freud or Jung, they have done so only from the popularizing books and various psychologistic blurbs about father, mother, childhood, love, etc.

In any case, we can imagine a few of them getting together to make a movie about America. Since they mistrust fiction, they will begin by photographing real-life situations. They will shoot, for instance, a religious gathering, where the believers go through their open-hearted confessions, mystical passions, and trances. Since the movie-makers sincerely believe that religion and mysticism are bad for the lucid mind, they will slant the essence of this gathering by presenting it as ridiculous circus fare. It will be cruelly funny, as most private passions are when they are blown up out of their proper context and dragged into the blazing sunlight to entertain the outsider.

Another Corruption

Then they will film a few scenes at a homosexual party, with men dressed as women. This—so their social minds tell them—will reveal

---

1. Is Mekas' construct of an imaginary situation a way of warding off criticism of his critique? Or is it a way of gaining license to comment in ways that would not otherwise be legitimate? And if it is neither of these things, why has he chosen this rhetorical device around which to structure his review?

another corruption of twentieth-century man. In no case should a homosexual be shown as emotionally honest and sincere. Neither can there be any sadness or tragedy in his life. He is a freak.

They will then photograph a striptease hall. Being puritanic and healthy and pure-minded, they will expose the "dirtiness" of all this striptease business. Striptease can mean nothing but a degeneration of sex. Just look at Paris. They will expose it with the same cynical disgust they expressed toward homosexuality. To them, there is nothing complicated about men or women. They know all the answers.

They will take many other scenes like this from real life. To tie everything together, they will introduce a heroine. To give a modern touch, they will make her into a Freudian character. By that our authors mean they will let her constantly talk about mother, father, childhood, love. That will give the movie some real psychological depth. They will also write a poetical commentary to it. Everybody can write poetry if they just try. Then a thick layer of loud music will be poured over it, and the cake will be ready to serve. The critics will acclaim it as one of the most truthful movies ever made. Everybody will swallow it whole—the cake, the platter, and the wrapping paper as well.

They will call this tutti-frutti "The Savage Eye."

Paul V. Beckley, *NEW YORK HERALD TRIBUNE* June 7, 1960

"The Savage Eye" is a nakedly naturalistic, even cruelly explicit, study of the disease of loneliness,(1) ending on a note of universal compassion that implies extraordinary sensibilities in those who made it. It is a film of powerful present impact on any audience, and one

---

1. What do you think is meant by the adjective "naturalistic" here? How would a "naturalistic" study differ from a "realistic" one?

can readily see it as a rich vein of source material for any future historian of our times.

It deems loneliness as a major disease of our era, a concomitant of concrete, of endless window reflections, the implication being that loneliness is never perfect except in a crowd—a Boone who could feel bustled by the sight of a neighbor's chimney smoke might feel isolated in Times Square. It does not pretend to categorize the body of our society, but focuses on a segment of it and thus becomes a document of the misery one hopes is but a fragment, (2) the misery of the disenchanted in a land proverbially bountiful. Like so many words by younger film makers, it peels off the layer of materialism to look at the spiritual emptiness that may lie under it.

Its heroine is a divorcee, who steps out of a plane in Los Angeles after being "nine years, sixty-four days married" and joins others like her in an apartment court to live on "bourbon, cottage cheese and alimony." The cameras follow her as she "endures the day with ceremony," dreaming through the rites of a beauty parlor or picking over hats in a women's shop or straying into a bar for an afternoon Martini. She goes on a date with a man who makes her feel uncomfortable, but no longer alone; sees wrestlers sweating in a smoky ring, or a stripper in an alcoholic haze.

Throughout, the camera studies with a kind of compassionate horror the lost people who surround her, (3) ventures into an animal cemetery—the narrator says, "Pity the pets who bear more than their natural burden of human love"—to see a dead shepherd dog in a coffin, legs folded but ears stiffly erect. At the wrestling match an elderly lady shouts disdain through a megaphone made of a paper cup with the bottom torn out, ostensibly because the performers fail to snap any bones. One feels an echo of Romans turning thumbs down in the Circus Maximus.

Although an independent film, it is not the work of gifted amateurs, but of Ben Maddow (scenarist of "The Asphalt Jungle," "Intruder in the Dust" and "The Unforgiven), Sidney Meyers (director of "The Quiet One") and Joseph Strick, who has written

---

2. Is the film as document synonymous with the documentary film?

3. How does the camera do this? Is "camera" a technical term here?

scripts, directed, produced and edited previous films.(4) The photography is by Haskell Wexler, Helen Levitt and Jack Couffer. Miss Levitt (trained under Henri Cartier-Bresson) has been credited not only for her photography here, but also for her influence on the overall photographic style—if so, her contribution is a major one. Certainly one feels a feminine influence is strong in this picture.(5)

Couffer is a naturalist by training and worked on Walt Disney nature films. However pervasive the feminine eye in this picture, the naturalist's is also very strong.

Barbara Baxley plays the central character, and if her acting is meticulously real, one might suggest that her performance deserves recognition as above and beyond the call of beauty, for the unrelenting cameras dote on close-ups so large the lens acts as a kind of magnifying glass, enlarging the pores and ordinarily unseen blemishes, reminding one of Gulliver's discovery that to a tiny eye even a beautiful Brobdignagian heiress may have an unlovely skin.(6)

Gary Merrill is the narrator, and, although he never appears on the screen, acts as a character in the script, carrying on tags of conversation with Miss Baxley's mind. If the script does not quite integrate him into the cast, it does make of his voice a kind of superimposed omniscience reflecting an alphabet of attitudes toward life and in the end giving the film form and direction. If the narrative becomes at times a trifle precious—"the sky smelled of cigars and coffins" or "your blind company searching in stone libraries for the green page of illusion"—it also manages a fine edge of irony, a hammer head bluntness and much real poetic insight.(7)

---

4. Is our attitude toward *The Savage Eye* altered in any way when we are told that the film makers are not amateurs—as we might have expected, knowing it to be an independent production—but professionals?
5. How does feminine influence exert itself in the film?
6. Are we being told here that the exposure of Barbara Baxley's physical imperfections was excessive? And if we are, what is being suggested about our expectations in regard to the beauty of film stars?
7. Has Beckley sufficiently clarified the narrator's role in the film? What does the critic imply when he calls this voice a "superimposed omniscience"?

Another major expressive instrument is the musical score by Leonard Rosenman, which usually substitutes for natural sound and thus becomes a crucial means of artistic control, of expressing the attitudes of the makers of the film. In the stripper sequence, for example, her act has not been backed by the customary musical bumps and grinds, but rather Rosenman's score with calculated severity employs discords and drumbeats out of time with her movements to wash her with a kind of mixture of absurdity and pathos—scarcely provocative. (8)

---

8. How realistic or documentary is this technique? Are we being offered at least partial insight into why the film has been called a semi-documentary?

The Seventh Seal, Courtesy of *Janus Films*

THE SEVENTH SEAL

CUE

October 18, 1958

From Sweden—An Allegory of Man's Fate

The Seventh Seal—(Janus) At the Paris, in Swedish with English titles. The lovely little marble bandbox on West 58th Street celebrates its 10th anniversary this month by presenting a rare and quite beautiful movie prizewinner. "The Seventh Seal," filmed in Sweden by writer-director Ingmar Bergman ("Smiles of a Summer Night"), is a strange, powerful, exquisitely poetic allegory of man in search of God, faith, and truth in a world beset by superstition and ignorance, bewilderment and confusion. Set in Sweden in the 14th Century, the picture is like a medieval tapestry—pure poetry in mood and movement, in the rhythm of its sequences and symbolism of its props and players, in the marvelously well-composed proportions of its colorful images, in the delicately pencilled light and deep rich shadows of its photography. (1)

---

1. While one art is often used to explain another (e.g.: sculpture as frozen dance), frequent critical confusion arises from shared

The film's protagonist, who seeks to find himself in his search for God, is a knight returned from the Crusades, wearied, disillusioned, tormented by doubts. With his squire at his side, he is first seen at a lonely seashore where he is met by black-cloaked Death, tall, guileful, eternally patient. They play chess for the knight's life, with the understanding that as long as the game endures the man may live. The warrior journeys through his plague-ridden country, while the game continues at intervals. The tormented soldier seeks God in the likely, as well as unlikeliest places; and fails again and again to find Him. Instead, on all sides, he sees cynicism and bitterness, stupidity and bigotry, avarice, hatred, hypocrisy, witch-burnings, disease and death. He can find no hope, no faith, no meaning; even Death will offer no relief—only nothingness.

Author Bergman's allegory—presented in the form of a medieval legend with its obvious modern application to soldiers today,(2) returning from the wars and finding the world sick, diseased and losing hope in the threat of a world-destroying Bomb—ends on a note of thin hope. He had drawn his picture's title from the 8th Chapter of the Book of Revelation: "And when he had opened the seventh seal, there was silence in heaven . . . and there fell a great star . . . and the name of the star is called Wormwood . . . and it fell upon the fountains of waters . . . and many men died of the waters because they were made bitter."

The picture has certain obscurities, but it is, nevertheless, a deeply moving drama, not perhaps for the usual "entertainment-minded," but a richly rewarding experience for those who have a taste for

---

vocabularies which shift in meaning as they shift in context. A theme in music is hardly comparable to a theme in literature; and the rhythm of painting is quite distinct from that of music. Here the reviewer discusses film with the language of poetry (rhythm, mood, symbolism, images) and with that of visual art as well (images, pencilled, shadows). Is it helpful to view the film as poem? As drawing? Is this simply metaphor or are we being told something about the nature of film?

2. How obvious is this application? How do we distinguish between the film's suggestion that it has "modern application" and our own feeling that its situations and statements apply to the present?

such poetic cinematic allegory as this is. (3) The cast, largely unknown here, includes several top Swedish players: (4) Gunnar Bjornstrand, Bengt Ekerot, Nils Poppe, Max von Sydow and Bibi Andersson. The photography is by Gunnar Fischer, and it is extraordinary.

---

3. Is "poetic" being used here in the same sense as "poetry" was in the first paragraph? Are we being told the film is literary?

4. In the introductory chapters, we suggested that part of the "convincingness of European films can be explained by the introduction of new faces, people we do not know and can associate only with their immediate roles." Can you conjecture as to whether or not your response to *The Seventh Seal* is significantly altered by your present familiarity with Max Von Sudow and Gunnar Bjornstrand? Do you think there is a lessening of ambiguity? Similarly, is *The Seventh Seal* a different film for you that it was for this reviewer because you know Ingmar Bergman and have probably seen other of his films?

Arthur Knight, *SATURDAY REVIEW*
October 18, 1958

That horror can exist without monsters or camera tricks is amply illustrated in "The Seventh Seal" (Janus), a new Swedish import directed by Ingmar Bergman. Essentially, it is a morality play set against the Black Plague that raged through Europe in the middle of the fourteenth century. A knight returns to Sweden from the Crusades beset by doubts, searching for the meaning of life and religion. He plays a game of chess with Death, not to win but to prolong his search. His quest leads him to Breughel-like inns and fairs, to corrupt clergymen and innocent fools, to lechers, knaves, and brutes, until he finally learns in his last desperate encounter with Death itself that there is neither an answer to life nor any escape from Death. The happy man is the fool who never questions, merely accepts. Significantly, his name is Joseph; his wife is Mary—and with their child they move in simple contentment toward the future as this strange and beautiful film draws to a close.

But the beauties of "The Seventh Seal"—both a physical beauty and a boldness of conception—are accented by the terror that Bergman produces with the simplest of means. We are told of the Black Plague, and we see a great hawk hovering motionless in an empty sky. We are told of Death and we see two horses standing alone, riderless on a rocky beach. A man sits huddled in a cowl, and for a moment the camera reveals his plague-ridden face. A band of flagellants make their way across a plain, and the camera holds upon the desolation in the wake of their passing. As the Knight makes his confession in a lonely church, his confessor turns and it is Death. These are moments of psychological, not physical, horror. They bring to us a touch of the supernatural, the terror that comes from not understanding, not knowing. It is the quality that has distinguished all great horror fiction and the few great horror films. "The Seventh Seal" is not a horror picture; but in the end, when the light returns, it produces the same sensation of having been purged and cleaned. (1)

---

1. Since Arthur Knight says quite clearly that *The Seventh Seal* is "not a horror picture," is it useful to place the film in such a context?

Andrew Sarris, *FILM CULTURE* No. 19, 1959

> "And when he had opened the seventh seal, there was silence in heaven about the space of half an hour."
>
> "Revelation"

> "A free mind, like a creative imagination, rejoices at the harmonies it can find or make between man and nature; and where it finds none, it solves the conflict so far as it may and then notes and endures it with a shudder."
>
> GEORGE SANTAYANA, "Art and Happiness" (1)

Although Ingmar Bergman's *The Seventh Seal* is set in medieval Sweden, nothing could be more modern than its author's conception of death as the crucial reality of man's existence. Appearing at a time when the anguished self-consciousness of Kierkegaard and Nietzsche has come back into favor as a statement of the human condition, *The Seventh Seal* is perhaps the first genuinely existential film. (2) The plight of the individual in an indifferent universe would have seemed a fatuous subject for an artist a generation ago when human objectives barely extended to the next bread line, and when, it now seems ages ago, Edmund Wilson could reasonably denounce Thornton Wilder's metaphysical concerns in *The Bridge of San Luis Rey* as socially irresponsible. Liberal reform, Marxist determinism and the Social Gospel of Christianity were variously hailed as the formulas of blissful world, but something went wrong with these collective panaceas partly because thinking men discovered that endless problem-solving reduced life to its one insoluble problem, death, and partly because population explosions, the hydrogen bomb and the Cold War scuttled the idea of Progress as a cause for rejoicing. Quite obviously, the time has come to talk of other things beside the glories of social reconstruction.

Ingmar Bergman, the son of a clergyman, is aware of the decline of religious faith in the modern world, but unlike Dreyer, he refuses

---

1. Sarris prefaces his discussion with two quotations, one clearly relevant to the film, the other more tenuous in its relations. Does the coupling of the two give Santayana's statement a pertinence which perhaps it would not otherwise have?

2. Is it legitimate to call this an "existential" film? Is the film existential in the same sense as is Camus' *The Stranger?* Or is it merely a film in which an existentially oriented critic can find existentialism? Further, does the perception of the film as existential constitute a convincing argument for its pertinence to contemporary life?

to reconstruct mystic consolations from the dead past.(3) If modern man must live without the faith which makes death meaningful, he can at least endure life with the aid of certain necessary illusions. This is what Bergman seems to be saying in *The Seventh Seal,* a remarkably intricate film with many layers of meaning.

The Biblical context of the Seventh Seal is never fully retold on the screen, but enough excerpts are provided to keynote the theme of the Last Judgment. A hawk suspended in flight opens the film with a striking image of foreboding against a rising chorale of exultant faith.(4) After ten years on a Crusade to the Holy Land, a knight and his squire return disillusioned to Sweden. Riding north to the knight's castle further and further away from Christianity's birthplace where God has died in their hearts, the knight and the squire are cast allegorically into the void of modern disbelief.

They first appear on a lonely beach, the knight seated by his chessboard, the squire flung awkwardly in a lackey's sleep. The two horses prance against the rushing waves as sun, sky and sea converge on the distant horizon. In the midst of a dazzling progression of sun-setting dissolves, the black-hooded figure of Death confronts the blond knight. Bergman's editing is ambiguous here for one cannot be sure that Death has actually materialized out of space. Nor is there any camera trickery involved in Death's subsequent manifestations. Death is presumably too real for magic lantern effects.

The knight challenges Death to a game of chess, the knight's life to be staked on the outcome. As the game begins with Death taking the black pieces, Bergman composes the first of his many tableaux inspired by medieval church murals. Death and the knight resume their match at fixed dramatic intervals later in the film. Bergman's fable is shaped by this chess game, not so much in the symbolism of the moves, most notably Death takes knight, but in the expanding

---

3. Does knowing Bergman is the son of a clergyman help the filmgoer? Could Bergman be equally "aware of the decline of religious faith in the modern world" if he were the son of, say, a doctor, a lawyer, an Indian chief?

4. Notice that Arthur Knight describes this same bird as a "great hawk hovering motionless in an empty sky" and implies the image is an emblem of horror. To what degree does Sarris share this perception?

meanings and ambiguities of the two players. While seeking God in the world of men, the knight relentlessly pursues the enigma of his antagonist.

As the knight and the squire continue their homeward journey, towering overhead shots of the two riders alternate with pulsating images of the sun. This cosmic technique would be pretentious for a lesser theme, but here in the beginning, Bergman is suggesting the dimensions of the universe in which his drama will unfold. (5) Once the philosophical size of the film is established, Bergman's camera probes more intimately into his characters.

The fact that the squire does not share the knight's first encounter with Death is consistent with Bergman's conception of the knight's solitude in his quest for God. Since the squire is a confirmed atheist, the knight cannot seek consolation in that quarter. Indeed, the squire's bawdy songs and low comedy grimaces stamp him as the knight's Sancho Panza until a startling incident transforms him into a co-protagonist. Dismounting to ask a hooded stranger the way to the next town, the squire lifts the hood and beholds the death skull of a plague victim. The squire's reaction is that of a forceful intelligence, and he displays an unexpected flair for irony when he tells the unsuspecting knight that the stranger said nothing but was quite eloquent. Bergman achieves his shock effect here with the aid of a dog frisking about its dead master before the squire lifts the man's hood. This is more than a trick, however, and Bergman later develops the flickering idea involved here.

Bergman adds to his chess pieces as the knight and the squire ride past a carnival wagon in which an actor, a juggler, the juggler's wife and their infant son are asleep. Emerging from the wagon into a sunlit world less intensely illuminated than the world of the knight and the squire, the juggler is awed by a vision of the Virgin Mary walking the Christ Child. He calls his wife to describe this

---

5. While there can be no argument about the expansiveness of these shots, can we be equally sure of the significance they embody? Is there a suggestion here that "towering overhead shots" alternating "with pulsating images of the sun" always constitute "cosmic technique"? There is similar photography, for example, in *The Endless Summer.* Are there "cosmic" overtones in this film? And if so, are they "pretentious" in a movie about surfing?

latest miracle of his imaginative existence, and as always, she is kind but skeptical. (Bergman has a priceless talent for establishing states of being in quick scenes.) The juggler and his wife are suggestively named Jof and Mia at slight variance from an explicit identification with Christ's parents. They are never quite that, but when Joseph observes wistfully that his son, Michael, will perform the one impossible juggling trick, the screen vibrates with Bergman's first intimations of immortality.

Bergman returns to his central theme as the actor steps out of the wagon to announce that he will play Death in the religious pageant at Elsinore. Donning a death mask, he asks (vanity of vanities!) if the women will still admire him in that disguise. As the pompous director of the troupe, he orders Joseph to portray the Soul of Man, a part Joseph dislikes for theatrical reasons. When the actor returns to the wagon, hanging the death skull on a pole outside, the camera lingers on this symbol long enough for the sound track to record the pleasant laughter of Jof and Mia before cutting back to the couple whose merriment operates both as a conscious reaction to the departing actor and as the director's expression of their irreverent attitude towards death. In all this symbolic by-play, Jof and Mia convey a wondrous innocence, and the scene ends on a note of emotional recollection as Mia's avowal of her love for her husband is underscored by the same musical motif which accompanied Jof's vision of the Madonna. (6)

Bergman shifts from the sunlit innocence of the carnival wagon to the ominous atmosphere of a medieval church. While the knight pursues his quest for God at the altar of Christ, the squire exchanges blasphemies with a morbidly cynical church painter whose fearsome murals of the Dance of Death, the Black Plague and religious flagellations are the visual inspiration of *The Seventh Seal*. This circular recognition of a predecessor typifies Bergman's concern with the role of art in transcending the existential limits of human life.

Unable to find solace at the altar, the knight advances towards a hooded figure in the confessional chamber. The knight's unrecognized confessor is Death, and in an electrifying passage of self-revelation,

---

6. Notice the careful intelligence at work here. Is Sarris' accumulation of evidence from the film helping us to understand what he meant in his earlier generalizations?

the knight confesses all the agony of a mortal man seeking God while unwilling to embrace a religion of fear. Death, the confessor, offers no consolation, no guarantees, no answers, and in his tactical role, lures the knight into revealing his chess strategy.

The knight's outrage when he discovers the deception may well be shared by the audience. Why should Death cheat on certainties? It is possible that Bergman is intensifying the horror of life by suggesting ultimate nothingness with intermediate stages of accident and caprice. Since Death's timing follows no logical pattern, he might as well indulge in masquerades and linger over interesting chess games. Bergman suggests also that Death is everywhere—the church, the confessional chamber, perhaps even on the Cross.

The knight achieves heroic stature in his reaction to Death's hoax. Extending his hands before him to feel the blood pulsing in his veins, noting the sun still at its zenith, the suddenly exultant knight proclaims to his hitherto uncertain self the one certainty of an appointment to play chess with Death. Almost any other director would have sustained this great cinematic moment with either an immense close-up or a receding tracking shot to the ceiling of the church looking down upon mortal man in his fullest affirmation. Instead, Bergman truncates his effect with a quick cut to the squire entertaining the church painter with a Rabelaisian account of the Crusade. This abrupt transition from sublimity to ridicule is characteristic of Bergman's balanced treatment of the high-low dualism of human life.

From this point on, the fear-ridden world impinges upon the knight and the squire. The Black Plague is now seen sweeping across Sweden on a trail of hysteria, witch-burnings and religious flagellations. The knight asks a young woman condemned for witchcraft to lead him to the Devil, who might confirm the existence of God. The knight is answered only by a piteous wail which evokes the callous inhumanity of the period. The squire rescues a silent girl from a renegade priest who has degenerated into a robber of the dead. Ironically, this same priest, the closest human equivalent of evil in *The Seventh Seal,* once shamed the knight into embarking on the Crusade.

The various threads of the plot are woven together into the

---

7. Does Sarris convince you that the town does represent "many of the evils of society"?

fabric of a town which represents for Bergman many of the evils of society. (7) Art reappears in a musical pantomime of cuckoldry presented by Jof, Mia and the preening actor. The medieval approximation which Bergman attempts in this performance is carried over into the actor's flamboyant affair with a flirtatious blacksmith's wife. With dainty steps and cock-robin flourishes, the seduction in the nearby forest derives its tempto from a bawdy nonsense song rendered in the town by Jof and Mia, their faces gaily painted, their manner joyously abandoned. Their performance is meaningfully interrupted by the wailing of flagellants bearing Christ on the Cross. Bergman cuts with brilliant deliberation back and forth between the painful detail of the incense-shrouded procession and tracking shots of the soldiers and townspeople kneeling reverently in turn as the Cross goes past. The same soldiers who threw fruit at the actors (art) now kneel to their Saviour (fear).

The brutalization of a fear-crazed society reaches its climax in an inn where the patrons suspend their discourses on the End of the World to laugh sadistically at Jof's grotesque dance on a table while the renegade priest brandishes a torch at the juggler's feet. (The ordeal of a performer deprived of his mask and the sanctuary of his stage is more fully explored in Bergman's *The Naked Night.*) Joseph escapes only because of the intervention of the squire, who slashes the priest's face. In a film drenched with death, this is the only instance in which blood is drawn.

Withdrawing from the discord of the town, the knight is moved by the innocent contentment of Jof and Mia to offer them his protection and the sanctuary of his castle. The knight, the squire and the silent girl share with the juggler's family an interlude of resignation. The knight consecrates this moment in his memory with sacramental bowls of milk and wild strawberries, Bergman's personal symbols of the bread and wine of human redemption. The final movement of *The Seventh Seal* is then performed in a forest of unearthly calm and tempest, and a castle of last judgement.

The knight's caravan takes on the spiritual contours of an Ark in a drowning world. Having assumed responsibility for Jof's family, the knight is now engaged in a selfless cause. The squire's instinctive humanism has gained him the loyalty of the silent girl he has rescued and the friendship of the cuckolded blacksmith he has pitied. Yet, the growing intimacy of the characters is itself an ominous portent of Death.

The rising tension is checked momentarily by an encounter with the errant blacksmith's wife and the actor. Here Bergman provides the last bawdy counterpoint to his major theme as the blacksmith is reconciled to his wife while the actor feigns suicide with a stage dagger. This apparently gratuitous scene is a fitting prelude to Death's manifestation in the forest. (8) When the actor climbs a tree to be safe from the wood animals during the night only to see Death saw down this medieval tree of life, the dark comedy of the incident confirms Bergman's sense of structure. The buffoonery of actor-blacksmith-wife is the film's last semblance of life unconcerned with death, and it is required for Bergman's graded shocks. However, one is suspended between horror and humor as the tree comes down with the actor screaming soundlessly and a squirrel hopping on to the stump chirping loudly. This image of animal life in the presence of human death expands the notion of individual mortality which Bergman touched upon in his earlier conjunction of the dog and the plague victim.

The caravan next encounters the witch, who is to be burned in the forest. Still searching for God, the knight asks her once more for the whereabouts of the Devil. The girl raves that the Devil is in her eyes, but the knight perceives only the reflection of her terror. When he asks an attending monk why the girl's hands have been broken, the monk who turns his face is Death, now cynically inquiring when the knight will stop asking questions. In this stunning moment of recognition, the knight's destiny is revealed. He must continue his quest despite its futility.

Although the knight has given the witch a drug to ease her pain, her last moments on the stake are filled with wild despair as she realizes that the Devil is not going to claim her from the emptiness which lies beyond the flames. The squire confronts the knight for the first time with evidence (?) of the void, but the knight refuses to abandon hope. One would lose all sympathy for Bergman's characters if they treated the witch's ordeal as merely a test of God's existence. Fortunately, Bergman never loses his human perspective on death even when the renegade priest is stricken by the Plague. The silent girl he once menaced rushes towards him until the squire

---

8. Note the successful effort here to relate "apparently gratuitous scene[s]" to the work of art as a whole.

restrains her, virtually pleading that any help would be futile. Dying never becomes a casual process for Bergman. The actor, the witch, the renegade priest all achieve a form of moral purgation in the inescapable self-pity they arouse in their audiences, both real and fictitious.

When Death confronts the knight for the final moves on the chessboard, the once stark tonal contrasts between the two antagonists have merged into relativistic grayness. Gone is the sun and the sea and the sky. Death has enveloped the forest and no longer makes striking entrances with his black cloak. Jof "sees" Death at the chessboard and takes flight with Mia and Michael. Fearing Death's intervention, the knight knocks over the pieces to allow Jof and his family to escape. Inscrutable to the end, Death does not indicate whether he has been taken in by this diversion, or whether he is tolerant or indifferent, or whether, after all, he *is* actually controlled by a Higher Power. Once Death has achieved checkmate and has claimed the knight and his friends at the next meeting, he still denies he possesses any secrets of the after-life, and in a dissolving close-up, his face is slowly and memorably transformed into a hollow mask.

While Jof and Mia are fleeing Death's storm in the forest, the knight leads his remaining companions into his castle where the knight's wife waits alone, a medieval Penelope who seems as weary of life as does her tortured husband. Here Bergman resists the beguiling temptation to sentimentalize the knight's attitude towards death. Having performed a noble service for Jof and Mia and having retained his wife's love for the ten years sacrificed in a futile search for God, the knight might be allowed to meet Death with the lofty grandeur with which most doomed film heroes crash into oblivion. Instead, when Death appears at the long banquet table to claim the knight and his guests, the knight prays hopelessly and, at last, unconditionally, to a God who must exist if life is not to end in senseless terror. The squire remains true to his own colors as he scoffs at the knight's quest for God. Accepting Death under protest, the squire acclaims his life without God, but significantly the last words are spoken by the silent girl: "It is done."

This elliptical declaration of awareness, perhaps miraculously extracted from the text of Revelation, is less meaningful than the glowing expression in her eyes as she awaits the end of her earthly servitude. The silent girl, more than any of the other characters, has been defeated by life, and in her defeat, has embraced the prospect of death. When we first see her, she is about to be raped and murdered. She passively accepts her role as the squire's housekeeper, and is always seen either bearing some burden or accepting the squire's protection. One almost suspects Bergman of a class statement in his conception of this memorable, yet elusive, character.

Yet, all of Death's victims in the forest and the castle have failed in some way. The actor is impaled on his vanity; the witch deluded into a pointless martyrdom by the ignorance of society; the renegade priest stripped of the last vestiges of self-induced consolation; the knight tortured by endless doubt; the squire limited to the easy wisdom and cynicism of the world; the blacksmith and his wife enmeshed in trivialities; the knight's wife deprived of the passion which might once have resisted Death. Strangely, there is little sense of regret. None of Death's victims ever suggest that they would have lived their lives differently if they had another chance. The knight is not even sorry that he embarked on the Crusade. One hesitates to suggest pre-destination in such an agnostic context, but it is difficult to recall significant opportunities for moral choice in any of Bergman's films released thus far in America.

When Jof and Mia emerge once more into the sunlight, the Black Cloud of Death is safely past. (Some critics have translated this cloud into the H-bomb, but the analogy is both labored and unnecessary. More substantial social parallels can be derived from the scenes of fear and doubt; the squire's description of his outlook as "modern" is deliciously ironic.) Against the distant sky, Jof sees the Dance of Death, Bergman's majestic summation of medieval imagery. As Death leads his six victims, hand to hand, in the fierce merriment of their last revels, *The Seventh Seal* soars to the heights of imaginative cinema.

It is not until Jof describes the Dance of Death that we realize that his vision is inspired by a creative imagination rather than a Divine Revelation. The people he identifies in the Dance of Death—Death, the knight, the squire, the actor, the blacksmith and his wife, and the renegrade priest—are not entirely the same people Death confronts in the castle. Jof has never seen the knight's wife, and her absence from his vision is quite logical. The omission of the silent girl is more puzzling. At least two interesting theories suggest themselves. The silent girl's final expression of acceptance slowly dissolves into the watchful expression of Mia. The two women look very much alike, and whatever this means—Jof developing a mental block in imagining death for someone resembling Mia, Jof unconsciously admiring the silent girl, Jof even absent-mindedly overlooking the existence of this girl—a clear link has been established between these two archetypes of woman.

The second theory is almost frighteningly intellectual. Since Jof calls off the names of the Dancers, it is possible that the unnamed silent girl cannot operate in Jof's artistic imagination. Except for the witch, all the other recurring characters are assigned proper names, but the silent girl, like the witch, remains an abstract being beyond Jof's ability to recall in his creations. (9) This theory raises the question of Bergman's immersion in the technical philosophies of logical and linguistic analysis, a question which can be answered ultimately only by Bergman himself. (10) Yet, it is quite clear from his interviews and his past films that he has been influenced by the irrational ideas of illusion and existence expressed in the works of Camus, Sartre, Anouilh, Strindberg and Pirandello.

If Jof and Mia represent the continuity of man, they do so because of certain transcendent illusions—love, art, contentment and the future of their child. These futile distractions from imminent death make life endurable if not justifiable. Yet, the knight and the squire are also aspects of man, the knight as the questing mystic, the squire as the earthbound philosopher. It is possible to identify Bergman in some measure with all three characters since *The Seventh Seal* is a unique amalgam of beauty, mysticism and rational logic. (11) What is most remarkable about Bergman's achievement is that he projects the most pessimistic view of human existence with an extraordinary vitality. Conceding that life is hell and death is nothingness, he still imparts to the screen a sense of joy in the very futility of man's illusions.

For all its intellectual complexity, *The Seventh Seal* is remarkably

---

9. Sarris never tells us which theory seems more valid. Is he denying his responsibility as a critic?

10. Is Bergman the final authority on his film? For example, if Bergman supports Sarris' first theory, does that mean Sarris' second theory is no longer valid?

11. If we can say that Fellini's *Juliet of the Spirits* is also an "amalgam of beauty, mysticism and rational logic," can we then identify Fellini with the squire, the knight, and Jof? Is our aim in this experience to know Bergman?

entertaining. In the high level of acting we have come to expect in Bergman films, Gunnar Bjornstrand as the squire, and Bengt Ekerot as Death, provide truly remarkable performances. Bjornstrand, previously seen here in *The Naked Night* and *Smiles of a Summer Night,* displays classic range in the sublety and force of his widely dissimilar characterizations. Bengt Ekerot's playing of Death is so uncanny that it is difficult to imagine this unfamiliar actor in any other role. Max von Sydow has the most difficult part as the mystical knight who must communicate from the depths of his soul, but in his dramatic scenes, he fully captures the tortured nobility of his character. Nils Poppe, Sweden's leading comedian, is very moving as Jof through the counterpoint of his comic personality and his cosmic problems. Bibi Andersson as Mia heads a gallery of unaffectedly beautiful women which includes anonymous faces in Bergman's crowd scenes.

Bergman's camera technique is fully equal to his theme. (12) Except for a glaring process shot in the opening scene, his medieval images are clear and solid in the best tradition of realistic cinematography. Bergman is at his best in intimate scenes where his unobtrusively moving camera builds up tensions before his editing exploits them. One is always aware of the meaningful texture of faces as they react to the uncertainties they confront. Bergman indulges in the sun dissolves endemic to Swedish cinema, and the reverse cloak opening of a frame which Hitchcock invented, but which Bergman gives a special flourish in many of his films. In this instance, Death's black cloak must have been irresistible.

Bergman's overall editing maintains a steady flow of images to create visual progressions fo reach successive plot development. The plastic symbol of the death skull reappears in each shot at a different expressive angle, and Death himself never repeats the choreography of his comings and goings. Bergman's economy of expression actually makes it difficult to absorb all the meanings in each scene. Instead of fully developing his ideas in long, obligatory confrontations of characters, Bergman distributes fragments of what he is saying into every incident. Yet, a great deal that is implied is left unsaid, and it is possible that *The Seventh Seal* will be a source of controversy for years to come, and that like all classics of the mind, its interpretations will vary with the minds and times of its critics. (13)

---

12. Can the technique of a film ever be unequal to its theme?
13. Is Sarris providing here an answer to question 2 above?

STAGECOACH

John Mosher, *THE NEW YORKER*
March 4, 1939

The View Is Nice

The movies I've seen lately suggest that kind of party you get caught in out in the country, where you have to be thankful there is at least some scenery.(1) It's the landscape that saves your life. For the sake of the view, you forgive all. In "Stagecoach," the view is certainly something, and it hardly matters at all what goes on. The credit for the valuable things in this film unquestionably belongs to the cameramen, the Messrs. Glennon and Binger,(2) both of whom, I discover, were involved in the making of "The Hurricane," which had its

---

1. How does the tone of this review provide additional meaning to this critic's explicit statements about *Stagecoach?*

2. Notice, in this 1939 review, how the cameramen are credited with providing beautiful landscapes. In 1969, it is more usual to credit this kind of accomplishment to the director. What does this tell us about the change in our concept of the director?

pictorial moments, you may remember, and to a Mr. Ned Scott, evidently a stranger without any recorded history, who is held responsible for the "still photography." Being an old-fashioned "Western" with a story of Arizona and New Mexico, "Stagecoach" at least provides an opportunity for the camera experts to focus on handsome mountains, deserts, valleys, streams, and beautiful horizons. Toward the end, for a big climax, John Ford has directed an Indian battle—arrows flying straight into the coach and missing heroes and heroines by mere inches—which must have forced the cameramen, except Mr. Scott, I assume, to whisk about with their implements. The narrative follows all the classic rules of "Westerns," including the inevitable expectant mother, always present on these difficult journeys, whose great experience complicates the general scuffle and harasses the valiant. The actors and actresses are mostly familiar persons, like Claire Trevor, and some genuine Apaches, so we are told, have bolted out of the reservation to contribute their little bit toward the progress of art.

Howard Rushmore, *THE DAILY WORKER*
March 4, 1939

You'll comb the Hollywood hills many a day to find a more brilliant team than Walter Wanger and John Ford and if there are those who doubt that statement, let them take a cinematic ride in "Stagecoach" current at the Music Hall. You'll not only enjoy every moment of the trip, but you'll see what happens to a film when a director and a producer of four-star caliber let loose their talents.

They have taken a mediocre plot, a sort of Wild West "It Happened One Night" and transformed into shear celluloid drama that hasn't a single dull moment. They have taken a cast of more or less average ability and inspired them to act with such vigor that at least two of them can easily be nominated for the coveted Academy Award "Oscars."

And thrown in for good measure is 1939's best photography to date by the lens of Bert Glennon and Ray Binger. In short, partner, "Stagecoach" is a powerful good motion picture.(1)

Characters Make the Story

Ford has done wonders with the material in the script. There isn't anything new about a motley array of humans in a bus or airplane or stagecoach having a lot of trouble together, but as in "It Happened One Night" the result is perfect drama. The Wells-Fargo six-horse buggy that rolls through the sagebrush contains: a Southern gentlewoman about to become a mother, a gambler, a crooked bank president, a prostitute, a booze-soaked doctor, a sheriff and his captive, Ringo Kid, the outlaw.

Each character is a vivid one, sharply etched under the masterful Ford directorial chisel. And of the lot, the outlaw and the lady of Easy Virtue become the most real and humane persons as the ordeal of fire gets underway. And as Indians attack, their love story is sung to a Winchester symphony and Claire Trevor as the woman of ill-fame and John Wayne as the outlaw emerge as two characters we venture to say will be long remembered.

First-Rate Entertainment

And Thomas Mitchell as the doc who likes his rye is our candidate for the Academy supporting-role award. His performance is downright amazing. When the lady from Virginia gives birth to a baby in the relay station, Mitchell's emoting attains a real high in screen acting. He is aided by John Carradine, the gambler who gives his life for chivalry, Louise Platt as the young mother, Donald Meek as the whiskey salesman and Berton Churchill as the embezzler.

It is a film of not only first-rate entertainment, but of social significance.(2) Ford and Wanger have taken care to show that society's

---

1. What elements does Rushmore isolate as central to the success of a film? What elements does he see as peripheral?

2. Rushmore makes clear that social significance is one of his criteria for excellence. He sees this social significance, moreover, as informing the film. Do you agree? Or is this a case of the critic's own *intellectual commitments* introducing distortion into *Stagecoach?*

outcasts often have qualities which the elite lack. The banker, the villain of the piece, spouts in approved Hoover fashion. "We've got to balance the budget—what this country needs is a real business man for president." Neither Mr. Wanger nor Mr. Ford attempt to cloak their sympathies, which, as the public knows, have long been on the side of democracy and there are a number of brief scenes which prove they aren't afraid to bring out that fact on celluloid. (3)

In this connection, we'd like to see them team up and do the Indians justice for once. It's true that the picture avoids most of the vicious horse opera presentation of the only 100 per cent Americans, but Geronimo was a real leader of his people and didn't spend his time pursuing the Wells Fargo stagecoaches. All this helped the plot, but not our understanding of a noble and courageous people. (4)

But otherwise "Stagecoach" stands out as all wool and a yard wide from any standard of movie criticism whether it be entertainment, suspense, acting or direction.

---

3. Does Rushmore weaken or strengthen his case for the film's social substance by citing the past commitments of its writer and director?
4. Is Rushmore admitting here that his desire for the truthful representation of Geronimo is extra-aesthetic?

CUE

March 4, 1939

In contrast to *The Oklahoma Kid,* which depends mainly on melodramatic action for its thrills, *Stagecoach,* similarly concerned with pioneering days in the Far West, is an engrossing drama of two brief days in the lives of a group of persons traveling by stagecoach through hostile Indian country.

Its excitement comes from the skillful characterizations of each member of this group, whose fortunes are linked in the common danger of the journey.

Behind the adventures which befall them as they race through the Arizona Monument Valley country, is once again the larger theme of daring and indomitable courage which characterized our early western settlers.(1)

The dreaded Apache chief, Geronimo, has escaped from the Indian reservation and is on the warpath again. Smoke signals spiral from the hills, communications have been cut, and the coach's promised military escort has failed to arrive. But the stagecoach must get to Lordsburg. There is nothing to do but try to break through.

The passengers include a prospective young mother planning to rejoin her husband, a lieutenant of cavalry; a dance hall girl driven from the frontier town by the outraged ladies of the Law and Order Society; as well as a drunken medical practitioner, a gentleman gambler, a pious whiskey drummer, a banker embezzling his institution's funds, and a young outlaw bent on avenging his brother's murder.

Each, for imperative personal reasons, must get through to the next town. For the next 48 hours these people, united by their need and isolated in their peril, learn tolerance and understanding as heroism and sacrifice crop up in unexpected places. For those who like their westerns fast and exciting there is plenty of action. But there is something bigger here (2)—a gripping drama, superbly told, embellished by excellent writing, with splendid performance and direction.

First honors go to young John Wayne, a cowboy actor who plays his first big time role as the outlawed Ringo Kid. Others who contribute toward making *Stagecoach* an epic of the Old West are Claire Trevor as the girl, George Bancroft as the sheriff, Louise Platt as the young mother, Thomas Mitchell in the doctor's role (much like his part in *Hurricane*), John Carradine, Donald Meek, Berton Churchill, and Andy Devine as the driver of the coach. John Ford *(The Informer, Arrowsmith, Lost Patrol, Mary of Scotland, The Hurricane)* directed.(3)

---

1. Does the phrase "once again" tend to diminish the reviewer's claim that the film conveys "the larger theme of daring and indomitable courage"? Why do you think the reviewer refers at all to a "larger theme"?
2. And what is the implication of "something bigger here"?
3. Who is this reviewer's audience? How do you know?

George N. Fenin and William K. Everson, *THE WESTERN: FROM SILENTS TO CINERAMA* (New York: The Orion Press), 1962

John Ford's *Stagecoach* of the same year [1939] appealed less to a nation's pride in design, but far more so in its ultimate execution. A sort of *Grand Hotel* on wheels, and based on the above-average Western novel *Stage to Lordsburg* by Ernest Haycox, it followed a familiar pattern: a group of widely assorted characters (perhaps too much of a cross section to be completely logical) are placed in a dangerous situation—Geronimo is about to attack. This situation forces their true characters to rise to the surface. In keeping with tradition, too, those who display the most nobility are the social outcasts (a gambler, an outlaw, and a prostitute), while the most "respectable" member of the party (a banker, played by Berton Churchill) turns out to be least worthy, a man with neither courage nor principles. (1)

Author Ernest Haycox is said to have been influenced by de Maupassant's *Boule de Suif* in his creation of the dance-hall prostitute who is the heroine. Certainly, there are superficial similarities in both the action of the two tales and in the conception of the heroine's character. The basic differences, of course, are stressed by the fact that Haycox's heroine redeems herself in the eyes of all by her courageous actions during the Indian attack, while de Maupassant, less sentimentally, more cynically, and perhaps more honestly, shows the passengers turning on her, despising her again, once crisis and her own usefulness are past. (2)

Although designed more as a Western melodrama than as an his-

---

1. Note that what Rushmore has seen as expressive of the director's social commitment, Fenin and Everson see in relation to tradition. Must we choose, or can both be right?

2. Are the novel and film being treated as if they were synonymous here? And is the introduction of a discussion of the novel useful to our understanding of the film?

---

torical Western, nevertheless, its carefully etched backgrounds—the establishment of telegraphic communication, the patrolling of the frontier by the cavalry, the role played by the stagecoach in the opening up of the West—made it a far more important contribution to Hollywood Western lore than *Union Pacific.*

Film historians—in particular, some European critics—have tended to overrate *Stagecoach* as a film and to regard it as the yardstick by which all Westerns should be measured. The reasons for this exaggerated evaluation are at least partially sentimental, (3) for the theme itself was an obvious one. (4) It was John Ford's first sound Western, and the first for which he was to use Utah's Monument Valley for his principal location. It was also a film that rescued John Wayne from the rut of "B" pictures in which he had marked time since *The Big Trail,* a decade earlier. (Wayne still had to complete a series of "B" Westerns at Republic following *Stagecoach,* but it was certainly this film which paved the way for his ultimate success as a star of big-budget Westerns.) *Stagecoach* should be seen in its true perspective as a film more important in the development of Ford than in the development of the Western itself. Certainly it was one of the most flawlessly constructed and beautifully photographed of all Ford Westerns. Even the ending—the time-honored duel in the streets—though perhaps anti-climactic after the magnificently staged chase across the salt flats, was so well photographed and directed that it still sustained interest. The whole film, however, was far more a matter of Ford's lovely, sentimental images and sweeping action, and Yakima Canutt's brilliant second unit direction of stunt sequences, than a completely *true* picture of the times. (5) William S. Hart pointed out somewhat scornfully that such a prolonged chase could never have taken place, the Indians being smart enough to shoot the horses first! (6)

---

3. Why must those who "overrate" *Stagecoach* be seen as "sentimental"? Can't they simply have poor taste?

4. Notice the assumption that a great film cannot have an obvious theme. Do you agree?

5. It would be interesting to know what constitutes a "sentimental image" in the eyes of Fenin and Everson. Does "sentimental" seem to mean "untrue" in this context?

6. And if it could never have taken place, does this make the chase less effective as cinema?

TREASURE OF SIERRA MADRE

Howard Barnes, *NEW YORK HERALD TRIBUNE*
January 24, 1948

Great Day for the Hustons

A savage, unrelenting and considerably entertaining film has come to the Strand. "The Treasure of the Sierra Madre" takes the novel by B. Traven and converts it into a florid melodrama of 1920.(1) Humphrey Bogart plays a bad man (2) who gets his just deserts as a trigger-happy prospector in the Mexican hills with a fierce intensity. Walter Huston is nothing short of magnificent as an aging gold miner, who knows most of the tricks of sneaking that curious stuff one finally sees in jewelry stores out of bandit-infested territory. John Huston, his son, has staged the production superbly.

---

1. Melodrama is almost inevitably a pejorative term. Does it function as such here?
2. In saying that Bogart plays a "bad man," Barnes is implying a lack of complexity in the film. Does it seem to you all that simple?

It is the elder Huston who takes top honors in "Treasure of Sierra Madre." His authoritative portrayal of an old man who can smell gold, but knows that it leads to killing, is one of the great performances of the current cinema. Whether young John put him through his paces or not, as this reviewer firmly doubts, he gives a vastly engaging characterization which is cause enough to go to the Strand.(3) From the moment that he tells a couple of foot-loose Yankees about prospecting in a Tampico flophouse, until the final sequence of riotous laughter as he discovers that a fortune has been blown away, he holds this Warner Brothers production to a key of high excitement.

The picture is too long,(4) as is commonly the case with recent offerings, but it manages to conserve its suspense and terror. Mostly this is due to the fact that the central theme is kept in the forefront throughout the exposition and that there is no extraneous romantic nonsense. "The Treasure of Sierra Madre" is merely concerned with the story of men wresting treasures perilously out of a wilderness. Kipling wrote a similar tale. It still has its obvious overtones of violence and dramatic shock. There are splendid pictorial fragments in the work, as the prospectors fight off bandits and contemplate double-crossing each other. They are held in a precise and striking unity.

Huston has been so fine on stage and screen for so many years that it may be belittling him to say that his performance in "The Treasure of Sierra Madre" is one of his best. It is. He plays with such perfect understanding of the somewhat flamboyant aspects of the script that he is the magnet of the production. Bogart has the bigger scenes in the work, as he tries to kill a partner who has saved his life and gets left for the vultures by some bandits, but he is in no way comparable to his elder colleague. Tim Holt is good as one of the gold-mining trio and Bruce Bennett has a fine bit as a Texan interloper. In any case, "The Treasure of Sierra Madre" is a superb below-the-border thriller, calculated to awake film-goer's interest again in rugged location screen melodrama.

---

3. In a film, can we ever know with any assurance to what degree a director has controlled the performances of the actors? And does it qualify any commitment we might have to either *auteur* or actor?
4. By what criteria can a film be too long?

Bosley Crowther, *THE NEW YORK TIMES* January 24, 1948

Greed, a despicable passion out of which other base ferments may spawn, is seldom treated in the movies with the frank and ironic contempt that is vividly manifested toward it in "Treasure of Sierra Madre." And certainly the big stars of the movies are rarely exposed in such cruel light as that which is thrown on Humphrey Bogart in this new picture at the Strand. But the fact that this steel-springed outdoor drama transgresses convention in both respects is a token of the originality and maturity that you can expect of it.

Also, the fact that John Huston, who wrote and directed it from a novel by B. Traven, has resolutely applied the same sort of ruthless realism that was evident in his documentaries of war is further assurance of the trenchant and fascinating nature of the job. (1)

Taking a story of three vagrants on "the beach" in Mexico who pool their scratchy resources and go hunting for gold in the desolate hills, Mr. Huston has shaped a searching drama of the collision of civilization's vicious greeds with the instinct for self-preservation in an environment where all the barriers are down. And, by charting the moods of his prospectors after they have hit a vein of gold, he has done a superb illumination of basic characteristics in men. One might almost reckon that he has filmed an intentional comment here upon the irony of avarice in individuals and in nations today. (2)

---

1. Crowther suggests Huston has learned how to make things look real from his experience with documentaries. This raises the question of what it is that makes art look like life. In focusing on Huston's documentary background, is Crowther implying that it is largely the film quality (the movie's visual resemblance to, say, a newsreel) that fools us into thinking we are seeing reality? And if this is so, what has happened to the role of plot, of dialogue, of acting?

2. Suppose this comment were "intentional"? Would it gain any validity?

But don't let this note of intelligence distract your attention from the fact that Mr. Huston is putting it over in a most vivid and exciting action display.(3) Even the least perceptive patron should find this a swell adventure film. For the details are fast and electric from the moment the three prospectors start into the Mexican mountains, infested with bandits and beasts, until two of them come down empty-handed and the third one, the mean one, comes down dead. There are vicious disputes among them, a suspenseful interlude when a fourth man tries to horn in and some running fights with the banditi that will make your hair stand on end. And since the outdoor action was filmed in Mexico with all the style of a documentary camera, it has integrity in appearance, too.

Most shocking to one-tracked moviegoers, however, will likely be the job that Mr. Bogart does as the prospector who succumbs to the gnawing of greed. Physically, morally and mentally, this character goes to pot before our eyes, dissolving from a fairly decent hobo under the corroding chemistry of gold into a hideous wreck of humanity possessed with only one passion—to save his "stuff." And the final appearance of him, before a couple of roving bandits knock him off in a manner of supreme cynicism, is one to which few actors would lend themselves. Mr. Bogart's compensation should be the knowledge that his performance in this film is perhaps the best and most substantial that he has ever done.

Equally, if not more, important to the cohesion of the whole is the job done by Walter Huston, father of John, as a wise old sourdough. For he is the symbol of substance, of philosophy and fatalism, in the film, as well as an unrelenting image of personality and strength. And Mr. Huston plays this ancient with such humor and cosmic gusto that he richly suffuses the picture with human vitality and warmth. In the limited, somewhat negative role of the third prospector, Tim Holt is quietly appealing, while Bruce Bennett is intense as a prospecting lone wolf and Alfonso Bedoya is both colorful and revealing as an animalistic bandit chief.

To the honor of Mr. Huston's integrity, it should be finally remarked that women have small place in this picture, which is just one more reason why it is good. (4)

---

3. Is Crowther saying that our experience of "action" is non-intellectual?

4. Crowther presents as a criterion of integrity (and we can assume

integrity is a positive value) Huston's failure to live up to the convention of screen romance. Do you share this judgment?

James Agee, *THE NATION*
January 31, 1948

Several of the best people in Hollywood grew, noticeably, during their years away at war; the man who grew most impressively, I thought, as an artist, as a man, in intelligence, in intransigence, and in an ability to put through fine work against difficult odds, was John Huston, whose *San Pietro* and *Let There Be Light* were full of evidence of this many-sided growth. I therefore looked forward with the greatest eagerness to the work he would do after the war.

His first movie since the war has been a long time coming, but it was certainly worth waiting for. *The Treasure of the Sierra Madre* is Huston's adaptation of B. Traven's novel of the same title. It is not quite a completely satisfying picture, but on the strength of it I have no doubt at all that Huston, next only to Chaplin, is the most talented man working in American pictures, and that this is one of the movie talents in the world which is most excitingly capable of still further growth. *The Treasure* is one of very few movies made since 1927 which I am sure will stand up in the memory and esteem of qualified people alongside the best of the silent movies. And yet I doubt that many people will fully realize, right away, what a sensational achievement, or plexus of achievement, it is.(1) You will

---

1. Agee fears that the film will generally go unrecognized as the achievement he feels it to be. The reviews of the film lived up to his worst expectations. What is there about *Treasure of Sierra Madre* that makes it so easy for viewers to dismiss it as trivial?

seldom see a good artist insist less on his artistry; Huston merely tells his story so straight and so well that one tends to become absorbed purely in that; and the story itself—a beauty—is not a kind which most educated people value nearly enough, today.

This story and Huston's whole handling of it are about as near to folk art as a highly conscious artist can get; (2) both also approach the global appeal, to the most and least sophisticated members of an audience, which the best poetic drama and nearly all the best movies have in common. Nominally an adventure story, this is really an exploration of character as revealed in vivid action; and character and action yield revelations of their own, political, metaphysical, moral, above all, poetic. The story unfolds so pleasurably on the screen that I will tell as little as possible of it here. Three American bums of the early 1920s (Walter Huston, Humphrey Bogart, Tim Holt) run into lottery luck in Tampico and strike into the godforsaken mountains of Mexico in search of gold. The rest of the story merely demonstrates the development of their characters in relation to hardship and hard work, to the deeply primitive world these modern primitives are set against, to the gold they find, and to each other. It is basically a tragic story and at times a sickeningly harsh one; most of it is told as cheerfully brutal sardonic comedy.

This may be enough to suggest how rich the story is in themes, semi-symbols, possible implications, and potentialities as a movie. Huston's most wonderful single achievement is that he focuses all these elements as simply as rays in a burning-glass: all you see, unless you look sharp, is a story told so truly and masterfully that I suspect the picture's best audience is the kind of men the picture is about, who will see it only by chance. (3)

But this single achievement breaks down into many. I doubt we shall ever see a film more masculine in style; or a truer movie understanding of character and of men; or as good a job on bumming, a bum's life, a city as a bum sees it; or a more beautiful job on a

---

2. Does Agee in this paragraph suggest in what ways this film resembles "folk art"? And if he does not and you must supply your own evidence, still, do you think the point is a valid one?

3. Is Agee saying that *Treasure of Sierra Madre* is so true that the only people who can really appreciate its truth are those the film is about?

city; or a finer portrait of Mexico and Mexicans (compare it with all the previous fancy-filter stuff for a definitive distinction between poetry and poeticism); (4) or a crueler communication of absolute desolateness in nature and its effect on men (except perhaps in *Greed*); or a much more vivid communication of hardship, labor, and exhaustion (though I wish these had been brutally and meticulously presented rather than skillfully sketched); or more intelligent handling of amateurs and semi-professionals (notably the amazing character who plays Gold-Hat, the bandit leader); or a finer selective eye for location or a richer understanding of how to use it; or scenes of violence or building toward violence more deeply authentic and communicative (above all in Huston's terrific use of listlessness); or smarter casting than that of Tim Holt as the youngest bum and that of Bruce Bennett as an intrusive Texan; or better acting than Walter Huston's beautiful performance; or subtler and more skillful collusions and variations of tempo (two hours have certainly never been better used in a movie); or a finer balance, in Ted McCord's perfect camera work, in every camera set-up, in every bit of editing, of unaffectedness, and sensitiveness. (5) (As one fine example of that blend I recommend watching for the shot of Gold-Hat reflected in muddy water, which is so subtly photographed that in this noncolor film the hat seems to shed golden light.) There is not a shot-for-shot's sake in the picture, or one too prepared-looking, or dwelt on too long. The camera is always where it ought to be, never imposes on or exploits or over-dramatizes its subject, never for an instant shoves beauty or special meaning at you. This is one of the most visually alive and beautiful movies I have ever seen; there is a wonderful flow of fresh air, light, vigor, and liberty through every shot, and a fine athlete's litheness and absolute control and flexibility in every succession and series of shots. Huston shows that he is already capable of literally anything in movies except the profoundest kind of movie inventiveness, the most extreme kind of poetic concentration, artiness, soft or apathetic or sloppy or tasteless or excessive work,

---

4. Agee says here that "all the previous fancy-filter stuff" is "poeticism," while this film is "poetry." Having said this, has he provided us with a meaningful distinction—one that we can apply to other experiences?

5. What do we learn here about Agee's criteria of film excellence?

and rhetoric whether good or bad. His style is practically invisible as well as practically universal in its possible good uses; (6) it is the most virile movie style I know of; and is the purest style in contemporary movies, here or abroad.

I want to say a little more about Walter Huston; a few thousand words would suit me better. Rightly or wrongly, one thing that adds to my confidence that the son, so accomplished already, will get better and better, is the fact that the father has done that, year after year. I can think of nothing more moving or happier than every instance in which an old man keeps right on learning, and working, and improving, as naturally and eagerly as a child learns the fundamentals of walking, talking, and everything else in sight until his parents and teachers destroy his appetite for learning. Huston has for a long time been one of the best actors in the world and he is easily the most likable; on both counts this performance crowns a lifetime. It is an all but incredible submergence in a role, and transformation; this man who has credibly played Lincoln looks small and stocky here, and is as gaily vivacious as a water bug. The character is beautifully conceived and written, but I think it is chiefly Walter Huston who gives it its almost Shakespearean wonderfulness, charm, and wisdom. In spite of the enormous amount of other talent at large in the picture, Huston carries the whole show as deftly and easily as he handles his comedy lines.

There are a few weaknesses in the picture, most of which concern me so little I won't even bother to mention them. Traven's Teutonic or Melvillean excitability as a poet and metaphysician sometimes, I think, misleads him—and John Huston; magnificently as Walter Huston does it, and deeply as he anchors it in flesh and blood, the Vast Gale of Purifying Laughter with which he ends the picture strikes me as unreal, stuck-onto-the-character, close to arty; yet I feel tender toward this kind of cliché, if I'm right that it is one. One thing I do furiously resent is the intrusion of background music. There is relatively little of it and some of it is better than average, but there shouldn't be any, and I only hope and assume that Huston fought the use of it. The only weakness which strikes me as fundamental,

---

6. When Agee states admiringly that Huston's "style is practically invisible," what is he implying about the role of style in film making? What is style?

however, is deep in the story itself: it is the whole character of the man played by Bogart. This is, after all, about gold and its effects on those who seek it, and so it is also a fable about all human life in this world and about much of the essence of good and evil. Many of the possibilities implicit in this fable are finely worked out. But some of the most searching implications are missed. For the Bogart character is so fantastically undisciplined and troublesome that it is impossible to demonstrate or even to hint at the real depth of the problem, with him on hand. It is too easy to feel that if only a reasonably restrained and unsuspicious man were in his place, everything would be all right; we wouldn't even have wars. But virtually every human being carries sufficient of that character within him to cause a great deal of trouble, and the demonstration of that fact, and its effects, could have made a much greater tragi-comedy—much more difficult, I must admit, to dramatize. Bogart does a wonderful job with this character as written (and on its own merits it is quite a character), miles ahead of the very good work he has done before. The only trouble is that one cannot quite forget that this is Bogart putting on an unbelievably good act. (7) In all but a few movies one would thank God for that large favor. In this one it stands out, harmfully to some extent, for everything else about the picture is selfless.

It seems worth mentioning that the only thing which holds this movie short of unarguable greatness is the failure of the story to develop some of the most important potentialities of the theme. (8) In other words, "Hollywood," for once, is accountable only for some minor flaws. This is what it was possible to do in Hollywood, if you were talented enough, had standing enough, and were a good enough fighter, during the very hopeful period before the November Freeze. God knows what can be done now. But if anybody can hope to do anything, I count on Huston, who made *San Pietro* and *Let There Be Light* as an army officer and *The Treasure of the Sierra Madre* as a Hollywood writer-director.

---

7. Agee gives evidence of how the actor may get in the way of valid film experience. Does he also suggest that with a well known actor this interference is inevitable? Consider here Agee's earlier remark concerning Huston's "all but incredible submergence in a role."

8. Which themes does Agee think are underdeveloped?

Viridiana, Courtesy of *Audio Film Center*

VIRIDIANA

Penelope Gilliatt, *THE OBSERVER,* London April 8, 1962

The Disgusted Genius

Buñuel's *Viridiana* (Curzon), the scorching anti-clerical masterpiece that won the Golden Palm at Cannes last year, must be one of the most impudent gestures in the whole history of the cinema. To have made it in Spain is as though Marx were to have written "Das Kapital" not in the British Museum but in the middle of the Stock Exchange.

Until Franco rashly suggested that he might come back to direct a feature, Buñuel had not worked in his own country since the mid-thirties. His "L'Age d'Or" and "Un Chien Andalou," two of the most brilliant and grimly mirthful works of the whole surrealist movement, were made in France; since then he has lived in Mexico so long that one hardly thinks of him as belonging to Spain at all.

Two or three years ago the obviously nettled Franco made overtures to him and to Picasso, and Buñuel, to everyone's surprise, calmly accepted. How the script ever got through one can only guess. I suppose it is possible that a Spaniard who knew nothing about

Buñuel, who is just the sort of person one would expect to be Franco's censor, might be deceived by reading a treatment into thinking that the tone of the film was going to be sympathetic to the Church and the social system. It would probably be equally possible, say, to describe "Guernica" so that it seemed to find some glory in war. But how the film came to be permitted as a Spanish entry at Cannes is much more baffling. (1)

Before the ponderous machinery of censorship ground into motion, however, Buñuel and the negative had both skipped the country. Franco now calls the film an outrage to Spanish piety and Spanish womanhood, and in Paris he has had it banned; in Curzon Street it is playing intact, and for everyone who responds to courage it is a time for lighting bonfires.

The heroine of the title, insultingly named after a local fifteenth-century saint, is a tense young kill-joy in modern Spain who is about to take her vows. The Mother Superior thinks she should have a last look at the world, so she reluctantly packs her hairshirts to go on a visit to her only relative, an uncle whom she has never met. Thirty years ago his wife died on her wedding night, and ever since then the tender fetichist has kept her wedding clothes in a trunk; the scene when he tries on her stays is worthy of Genet.

Next day, with the Hallelujah Chorus blaring on the gramophone, he persuades Viridiana to dress up in the clothes herself, then gives her a sedative and carries her gently to bed, where he means to make love to her but finds himself worshipping her instead, as though she were the stone image of a wife on a tomb. In the morning he asks her to marry him, and she responds so cruelly that he hangs himself. (2)

At this even Viridiana is obscurely aware of maladjustment, and she throws up the convent to devote herself to spending her uncle's wealth on a band of ungrateful beggars. The scavengers include several of Buñuel's recurring blind men and cripples, a sulky girl five months pregnant, and a man with sores who used to vex the others in

---

1. This is all very interesting gossip, but is it relevant to either our understanding or evaluation of the film?

2. What is the tone of Miss Gilliatt's plot summary? Is it appropriate to the film?

their days of robbing Church offertories because, they say irritably, he put his filthy hands into the holy water.

Their dislike of their busybody benefactress is lazy but implacable. They are happy to take anything she offers, but to their mind she is not doing her job properly: the beans are badly cooked. At one stage she dragoons them into a prayer meeting in an orchard, and the scene is brutally cross-cut with workmen putting electricity into the house. There is not much doubt about which Buñuel regards as more philanthropic. When their Lady Bountiful has gone away for an evening, the beggars at once break out and treat themselves to a pilfered banquet. One of them puts on the Handel record again, and in a riot of squalling babies, squealing women and tipsy cripples hopping to the Hallelujahs a girl throws up her skirt and pretends to be taking a photograph, freezing them into a grotesque parody of Leonardo's "Last Supper."

Buñuel uses visual blasphemy as a great writer can use a swear word, placing it so that it explodes. He also points out, incidentally, that there is as much eroticism in sacred music as there is in Wagner's "Tristan," which he used in the same way in "L'Age d'Or." The script of the film, ribald and terse, is very much his own; so is the way the camera is often lowered to look at people's feet, in a mocking impersonation of a nun's averted gaze. (3) After two rapes Viridiana is forced to recognise the real world, and she ends up reluctantly playing cards.

To Fascists and bigots this is obviously a very offensive film. (4) To most other people it will have the insolence of genius; we have been taking Bergman on the chin for years, and at last someone is speaking the truth about religious mania. Buñuel's greatest work has always come out of his disgust, and it is the marriage of piety and Fascism in his country that makes his gorge rise. What are we to make of a Christianity that runs on keeping people poor? Why should one respect the collusion in Spain of the godly with the greedy, who profit by suffocating peasants with superstition and clapping intellec-

---

3. Does this help us to understand what the critic means when she points to Buñuel's extraordinary use of "visual blasphemy"?

4. Where does this leave the filmgoer who finds *Viridiana* "offensive," but doesn't want to think of himself as either a "fascist" or a "bigot"?

tuals in gaol? "Being thoroughly normal and honest," Henry Miller once wrote of Buñuel, "he finds himself regarded as bizarre. . . . Perhaps, like Lawrence, he is only an inverted idealist. If you are sane and healthy you are an anarchist and you throw bombs."

LONDON TIMES

April 6, 1962

Buñuel's Masterpiece of Surrealist Film

When Señor Luis Buñuel's latest film was shown at Cannes last year opinion was divided between those who thought it brilliant but beastly and those who stopped short at the "brilliant". Now that it has appeared in this country, completely uncut (a rare tribute to our censors' broadmindedness) a less hurried and perhaps a fairer judgment is possible.

First, there is no doubt at all about the film's artistic maturity and technical mastery.(1) For years in Mexico Señor Buñuel has been doing wonders with short schedules and limited finances, but here, with the more generous allowance of time and money the film's Spanish producers (improvidently, as it now appears, for themselves) permitted him, he has surpassed himself. Seldom or never has the surface of a Buñuel film corresponded so exactly to its spirit: (2) the photography of Señor J. A. Agayo, by turns hauntingly beautiful

---

1. Does the critic offer any evidence of the film's "artistic maturity and technical mastery"?

2. When in this context the critic refers to the "surface" of the film, is he speaking merely of film quality?

and deliberately, savagely harsh, is always perfectly calculated in dramatic terms; (3) the music is selected with sinister aptness from Handel's *Messiah* and other unimpeachable sources; and the acting, usually a strong point in Señor Buñuel, is here really remarkable, particularly in the case of Señorita Silvia Pinal as the priggish (or perhaps saintly) heroine.

Why, then, should there be any doubt about the film? Mainly because here the anarchic surrealist and militant atheist in Señor Buñuel have broken out with a force greater than anything since his *maudit* classic *L'Age d'Or. Viridiana,* indeed, has every appearance of a personal testament, summing up its creator's whole *oeuvre* in one film. (4) The story moves with dazzling speed and certainty from its extraordinary opening sequence, in which the heroine, a novice on the point of taking her vows, is dressed up in her dead aunt's wedding gown, drugged, and nearly raped by her old uncle through her attempts at private charity with a group of unscrupulous beggars, to its brutally cynical—or, as Señor Buñuel would no doubt say, merely realistic—conclusion.

This last parenthesis gives the essence of the film's power to offend. If all these things were shown with bitterness, if the film could be represented as a savage and disillusioned attack on the way we live now, everything would be all right: we could shake our heads with the author and go away smugly uninvolved. But no. If anything is attacked it is Christianity, conventional morality, charity, liberal values, and all the things most audiences might be expected to be for. Like *Los Olvidados, El,* and *Archibaldo de la Cruz, Viridiana* blames society and all its most cherished institutions for perverting man's nature and making a world where only the animals (the wasp drowning in a water-butt, the dog being dragged along behind a cart) deserve sympathy.

It is a point of view, and one, the liberal must agree, which has as much right to be heard as any other. Certainly in this film it is ex-

---

3. Would it help if we were given some examples of "hauntingly beautiful" and "savagely harsh" photography?

4. If spring is here, can summer be far behind? If *oeuvre* is here, can *auteur* be far behind? Is it a virtue for a film to sum up a film maker's entire work?

pounded with a burning passion and sincerity which compel, if not acceptance, at least undivided attention and respect. (5) And whatever one's final attitude to the ideas put forward, the film itself remains unassailably a masterpiece, perhaps one of the last, and undoubtedly one of the most unexpected, in the chequered history of surrealist art. (6)

---

5. How does the critic know Buñuel is sincere?

6. This is the second use of "surrealist." Has the term been explained and if not, should it have been? Is *Viridiana* surrealist in the same sense as is *Un Chien Andalou*?

David Robinson, *SIGHT AND SOUND* Summer, 1962

"Thank God—I Am Still an Atheist": Luis Buñuel and Viridiana

> *Viridiana* is a direct continuation of my personal tradition from *L'Age d'Or*. With thirty years between them, they are the two films I have made with the most freedom.

The wonder is not that Buñuel, who is one of the greatest artists the cinema has produced, should have spent fifteen years in the wilderness. Between *Las Hurdes* (1932) and *El Gran Calavera* (1947)—though properly speaking it was *Los Olvidados* in 1950 which marked his return—he was virtually inactive, confined to unproductive administrative jobs in the studios or driven to refuge in the Museum of Modern Art, from which he was hounded by the first anti-Communist witch-hunts. (Not that he was known as a Communist; but as director of *L'Age d'Or* he was fair game for the Red-hunters.) (1) The wonder is rather that in the wilderness he was never tempted; never once, before or since, compromised; so that *Viridiana* still speaks as loud and as clear and with the same voice as *L'Age d'Or,* still asserting sanity and cleanliness in a world whose nature is to be mad and filthy. If there has been a change in the thirty years between, it is that the Swiftian fury of *L'Age d'Or* has given place to a calmer philosophic clowning, as cool and therefore as deadly as Voltaire.

> *It was not my intention to blaspheme, but of course Pope John XXIII knows more than I do about these things . . .*

The story of how *Viridiana* came to be made is now well known. Gustavo Alatriste proposed that Buñuel should make a film exactly as he wished. Then it was decided that the film should be shot in Spain, in co-production with the two most advanced new companies there. UNINCI began production with *Welcome Mr. Marshall* and recently produced Torre-Nilsson's *The Hand in the Trap*; Films 59 enjoyed considerable international success with their first features, *Los Golfos* and *El Cochecito.* Buñuel can hardly have been reluctant to identify himself with this renascence in the Spanish cinema; and the Spanish authorities were rashly delighted to welcome him home. They had, of course, underestimated their wandering son.

Somehow the script of *Viridiana* was put over on the censor, who requested only one slight change to the ending—a proposal which Buñuel gratefully accepted as a distinct improvement over the conclusion he had himself devised. The film was finished, and almost before anyone was the wiser, arrived in Cannes. The story goes that the censors never saw the film complete: it was barely ready in time for Cannes, so that with due apology it was submitted for appraisal in short sections, whose piecemeal effect must have seemed more or less innocuous.

At Cannes, of course, the film was a triumph, and the official Spanish representative proudly but incautiously stepped on to the platform to collect the Palme d'Or. The horse had bolted and the stable doors began to slam. The authorities were appalled; the Pope himself was

---

1. Again, gossip. Is there something about *Viridiana* that leads to this response? Or is there something about Buñuel?

said to have given voice to his disapproval. Officials were dismissed. A hue and cry was begun to find and destroy the negative. Trade agreements were invoked to prevent the film from being shown in France. The Spanish press was forbidden even to print its title. At 61, Buñuel was still as scandalous as he had been at 29, when *L'Age d'Or* provoked riots and bomb-throwing in Paris.

> *I don't see why people complain. My heroine is more of a virgin at the dénouement than she was at the start.*

The form of the story is comparable to *Candide* or *A Cool Million,* in that it is the progress of an innocent and her discovery of life in all its carnal and surreal monstrosity. On the eve of taking her final vows, Viridiana is bidden to visit her sole relative, Don Jaime. Her reluctance, her fear of facing the outside world, proves to be a foreboding. She finds that her uncle is a devout and gentle old patriarch who plays sacred music on the organ and does not acknowledge his only son because he was born outside the church's grace. The old man's strange pleasures include squeezing his plump body into the wedding garments of the wife who died on the night of their marriage, watching his housekeeper's little girl skipping, and caressing the phallic handles of the rope he has given her. Spying on Viridiana through a keyhole, the housekeeper, Ramona, discovers that the girl sleeps on the floor and that her luggage consists of a wooden cross, some nails and a crown of thorns.

Viridiana resembles Don Jaime's dead wife, and he asks her to put on the wedding dress. She does so; but when her uncle goes on to ask her to marry him, Viridiana angrily refuses. With Ramona's assistance, Don Jaime drugs the girl and carries her to bed. First laying her out like a corpse, he passionately kisses her, but stops short of worse assaults. Next morning, however, he tells Viridiana that she cannot return to her convent, for he has possessed her while she slept. She leaves the house notwithstanding; but Don Jaime has one last trick to outwit her. He hangs himself with the child's skipping-rope. His heirs are Viridiana and his natural son, Jorge.

The second part of the film opens with the Mother Superior's visit to the errant novice; and there is a characteristic Buñuel observation when the old lady puts on her spectacles, to transform her ascetic face into that of a fat old gossip, indecently curious to know Viridiana's motives for leaving the convent. Viridiana tells her that she intends to pursue Christianity independently and alone. This purpose she carries out by surrounding herself with a group of disciples—fearful old thieves and beggars and whores whom she feeds and clothes and teaches to pray. Her disciples quarrel viciously among themselves and cast out one of their number who is diseased. They are grandly, monstrously ungrateful: "The string beans were a little bitter today." But Viridiana blithely harvests virtue's own reward.

Meanwhile Jorge, Don Jaime's son, sets himself to build up the decayed estates; and a comic but clumsy sequence of cross-cutting contrasts vigorous, insolent images of manual work with the effete hypocrisy of Viridiana's beggars at their *angelus.* Jorge himself is normal and average and without complication. He dismisses the silly mistress he had brought to the mansion with him; and when the devout Viridiana promises to be a difficult lay, he turns quite easily to the lovelorn Ramona. (2)

One day masters and servants must all go to town, and the beggars are left in charge. Their good intentions easily collapse and they mischievously break into the house to organise an orgiastic feast. They gorge, drink, swear, blaspheme and copulate. The blind leader of the beggars tells tales of robbery in churches, of betrayal and informing. At the height of their merrymaking they pose around the table in the exact attitudes of the Last Supper; the cock crows, and a whore pretends to photograph them, using as a camera the chief instrument of her trade. The orgy mounts, the beggars perform a mad *jota* to the "Hallelujah Chorus." Suddenly the merrymaking comes to an end as the blind man flies into a fearful rage on learning that his woman is with another beggar. He lays furiously about him with his stick; and over the destruction the gramophone sings triumphantly "And He shall reign for ever and ever." The beggars discreetly but tipsily take their leave as the proprietors return.

When Jorge and Viridiana enter the scene of chaos, he is overpowered by one beggar while another—his trousers supported by the self-same phallic skipping-rope—rapes Viridiana. Jorge bribes the second beggar to kill the rapist, just at the moment that the police, called by Ramona, arrive at the house.

The epilogue is not so tense or furious as the ending of *L'Age d'Or* or of *Nazarin.* Viridiana sits, evidently sadder and probably wiser, in her room. Outside in the garden her religio-masochistic paraphernalia

---

2. Notice that Robinson's tone is very much like Miss Gilliatt's. In what ways does the film invite the adoption of this tone?

—the cross, the nails, the crown of thorns—burns on a bonfire. Ramona's little daughter curiously fishes the crown out of the fire, and it lies there flaming on the ground: the image recalls the last image—the hair blowing on the cross—of *L'Age d'Or*. There, however, the feeling was of putrefaction, here of purification. Indoors, Jorge plays at cards with Ramona, who is evidently his mistress: and the gramophone is now playing a crazy pop song, "Shake, shakemedown, shake," which dominates the whole of this last section of the film. There is a knock at the door: it is Viridiana, who is at last pleading for human companionship. Ramona makes to leave, but Jorge stops her and has her sit down with Viridiana. "All cats," he says, "are grey in the dark." (This was the censor's invention: Buñuel's script had Jorge and Viridiana left alone.) And so Viridiana is dealt a hand of cards. The camera rapidly draws back from the little group at the table. "I knew," says Jorge, "that one day my cousin would play cards with me."

> *It's no good telling people that all's for the best in this best of all possible worlds . . . I believe that you must look for God in man. It's a very simple attitude.*

Viridiana's picture of mankind does not present a very flattering image of God. Buñuel depicts men's viciousness in terms that are no less direct and no more amiable than those of *L'Age d'Or.* If there is a hero at all it is Jorge, who lives positively and (as a good surrealist) according to the dictates of desire. Yet one feels that Buñuel does not prefer him to the others (3) even to Don Ezekiel, the vicious little clown always good for a laugh and ready to cause trouble, or to the odious man with diseased hands (has he really venereal disease, or is it just the fallacy of the good that disease is the visitation of the wicked?) who repays Viridiana's kindness by abetting her rape.

The film's total effect is invigorating rather than depressing because Buñuel values them all alike as men, and likes them all because they are funny and human. If there is one whom he does not like, it is Don Amalio, the blind leader of the beggars. Buñuel has never liked blind men, linked as they are with false sentimental associations. In

---

3. From what source does Robinson's feeling about Buñuel's preference derive?

L'Age d'Or Modot kicked a blind man to the ground. Don Amalio can hardly be distinguished from the vile blind beggar in *Los Olvidados.* Don Amalio is Christ at the Last Supper; Don Amalio has been an informer; among the beggars it is Don Amalio who looks for all the world like a true bourgeois when he puts on the clothing Viridiana gives him. On the other hand, if there is one character whom Buñuel really admires, it must be that insolently proud beggar who rejects Viridiana and spits on her piety; and in the same breath demands alms from her. This is a noble independence.

Other men might be affected to pity by this picture of rot and corruption. But for Buñuel pity implies resignation, and resignation defeat. In a way the irresistible moral degradation of the beggars recalls the hysterical litany of woes that beset the Hurdes. It was not the viper that bit them that was deadly, but their efforts to cure the wound. In the same way it is Viridiana's piety and goodness which corrupt. In *Las Hurdes* too there was no pity, only the clear gaze of a man who is prepared to recognise the world for what it is, and in doing so makes the first and vital step to therapy.

> *If Christ came back, they'd crucify Him all over again. You can be* relatively *Christian but to try to be* absolutely *Christian is an attempt doomed to failure from the start. I'm* sure *that if Christ came back the High Priests and the Church would condemn Him.*

Buñuel admits no pity; and no panaceas. Nor does he accept the panaceas that are offered elsewhere. He is set, as he has always been set, against the soporifics of conventional morality and conventional sentimentality. (4) "I am against conventional morals, traditional phantasms, sentimentalism and all that moral uncleanliness that sentimentalism introduces into society . . . Bourgeois morality is for me immoral, and to be fought. The morality founded on our most unjust social institutions, like religion, patriotism, the family, culture: briefly, what are called the 'pillars of society'." The true answer is to live in the world and to seek God in man. The Christian virtues are unexceptionable in their argument, but in their application they are unreal, for the world is what it is.

---

4. Is this an insight from the film? Or is the critic merely commenting on the quotation from Buñuel which precedes this paragraph?

In recent years Buñuel has become more and more interested in the figure and the failure of the perfect Christian. Dr. Lizardi in *La Mort en ce Jardin* is a prototype. *Nazarin* really was Christ in modern dress. His attempts to practise Christ's principles invariably led to disaster. His mere presence among road-workers resulted in slaughter. Society being organised as it is, his martyrdom was inevitable. In the last shot, to the sound of the tambour of Calanda, he walks towards the camera like the other Christ at the end of *L'Age d'Or,* although this time he is victim instead of tormentor. In the final sublime moment when Nazarin receives human—not divine—charity, there seems to be an atonement of some kind. Like Lizardi and Nazarin, Viridiana's Christianity is destined to failure. Paradoxically it is her very piety which corrupts corruption. As in *Nazarin,* one feels at the end that there has been an atonement of man to man: Viridiana seems nearer salvation in human contact than in divine service.

But *Viridiana,* like all Buñuel's films, defies a simple interpretation. It is meant healthily to shock and disturb, and not to answer questions.(5) Buñuel's statements are of their nature ambiguous and paradoxical. "If the meaning of a film is clear, then it can no longer interest me," he says.

> *The film seems an involuntary imitation of dreams. The cinema might have been invented to express the life of the subconscious, whose roots penetrate so deeply into poetry . . .*

The critic of *The Times* wrote: ". . . the film itself is a masterpiece, perhaps one of the last, and undoubtedly one of the most unexpected, in the chequered history of surrealist art." Buñuel is still the surrealist of 1929:

> *les objets bouleversants,*
> *le cassage de gueules,*
> *la peinture fantastique . . .*
> *l'écriture automatique,*
> *l'anticléricalisme primaire,*
> *l'exhibitionisme,*
> *les plaisanteries pas drôles.*

---

5. How does the critic know what the film is "meant" to do?

By his own account his conception of the film was a matter of association.(6) The story was built up from unrelated images: "It was born out of one image . . . a young girl drugged by an old man . . . Then I thought that this girl should be pure and I made her a novice . . . The idea of the beggars came later."

The film's rich atmosphere is built out of images which are nothing if not surrealist: Viridiana's sleep-walking, ashes on the bed, dreams of black bulls and so on. Buñuel gives free play to his own private fetishisms. He admitted in an interview that the only image he recalled from *Les Anges du Pêché* was the scene in which the nuns kiss the feet of one of their dead sisters. *Viridiana* is full of feet—Rita's skipping feet; Don Jaime's grotesque boots and the novice's square-toed shoes marching side by side; the striptease of Viridiana's lower limbs. For no reason at all Francisco Rabal (Jorge) is seen washing his feet. (One naïvely polite English critic guessed that this was because feet are the natural focus for a nun's downcast eyes.) Only briefly does Buñuel indulge his entomological preoccupations, when Don Jaime carefully rescues a nasty little fly which has fallen into a water butt. Phallic references proliferate, however: a richly comic and vulgar scene has Viridiana innocently, instinctively recoiling from contact with a cow's teat.

> *Technique has no problems for me. I've a horror of films* de cadrages. *I detest unusual angles. I sometimes work out a marvellously clever shot with my cameraman. Everything is all beautifully prepared, and we just burst out laughing and scrap the whole thing to shoot quite straightforwardly with no camera effects.*

The real marvel of Buñuel is that he has the technical mastery to fulfill his ideas and his poetry. Technically *Viridiana* is unusually elaborate for its director. The camera moves a good deal; there's a tendency to show people in vistas seen through several rooms. The cameraman, José F. Aguayo, has the same sort of pictorial vigour as Figueroa, and the same ability to visualise the anti-beautiful beauty of Buñuel's conceptions.

---

6. Do we need Buñuel's account or does the film tell us all we need to know? And if we cannot understand *Viridiana* without additional, extra-film comment by Buñuel, does this mean the film fails?

With Buñuel, one never feels that technique is something interposed between conception and execution. (7) Problems of *mise en scène* seem to have no more existence for him than do problems of technique in a sketch by Picasso or Goya. Grandly independent of conventional techniques as of conventional ideas, Buñuel seems to have the ability simply to put pictures on the screen with the accuracy and certainty of a good paperhanger sticking up paper. Largely this is due to the assurance and precision of his conceptions. "If I plan and shoot two hundred and fifty shots, then two hundred and fifty shots appear in the finished film." A friend described his work on *Viridiana* thus: "Before each shot he would wander about with a viewer, all by himself, for half-an-hour, lining up and planning the shot while the crew sat drinking. Then he'd go over and say 'Right: that is what I want.' Then they'd go and get the shot, while he sat drinking." (8)

Thank God—I am still an atheist.

If Buñuel's creative life had ceased with *L'Age d'Or,* he would have had a safe place in film history. That film revealed unforeseen possibilities in the cinema for surrealism, for anarchy, for philosophy, for anger. Succeeding works in Mexico and in France represent a body of work which few directors have paralleled, but never excelled the first, extraordinary feature film. Now Buñuel has made his second masterpiece, his most authoritative work: "The second pole," in the words of Ado Kyrou, his most fervent admirer, "which sustains the wonderful Buñuel edifice."

The quotations from Buñuel are taken from a number of magazine interviews.

---

7. Here Robinson offers a criterion of film excellence. Does his statement imply that it is one which can be applied generally to film?

8. Could a director go through all these motions and still make a bad film?

SUGGESTED READINGS

What follows is a list of ten books which we have found helpful in our study of film. We have included only books available in English which, unfortunately, eliminates the great body of work now being done in France, and we have omitted the many full length collections of film writings by critics represented in this volume. Happily, such collections are now being published in great abundance, but their very numbers and frequency of issue would tend to make any compilation we could provide very quickly obsolete. We suggest that the reader pursue some of his favorite critics at greater length in the more representative context of an anthology of a single critic's work.

Arnheim, Rudolph, *Film as Art,* Berkeley and Los Angeles: University of California Press, 1957.

Containing essays written between 1933 and 1938, this book is a landmark in the history of film aesthetics. Technique, which Arnheim sees as central to film, is discussed in detail. In the final essay of the book, Arnheim sets forth the reasons for his by now famous (infamous?) bias against "the talking film."

Bluestone, George, *Novels into Film,* Baltimore: The Johns Hopkins Press, 1957.

A detailed study of the transformation of six novels into films, Bluestone's work is extremely helpful in clarifying the distinctive features of the film medium through comparison and contrast with the medium of the novel.

Eisenstein, Sergei M., *Film Form and Film Sense,* Cleveland: World, Meridian, 1957.

In this landmark in the history of film aesthetics, the director of *Potemkin* and *Ten Days That Shook the World,* and perhaps the most famous of Russian film theorists, presents his theory of film. His concern is largely with montage and film structure and his views are clearly and precisely given. Included are diagrams from *Alexander Nevsky.*

Huss, Roy and Norman Silverstein, *The Film Experience: Elements of Motion Picture Art,* New York: Harper & Row, 1968.

This volume is especially recommended for the reader who wishes to learn the language of film. Many stills and charts help to make some of the more elusive terms and concepts clear.

Kracauer, Siegfreid, *Theory of Film,* New York: Oxford, 1960.

For Kracauer, film is largely visual and from this point of view he discusses film technique. There is an interesting comparison of the novel and film as media.

Lindgren, Ernest, *The Art of the Film,* New York: MacMillan, 1948.

A very clearly spelled out volume on film technique as well as theory. Especially suitable as an introduction to both.

Manvell, Roger, *Film,* London: Penguin Books, 1950.

This short general discussion of films is first, a relatively early plea for the acceptance of film as art and second, an examination of the role of film in society. This is a very useful short reference work which includes an interesting if dated list of "Some Directors and Their Films." 192 stills.

Montagu, Ivor, *Film World: A Guide to Cinema,* Baltimore: Penguin Books, 1964.

Montagu discusses film from four perspectives: "Film as Science, Film as Art, Film as Commodity, Film as Vehicle." Particularly valuable are discussions of the physics of sound and optics and Montagu's analysis of film technique. This volume abounds in precise and clearly illustrated information.

Pudovkin, V. I., *Film Technique and Film Acting,* New York: Evergreen, 1960.

Two classic books, published in one volume, contain cogent and practical discussions of the roles of the director and the actor in film making.

Stephenson, Ralph and J. R. Debrix, *The Cinema as Art,* Baltimore: Penguin Books, 1965.

Essentially concerned with technique and the ways in which illusion is made to seem like reality, this book is especially useful for its detailed presentation of the vocabulary of film. 54 plates.